The Study of Ethnomusicology

Bruno Nettl

The Study of Ethnomusicology

Twenty-nine Issues and Concepts

University of Illinois Press
Urbana Chicago London

Manufactured in the United States of America

This book is printed on acid-free paper.

Library of Congress Cataloging in Publication Data

Nettl, Bruno, 1930–
The study of ethnomusicology.

Bibliography: p.
Includes index.
1. Ethnomusicology. I. Title.
ML3798.N47 1983 781.7 82-7065
ISBN 0-252-00986-X (cloth) AACR2
ISBN 0-252-01039-6 (paper)

For Wanda

Contents

The Study of All of the World's Music

List of Figures

Preface

How can one best organize the description of a field of inquiry or scholarship? Conventions come to mind: systematic, geographical, or historical accounting of the subject of research, be it art, social institutions, battles, animal species; or a history of the field, its major figures, ideas, publications; or again, a chronicle of the activities in which a scholar typically engages, field research, analysis, interpretation perhaps.

The task I have set myself here is to discuss the field of ethnomusicology in terms of a number of its central issues and problem areas of general concern that have for several decades been and continue to be subjects of debate and controversy, in the belief that such issues most clearly characterize an academic field. Each of the twenty-nine essays presented deals with a concept or an aspect of theory or procedure affecting the field of ethnomusicology as a whole, and not specific to the study of any one world area or culture. While this approach has not often been followed in the past, it surely has its precedents, at least in sections of major books by Merriam (1964), Hood (1971), Blacking (1973), and, much earlier, those of Lach (1924) and Sachs (1930). And if I may justly maintain that I deal with some issues to which these authors have not specifically addressed themselves, there can be no pretense that this is a comprehensive treatment. It is easy to find issues that I have not included: aspects of organology, the study of Oriental musical treatises, formal aesthetics. And there are obviously other ways in which concepts could have been combined into chapters.

The choices have been made on the basis of personal preference and background, but I believe that they reflect a broad view of the field, comprising directions regarded as central by several schools of researchers. Even so, while any book dealing with a field of inquiry is bound to reflect the particular interests and convictions of the author, this one probably does so to a greater degree. In contrast to my *Theory and Method in Ethnomusicology* (1964), which is largely a compendium of the approaches and techniques developed by others, and in the past, this group of essays is substantially a personal statement of what I think ethnomusicology has been and is all about. There are frequent references to the publications of others, but no attempt to summarize all that has been thought and done. The preponderance of illustration comes from my own experience, from the cultures with which I have had contact—the North American Plains Indians, the Middle East, and the fine art tradition of Western urban society. No attempt is made to cover the globe or to touch upon all types of music even in one society. There are occasional anecdotes, some true, others apocryphal combinations of real experience, presented in order to make some points rather simply or as a change of pace, occasionally for comic relief. I ask forgiveness for these moments of levity, asserting at the same time that the subject of this book is what I have been most serious about in thirty years of academic work. There are many personal opinions and interpretations, and the occasional mildly poisonous dart. The kinds of phenomena discussed are indeed those I consider to be central in the present, perhaps in the future; they have also for the most part been central in the past, and while this is not a history of the field, frequent reference to earlier publications supports my view that the present identity of ethnomusicology embodies its history.

Although I cannot claim to present new findings, I have some hope that the approaches, perspectives, and reflections in these pages will be of interest to specialists in ethnomusicology, and the book is in the first instance directed to them. While it is not constructed as a text, it is also directed to graduate students for whom it may serve as an introduction to ethnomusicological thought. Beyond this, I have tried to write something that will introduce the fundamental concepts, ideas, and issues of ethnomusicology to members of related fields and professions, in particular to anthropologists, musicologists concerned with the history of the Western tradition, folklorists, and specialists in area studies. My purpose is not to argue that ethnomusicology is a separate discipline. But I hope to show that it is a field of learning with an identity, characteristic problems and approaches, and a history of its own.

The reader may be nonplussed by a few of the chapter and subdivision titles; they are intended to amuse and attract, not to repel. The significance of each is made clear in the introductory paragraphs. The body of the work is presented in four groups of chapters, each representing one major component of the mainstream of ethnomusicological thought as I perceive it. But the close interrelationship of the various issues is obvious throughout, and their overlapping is one of the intriguing aspects of the field. It may be useful here to explain the organization in a bit more detail.

The Prelude concerns the definition of ethnomusicology, and Chapters 1–9 deal with the field as the comparative study of musical systems. Chapter 1 discusses the concept of music; Chapter 2, the concept of music-making; Chapter 3, the question of universals. Chapters 4–9 discuss various issues involving the analytical process; Chapter 4 the problem of identifying, in music, units somewhat analogous to languages; Chapter 5, comparison and comparative study; Chapter 6, transcription and visual representations of music; Chapter 7, a number of general problems involving description and analysis of repertories or bodies of music; Chapter 8, the identification and study of the individual musical work; and Chapter 9, the problem, already touched upon in Chapters 4–8, of determining degrees of similarity and difference among musics and musical artifacts.

Chapters 10–17 deal with various aspects of the study of music in culture. Chapter 10 discusses music in relationship to the culture concept, and the general problems of musical ethnography. Chapter 11 concerns uses and functions of music; Chapter 12, musical origins; Chapter 13, some aspects of musical change as studied in ethnomusicology; Chapter 14, oral tradition as the normal form of musical transmission and as an area especially of ethnomusicological study; Chapter 15, the study of music as symbol and as a system of symbols; Chapter 16, the use of geographic distributions in ethnomusicology; and Chapter 17, the question of what causes a society to have a particular musical style.

Chapters 18–22 deal with aspects of fieldwork. Chapter 18 attempts to sketch the general character of ethnomusicological field research, while Chapter 19 discusses the contrast between the outsider and the "insider" of a culture. Chapter 20 deals with the concept of preservation as a major component of fieldwork and of ethnomusicology at large; Chapter 21, the study of the individual in ethnomusicology; and Chapter 22, the relationship of fieldworker and informant or teacher in the sense usually labeled as "ethics." Chapters 23–27 then discuss some of the issues related to the concept of ethnomusicology as the study of all of the world's music; Chapter 23, the existence of social and musical strata in a society, with emphasis on the concept of folk music; Chapter 24, the role of the ethnomusicologist's personal or cultural values in research; Chapter 25, the study of learning and teaching; Chapter 26, the study of special and sometimes neglected components of a society's music, the repertories of women, children, and minorities. Chapter 27 discusses some of the special problems occasioned by the universal influence of Western culture, music, and musical thought in the twentieth century. Finally, the Postlude deals briefly with some broad trends in the history of ethnomusicology.

I have advisedly designated these chapters as essays. Each deals with its issue in its own way. In some cases the scholarly history plays a major role; in others I have tried to take a thin slice from the meat of an issue for exclusive discussion. Some chapters are in the main responses to specific viewpoints; in others I set forth a personal view with little reference to the work of others on the same subject. Where possible, illustrations from specific musical cultures or earlier scholarly literature are used for clarification. I have tried, here and there, to draw on some of the relevant literature from historical musicology, anthropology, and occasionally other disciplines. Throughout, it will be noted, the emphasis is on work done in the United States. Other literature is frequently mentioned, and there is no question of my respect for it. But just as the cultural background of scholars determines in essence their approach to learning, this book comes out of the context in which I have been working, and cannot but reflect it.

In a number of the chapters I have based a few pages or paragraphs on earlier publications of mine, but in no case has a paper or article simply been reprinted; the viewpoints and interpretations have usually been changed very substantially.

I am grateful for many kinds of help that I have received in the course of working on this project. Conversations with many colleagues at the University of Illinois and elsewhere have helped to clarify ideas and given food for thought. I obviously cannot list them all, but would like to mention Larry Gushee, Alex Ringer, Dan Neuman, Alan Merriam (before his untimely death), and Nazir Jairazbhoy. The anonymous readers who evaluated the manuscript for the publisher gave many helpful suggestions, as did Charles Capwell, William Belzner, and Stephen Slawek, who read the manuscript at various stages of completion. I wish to express my gratitude to the University of Illinois Research Board for making grants which provided the services of research assistants during 1978–79 and 1979–80, and which made possible the final typing of the manuscript. I particularly wish to thank Alison Arnold, my assistant in 1978–79, who did much bibliographic and editorial work, and Chris Goertzen, assistant in 1979–80, who among many other things made the suggestion which resulted in the final arrangement of chapters. I am happy to acknowledge the considerable help of a Fellowship for Independent Study and Research from the National Endowment for the Humanities, held during 1981–82, a portion of which made possible the rapid conclusion of the project. And finally, I wish to thank Bonnie Depp, who copy-edited the manuscript, the staff members of the University of Illinois Press, and particularly Judy McCulloh, for seeing the book through to publication beginning with advice at the time of the first draft, all the way to the final stages.

B.N.

Prelude

The Harmless Drudge

DEFINITIONS

For years, people have been asking me the question: "You're an ethnomusicologist?" Shortly after 1950 it was likely to be accompanied by expressions of wonder and of the belief that I was somehow involved with "folk" music, with "primitive music," and particularly with "ancient music," and also that I must have a great deal of companionship with a tape recorder. By 1960 the questioner would likely bring up participation in an Indonesian gamelan, or perhaps an ability to "play" many of the world's odd instruments. In the 1970s, the conversation might well include the term "ethnic" music or even the etymologically outrageous "ethnomusic."

I have always found it difficult to come to a precise, concise, and readily intelligible definition. Dictionaries differ considerably but espouse limited views. I could talk about my activities, but which of these gives a true perspective of the field? There were such differences between what I had studied as a graduate student of what was, before 1950, called comparative musicology (folk music of Europe and North America, American Indian and sub-Saharan African music); what I was teaching (mainly courses giving surveys of non-Western music, or of the music of entire continents); the subject of my recent research (specialized problems such as the social structure of musical life on an Indian reservation and the decision-making process of improvisors in the classical music of Iran); my major orientation (I was filled with wonder at the world's musical diversity and assumed that it resulted from the diversity of the world's cultures and lifestyles); what I hoped to do in the long run (find out why different societies engage in different kinds of musical behavior and produce different kinds of sounds); and what I hoped my students and their future colleagues and students would finally be able to do (control all conditions that affect music sufficiently well so that they could predict musical events from cultural processes). All of these, in a way, define ethnomusicology, in terms of the experience of one person over a period of time. In the century in which ethnomusicology can be said to have existed, since the first pioneer works of Ellis (1885), Baker (1882), and Stumpf (1886), attitudes and orientations have changed greatly. So has the name, from something very briefly called "Musikologie" (in the 1880s), to comparative musicology (through about 1950), to ethno-musicology (1950 to ca. 1956), quickly to ethnomusicology (removing the hyphen actually was an ideological move); and if we are not careful we may end up with ethnomusic-ology. The changes in name are indicative of even more changes and greater diversity of definitions.

There clearly is such a thing as ethnomusicology. But just as I find myself unable to give a single, simple definition, confident that most people in my field would subscribe to it, the literature of the field abounds in them. Perhaps more than members of other fields of study, ethnomusicologists have been much concerned with defining themselves. In a large number of publications Alan P. Merriam, the scholar most concerned with the associated problems of basic orientation (Merriam 1960, 1964: 3–36, 1969b, 1975), promulgated the need for ethnomusicologists to look carefully at what they do, have done, and wish to do in order to move in concerted fashion toward their goals. In a major essay discussing the history of definitions, Merriam (1977a) brings together a large number of separate statements defining the outer limits, the major thrust, the practicality, and the ideology of ethnomusicology (see also Simon 1978). There are various types of definitions: some tell what each ethnomusicologist must do or be, and some synthesize what the entire group does. Some focus on what has transpired in terms of research activity, and others, on what should in fact have been done or what must eventually be done. They define in terms of a body of data to be gathered and studied, or in terms of activities undertaken by typical scholars, or again by the questions that are asked of the raw material. Some seek to broaden limits, including within the scope of ethnomusicology all sorts of things also claimed by other fields or disciplines; others envision a narrow specialty. It would seem that finding order among all of these definitions (Merriam cites over forty, but that is just a start) would require one to become what Samuel Johnson called, referring to himself, the lexicographer, a "harmless drudge."

What, specifically, are some of these definitions, and how can one group them? In their briefest form, without elaboration or commentary: those statements which seek to define by material to be studied include (a) folk and what used to be called "primitive," i.e. tribal or possibly ancient music; (b) non-Western and folk music; (c) all music outside the investigator's own culture; (d) all music that lives in oral tradition; (e) all music of a given locality, as in "the ethnomusicology of Tokyo"; (f) the music that given population groups regard as their particular property, e.g. "black" music of the United States; (g) all contemporary music (Chase 1958); and (h) all human music. Those that define by type of activity include (a) comparative study (of musical systems and cultures); (b) the study of music in or as culture, or perhaps music in its cultural context; and (c) historical study of Oriental and "primitive" music. Those that define in terms of ultimate goals include (a) the search for universals; (b) the description of "*all* factors which generate the pattern of sound produced by a single composer or society" (Blacking 1970a:69); and (c) the "science of music history," aiming at the establishment of laws governing musical development and change. This sampling may provide an idea of the number and variety of definitions and approaches. Beyond these, however, the disciplinary identity is often discussed and called into question. Opinions: Ethnomusicology is (1) a full-fledged discipline; (2) a branch of musicology, or of anthropology; (3) an interdisciplinary field; (4) what musicology ought to be, but hasn't become. No wonder that preoccupation with identity is a major activity. When attending meetings of the Society of Ethnomusicology, the largest organization of the field, I am struck by the number of specialized papers that nevertheless begin with statements giving the speakers' definition of and general orientation toward the field.

Still, the types of definitions mentioned above fail to include yet another approach to defining, which is to state and to determine the configuration of the intellectual, methodological, and theoretical issues that confront a field. One may also define a field of research in terms of the kinds of things about which its people argue and debate; in a sense, this series of essays is a somewhat clumsy attempt to define ethnomusicology in terms of abiding issues, questions, and problem areas of general concern. It is, there should be no question, a personal attempt, stressing one author's point of view and experience. Self-definition, itself a major issue among ethnomusicologists, seems an appropriate place to start, for it is in many ways the most fundamental.

There may be many definitions, but what those who call themselves ethnomusicologists or, perhaps avoiding the professionalizing suffix, otherwise associate themselves with this field actually do, and who they are, is fairly clear. Can one make a composite sketch of the life of the typical American or Western European ethnomusicologist active in the 1960s or 1970s? It hardly seems fair to the great variety of backgrounds and personalities. And yet, many share at least a number of the following events and experiences:

(1) Initial background in music, as a student of performance, theory, or composition; in the United States, this may culminate in a bachelor's degree in music. (2) Some kind of exposure to the study of culture, broadly speaking; may be manifested in graduate study of anthropology, or of a field of area studies such as South Asia, Africa, the Middle East, or involve a period of living in a non-Western culture as a teacher (of English or of Western music), missionary, or member of the Peace Corps. (3) Develop-

ment of allegiance, often quite specialized, to the music of a particular culture or area—Plains Indian dances, Javanese gamelan music, North Indian classical instrumental music. (4) Graduate study in a program of ethnomusicology adjunct to a musicology, anthropology, or folklore department, usually involving the student in some kind of comparative study of a variety of musics. (5) Field research, leading to and/or following completion of the doctorate, for a fairly long period—a year is typical—in the major area. (6) Following fieldwork, analysis of collected data, almost always taking the form of some kind of reduction of the sound to paper, and manipulation of the written material to arrive at musical insights; development, with more difficulty, of a procedure for the analysis of human activities and attitudes revolving about the musical sounds. (7) In the course of this analysis, some attention given to the way in which the gathered material came into existence; this may involve traditional historical study or the reconstruction of history through conjecture based on analysis of contemporary data. (8) Teaching, which almost always includes a course in "musics of the world," or at least something going far beyond the scope of the ethnomusicologist's specialized research. (9) Periods of penury. (10) In middle age, the appearance of a new, second culture area as a focus for research. (11) Sometimes early, sometimes later, but surely at some point, an interest in generalizing about the world of music, a result of experience with several musical cultures.

WHAT THEY ACTUALLY DO

A typical ethnomusicologist's profile? Despite all diversity, a good many of my colleagues will surely recognize themselves here. The definitions cited above differ more in outer limits than in central thrust. The achievement of a variety of ultimate aims can be satisfied by similar activities. There is often a gap between what ethnomusicologists do and what, by their own definition, they claim to do or hope some day to accomplish.

What most of them do is to carry out research about non-Western, folk, and popular music. However we define these terms, they are what authors in such journals as *Ethnomusicology* and the *UCLA Selected Reports in Ethnomusicology* actually write about. The definition of ethnomusicology as the study of non-Western and folk music, although widely criticized, is descriptively correct. On the other hand, the definition as study of music outside one's own culture is not, for Asian and African ethnomusicologists (thus identifying themselves) do study their own music, but when they study the European music that is outside their own culture, they avoid the term, instead calling themselves music historians or general musicologists. It is one of the main curiosities of our history that in the 1970s few are willing to define their field in terms of what is actually done by its members.

They are interested in music as a component of culture. For some time—perhaps the period between 1950 and 1970 is the most indicative—ethnomusicologists tended to divide themselves into two groups, one concentrating on the music "itself," another on the cultural context. The two groups were frequently at odds. Those associated with music departments typically felt that they were properly studying the main point of focus, the music itself, in its cultural context. They looked down on these "contextualists" as amateurs unable to deal directly with music, relegating them to a kind of supporting discipline. Those ethnomusicologists espousing an anthropological approach considered their opposite numbers as naive, unable even to understand the musical artifact because they could not deal with it as a product of culture, and unwilling to deal with musical concepts, attitudes, or forms of behavior other than the piece of music itself. But while there surely are publications that deal specifically and only with musical sound and its analysis, and while certain ethnomusicologists have even recently been proposing analytical models for music taken by itself, I know of no ethnomusicologist who does not, in his or her total commitment, have a major interest in music as an aspect of human culture. Anthropologists, as a basic technique of their profession, know how to deal with the interaction of various domains in culture; musicologists are distinguished by their fundamental ability to make sophisticated analyses of musical artifacts. The difference between "musicians" and "contextualists" is one of emphasis and technique, but the difference in work actually carried out may be modest.

Yet the relationship of ethnomusicologists to others in the music world has sometimes become a problem of educational theory and even had an impact on the scholarly integrity of the field. In the various institutions that support music, there are many who wish to deal with what they consider ethnic music in various ways—performing, teaching, entertaining—not directly involving research. Frequently they too call themselves ethnomusicologists, although they should not be called "ologists" of any sort, for they are (at least at the moment they are engaged in these practical activities) not committed to the intellectual pursuit of knowledge. I do not propose to deal with their activities as issues of ethnomusicology, but I have, of course, no wish to denigrate what musicians and teachers who devote themselves to non-Western and folk music have accomplished, what they have contributed to music and to humanity. In their presentation of folk music to urban audiences, and of non-Western music to school children, in their use of African and Oriental sounds in the American and European concert culture, and in much else, they have done more to affect society than have the ethnomusicological researchers. If they have benefited from the teaching and writing of the scholars, well and good. On these pages they are accepted not as ethnomusicologists but as musicians and teachers, themselves definitively honorable designations. It is curious that so many of them should have tried to find solace in aspiring to the much more controversial label of ethnomusicologist.

Glances at relationships to anthropology and musical performance and pedagogy are logically followed by a look at the relationship to general musicology, for, in terms of ultimate goals, ethnomusicology is not easily distinguished from it. Musicologists also claim the study of music in culture. While only a small part of musicological research has directly involved such an approach, there are probably few thoughtful musicologists who would not subscribe to this ultimate commitment, perhaps using the term "culture" in a more general way than the technical sense of the anthropologist. So, given this character of musicology, it is problematic to define ethnomusicology as the study of music in culture. On the one hand, this does not specifically describe the bulk of its activity, and on the other, it is a commitment shared with all of musicology.

Fieldwork is regarded as the ethnomusicologist's indispensable tool. The prehistory of the field begins with statements based very considerably on speculation with only a smidgeon of supporting concrete evidence. Soon it moved to "armchair" research in which the ethnomusicologist analyzed materials collected and recorded in the field by others, usually anthropologists and missionaries. But as the twentieth century progressed, fieldwork became increasingly essential and, after World War II, a *sine qua non* of the ethnomusicologist's own style of life and study. Of course face-to-face investigation of exotic music and musicians was known earlier, and even in the "armchair" period most ethnomusicologists did go into the field or at least recognized the desirability of doing so.

Today it is taken for granted that each ethnomusicologist must have *some* field research experience, and that most studies are based on the researcher's own fieldwork. But considering economic and political developments of the 1970s as well as the increasing availability of recordings and other data not yet subjected to study, it is possible that in the future there will again be more research done with the use of other people's field data.

There is no doubt that the kind and quality of fieldwork on which given research is based have a profound effect on the conclusions. One cannot make a satisfactory research project out of inadequate fieldwork. Yet ethnomusicological publications rarely tell much about the procedures used in the field. They may give data such as names of informants, machinery used to record or film, questionnaires, but rarely the whole story. Fieldwork is shrouded in mystery, for something keeps the fieldworker from divulging much of his relationship to the people whose music he is studying. One reason is a disinclination to reveal the emotional impact of the relationships that develop, their intensity, their disappointments. For the moment, we only observe this fact, saving further comments for subsequent chapters.

It is a widely accepted basic assumption that an ethnomusicologist needs experience in the field, not only because it is essential for the gathering of data for a specific project, but because it is valuable in itself. There seem to be several beliefs on which this assumption is based. Exposure to another culture stimulates empathy with the strangeness, but also with the humanity, of another society of people, and with the complexity of the music and musical life in what may from a distance seem a simple situation. We believe that this feeling, once experienced, will carry over to further work not based on field research, help bestow an ability to evaluate publications by others that may be based on fieldwork, and provide insights necessary for guiding the fieldwork of students who investigate societies with which the teacher is not directly acquainted. All of this is, of course, tied to the fact that ethnomusicologists study cultures outside their own and to the resulting assumption that there is a dichotomy between one's own culture and all others, the latter in a certain sense all alike. Of course we know that they are not, but our approach to foreign cultures initially lumps them into a single category; we begin by dividing the world into categories of "ours" and "not ours," into "familiar" and "strange."

Ethnomusicologists engage in comparative study. It appears at least to be so. Whether in fact one can make significant comparisons and whether there is a good method for doing this are questions that the literature generally avoids, although here and there they become the subject of considerable debate (and of subsequent chapters here). After all, for some five decades, until ca. 1950, the field was called comparative musicology. Merriam (1977a: 192–93) believes that the change to "ethnomusicology" came from the recognition that this field is no more comparative than others, that comparison can be made only after the things to be compared are well understood in themselves, and that, in the end, comparison across cultural boundaries may be impossible because the musics and cultures of the world are unique. In his classic book *The Anthropology of Music* (1964:52–53) he also points out that most of the general publications of ethnomusicology do not deal with methods and techniques of comparative study (Wiora 1975 notwithstanding). At the same time, it is difficult to find specialized studies that do not in some way, at least by implication, make use of intercultural comparison as a way of gaining and presenting insights. The proponents of comparative study, accepting the criticisms given here, nevertheless appear to consider the benefits of the comparative view so great that they feel it worth their while to indulge it, even at the risk of sometimes using premature and inadequate data.

But the adoption of the term "ethnomusicology" as a replacement for "comparative musicology" may have causes additional to those suggested by Merriam. I do not question the reasoning of Jaap Kunst, who is generally regarded as the first to have used the new term prominently in print (Kunst 1950:7); he did so, he says, because comparative musicology is not *especially* comparative. But why then was the new term adopted so quickly, and particularly by Americans, who seem to have been the first to adopt it officially?

The participation of a number of anthropologists in the American leadership of comparative musicology seems likely to have favored the use of a term paralleling the names of several anthropological subfields: ethnolinguistics and ethnohistory, with others, such as ethnobotany and ethnoscience, coming later. Among academic disciplines anthropology had greater prestige than did musicology, often misunderstood even in the 1950s. Musicologists, after all, were the academic Simon Legrees for students of musical performance, and musicological study was frequently regarded as the refuge of the unsuccessful player or composer. The new term attractively symbolized association with anthropology or something that sounded anthropological. Nationalism may also have played a part. Americans were proud of their significant contributions to non-Western and folk music research between 1930 and about 1955, in comparison to their more modest work as historians of Western music. They needed a term that expressed their special role, that was not simply a translation of the established German term, "vergleichende Musikwissenschaft." The fact that one was dealing with a special kind of music, low in the hierarchy of musics with which the conventional musicologist dealt, may also have stimulated the need for a special term, a whole word, "ethnomusicology," instead of a term designating a subfield of musicology that dealt, by implication, with "sub-musics" worthy only of being compared with the great art music of Europe.

But whatever the attitude toward comparison and its role in the development of a self-image, ethnomusicologists use it to generalize about world music. The specialist in the music of East Africa, Thailand, the Navaho, or Croatia tries to see it in a world context. When serious discussion of musical universals takes place, it is among ethnomusicologists. When general comments about the history of world music are made, they usually come from ethnomusicologists, from a vantage point of direct experience with at least two or three musical cultures and of a literature that describes a good many others. When the function of human music at large is discussed, it is in the same forum. Ethnomusicologists are moderately effective here; before their advent, the same generalizations were made by philosophers and sociologists and historians of European music, and they could often be falsified by mere reference to standard descriptions of non-European cultures. Most of the relevant statements involve observations of change and its processes, or questions of origin, and thus we may conclude that most of the generalizing done in this field has some kind of relevance to history. A characteristic of the comparative stance is a diachronic view of the subject.

A CREDO

Beyond brief definitions, a profile of the typical individual, and an account of shared characteristics, we can also identify some beliefs that characterize the person who is devoted to research in ethnomusicology. There seems to me to be an underlying creed leading to the configuration of persons and activities that comprise this field. It consists of four beliefs, or groups of beliefs, which happen to overlap or coincide substantially with the activities given above.

1) We endeavor to study total musical systems and, in order to comprehend them, follow a comparative approach, believing that comparative study, properly carried out, provides important insights. Our area of concentration is music that is accepted by an entire society as its own, and we reserve a lesser role for the personal, the idiosyncratic, the exceptional, in this way differing from the historian of music. We are most interested in what is typical of a culture.

2) We believe that music must be understood as a part of culture, a product of human society, and while many pieces of research do not directly address the problem, we insist on this belief as an essential ingredient of our approach. We are interested in the way in which a culture musically defines itself, but also in the way it changes its music, and thus we also stress the understanding of musical change, less in terms of the events than in the processes.

3) We believe that fieldwork, face-to-face confrontation with musical creation and performance, with the people who conceive of, produce, and consume music, is essential, and stress concentration on intensive work with small numbers of individual informants.

4) We believe that we must study all of the world's music, from all peoples and nations, classes, sources, periods of history. The fact that we have not done so results from convenience of certain sources, location of peoples, availability of time, and other incidental factors.

I don't know whether this is a credo for all ethnomusicologists. My colleagues, typical nonconformists among musicians and music scholars, are unlikely to accept any doctrine. But I have chosen these four areas of belief as the basis of my organization of these essays.

Yet there are also some other, perhaps more fundamental beliefs that define the core of ethnomusicological thinking and that must somehow be made part of the credo, for they seem to determine what kind of person goes into ethnomusicological research, and what kind of an individual he or she may become.

Ethnomusicologists seem to be driven by two major but apparently conflicting motivations. They search for universals, hoping to generalize intelligently about the way in which the world's cultures construct, use, conceive of music. They try to understand human music in the context of human culture as a unitary phenomenon. And yet they never cease to marvel at the incredible variety of manifestations of music. They delight in imparting to the world the strange facts uncovered by musical ethnography and analysis: that among the Sirionó of Bolivia, each person may sing only one tune all of his or her life, identifying the individual with a personal musical stamp (Key 1963, Stumpf 1886:411); that in the classical music of India there is an almost incredibly complex interaction of melody and rhythm maintained over a sustained period by a musician who manipulates the rhythmic cycle in juxtaposition to improvised rhythmic units; that downtrodden minorities have special uses for music in their struggles for improvement. Despite their interest in human universals, ethnomusicologists revel in their knowledge that most generalizations about structure and use of music can be overturned by reference to this or that small society. They vacillate between a view of music as a unified human phenomenon and as an emblem of the infinite variety of human cultures.

Fundamentally, ethnomusicologists must be relativists. They become attached to cultures which they study and with which they identify themselves, they have special loves, obligations toward the musics they regard as an ethnic or family heritage. They may consciously or tacitly believe in the intellectual, technical, aesthetic, or artistic superiority of certain musics and be able to make a good case for this belief, preferring the classical music of Europe or Asia because of its complexity, or the music of "simple" folk because of its presumably unspoiled nature. But, at the bottom line, at some level of conceptualization, they regard all musics as equal. Each music, they believe, is equally an expression of culture, and while cultures may differ in quality, they are bound to believe in the fundamental humanity, hence goodness, of all peoples. They believe that each culture and each music must be understood first and foremost in its own terms. They consider all musics worthy of study, recognizing that all, no matter how simple, are in themselves inordinately complex phenomena. And they believe that all musics are capable of imparting much of importance to the peoples to whom they belong, and thus also to the scholars who study them.

But there is a sense in which ethnomusicologists are not relativists. Taking a sympathetic view of the music of all peoples, they come to believe in the right of each society to determine its own way of life, and they are likely to become dedicated to the improvement of living conditions for the people with whose music they are concerned. This may move them in the direction of social and political activism, and perhaps more typically, of a kind of musical activism, to the determination that the musics of the world's peoples must be protected, preserved, taught, treated with respect. Although they may wish to study their subject dispassionately, they are in the end often unable to avoid the results of extended contact with humans and their works in a foreign society. They try to bring an understanding of their musics to their own society, believing that the teaching of their subject will in a small way promote understanding of these "strange" peoples, that it will combat ethnocentrism and build respect for the traditions of the world's societies. In their quest for knowledge of musical cultures, they try to be neutral, but they typically try also to err on the side of showing that the music of the downtrodden of the world, of lower classes in rigidly stratified societies, of isolated, tribal, technically backward peoples, is something innately interesting, something worthy of attention and respect, something indeed magnificent. These attitudes are not a prerequisite of graduate study, not part of the definition of the field; they are, of course, also found among members of other professions. But there are few ethnomusicologists who do not share them.

What now is the role of ethnomusicology among the various fields of inquiry, and what is its single major contribution? What is its main thrust, past and future? The view I represent may perhaps offend members of other fields and disciplines who will perceive encroachment on their territory. The value and the contribution of ethnomusicology seem to me to be essentially and very broadly historical. We engage in comparative study, in the study of music as a part of culture, in a holistic approach to music. We do this ultimately because we wish to know how things came to be, in a somewhat broader sense than that of the historian. We wish to know how and why things musical—songs, styles, repertories—change and develop. We would like some day to be able to predict what the musical future will be: the future of a tune subjected to intercultural contact, of a style confronted by a compatible kind of music emanating from a dominant society; the effect of the exceptional individual, of social and political movements, of isolation, of multifaceted contacts, of the limits of the human mind, of geography and the weather. In this respect we differ only in degree, not in essence, from the scientist who learns that the combination of two substances will normally bring about an explosion. But dealing with infinitely more complex phenomena, we are far from having the scientist's degree of knowledge and control.

As we examine the issues that ethnomusicologists confront, it may become evident that this is a field which frequently asks questions that are fundamental to musicology. In dealing with all peoples, phenomena, times, and processes, it casts the widest net. In the nature of its central thrust, I personally regard it as an area belonging in the first instance to musicology, and not as an adjunct, but at the center. Of course, many of the scholars who contribute to this central area of musicology regard themselves not as musicologists at all but as anthropologists, folklorists, sociologists, linguists. Yet, in engaging in ethnomusicological work, they are contributing to this central core of musicological activity, a core we may label the "science of music history"—perhaps yet another definition of ethnomusicology. It is, of course, true that they are at the same time making contributions to other fields, but their findings are not as central to these as they are to musicology. We may rightly argue that ethnomusicological theories, methods, and insights, wherever else they also belong, and even when they only tangentially seem to concern the sound of music, are and properly should be part of the basic stuff of musicology.

The Comparative Study of Musics

Chapter 1

The Art of Combining Tones

THE COCKTAIL PARTY

In American academic society few people can define music, and they differ greatly in what they think is significant about music. Let me present a cocktail party conversation, as I remember it, resulting from my confession of working in ethnomusicology. "Studying American Indian music!" says one amazed person. "I didn't know the Indians even had music." I try patiently to explain. "Oh yes, I knew they had chants, but is that really music?" From an elderly gentleman: "I spent a year in Africa, heard a lot of singing and drumming but that isn't music, is it? After all, they don't write it down, maybe they make it up as they go along, they don't really know what they are doing." More explanation. A lady joins in the conversation: "A few days ago, I heard some ancient music from the Middle East which didn't sound at all unpleasant. The commentator said it sounded good because, after all, it is from the cradle of our own civilization." A young man has added himself. "But these sounds that the Chinese make with their instruments and voices, or the Indian chants, how can you call them music? To me, they don't sound like music. For example, they don't have harmony." And the old gentleman: "My teenage boys play their records all day, but hardly any of them sound like music to me."

(Time for that second Scotch.)

The ethnomusicologist deals with music but may find it hard to determine whether something is actually music. The problem of defining music and the scholar's position toward it as a concept, and as a body of audible and recordable sound, is actually among the major issues of ethnomusicology. Not frequently brought out into the open (but see Merriam 1964:27–28), the question is often found lurking behind and between the lines of even the most specialized publications. Evidently it is up to us to determine what music is in an interculturally valid way. In many languages there is no direct translation of the term, and there are societies which do not even have a concept of it that is in any way compatible with that of Western society. Even in Western culture defining music is difficult.

In a complex society one may find definitions in at least three ways: by asking the society's own "expert," who has thought about it long and hard (that is, perhaps, by looking in the dictionary); by asking members of the society at large in order to determine whether there is a consensus (possibly using a questionnaire and distributing it widely); and by observing what people do and listening to what they say without imposing one's self on their thoughts by asking questions (for example, by going to concerts and record stores, or, better yet, attending cocktail parties).

Many music dictionaries published in Europe and North America avoid the definition of music in its most fundamental sense. Wisely, perhaps, their authors assume that the readers know what they and the people with whom they associate think music is. The fifth edition of *Grove's Dictionary of Music and Musicians* omits it, the *Harvard Dictionary* (Apel 1969:548) discusses the phenomenon of music without specifically attempting a definition. When they discuss the term, music encyclopedias usually suggest that music is made up of tones, that it has emotional impact, and also that it is an art, in the sense that it is something people *do,* as well as a science, that is, something about which they think in a systematic, disciplined fashion. Thus *MGG* (Blume 1949–79:9:970) simply states that music is "that one among the artistic disciplines whose material consists of tones" (my translation). By contrast, the latest edition of the *Riemann Musik Lexicon* (Riemann 1959–67: 3:601) gives a complex, convoluted definition of ten lines, perhaps indicating that the author had difficulty circumscribing his subject. He should be forgiven, for it is well known that those things most basic to a society are frequently the ones hardest to define simply and clearly, constituting, as it were, the axiomatic part of the culture.

A dictionary of the English language cannot avoid giving definitions. The *Oxford English Dictionary* states that music is "that one of the fine arts which is concerned with the combination of sounds with a view to beauty of form and the expression of thought or feeling." A dictionary directed to young students, *Webster's Intermediate Dictionary,* says that it is "the art of combining tones so that they are pleasing, expressive, or intelligible." In these and other dictionaries, including those of other European languages, music is discussed in terms of tones (which, to the Western thinker on music, appear to be its basic building blocks), beauty and intelligibility (relating to music as art and as science), and expressiveness (giving the sense that music is a kind of communication). There appears to be a consensus, but it is surely culture-specific, for there are societies and musics where these criteria make no sense at all.

What now do people in a typical American town or city who have not made a specialty of this field consider music to be? No results from a questionnaire appear to be available, but some interviews enable me to state very tentative findings. While not actually giving definitions, they indicate something about the outer limits of music (see Nettl 1963). Urban Americans have a number of rather specialized conceptions of music, but when pushed, they appear to believe that almost any sound is potentially musical, accompanying this conception by evaluation. The point is that music seems to Americans to be innately a "good" thing, and therefore it is probably good for a sound, or even a lack of a sound (silence), to be accepted potentially as a component of music. Sounds that are "good" are sounds that may be included in music. Thus the sound of coins about to be paid is "music to my ears," a person whose speech one likes is said to have a "musical voice," and a language whose sound one dislikes is said to be "unmusical." At the same time, Americans think of music as something associated with particular social contexts, such as concerts, and thus any sound produced in a concert is likely to be accepted as music. If asked to consider the matter, people will often accept any sound as music, including animal sounds, industrial noises, and of course any of a vast number of humanly produced sounds made on instruments, with the body, and with the voice, including speech. Twentieth-century Americans like music, and they like to feel that much of their world can somehow be related to music. This is all probably true of urban Europeans as well.

So, having been asked to consider what their conception of music really is, people show themselves to be broad-minded. But let me return to the cocktail party and think of it as a field experience; by masquerading as a fieldworker, I can use what I hear to construct some idea of the conceptualization of music that this society holds when its members are not artificially being asked to consider the matter carefully. I had to defend my interest in non-Western music because my friends wondered whether it was actually music. There is a curious disparity in what people include under the heading of music when given time to consider the question, and what they will accept when giving quick reactions. In the latter, they showed themselves to be more narrow-minded. Outer limits are broad; the central thrust of opinion is narrow. A fieldworker early learns this major lesson: he or she may get one kind of answer when asking a question that has no place in the culture and another when observing the society's behavior. Asking for a definition of music is in the first category. Indeed, our music dictionaries' silence indicates that people are not used to answering the simple question "What is music?" and when confronted with it, they do not give answers reflecting the way they act. An analysis of the cocktail party conversation may give us a more reliable perspective of the way urban, middle-class Americans actually use the concept of music in their lives.

Not interested in defining music, my friends, in their questions, nevertheless divulged some of the criteria they ordinarily use by telling me what characteristics the activity and sound that they call music should have in order to be accepted as true and proper music. "Indians have only chants, not music," implies that a certain level of complexity, as perceived by the Western listener, is a necessary feature. What my friends colloquially called "chants" have only a few tones and no harmony, and that kind of sound is not fully acceptable to them as music. The same kind of thinking concerns the concept of harmony; in Western urban society we can conceive of music without a background of chords, or without two or more simultaneous sounds, but we consider such a texture as clearly exceptional. Some music, but not very much, may lack harmony, but in the general view of my compatriots, a people whose music has no harmony at all may not really have music. Here is a new component in our exercise of defining: music must have certain traits in order to be acceptable, but some of them need be present only in the mainstream of a repertory. Minority repertories in which they are absent are nevertheless accepted. Some other societies seem also to follow this approach. In certain North American Indian repertories one hears that there were some songs with harmony (Nettl 1961). While these were accepted as part of the musical material of the culture, the use of harmony was never extended to the mainstream of Indian music. In some North American Indian cultures, occupying a role opposite to that which it has in urban Western music, harmony of a sort was acceptable if it did not become central; in the West music without harmony is acceptable as long as it stays outside the mainstream.

The idea that music is intrinsically good and pleasant was suggested in my interviews and in some of the dictionary definitions, and, indeed, my friends at the party brought it up as well, expecting music to please. As pointed out, our society believes that music is in itself something good, and with this goes the belief that we should enjoy its sound. Confronted with something whose sound they dislike, my friends immediately questioned whether it could be music. Critics have had similar reactions to new or strange music. As a related point, the dictionaries implied that music must normally be composed and notated by individuals who are trained and who give thought to their work. The idea of preconceived structure, of music's being something created by people who know what they are doing, was also important to my friends, and is tied to the more formal definition of music as a science. The significance of this criterion explains much of how Western urban society understands musical structure and activity of the past and present. Among other things, it explains at least in part why Western society considers "composition" to be a more noble activity than "improvisation," which, according to our music dictionaries, is regarded essentially as a craft rather than an art.

Perhaps most intriguing is the skepticism that my friends at the cocktail party displayed over the possibility of another culture having music at all. They were not surprised at the existence of sounds such as singing, but had second thoughts about calling it music. This reaction has several possible implications. First, it is conceivable that our society, assuming now that my friends are representative of it and give reactions that are generally acceptable, regard music as so important to our way of life that they cannot see quite how another society could also have it. We are, after all, a rather ethnocentric lot. Music, being a priori a "good" thing, must belong exclusively to ours, the only truly acceptable culture. Second, our tendency in Western society is to feel that other peoples do not know how to do anything properly if they have not adopted our way of doing it. In technology we expect machinery of all types; in agriculture, crop rotation; in religion, Christianity or Judaism; in political structure, democracy of a sort; in marriage, monogamy. And, in the case of music, the implication is that if a society does not have at least the central components of our kind of music, it may not truly have music, just as a society is not considered to have marriage in a sense acceptable to us if it permits polygamy or arranged partnerships. My friends, who love their own music, may know better, but they cannot get themselves to admit that other cultures have something so close to their hearts as music. Or, to put it more bluntly, they may have doubted that the world's savages can have created something which is so valuable as music. To be sure, this viewpoint has been rapidly receding in the last few decades.

There are some obvious contradictions between the formal definitions of music in our society and these informally derived ones. Dictionaries stress tones, but my friends stress harmony. The dictionaries imply that music is somehow a universal language, whereas my friends hold that it is culture-specific. But the definitions agree in some respects. Music is "pleasant" to my friends, "expressive" to the authorities; it is an art and a science in the dictionaries, and to my friends, something in which one must be skilled and therefore produce something complicated.

Amazing, what one can learn at a cocktail party.

DO THEY REALLY HAVE MUSIC?

If we have trouble in our own culture, determining the definition of music for other cultures is even more of a problem. The concept of music is not universally present or everywhere the same. Even within one society a particular sound may be regarded as musical in one context and as non-musical in another. (For a thorough discussion of this issue, see Robertson-DeCarbo 1977:36–40.) It is important to point out that the languages of other cultures often do not have a term to encompass music as a total phenomenon. Instead, they will very likely have words for individual musical activities or artifacts such as singing, playing, song, religious song, secular song, dance, and many more obscure categories. Most ethnomusicological studies do not actually speak to the question of the definition or conception of music in any one society, taking for granted the existence of the concept in the absence of an actual term for music. Merriam (1967a:3, 1964:3–84) discusses this matter at length, but ethnomusicologists have often been unaware of it, not speaking the language of the people whose music they are studying, not bothering to think about it when observing a plethora of interesting musical activity.

Indeed, the fact that a society has no general word for music may well mean that it does not regard as closely related all of the activities ethnomusicologists usually put together under that term. According to Ames and King (1971:ix; Ames 1973b:132), the Hausa of Nigeria have no term for music; there is a word, *musika,* derived from the Arabic *mūsīqī,* in turn derived from the Greek word, which is used for a very restricted body of music. This may mean that the many musical activities in which the Hausa engage are more important as components of a variety of cultural contexts, and thus verbally associated with these, than as a complex of structurally similar phenomena. The same seems to be true of many American Indian societies that have no word to tie together all musical activities. Each culture seems to have its own configuration of concepts. The Blackfoot thus do have a word that can roughly be translated as dance, which includes music and ceremony and is used to refer to religious and semireligious events that comprise music, dance, and other activities; but this word does not include certain musical activities such as gambling that have no dancing at all. They have a word for "song," but not instrumental music. A similar attitude was evidently once found in India; the word *sangit* or a derivative of it, is used to translate "music" rather accurately, but dance may also be included in that term. According to McAllester (1954:4), the Navaho have no word for music or for musical instruments. Keil (1979:27–29) searched in vain for a specific term for music in a dozen languages of West Africa. But the absence of a term for music is only one of the characteristic difficulties. Although a society has a word roughly translatable as music, the word may include things we in Western urban society, despite our own loose definition, do not include as musical, and it may specifically exclude phenomena that we regard as music.

For example, in Iran the Persian term now generally used to translate "music" is *mūsīqī,* borrowed from Arabic. It refers primarily to instrumental music, although it is also used for vocal music. The latter is more usually called *khāndan,* a word translated as "reading," "reciting," and "singing." The singing of the Koran, whose structure and sound are not very different from the singing of secular classical and folk music, is not readily admitted as belonging to *mūsīqī;* nor is the recitation of prayer or the muezzin's call to prayer. The reason for the exclusion of the most specifically religious singing from the main category of music has to do with the opinion that music is in certain ways an undesirable and even sinful activity and that as a concept it must be kept separate from religion. Indeed, one of the first acts of the Ayatollah Khomeini upon proclaiming the Islamic Republic of Iran in 1979 was to outlaw certain kinds of secular music and to reduce the educational budgets for music, but all of this affected much less those sounds classed as *khāndan* and not as *mūsīqī*. On the other hand, the singing of the nightingale is regarded by Persians as at least closely related to human singing and, indeed, as a model for it. The Iranian classification is therefore overlapping. Instrumental music is *mūsīqī;* Koran singing and prayer are *khāndan;* folk song, popular song, classical vocal music, and the nightingale are in both categories. The barking of dogs is in neither.

According to Merriam (1964:64–65), the Basongye of Zaire include as music what Westerners regard as singing, exclude bird song, and are not sure about the status of whistling and humming. Keil, on the other hand (1979:28–30), questions the possibility of deriving such a definition where, as among the Basongye, there are no terms to correspond to "music," "sound," and "noise" and points out that, among the Tiv of Nigeria, a large set of specific terms substitute for our holistic idea of music. Some cultures may have no interest in being holistic.

By the same token, Western society, in its Anglo-American form, may appear quite arbitrary in what it includes as music. Birds sing, we say, but not donkeys and dogs (although the latter, to a dog lover, might well produce "music to my ears," reinforcing our contention that music symbolizes goodness and happiness). The sounds made by dolphins, acoustically as similar to human music as is bird song, are said to be "language" (see Truitt 1974:387–92, also Sebeok 1977:794–808), but the sound of birds, also communication, is not. Among the sounds produced by humans, it is clear that we are similarly arbitrary. The sound of a machine is not music unless it is produced in a concert with a program that lists its "composer" and with an audience which applauds (or at least boos). In the academic "new music" culture, even the presentation of art works on slides, in a concert listed as a general musical event, may be regarded as music and treated as such by an audience.

WHAT IS THIS THING?

I should like to touch upon three thoughts somewhat tangential to the definition of music per se. First, the value of music in a society seems to be a major factor in determining the breadth of its definition of music. Second, the widely held view of music as simply a type of sound is a basis of operations too narrow for acceptance by ethnomusicologists. Third, the relationship of music and language is an important ingredient in the derivation of definitions of music as used in various of the world's societies, and in the field of ethnomusicology.

Obviously, all cultures regard music as at least minimally valuable. But some consider it as supremely valuable, others more or less as a necessary evil. For example, the Blackfoot Indians traditionally believed that they could not live without their songs, for these were a major component in the relationship of humans to the supernatural. Muslim society in the Middle

East likes music, but believes that there is something a bit wrong with this state of affairs and thus relegates much of it to low status (see e.g. Zonis 1973:7). The Basongye value music itself but then proceed to degrade its practitioners (Merriam 1973:268), something also true of the Hausa of Nigeria, who accord musicians low social status while allowing some of them a high standard of living (Ames 1973b:155–56). Modern urban Americans, as we have said, consider music a good thing but not, at least theoretically, as something essential to life. Certain societies regard music as something specific to humans (Blacking 1971b:37, 71; Merriam 1964:64), while others such as the Blackfoot (Nettl 1967c:158) would assert that other beings, spirits, the supernatural, animals, may also produce music.

These may be interesting observations, but one may ask what they have to do with defining and delimiting the concept of music. I suggest that a society which considers music to be valuable may include a great deal within its conception of music, but it places ceremonial activities and dance in the same category of thought, unafraid to put things with music that might, to a member of another society, not appear to be obviously musical. Unlike Middle Easterners, they regard music as a good thing and do not fear for the integrity and reputation of whatever else is included. In Western society music is associated with good and with happiness. Sounds that somehow symbolize happiness to us (e.g. bird song) are called musical while those we consider uphappy or neutral (again the barking dogs) are not. But the concept of music is extended by Europeans to the whistling wind, musical speech, orchestration of political strategy, and by some American Indian peoples to the supernatural sources of creation. By contrast, Middle Easterners, according music lower value, wish to restrict the concept by excluding its religious forms. The point to be contemplated is that perhaps societies do not first develop the concept of music and then decide upon its attributes but, rather, faced with the existence of musical sound, accord it function and thus value, and then proceed to build a definition of the concept, using value as a criterion.

Members of Western society often define music with specific reference only to the sounds one hears and to their representation in written notation. But ethnomusicologists have reason to define music more broadly. The issue here is whether there is, or should be, for ethnomusicologists, a special definition of music that guides their work. In these essays we must address ourselves to the problems faced by the ethnomusicologist, but we may also ask whether music might not be defined in modern society in such a way as to take into account the different concepts of music and sound in other cultures. Merriam has suggested a rather definitive grouping of three areas equally central to ethnomusicological work, labeling them concept, behavior, and sound (Merriam 1964:32–33). Concept involves the way people think about music in the broadest terms, considering, for example, what power it has, what value, what fundamental function; behavior includes the musical and nonmusical acts of musicians, the activities that precede, follow, and accompany the production of sound; thus sound, which we usually call the music "itself," is in this context no more the primary focus of attention than the other parts of the tripartite model. One of the central issues of ethnomusicology revolves around the degree to which the three parts command equal attention. Thus in a sense the definition of music also determines the definition of ethnomusicology.

Music has much in common with language, and the two are almost inseparable as ingredients of the activity perhaps most centrally observed by ethnomusicologists — singing. The relationship of language and music is an important aspect of ethnomusicological literature, extending from comparative studies of two systems at large and parallel characterizations of music and language in one society, on to many other specialized kinds of study. There are attempts to reconstruct the prehistory of music as an offshoot of early language development, studies showing the influence of linguistic structure on musical structure, investigations of song texts as related to melodies (see e.g. Bright 1963; Blacking 1972; Nettl 1956b:134–37; Herzog 1934, 1945). Music has been studied as a symbolic system analogous to language, and the methods of language study have been applied to music (Nattiez 1973, 1975; Ruwet 1966, 1967). But the closeness of the relationship seems also to get in the way. In many publications Charles Seeger questions the ability of musicologists to use speech as a means of communicating ideas about music, and at the very least he cautions scholars to be constantly on guard against unknown and imponderable factors introduced into their work as a result of dealing with one form of communication in the mode of another, that is, talking about music (C. Seeger 1977b:16–30). Music and language are different and separate forms of communication, and of course musical communication is multifaceted, to say the least (Blacking 1971b:42–52). The study of music-language relationship separates the two systems, but if we are to define music, we must remember that a broad area of communication may lie between speech and music. This middle ground includes, for example, certain kinds of dramatic and religious expression, and instrumental signaling of messages (see List 1963b). Or, among the Shuar of Ecuador, Belzner (1979) has identified a continuum of types of sound communication including several kinds of ceremonial speech with song-like rhythmic patterns. Drawing a sharp line between speech and music is hardly possible there. These phenomena are relevant to the definition of music, as societies may or may not include them. They are important, as well, for the ethnomusicologist's own conceptualization of music. If music can be defined, it cannot easily be circumscribed, its boundaries are unclear, and one may have to accept certain phenomena as both music and something else, the latter usually being language. Indeed, since so much music is singing with words, we may have to consider the possibility that it is not, after all, really separable from language.

THE ETHNOMUSICOLOGIST AS A GLUTTON

Despite all of these definitional problems, musicologists and ethnomusicologists seem to have little trouble agreeing on the things that are within their purview for study. Although defining the concept of music is basic to any understanding and study of the subject, it is not, after all, the ultimate aim of the ethnomusicologist. The task is more typically one of studying the definitions provided by the world's musical cultures in order to shed light on their way of conceiving of music. Even so, we need a working definition that states with what phenomena we should deal, and this need not be one which is universally acceptable. In practical terms, ethnomusicologists have arrived at such a definition from two assumptions: (1) All societies have music. (2) All humans can identify music—though not necessarily understand it—when they hear it. The definition includes these components: When they find that a musical sound is considered as speech, ethnomusicologists nevertheless regard the phenomenon as sufficiently musical to include it in their area of study. When the concept of music does not appear to exist in a culture, or when it is extremely restricted so that certain phenomena regarded as music by the ethnomusicologist's own culture fall outside it, these phenomena are accepted as music without reservation. When a society includes in its purview of music something that Western ethnomusicologists do not recognize as music, they also accept this for study, perhaps with certain reservations.

Having frequently served on the program committees of ethnomusicological societies, I do not remember that a paper was ever considered as unacceptable simply because the committee did not think that it dealt with music, the author notwithstanding. This is related to the fact that ethnomusicologists as a group take a broad view, including everything conceivable in their scope of study. Having decided that one must look at the conceptualization of music in each culture and consider the possibility that such a thing is not even extant in some societies, they have nevertheless decided for themselves that all cultures have music. They have discovered that all cultures have forms of sound communication other than their spoken language, and much of this is arbitrarily accepted as music. Defining music as human sound communication outside the scope of spoken language makes it possible for us to include, for musical study, such "nonmusical" events as Koran reading, African drum signaling, and Mexican Indian whistle speech, all of which have been dealt with in the journal *Ethnomusicology*.

These assumptions make ethnomusicologists appear not only gluttonous but also a bit ethnocentric. Curiously, the gluttony may be a function of the desire to avoid ethnocentrism, but the avoidance turns out to be only partial, for with the insistence that they know what music is, ethnomusicologists automatically include in their work anything that sounds to them like music, yet they may only grudgingly include what does not fit their own model. Wachsmann puts it more elegantly (1971b:384): "I could say to myself that those phenomena outside my own immediate culture to which I now attach the label 'music' because I recognize and acknowledge them to be music, are merely so labelled because, rightly or wrongly, they seem to me to *resemble* the phenomena which I am in the habit of calling music in my home ground. I am used to thinking of a (more or less) certain group of phenomena as music; this group embraces a number of different properties which I cannot clearly define, yet I have no doubt that they belong to this group 'music.'"

It probably could not be otherwise. Ethnomusicology as understood in Western culture is in fact a Western phenomenon. It is practiced by members of non-Western societies, but only to the extent that it occurs in the Westernized sectors of these cultures, the result of Western-derived educational training. Non-Western musical scholarship such as the theoretical traditions of India and China is regarded as material for ethnomusicological research rather ethnomusicology in itself, but traditionally, Western musical scholarship is not similarly used. With all of its pejorative connotations, ethnocentrism has its uses. To respect all cultures and to study them on their own terms is desirable, but to strive for an interculturally valid approach *equally* derived from all of the world's societies may not be. To regard all languages as equally expressive is a valuable view, to which I readily subscribe. But it does not necessarily lead to the adoption of Esperanto.

Each society divides the world it knows into areas, domains, and categories. In Western society we recognize language, literary art, music, dance, and drama as more or less separable domains for which we have developed scholarly disciplines: linguistics, literary scholarship, musicology, art history, choreology. If there are societies that draw the lines at different points or not at all, they have or will have developed scholarly ways of viewing their culture, ways that correspond to their conceptual classifications and, like ethnomusicologists in the West, view the rest of the world through their own eyes, hoping that some insights will come from this also essentially ethnocentric approach. If ethnomusicology has developed a definition of music for itself, that definition is surely part and parcel of the Western background of the field.

Chapter 2

Divine Inspiration and Tonal Gymnastics

THREE CONTINUUMS

Schubert is said to have composed a song while waiting to be served at a restaurant, quickly writing it on the back of the menu; Mozart turned out some of his serenades and sonatas almost overnight; and Theodore Last Star, a Blackfoot Indian, had visions in which, in the space of a minute or two, he learned from a guardian spirit a new song. But, then, Brahms labored for years on his first symphony; Beethoven planned and sketched ideas for his Ninth for over two decades; and William Shakespeare, an Arapaho Indian, said that when he took a bit from one song, something from another, and a phrase from a third, making up a new Peyote song, it might take him a good part of an afternoon. The xylophonist of a Chopi orchestra makes up music as he goes along, but he is constrained by rules articulated by his leader (Tracey 1948:109). The great North Indian sitarist sits down before his audience and makes up a new piece of music on the spot, but he can only do this because he practices memorized exercises for hours every day. A Kentucky mountaineer sings "The Two Sisters" in a tavern, his friends admiring a new twist in the refrain but insisting that only he can sing the song correctly. "She's never played like this before, she makes the Suite live like no one else," exclaims the Bach-lover, overjoyed, after the cello recital.

In some sense, each of these musicians has created music, but music scholars actually know very little about the way in which music comes about, especially in its innovative aspect, which they perhaps most admire. They believe that when music is produced (in any sense of the word), something new is being created. There is innovation in the composition of a symphony, the jazz improvisation of a new version of a well-known show tune, the unique rendition of a Japanese chamber work that has been handed down with little change for generations, the reading of a string quartet. Ethnomusicologists must deal with what is new, new in a sense generally understood by them, but also new within the specific framework of the culture that produces a particular item of music.

Cross-culturally speaking, what may be judged as new composition in one culture would be regarded as simple repetition or variation of something extant in another. Judging the degree of innovation is a tricky business. The Persian improvisor who by the standards of European composition gives his audience something different each time he performs is not, in his own manner of musical thought, doing something really new but simply "playing a particular mode." The Plains Indian who is learning a song in his vision may think of it as a new song, even if it sounds identical to a song learned by one of his friends in another vision. The South Indian musician with a penchant for giving her audience unexpectedly strange vocalizations runs the risk of rendering something outside the realm of propriety and being criticized for not knowing her basic material. The American composer who writes a piece that could conceivably be mistaken for something by Hindemith or Stravinsky is criticized for presenting something belonging in the past.

The task of ethnomusicology is not so much to probe the essential nature of musical creation; such an ambitious job is better left to a consortium of academic disciplines. It is a task, however, to examine the ways in which various societies conceive of and evaluate musical creation and to derive an analytical system that will permit them to be compared. Considering the lack of terminology in most languages for discussing creativity, and the incompatibility of the concepts, it is a particularly thorny problem. A good deal of literature speaks to the issue, some of it highly theoretical (e.g. Meyer 1967), some by surveying much extant literature and giving examples of concepts and techniques known in different societies (e.g. Merriam 1964:165–84), some by concentrating on aspects of the concept: the role of composer in his society (List 1968); improvisation (Ferand 1938); performance as creation; the vast literature on what is called performance practice, beginning with a landmark work by R. Haas (1931); definitions of the raw materials for use in creating music in a particular culture (e.g. Powers 1970, Elsner 1975); and much more. Here we suggest some further ways of examining the problem. It seems convenient, initially, to think of it in terms of three intersecting continuums.

1) To some extent music is inspired, in the sense that we cannot analyze the way in which it finds its way into the thinking of a musician; it is also the result of the manipulation and rearrangement of the units of a given vocabulary, of hard work and concentration. The concept of inspiration, sometimes divine, and of acquiring music directly from supernatural sources, is very widespread among human societies, simple and complex. Haydn worked regular hours and depended on some kind of inspiration; when it did not come, he prayed for it (Nohl 1883:173), like the Plains In-

dian seeking a vision who is also, in effect, praying for songs. At the other end of the line is the concept of composition as an essentially intellectual activity, in which one conscientiously manipulates the materials of music, structuring them carefully in ways that will make it possible for the listener to comprehend the structure, or even arranging them in ways that satisfy certain principles which are not audible and which can be perceived only through careful analysis of a score.

The twentieth-century Western serialist composer is careful to include all units in a predetermined vocabulary, being precise in their manipulation so that they remain intact, following the rules set by himself. The listener is likely to be unaware of all the care that has gone into the preparation of this complex structure. The approach is not limited to societies with written notation and music theory. The American Indian composer of Peyote songs is equally careful, using and abiding by a general structural principle that governs the song, musically making clear a number of intricate interrelationships, deriving phrases from earlier ones, all within a rather rigidly defined framework. But it seems unlikely that the Indian listener understands how this piece has been put together. The two ends of the continuum merge: Mozart's music sounds divinely inspired, was often composed quickly, yet has incredible consistency and complexity. The songs of the Yahi of California, sung by Ishi, the last "wild" Indian, ten seconds long and using only some three or four tones, exhibit considerable sophistication in their internal interrelationships, with a logic like that of Mozart. An Iranian musician says that his improvised performance comes "from the heart," but analysis demonstrates highly structured and sophisticated patterns unique to the performer. An Indian improvisor learns a vast repertory of melodic and rhythmic units that can and must be interrelated in many ways, exhibiting her skill in showing the multitude of combinations she can control; yet in her culture this music is considered spiritual and related to another level of consciousness. Everywhere we find some portion of both ends of the continuum. The proportions vary by culture and individual, and in the creator's and the analyst's perceptions.

2) Improvisation and composition are frequently regarded as completely separate processes, but they may also be viewed as two forms of the same kind of thing (Nettl 1974b). The phenomenally quick though by no means careless composition of a sonata by Schubert may well be related to the rapid combination and rearrangement of materials in an Indian improvisation, and the fact that Schubert used paper and pencil may in some respects be incidental. On the other hand, the gigantic labor involved in the careful composition of a symphony, with the use of sketches and planning diagrams, has just a bit in common with the technique of the Yahi Indian composer who, within the strictest possible limits, nevertheless finds a large number of ways of relating to each other two short phrases that make up a song. For that matter, the many readings of a Beethoven sonata by a

Horowitz are comparable to the twenty different ways in which an Arabic musician may render a maqam in the *taqsim* form in the period of a year, or of his life. It may be rewarding to consider improvisation and composition in essence, if not in specific nature, as aspects of the same process. The extreme forms of both appear at opposite ends of a continuum. The one relies on speed, quick decision-making, and risk-taking in public, in front of an audience that wants to see the musician deal with his issues immediately. The other is characterized by laborious processes and the careful, thoughtful solution of complex problems.

3) The third continuum involves us in the course of events in the creation of a piece of music or of a performance. It has been suggested (Lindley 1980) that one could divide the process into precomposition, composition, and revision. In the case of the typical composer of European classical music, precomposition involves the learning of the basic materials, the theory of music and the extant forms, as well as advance planning of a general sort. While composing, what the musician first writes down may be a finished product but is more likely to be simply a draft. Once this is completed, revision in several stages is usually in order. This description of events in formally composed music has been used to distinguish what some may consider true composition from improvisation and also from the creation of music relying entirely on oral tradition. The role of notation in the process of composition is sometimes misunderstood and overestimated. There are, to be sure, composers for whom work with pen and paper is an intrinsic part of creation; one can hardly see how "The Art of the Fugue," "Meistersinger," or "Wozzeck" could have been put together otherwise. But there are also composers who work things out in their minds (or at the keyboard, as reputedly did Haydn and Stravinsky), and then write down a relatively finished product. While many non-Western societies have musical notation, these seem substantially to have an archival or preservative role, perhaps serving as mnemonic devices for performers rather than as something to aid composers in controlling and manipulating their structural building blocks.

It is widely believed that there is a difference, in *essence,* between composing art music, with notation or at least a background of theory, and folk or tribal music. The latter is often, but I think improperly, labeled as improvisation, as for instance by Knepler (in Brook and others 1972:231), who regards true composition as the "synthesis" or "the linking together of musical elements stemming from different spheres." The difference between "art" music and others has been a major paradigm in musicology. Earlier ethnomusicologists insisted on its significance. Thus, Bartók: "Whether peasants are individually capable of inventing quite new tunes is open to doubt" (1931:2). Yet to me there seems no reason to regard composition in cultures with oral and written traditions as different species. The precomposition-composition-revision model, while most readily applied to Western composers who depend heavily on notation, also works for those who have none. In classical Indian music, for example, the improvisor learns the ragas and the talas, the materials for and ways of dealing with melody and rhythm, and certain kinds of pieces that enable him to internalize techniques for improvisation. In the context of Indian performance, this is precomposition, and so also is a group of decisions as to what raga and what tala to perform on any given occasion, as well as some completely mental but nevertheless specific planning. Composition itself takes place during performance, and only what is performed constitutes the complete composition. But, revising like the composer with his manuscript, the improvisor, sometimes moving away from an intended goal, must make constant adjustments to return to what was in mind in the first place. Mistakes must be covered up, quick adjustments made, unexpected slips absorbed in the structure that the musician has determined in advance.

In most cultures, and perhaps everywhere, we find the composer being inspired but also perspiring, the contrast of improvisatory decision-making and planning with preparation, execution, and revision. One might use these continuums as initial devices for the comparative study of composition, and perhaps also of performance.

GIVEN AND ADDED

Having now suggested that at some level of conceptualization all musical creation everywhere, including composition, improvisation, and performance, is broadly alike, we must also recognize the fact that different societies have quite different views of what constitutes musical creation. In many cases, however, there is the recognition that something already exists, in the most general sense of the word, and that the composer has the job of translating this "something" into acceptable musical sound. A few examples show great variation. The Pima Indian seems to feel that all songs exist already, somewhere in the cosmos, and that it is the task of the composer to untangle them (Herzog 1936a:333). The Eskimo sings: "all songs have been exhausted. He picks up some of all and adds his own and makes a new song" (Merriam 1964:177), specifying that songs exist as material for new ones, to be created by recombining material already extant. In quite a different way traditional Western composers learn a basic body of music theory, comprising a kind of vocabulary and the rules for its use, on which they are to draw for composing new music. The Iranian musician begins his career by studying and memorizing the *radif,* a body of music that he then uses as inspiration for improvisation and composition of set pieces, avoiding going beyond its bounds. In each culture the musician is given something and has the job of adding something else, but the nature of given and added varies greatly.

It may be helpful to look at the balance between them and at the way in which innovation is identified and evaluated in a society. The concept of innovation itself has received considerable attention from anthropologists, beginning with the classic work by Barnett (1953), but it is usually treated as a way of working toward an understanding of culture change. Musicologists deal constantly with innovation; just as Western musicians accord highest value to doing something "new," music scholars typically concentrate on what is new in each period, style, composer's opus (see e.g. Meyer 1967:pt. II). The issues inherent in identifying what is new have not frequently been touched upon. In their verbal and behavioral responses to music most cultures place less value on innovation than does the European-derived West. Given the difficulty of distinguishing what is in fact "new" and what may be perceived as "new" in a society outside one's own, it nevertheless seems that there are many societies in which musical innovation is very restricted. For them, in terms of practical music-making, this may be interpreted to mean that what is given accounts for a very large proportion of the universe of music, and what is added, very little.

Anglo-American and many European folk music repertories seem to fit this model. A song, once composed, remained intact, as indicated for instance by the broad similarity of tunes collected in places and at times far apart (Bronson 1959:72). One learned the songs from one's parents and friends, and then sang them, introducing minor variations and gradually developing variants that were still clearly recognizable as forms of the original. New songs might be composed, but they were cast in the rhythmic, melodic, and textually formal mold of the previously existing material. But comparison with the Persian *radif* seems instructive. It is a large repertory memorized precisely, and variants are rarely introduced in it, but when it gives rise to improvised performances, what is new in these is greater in scope than the innovation in variants of an Anglo-American folk song. Yet the *radif* exerts a greater degree of control over what may be created, for new songs quite different from what already existed were often accepted into the Anglo-American repertory. In the Persian classical system, so great a degree of innovation would have been unacceptable. Now the *radif* in itself contains more music, and if you will, more variety of all sorts, than the basic few tunes (only forty, in a sense, according to Bayard 1953) of Anglo-American folk music, suggesting that the size or amount of the material given correlates inversely with the amount of innovation permitted. This thought would have to be tested in many ways, perhaps on two musical cultures similar in most ways and contrastive only in regard to the mentioned variables.

Let me propose illustrations. It is likely that the musical forms of the Plains Indians were at one time relatively varied, but at that time new songs came into existence rather infrequently. By contrast, in more recent times the forms available for use, the "given" materials, have shrunk in scope, but at the same time the number of new songs constantly appearing increased. In European music of the nineteenth century it would seem that what is given, including the quantity of harmonic scales, modulatory techniques, and forms, is vast. Each composer similarly takes upon himself a huge set of vocabulary-like elements and characteristics on which he draws over long periods. Innovation in the sense of departure from these given traits, seen on a worldwide basis, may not really be very great. In nineteenth-century music one can, for example, very quickly recognize styles and composers—a few notes or chords will suffice—testifying to the consistency of what is given. In each piece the proportion of what is given seems to me very great, and departure in the course of a piece seems not to be so great when viewed in intercultural comparison, the—to us—very radical innovations in each composition notwithstanding. And the performer (as creator) is given a score, a blueprint much more detailed than that handed down in oral tradition or in earlier periods of Western music history when the available vocabulary was more compact.

Not only the quantity but also the nature of what is "given" seems to vary among the world's cultures. It is difficult to enumerate comprehensively. In some societies, such as American Indian, it may be simply all music that a composer has already heard. One is not given the components in separately packaged form. In others, the basic materials for composition are separated from the music itself. In Western culture this is in part a practical theory of music that one learns before being permitted to compose, a vocabulary of materials and analytically derived rules for its use. In the jazz community it is audible materials which are not in themselves music but which the composer must abstract from music he has heard. The American Indian composers of Peyote songs appear informally to learn rules for separating a song into its component phrases and then recombining them in new ways. In the art music culture of India it is the material a musician learns for improvisation—the nature of ragas and talas, the exercises that juxtapose the two, etude-like pieces called *varnams* which contain, South Indians say, the grammar of a raga. In Persian classical music it is the *radif,* a unit the composer then breaks up and subdivides into components for creation. What is also given is optimum lengths, options of all sorts, socially acceptable ways of combining large units. All this is, of course, a mere smattering from a vast array of phenomena.

NEW AND GOOD

Despite much speculation, little is known about that aspect of composition which is designated as inspiration. In the assessment of its degree of importance, there may be a genuine difference between certain traditional and tribal societies and those others in which professional music-making, notation, and technology have become major ingredients. While the American Indians who thought that they dreamed songs in visions certainly did engage in musical gymnastics, manipulating tones and phrases, they did not recognize or at any rate stress that activity, considering music as something which in essence comes from the supernatural. While the composer of new music in an American university may at least recognize a kind of agnostic counterpart of divine inspiration, the idea of talent, in part a fortuitous event or one resulting from genetic inheritance, he or she usually stresses the gymnastic aspect of dealing with the materials in ways that show expertise and ability to do the difficult. In some societies, including our own, the essence of musical creation is to accomplish the difficult.

The concept of "divine inspiration" (according to which music-making should be easy) and the "athletic view" of music (according to which music-making—composing, improvising, performing—must be difficult to be truly great) represent a broad contrast. But the two concepts, supernatural and virtuosic, are also related. The ubiquitous use of music in religion associates it with things that are otherworldly, are not natural, "do not come naturally," are not easily explained, are so difficult that the ordinary human cannot understand them. In European folklore we find the concept of the musician, usually a violinist, in league with the devil (Halpert 1943), who is able to play "devilishly" difficult music, cast supernatural spells over other humans because of his incredible musical skills, able perhaps to seduce women with the uncanny sound of his instrument. And there is Orpheus, who can even defeat death with his superior musicianship. Elsewhere again, the supernatural is manipulated by the musician who performs the right music, at the right time, flawlessly. The "athletic" view of music, so developed in the urban West, may in fact have its roots in the belief that music is divinely inspired.

The criteria for acceptable innovation have rarely been spoken to in ethnomusicology. We believe that music-makers innovate, but when do they and their audiences agree that something new has come about, and how much newness will they accept? In the "new" Western music of the 1960s, it almost seems that anything new was provisionally accepted as good. It may have been different in the nineteenth century, if we are to believe the apocryphal story of Camille Saint-Saëns, who described a colleague's music as containing much that was good and new, though what was good was not new, and what new, not good. But in the 1960s innovation was a supreme value, and in music, therefore, one was driven to try to depart from norms. Audiences and critics tended to pay attention to that aspect of a piece which struck them as new, and avoided relating it to earlier models. By contrast, in traditional Persian society, where radical innovation was not valued, thought-out composition was not stressed. Rather it was improvisation, viewed not as the creation of new material but simply as the performance, in slightly changed and personalized form, of something that already existed. In traditional India, where radical innovation is also not prized, its threat, resulting from contact with other cultures (as for instance from the traveling of musicians to Europe and America), may be criticized and included in the concept of pollution, which Indians fear greatly. In the rituals of the Navaho and tribes of the Northwest Coast of North America, mistakes were punished and innovation inhibited (McAllester 1954:64; Herzog 1938:4–5, 1949:106–7).

The criteria for innovation lead quickly to a consideration of the concept that in many societies there are distinctions between what is good music (or music-making) and what is unusually good, barely acceptable, or beyond the pale of music. In our twentieth-century view of nineteenth-century European concert music, part and parcel of twentieth-century musical culture, we distinguish rather easily between a small number of star composers (of course, Beethoven, Schubert, Wagner, Brahms, and a number of others) and a large number of unknowns whose music, once regarded as acceptable fare, is now totally forgotten. We have a middle ground, a group of minor masters (Bruch, Borodin, Lortzing) whose works are tolerated and occasionally loved. There is a fine line between the "stars," all of whose music is accepted as the work of genius, even their less distinguished creations mentioned in hushed tones, and the others, whose work is only very occasionally regarded as close to the creations of these "stars." While there is little of substance on which one can base these suggestions (but see Mueller 1951 for supporting data from symphony orchestra repertories), it would seem that certain composers have, over a period of time, moved in and out of the "star" category. Mahler, Bruckner, Weber may be cases in point. But the structure seems to have remained essentially intact for some decades. What makes the music of the "stars" so great? In Beethoven's last quarters, Wagner's "Meistersinger," Bach's "Art of the Fugue," we sense the athletic view, seeing incredible control of a large diversity of materials. Only by exception is broad stylistic innovation a criterion for identifying the greatest masterpieces. But innovation on a smaller scale is more often a factor. The superstar sounds less like anyone else than does the average musician, and his works sound less like one another, yet his imprint may be readily perceived in a selection of a few measures of his music. In these senses, what he does is new because it is different, unique, not necessarily because he changes the direction in which the music of his contemporaries moves. Of course, such observations and many speculations in a large literature not withstanding, we do not really understand what it was that made him a star (see e.g. Meyer 1967:22–41).

The star system is found also in the classical music of Iran in the twentieth century. Indeed, the line between stars and others seems to be more pronounced there than in Europe, star performers being accorded relatively more status, license, money. The nonstars are readily ranked from acceptable to incompetent, but none has a high place in society. What distinguishes the "stars" among the improvisors, who are in fact the most significant composers in Iran, is their ability to do something new within very strict confines. Radical innovation, contrary to the recent "new music" culture in the West, almost automatically places one outside the category. Ability to hold on to the tradition is a more important criterion. Yet, if one examines the work of those improvisors who are most respected, one sees that their performances contain more of innovation; there are more changes in the flow of the music, the various improvisations based on one model differ more among themselves, but as in the case of the great European composers, the personal stamp seems more pronounced.

In the case of the Blackfoot Indians, it is more difficult to speak of the characteristics of individual composers. In recent times variety in composition has decreased as has the number of composers, the practice of composition in dreams and visions on the part of many or most men having declined. These trends coincide with the development of a class of specifically designated and somewhat professional song-makers. The Blackfoot appear not to separate stars from other song-makers, and if anything distinguishes certain individuals, it is their productivity. The best song-makers are those who make up the most songs. But if one examines those songs said most frequently to be "favorite" songs of the tribe, it is likely that they, as a group, are very slightly different from the norm (Nettl 1967c:298) and thus can be interpreted as being innovative.

Clearly, an understanding of the nature of musical creation is a major issue in the world of music, a problem that is largely unsolved. Ethnomusicology can bring to its solution some insight into the way musical creativity is perceived in the cultures of the world, into vast differences and what is held in common. It is obvious that one cannot deal only with the musician's work, his concepts and techniques, but must also address the ways in which the values of a society are expressed in a people's evaluation of what is new and what is good in music.

Chapter 3

The Universal Language

ETHNOMUSICOLOGIST'S BACKLASH

"What do you expect to do as an ethnomusicologist?" I asked the new graduate student in the Anthropology Department. "To study universals," she said without hesitation. In 1970 this sounded anachronistic, for in my college years, about 1950, the idea that there was much that all cultures shared was presented as ancient and abandoned history. If it was here again, rearing its head, anthropology and ethnomusicology must have come full circle, for the belief in universal traits of music seemed characteristic of scholarship of the nineteenth century. Wilhelm Wundt, one of the last to have tried his hand at a complete culture history, told us that all primitive peoples have monophonic singing and use intervals rather like those of nineteenth-century Western music, major and minor seconds and thirds, singing that came from speech in which the duration of unwavering pitch, the note, became sufficiently long to be perceived and repeated (1911:4:464–66). Most musicians of his time and later were probably attracted to such a view, and even the teacher of music appreciation in North America as late as the 1930s and 1940s was quite prone to consider music as a "universal language." In contrast to the languages of the world, which were mutually unintelligible, music of all kinds was thought intelligible to anyone. So, in the Western world, we developed books called "*The* History of Music" and courses called "Introduction to *the* Art of Music," which dealt with only one kind of music. The assumption seemed to be that the basic principles of this kind of music were universally valid, either because it was the only "true" music or because all other kinds of music simply represented its generative stages, or perhaps degenerations.

Anthropologists and comparative musicologists, when they became established early in the twentieth century, saw it as their job to cry out against this unified view of culture. Finding ethnocentrism distasteful, they were fascinated by the diversity of human culture, by the many sounds, systems, and uses of music. And so, when I was a graduate student, had I been asked what I wished to do, I would have answered, "to discover musical diversity but to show that all musics, at some level, are equally good."

Surely, in the development of a general methodology of ethnomusicology as promulgated by leaders like Hornbostel, Sachs, Herzog, Kunst, Merriam, and Hood, the non-universality of music looms as a major point of agreement. All musics were not alike, and the approaches used to understand Western music did not suffice for that of other societies; it was to show this that they were all in business. In a backlash against musical ethnocentrism the ethnomusicologist practiced gamesmanship, answering generalizations about music with a parody of the well-known "not in the South," insisting that it was "not so among the Cherokee," or "different in Japan." The task was to prove facile generalization wrong, even immoral. When not engaged in gamesmanship, the ethnomusicologist tried seriously to show, in teaching and writing, that musics, like languages, were not universal; music, the *non*-universal language, became in effect a battle cry (Herzog 1939).

And then, having got their fill of diversity, ethnomusicologists began in the late 1960s to return to the study of universals. Panels and special issues of periodicals (e.g. *Ethnomusicology,* vol. 15, no. 3, 1971, *The World of Music,* vol. 19, no. 1/2, 1977) have been devoted to the subject, and some of the leading scholars of the field (Seeger 1971, Wachsmann 1971b, Harrison 1977, McAllester 1971, Harwood 1976, Blacking 1977, Hood 1977) have had significant things to say on it. They had distinguished models, as other disciplines had developed new culture heroes who clearly also renewed interest in what tied humans together. Indeed, the interest of ethnomusicologists in universals seems to have followed similar trends in linguistics and anthropology. Noam Chomsky showed the underlying structure of all human languages, developed the idea that a deep structure, an ability to learn language, was present in all humans (Lyons 1977:131–33). Lévi-Strauss asserted that all mythologies are basically alike, as are all customs involving basic human needs, their task to bridge the universal contrast between humans and animals, men and women, parents and children, us and them, nature and culture (Leach 1970:53–86; Lévi-Strauss 1963:208, etc.). Speaking frequently and understandingly of Wagner and Chabrier, symphony and fugue, he knew, of course, that the South American Indians whose myths he discussed have music that is incredibly different. Yet, because the structure and functions of all human brains are alike, he found it possible to speak of these myths and of Western art music in one breath, as if an understanding of this music could provide comprehension of all music as easily as the Indian myths can provide an understanding of the concept of myth.

Perhaps it is so. In the 1940s it was necessary for ethnomusicologists to point out that music is indeed not a universal language. But non-universality in the end was widely accepted and finally overstated by those opposed to comparative study, and so later it again became important to seek ways in which the various musics of the world are alike. First, musics had to be liberated, as it were, from Western ethnocentrism; ethnomusicology had to make clear their independence, had to urge their acceptance on their own terms and not simply as evolutionary waystations to something greater and more perfect. This mission accomplished, ethnomusicology had to return to seeing them as part of a single whole.

There seem to be two approaches to the identification of musical universals. One involves the search for specific features that musics have in common; the other, establishment of a conceptual framework for musical analysis and description broad enough to subsume all imaginable differences. In this chapter we follow the first approach.

Seekers for universals have a dilemma. They must somehow define or conceptualize music, and do this on the basis of empirical evidence from the musical systems of the world. But to give a definition of music and then equate it to a statement of universals is not enough. They must find those features that (1) fit the definition of music, (2) are found everywhere (a term yet to be defined), and (3) exclude what could conceivably be regarded as music but is not actually done in the cultures of the world. In other words, the task is to state the outer limits of music, and then to ascertain what within these limits has been selected by humans for musical expression. To be practical: if we heard music whose scale consisted of seven tones separated by quarter-tone intervals, we would, given the ethnomusicologist's gluttony, have to include it as music—but no human culture has accepted this structure of sound as anything approaching a cultural, personal, or contextual norm.

THREE TYPES OF UNIVERSALS

In the context of this discussion, what is "everywhere"? We wish to ask whether there are musical traits present in every instant of musical sound, others found in every musical utterance, in the musical experience of every human, in the musical experience of every human community, in every culture, or in every musical repertory. This group of distributions may lead us to a typology or perhaps a hierarchy of universals. There are at least three types.

If there is anything that is present in every instant of music, it involves the definition of music. Having decided what music is, we would expect that we could identify it instantly when we hear it, could distinguish it immediately from all other kinds of sound—speech, animal sounds, random noise, wind, machinery. But this is impossible, even after prolonged listening, and even given an interculturally valid definition. One surely cannot distinguish certain kinds of speech from singing even after hearing a total performance, or certain electronic music from factory sounds, except on the basis of the social context. All of the formidable difficulties of defining music that we encountered earlier are here again, and except in the most theoretical sense, there is no way of generating from this approach a meaningful test of universals.

For a second approach, we make the requirements less stringent and ask whether there is anything that is present in every musical utterance. In order to address this question, we must hypothesize that the concept of a musical utterance is itself a universal phenomenon. In Western culture it would be a song, a piece, a symphony, a march, a mass, some kind of a culturally accepted unit of musical thought. Elsewhere there are similarly definable units, long and short. One begins to make music and, at some point, comes to an end, by design or because the context has ceased to exist. Or one repeats. Now, are there things that all musical utterances have in common? (Well, almost all; no one seems to have heard enough of them, so we can't be sure.) Here are some suggestions.

There is a more or less clearly marked beginning and ending. There is some redundancy, some repetition, balanced by some variety, articulated through rhythmic, melodic, textural means. There is a level of simplicity and levels of complexity beyond which the overwhelming majority do not extend. Even those most complex units that exceed such limits may not be regarded properly as music by the people from whose cultures they emanate. Music must evidently fall within some kind of perceptual band, even if, theoretically, it could go further. The musical utterance consists of smaller units which are fairly well marked, and for which one may substitute others from a given cultural repertory in order to produce new utterances. These may be (and in Western culture have been) defined as tones, notes, motifs, chords, phrases, sequences, and in a sense they are comparable to phonemes and morphemes in language, a lexicon from which, given certain rules, a music-maker may draw to create old and new musical utterances. A musical utterance always consists of more than one minimal unit.

These are just examples, and others would no doubt be equally general. This second category of universals still does not tell us *how* humanity has chosen to structure its music; like the first type, it mainly tells us simply *that* humans have music.

For a third and somewhat more feasible approach, we ask whether there is anything that is found in each musical system, whether musics or musical dialects are all in some way alike, whether there are any characteristics or traits present in all of them, even if these are not found in all musical utterances, or all pieces, to say nothing of all instants of musical sound. The question includes musical sound as well as the concept and behavior parts of Merriam's well-worn model.

First the sound of music, with the caveat that many musics are unknown to the ethnomusicological population, and many more, to me. Even so, all cultures have singing. In the vast majority of vocal musics the chief melodic interval appears to be something close to a major second. We are not speaking, of course, about accuracy in tuning. Intervals of that general scope, including anything from five quarter tones to three quarters, surely make up the bulk of the world's melodic progressions. Only in rare instances do we find cultures in which many pieces progress exclusively by half or quarter tones or, for that matter, by thirds and fourths. (Some South American Indian peoples seem to be a major exception.)

In the vast majority of cultures musical utterances tend to descend at the end, but they are not similarly uniform at their beginnings. All cultures make some use of internal repetition and variation in their musical utterances. Indeed, it has been suggested that one characteristic of music is its unusually large degree of redundancy (Lomax 1968:13–15). All have a rhythmic structure based on distinction among note lengths and among dynamic stresses. All of the mentioned features are universals in the sense that they exist practically everywhere, but also in another sense: they would *not* have to be present in order for music to exist, and thus are *not* simply a part of the definition of music. It is, for example, conceivable for a musical system to use only perfect fourths, or only notes of equal length, but there is no such music. Evidently humanity has decided not only to make music but, despite the vast amount of variation among the musics of the world, to make it in a particular way.

Universals in the conceptualization of music and in musical behavior are harder to isolate, but let me attempt a short list. Surely first among them must be the association of music with the supernatural. All known cultures accompany religious activity with music. McAllester (1971:380) sounds a similar note when he says that everywhere "music transforms experience." Further, there is the conception of music as an art that consists of distinct units of creativity which can be identified, by place in ritual, by creator or performer, by opus number. One does not simply "sing," but one sings *something*. Music is composed of artifacts, although cultures differ greatly in their view of what constitutes such an artifact. The visual arts and perhaps literary art are presumably similar, but in at least some societies dance seems not to be. In some cultures one may simply "dance," or dance a specific *kind* of dance, but not necessarily *a* dance.

Also in this category of universals is the musical association with dance and speech. There is no culture that does not have *some* dance with musical accompaniment, nor one whose singing is completely without words, without poetry. These, then, are a few universals of the sort present in all or at least the overwhelming majority of musics, in practically all cultures, but not in each musical utterance.

The musics of the world, viewed as self-contained systems, have common properties. The presence of differential levels of musicality in every society, the fact that all population groups have tradition-carrying networks, the existence in all societies of a repertory of children's music, could all be examined from the point of view that they are musical universals. Let me briefly concentrate on only one such issue, the overall general and internal structure of a music, of a musical repertory. Musics, as systems, seem to have some things in common.

It goes without saying that in each society limits are placed on musical creativity. We have seen that certain sounds are accepted as being proper music and other excluded. But there also seems in each music (considering that few have been described in these terms) to be a gray area, a group of pieces or musical utterances, if you will, that reside at or beyond the boundary of music. People, it seems, tolerate a certain but limited amount of intolerable music-making. All musics seem to have a wide band of relatively exceptional materials at their borders and, as indicated in Chapter 2, some of it is only arguably accepted as music.

Thus in contemporary Western culture a good deal of electronic and similar-sounding music exists, but it is not used or tolerated by the majority. American Indian music is generally monophonic, but a few polyphonic utterances, for specific social purposes, were permitted here and there (Nettl 1961). Even Bach seems to have written the occasional tabooed set of parallel fifths. The exceptional material often has certain special and significant social uses and functions.

If each repertory has such material at its borders, meriting special attention, it seems also to have a mainstream, a unified style clustering in the center, composed of a large number of utterances that are very much alike. These are not necessarily the most valued, however, for what is best or greatest—either as music or because it has special social or religious significance—is also likely to be somehow exceptional.

The immediate reason for the high value of the exceptional is different for each culture. In the West it may be the value of innovation; in Iran, the value of individualism and surprise; among the Blackfoot, the importance of music in forging group identity. But the three repertories exhibit striking similarities in the structure and social role of that which lives at the boundary of the musical mainstream. We may not have arrived at a legitimate "universal," but at the very least one can suggest that there is no difference in essence between Western and non-Western, urban and tribal, musical repertory structure.

THE FOURTH TYPE

The fourth approach to the study of universals is less problematic than the first three. It asks, simply, whether there are features shared by a healthy majority of musics, though by no means all. In other words, one can look for what is extremely common, substituting the concept of statistical universals for what is sometimes described as a "true" universal. This expedient allows one to avoid dealing with cultures that do not share in the worldwide mainstream. Since we know a great deal about a few musics, a bit about many, hardly anything about some, and nothing about an unknown number from the past, we can, without unduly bad conscience, gloss over such areas of ignorance. We can satisfy our quest for ways in which humans have chosen to make music, establish conceptual and sonic boundaries for their music-making, not the result of physical coercion or other essentially nonmusical factors. For the time being, we need not even account for those cultures that do not share these "limited" universals, taking them to be historical accidents or aberrations. This type of universal is not concerned, as are the others, with physiological or perceptual limitations to which all humans are subject (see Harwood 1976:525–28). It is a bit like a consensus of the world's societies.

Examples: tetratonic and pentatonic scales composed of unequal intervals, often major seconds and minor thirds; singing in octaves; stanzaic structure of songs and pieces; the use of idiophones and of sound tools termed by Curt Sachs (1940:63) as the "oldest" layer of man's musical instruments; the concept of musicianship. Most cultures have some sense of a musical specialist who, for whatever reasons—religious, aesthetic, social—knows music better and is able to produce it more adequately and in larger quantity than others.

Were we to continue this line of thought, our next step would be to find fairly widespread non-universals, then other traits with more limited distribution. But our fourth category is the last one that we could conceivably call a "universal." We have moved from the components of the definition of music itself to the essential characteristics of the musical utterance, on to the characteristics of total musical cultures or musics, and then on to traits generally typical of world music. Clearly, we are dealing with concentric circles. It remains to ask what it means that such phenomena exist.

Why, for instance, are there such "universals" of the fourth type? Of course we can only speculate. Demands of human physiology and anatomy do not provide a very convincing argument. The theory that there is a unilinear cultural evolution from which a few societies diverge, like mutations, or perhaps remain behind, also finds few adherents. Perhaps most convincing is the argument that most human societies have, for millennia, been in direct and more often indirect contact with each other, and that there is a single world of music, rather like a single language family which has spawned many variants (Lyons 1970:145). If so, it is interesting to view the structure of the world of music as a macrocosmic musical repertory with some of the structural features of smaller repertories mentioned above: a mainstream—the many repertories characterized by the universals in this fourth type such as pentatonic scales—and borders of material that might not even be considered properly music by the mainstream. In the case of the global macrocosm, these sidestreams might on the one hand be the ditonic and tritonic scalar style of the world's simplest music (Sachs 1943:32–34), and on the other, a group of exceptional, highly prized classical systems straining the perception of the average listener and the abilities of music-makers.

Rather a fantastic speculation. But it may be significant that before one spoke explicitly of universals, and before one used the expression "musics" of the world, rather than speaking of the "music" of the world, George Herzog (1939), putting forward the view that one must study the music of each society in its own terms and learn it individually, referred to "music's dialects" rather than "music's languages." There are musical systems, there are musics, but they are more readily connected, more readily understood at least in some respects by the novice, than are true languages. Despite the enormous variety of musics, the ways in which people everywhere have chosen to make music are more restricted than the boundaries of the imaginable.

Chapter 4

The Non-Universal Language

THE LANGUAGES OF MUSIC

Emerging from the concert of electronic music, the elderly musicologist was angry. "This simply is not music," he exclaimed. I tried to calm him: "It certainly sounds strange. One must learn how to listen to it, find the meaning of its various components." "Oh, you ethnomusicologists, always making excuses. You can play Chinese music, or Polynesian music, and it will sound strange to me, but I will know that it is music. But this, this *is not music,* you can say what you want." My friend seemed to equate the liking of music with understanding it, or to follow the adage, "to understand is to forgive." Perhaps he felt that music, something which this culture defines as pleasant and which one is expected to like, is understood if it is simply enjoyed. In this society it really works that way; people often listen to Japanese, Javanese, Indian music, making comments about it that would be totally unacceptable to an Asian musician, but satisfied that they understand it because they enjoyed it.

The electronic concert took place in the 1950s, at the time that Mantle Hood was developing his concept of bi-musicality (Hood 1960), a concept based on the premise that the world consists of a series of musics, each of which, like a language, must be learned and understood. Followers of Mantle Hood as well as my friend who did not like electronic music find themselves at times at the borders between musics, recognizing certain incompatibilities on the two sides of the line, questioning the emotional and technical dislocations they occasion, responding with disgust or enthusiasm. Both cases illustrate a way of looking at the world of music which is rather like that of linguists viewing the world of language, seeing a group of more or less discrete systems of communication. The main approach of musicologists to the world of music has all along followed this line. The concept of music as the "universal language" has never played a great role, nor has the belief that associated or neighboring styles merge gradually and imperceptibly.

Most publications deal with bodies of music and attempt to characterize these as self-contained units. The work of one composer, one nation, one period, the musical style of a tribe or an Asian nation, are dealt with as if they were systems somewhat analogous to languages. But this widespread view has rarely been the basis of an explicit theory, though, as in many cases, Charles Seeger's work is an exception (1953a). Without pretending that language and music are alike, there are sufficient similarities to have permitted ethnomusicologists to take certain cues from the study of language in order to gain insight into the world of music (see Bright 1963, Feld 1974, Powers 1980).

If we are to find the typical characteristics of a music, we should first ask how one goes about defining what comprises it. What it is that belongs to a language is determined by linguists in various ways. One is the recognition of the existence of units known as speech communities (Bloomfield 1951: 42), groups of people who communicate with each other regularly and consistently. The body of vocal sounds they use is a language, a dialect, or some unit that can be studied by linguists as a self-contained system. At the same time the total linguistic inventory of an individual person may also be a unit worthy of study. Known to linguists as idiolect, it too is a way in which the content of language can be circumscribed. In contrast to these essentially social definitions of language, structural approaches view a language as consisting of a phonology and a grammar, that is, characteristics of structure which are imposed on meaning and content of thought. One may further define a language in terms of its content, a set of words or perhaps of culturally or structurally acceptable statements. In a certain sense the content of a dictionary is the content of a language, and all of the words of a language, a kind of definition and circumscription of the language.

Linguists, like musicologists, have had to deal with the problem of boundaries, asking whether a traveler across India moves imperceptibly from one language to another, uncertain when he has made the transition from Tamil to Telegu country, and whether Old English changed rather suddenly to Middle English. Taking an essentially historical perspective for the study of separate languages, linguists at one point believed that "sound laws admit of no exceptions," implying that there are sharp boundaries, that the speech of one community can be obviously classed as belonging to Language A, and that of a neighboring community to the related but separable Language B. They would insist that languages that seem to border on each other on the map such as Czech, Slovak, and Polish really can be separated. Others, by contrast, believe that "every word has its own history," implying a gradual merging of one language into its geographical or chronological neighbor, the boundary for any two words occurring at different points on the map (Anttila 1972:291).

Some of these ways of defining and finding the borders of languages can be suggestive for the musicologist. The idea of a music community, for example, is well developed. A large proportion of ethnomusicological work claims to report upon the repertories of communities of people in which there is frequent exchange and communication of musical material. As a matter of fact, while there is no reason to doubt the applicability of a published repertory to a music community, little by way of evidence is usually presented. The typical collection of the music from one tribal group or village is a collection made with a very small number of informants, sometimes only one, and broader questions such as the degree to which the repertory is evenly distributed throughout the village or tribe, or the music community, are often ignored (see Brailoiu 1960, the classic study of a village repertory). But the unit of music in most ethnomusicological publications is determined by a social group that communicates in ways other than musical, such as a group of people who also share a language. Musical communication within the group is normally assumed rather than proved, and across cultural or linguistic boundaries it has usually been neglected.

The use of a single individual to determine the content of a music has been more widely accepted by scholars than has the linguistic analogue. There are several criteria for defining a musical idiolect. We can ask what music one individual knows, but we must first also define knowledge. It may mean ability to perform, or to recognize, some kind of identification with self, admitted liking, or claimed understanding. The concepts of active and passive repertories, developed in folklore, would be useful to musicologists. In the case of language one can test informants' understanding of utterances, and one can check consensus by asking groups of informants to make statements, such as giving the word for "mother" or "father" and then comparing them. The latter approach could conceivably also be used for music, but there is difficulty in finding minimal units analogous to words that can be used to construct a lexicon circumscribing and defining one music. One might use such units as intervals, brief rhythmic motifs, chords, all possibly related in length or scope to the phoneme of linguists, but they might not be units with significance in the culture. We could take units which the culture itself presents as separable, songs and pieces, but for which the collector of linguistic texts has no equivalents smaller than proverbs, tales, song texts. Despite these problems, defining a music through individual informants may bear more examination.

Let's use our imagination. We begin by inquiring into "musical understanding." If you, dear reader, are an American with some academic pretensions, you are likely to claim that you understand "Barbara Allen," a Beethoven symphony, records by Louis Armstrong and Elvis Presley, and a Gregorian mass. No matter if your professor of music history denies you the privilege unless you can make a thorough analysis; and no matter if specialized aficionados of jazz, rock, and early music believe that you lack true understanding. You claim a certain degree of it. But are you likely to accept all of these kinds of music as somehow belonging truly to yourself? One could construct a test in which you are confronted with the mentioned pieces, and also with excerpts of African, Chinese, American Indian, and electronic music, and then might arrive at a structure of your musicality. The test might find you identifying yourself with Armstrong and Presley, claiming some affinity with Beethoven, somewhat less with medieval and African music, and none, though attraction, to Indian and Chinese music, and in the end throwing up your hands at the electronic excerpt. Concentric circles—and if this model doesn't fit you, something similar probably would. The structure of the given grouping might give us some important insights. Thus: electronic music in the context of Western culture is a new music, a new musical language, and society is being asked to learn it but has not yet done so. African music has a long-standing affinity with Western music, as long ago suggested by Richard Waterman (1952). The musical building blocks of Armstrong, Presley, Beethoven are in important ways the same.

Our little exercise has defined a music, *your* music; we can look at literature dealing with the musical knowledge of individuals in other cultures as possible support, including some of the world's simplest repertories, those inevitably presented as the extreme contrast to Western classical music. Ishi spent his last five years teaching what he could of his culture to anthropologists. He also sang all of the songs he knew or could think of, and produced a total of about sixty-three. By contrast, a concert violinist has memorized many dozens of pieces, holding lots of them in his mind at one time. Again, the man on the street, if pressed, can perhaps sing a few songs, although he recognizes many.

It was long believed that in a typical folk or tribal culture, musical experience was homogeneous and thus most people could sing most of the songs of the tribe. But such generalizations pale in the face of enormous cultural variety: thus the Sirionó were described in precisely the opposite terms (Key 1963:18), as each person tended to sing all of his or her songs to a single, personal tune. Somewhat similarly, an Iranian folk singer may sing only one song type and one melody type, constructing an entire musical life on one tune and its variants. Again in contrast, the men of the people of Yirkalla in northern Australia (R. Waterman 1956) appear to learn the same songs, the idiolect of each man being essentially the same, but they learn the songs gradually, and only old men seem to have at their command the entire repertory, a credible sampling of the entire music. If we use the idiolect as basis, the musics of the world differ widely in scope, size, and internal interrelationship.

CONTENT AND STYLE

In the literature of musicology and ethnomusicology, musics are described most frequently in terms of their style. It is customary to begin with a music community or a musical idiolect, and then to take what is typical within it, bestowing upon that portion the concept of a music (a "style," as it is frequently put), and finding reasons to lay aside that whose character departs radically from the norm. Then, for example, a music is described as a system in which a particular kind of scale is very common, other kinds less so, a few more, barely present or absent; similar statements can be made about other characteristics. Once the style is characterized, the assumption is that any new piece that fits the characterization can become a part of this music. Indeed, a really first-class, comprehensive description of a musical repertory should make it possible for an intelligent reader to synthesize the musical style, to be able to compose new pieces that merge with it without trace. But there is no literature that tests this assumption. Ethnomusicologists have here and there composed pieces in the style they study, sometimes, like Jon Higgins, American singer of South Indian music, in improvised repertories. In such instances the special circumstances have usually been known to the informants who react, probably making it impossible to compare the reception of such material with that of new songs entering the repertory in completely traditional ways. This process should theoretically be feasible, but as a matter of fact it is quite possible that new songs synthesized from a description might not be accepted in a traditional music. There are probably certain rules that must be observed in the introduction of new music, rules that have to do with the way the society works and that may be completely independent of the musical system as defined by characteristics of style.

This thought brings us to defining a music by its content. We may regard musical ideas, motifs, lines, tunes, as analogous to words or concepts in a language. If a tune retains its integrity through changes of scale, mode, meter, form, and singing style, that aspect of it which remains constant—and this is often very difficult to pin down—can be regarded as content. A musical culture may define as "new" and therefore extraneous any material not related to musical thought, or musical content, already extant. And so, rather than accepting anything that conforms to style, a culture might not consider a newly introduced tune to be part of its music unless it also can be related to specific extant musical works. Similarly, a new word does not enter a language even though it may fit the phonology unless there is a way in which the culture can make use of its meaning or conceptualization.

Circumscribing, defining, or enumerating the content of a music is indeed difficult. A few publication types qualify as attempts, although this is not their purpose. The thematic catalogues of the works of individual composers are a case in point. Perhaps even more applicable are the comprehensive inventories such as W. Haas's (1932) attempt to put into musically logical order all of the themes by Beethoven. Otherwise, there are brief statements indicating recognition of the problem: Samuel Bayard (1953:130–32) asserts that the overwhelming majority of American folk songs belongs to a very limited number of tune families, implying that there are perhaps forty tunes, ideas, musical equivalents of words, if you will, that comprise this music. The Peyote songs of North American Indians appear to make use of a limited number of musical motifs that are interchanged and alternated in a number of ways, and an inventory of these could serve as a statement of the musical content of this repertory, and a way of defining it as a music. A listing of this content in some kind of systematic form would be the musical equivalent of a dictionary or lexicon. Indeed, there have been occasional attempts to make inventories of this sort, such as Bartók's listing of motifs in Romanian bagpipe tunes (1967).

In our considerations of universals, we suggested that musics as systems share in certain overall structural traits. Thus it seems that all musics tend to have a mainstream, a homogeneous core, and then one or several easily distinguishable sidestreams or minorities. Let us take the subject a bit further. One example: in 1967 about 90 percent of the Blackfoot Indian repertory consisted of songs in the "classical" Plains Indian style, which included the well-known characteristics of the typical "incomplete repetition" form (e.g. AABCD, BCD), descending contour, high tessitura, vocal tension, pulsations, falsetto, and drumming off the beat (Nettl 1954a:24–33). The remaining 10 percent was a large group of gambling songs in a completely different though not totally incompatible style. Or another example: if there is such a thing as "Western" music, the one most prominent thing that holds it together is a system of harmony, usually called "functional harmony," present in the mainstream in all forms of acceptable Western music, popular and classical, composed from the seventeenth century to the twentieth. But sidestreams, among which one could include monophonic folk and liturgical music, "new" music, music of medieval origin with a harmonic base different from the functional system, constituting minorities, are all present in our contemporary perception of what Western music is.

The point is that in each of these musical languages, some style features dominate and coalesce into a mainstream, but material not sharing these characteristics but nevertheless generally compatible is permitted to exist and is accepted as part of the music. One may hypothesize that such a structure is essential to the existence of a musical system. Conceivably it is a reflection of the changeable nature and essence of culture, and the function of the disequilibrium that is both a prerequisite and a result of change.

CENTERS AND BORDERS

One of the major difficulties in dealing with the world of music as a group of musics is the question of boundaries. The development of musical areas analogous to culture areas in North America and Africa (Nettl 1954a, Merriam 1959a) was a practical application of the concept of musics. In these areas it has been relatively easy to find central points in which the main characteristics of music are concentrated, but it has been difficult to find the precise points on the map between one area and another (Nettl 1960). Anthropologists have dealt with this problem in a broader context (see e.g. Barth 1969). The historian of European music, interested in the fact that the culture moves periodically from one musical language to another, just as it moves from using Old to Middle English and eventually to modern English, finds little difficulty in identifying the centers of periods (Mozart, Schumann) but has trouble in establishing precise boundaries between them (Schubert, classicist or romanticist; or Debussy, or Monteverdi). Indeed, the standard periodization in the history of European music now generally accepted was at one time not at all taken for granted. There was much variety. Thus one found Guido Adler providing a scheme with four periods (1930), and Einstein (1947b), Lorenz (1928), Sachs (1946), and Clark (1956) all providing different opinions of when the languages of music changed. We will have some occasion to refer to this question of spatial and temporal distribution later in Chapters 14 and 17, but I want to point out that it is also a factor in the question of dividing the world into a group of discrete musics. Musical systems far exceeding cultural boundaries have also been proposed, like the time-honored relationship of North African, Middle Eastern, and South Asian music on the basis of improvisatory models (Lachmann 1929).

There are two other areas of concern to which we should briefly direct attention. While the concept of bi-musicality is usually taken as a fruitful approach to fieldwork, the fact is that many cultures have been and are natively bi-musical (or poly-musical), recognizing and keeping separate two or more musics in the same way in which bilingual people handle two languages. In India some musicians seem to have managed to keep classical and folk musics separate, obeying for each its own set of rules. Some of the folk singers of northern Iran, specialists in two or three rather rigidly circumscribed repertories or genres of song, seem to keep these systems from affecting each other. In the nineteenth and twentieth centuries Western music has come to be known to the members of most societies, leading to a variety of ways of dealing with the matter of musical boundaries. In some cases, such as cities of West Africa, there has emerged a single, new musical language or system resulting from the compatibility of Western and traditional African. This compatibility has also been a major concept in explanations for the growth of an essentially discrete Afro-American music, with its emphasis on those elements that are shared by traditional West Africa and Europe. The Blackfoot Indians consider themselves bi-musical, speaking of "white" and "Indian" musics, and holding these separate despite the fact that certain elements of Western culture have come to influence the traditional "Indian" material (Witmer 1973). Bi-musicality here accompanies and symbolizes bi-cultural society.

The view of the world as a system of musics with centers and boundaries must also take into account the rapidly increased accessibility to most people of a large variety of music, much more than was available before. This change is particularly pronounced in non-Western societies, which now have access to Western music along with their older traditions, plus perhaps a larger spread of national or regional styles. The idea of the world of music consisting of a large number of discrete systems, more or less acceptable for the past, may not work in the present, when there is much less to keep the musics of the world separate. In the North American city one can easily hear classical, popular, jazz, all kinds of folk and non-Western music on the radio, on records, even in live performance. The same in various proportions is perhaps true in all cities of the world, including those of non-Western nations, with varying but equally complex configurations of bodies of music. This may be interpreted as a society learning more music, becoming bi-, tri-, multi-musical, acquiring second, third, fourth musical languages, or alternatively as the expansion of a single musical system that is enriched by adding materials and styles. The latter interpretation seems to accept a model of a music as something that has no internal structure, being simply the music experienced by a self-defined population group. The first, on the other hand, returns us to the question of what it means for a society actually to have, to possess, a music. Of course we would have to refine our analytical tools and our field techniques in order to see just how the various musics in the society are distinguished by the people who use them, and whether these distinctions are reflected in musical structure, style, and content.

These are questions for the future. For the moment, it seems useful to continue the concept of the world of music as a collection of musics, to accept the fact that a society may have several musics, that a given group of people will regard one music as intrinsically its own and yet claim to share others, and that a music is distinguished by more than simply acceptance by a group of people, that is, it also has a logically consistent style or content which defines it. A central problem for future research is the degree to which social function, style, and content coincide and correlate, and the degree to which the cultural characteristics of a music community are reflected in the traits of the music it claims as its own. The way in which the world of music is divided into musics, and the criteria for the divisions, are major issues that have perhaps not been given sufficient explicit recognition.

Chapter 5

Apples and Oranges

A STATE OF CONFLICT

In 1953 I tried to present a panorama of North American Indian musical styles with a few examples for a class of students. There was a dearth of readily available records, but I tried to compare those that I had and surprised the students with the interesting variety of styles. Although they had at most heard some songs of the Plains Indians, it was clear to them that the purpose of the exercise was to exhibit this variety, which struck them as important, and which could only be illustrated through comparison.

Twenty-five years later I tried the same thing, for another class of more knowledgeable and sophisticated students who had heard much more Indian music. Their attitude was different. They questioned the purposes of the comparison, wanted to know what valid conclusions one would draw from it, whether we were looking for differences or for similarities. They criticized the parameters upon which comparison was made and wondered whether a comparative examination of thirty examples was at all a good way to provide an introduction to this music. They were suspicious of comparison and justified their suspicions by saying that I was comparing apples and oranges.

In his article outlining the history of definitions of the field, Alan Merriam (1977a) suggests that there has been a gradual trend from one concept of ethnomusicology as a comparative field to another in which comparative study is criticized, avoided, postponed. Beginning with Guido Adler (1885: 14), who in the first outline of the subdivisions of musicology stated that the purpose of this branch was to compare in order to provide groupings and classifications of the world's music, Merriam goes on to cite Hood (1963a: 233, and in Apel 1969:299) to the effect that comparisons are premature until satisfactorily accurate descriptions of musical systems are available, also quoting Meyer (1960:49–50) and Blacking (1966:218), who believe that comparison may result in the improper interpretation of similarities and differences. Whether ethnomusicology is in principle a comparative field or not, there is no doubt that the nature and the role of comparison have all along been central issues. They will arise many times in these essays, in specific contexts, and I wish here only to address the question in general.

We are in a state of conflict. In the 1970s it seems that a few ethnomusicologists have, on the one hand, gone more deeply than before into intercultural and to an extent intracultural comparison. Usually without saying so, they were trying to develop comparative methods, something rarely touched upon by the early scholars who, calling themselves "comparative musicologists," nevertheless seemed to take methodology for granted. On the other hand, in print, but even more in face-to-face discussion, I have been impressed by the degree to which comparative study is criticized and viewed with suspicion.

Of course the concept of comparison is problematic. To note that two things are in one way alike does not mean that they are otherwise similar, spring from the same source, or have the same meaning. There are some respects in which no two creations of mankind can really be compared. But on the other hand, I would maintain that even apples and oranges can very well be compared, turn out to be alike in being round and in being fruits and in being about the same size, different in color, taste, texture. The fact that, to itself, an apple may not feel the least bit like an orange and doesn't know how it is to feel like an orange, is irrelevant for some considerations, though crucial for others. The question is whether we can find systematic, elegant, and reliable ways to carry out the comparison, and whether, having done so, it has been worth the effort. Thus there is little discussion in the literature of ethnomusicology about comparative method. Many of the studies that use comparison do so by implication rather than explicitly, and the conclusions based on comparative work have their great limitations.

But before moving on to discussion of these difficulties, it is important to point out that comparative studies have a long history in ethnomusicology, as described in Wiora's small but definitive book (1975). This history includes distinguished studies carefully executed, with criteria, method, and purpose clearly laid out. At the same time, one can find but surely cannot support random comparisons, made for capricious reasons, perhaps of the music of Tibet with that of Portugal, but these make even the most devoted comparative musicologists cringe. While the concept of comparison appears basic to the early development of the field, it is also true that ethnomusicologists have not often set out systematically to make comparisons. Adler, in the classic article (1885), clearly felt that the immediate need was to classify the musics of the world in an ethnographic, that is, descriptive manner, in order to see what the universe of music contained, clearly implying that this was best done through a series of comparisons. Such a statement, made *ex cathedra* by one of the founders of musicology, might have been taken as a mandate to "go forth and compare," and to a certain extent the early period of ethnomusicology, through the early twentieth century, is marked by a general if not systematically controlled comparative approach. The work of this period is a clear contrast to earlier publications on non-Western music, such as those of Amiot (1779), Kiesewetter (1842), and Villoteau (1809), which approach their subjects with particularist zeal. Beginning at the turn of the twentieth century, E. M. von Hornbostel did not engage very much in comparison as such, but nevertheless provided a series of studies covering many parts of the world all based on a single analytical model, suggesting that comparative study was the ultimate purpose to which these descriptions would be put. His career, encompassing studies of the music of five continents, is itself an exercise in comparative method. Likewise, the first general works on tribal or "primitive" music, Stumpf (1911) and Wallaschek (1893), are also basically, if not always explicitly, comparative. Later scholars coming out of Hornbostel's circle also sustained an interest in comparative study (see also Bingham 1914). See, for example, the comparison of Pima and Pueblo musics in George Herzog's dissertation (1936a), that of Yurok and Papago music in Schinhan's thesis (1937), and Helen Roberts's comparison of the styles and instruments in North American Indian culture areas (1936). One need, of course, hardly point out that comparison saturates the many works of Curt Sachs (e.g. 1953, 1961, etc.).

The comparative approach of the early ethnomusicologists goes hand in hand with that of anthropologists of the same period. Around 1900 the purpose of anthropologists' comparisons appears to have been primarily that of historical reconstruction, and the notion of *a* comparative method, hardly ever defined but nevertheless accepted, runs deep in the literature. In an important statement of the history of comparative anthropological study, Oscar Lewis (1956:260) very simply says, "Most anthropological writings contain comparisons." One could, of course, equally maintain that all ethnomusicological writings contained comparisons. But in anthropology the concern for comparative method and for the intellectual problems involved in making comparisons goes back to the early days of the field (see e.g. Tylor 1889). Shortly after 1900 Central European anthropology began to make a specialty of comparative study, its methods specifically reflected in some of Hornbostel's and much of Sachs's work. Interestingly, while anthropologists and linguists engaged in comparison for specifically historical purposes, musicologists seem to have done so equally for the purposes of perception and analytical understanding.

The broad comparisons and generalizations of early ethnomusicology, based inevitably on a small sample of evidence, may have made later scholars hesitant to pursue comparative method. A period of specialization followed. Spurred by greater opportunities for extended and efficient field research, the ethnomusicologist became more involved in one culture. Broader exposure instilled a respect for the intrinsic value of non-Western musics, particularly those of the Asian civilizations, which would only be satisfied by lifetime devotion to one culture. Indeed, this kind of study showed that the musics of the world are in certain respects not comparable. While one can compare those elements of a music that are basically alike, one must admit the existence, in each music, of elements that are so distinct as to make comparison a matter of great methodological and conceptual difficulty. The comparative techniques that had been established by Hornbostel and his school—counting tones and intervals in scales, providing typologies of rhythmic units, and so forth—went only so far. But it began to be realized that one must also study each music in terms of the theoretical system that its own culture provides for it, be this an explicitly articulated, written system or one that must be derived from interview and analysis; and that one must study musical behavior in terms of the underlying value structure of the culture from which it comes. Thus the period after 1940 showed a marked decline in concern for comparative work in ethnomusicology. But some thirty years later it began again to rear its head.

Anthropology, which had in many cases served as a model for ethnomusicology and preceded it in approach and method by a decade or two, seems to have experienced a similar fate. A discipline that in the nineteenth and early twentieth centuries thrived on comparison, particularly for the purpose of deducing historical processes, it began to move in the direction of specialized ethnography early in the 1900s. But by the middle 1950s it had again begun to stress a comparative approach, as shown by the renewed emphasis on comparative study in some of the recent summaries of the field (e.g. Naroll and Cohen 1973, Keesing 1976) and the development of a specialized literature on comparative method (e.g. Śarana 1975).

KINDS OF COMPARATIVE STUDY

Anthropology can provide various broad kinds of classification for types of comparative study. Let's look at one published about the time ethnomusicologists began to turn away from comparison. In his bibliographical and analytical study of research, Lewis (1956) surveyed 248 publications (almost entirely of American and British origin) from between 1950 and 1954 that are comparative in nature. Of these, as many as 28 deal with the theory and methodology of comparison. Lewis does not indicate the proportion of comparative studies in the total anthropological corpus of his five-year period. But it is reasonable to assume that these 248 publications occupy a rather substantial slice of the whole, and that some of the 28 theoretical and methodological pieces are among the important works of theory of the period.

Lewis classifies the studies further, finding six dominant aims: (a) establishing general laws or regularities, (b) documenting the range of variation of a phenomenon or (c) distribution of a trait, (d) reconstructing culture history, (e) testing hypotheses derived from Western and (f) from non-Western societies. Furthermore, 34 studies involved global or random comparisons; 33, comparisons between continents and nations; 31, comparisons within one continent; 31, within one nation; 70, within one culture area; and 34, within one group or culture. Considerably more than half involved the Western hemisphere.

How did comparison fare in a similar period in the history of ethnomusicology? The prominence of the journal *Ethnomusicology* within its field makes it perhaps a reliable sample for following Lewis's approach. A survey of volumes 2–17 (1958–73) reveals a total of approximately 270 articles. While it is difficult for us (as it must have been for Lewis) to segregate "comparative" studies, it seems that only 43 of the articles are clearly (though not in all cases even primarily) addressed to the question of comparison of repertories or of segments of repertories, or of cultures. Of these, 13 articles are primarily theoretical. Nineteen contain comparisons within one culture area and 11 are in some sense historical, comparing repertories from different periods or of different areas (such as African and Afro-American) with the purpose of providing historical insight. All of this is perhaps curious in a discipline that has been greatly influenced by anthropology with its comparative orientation, a discipline that long called itself "comparative musicology," and particularly in a field within anthropology that lends itself, perhaps better than many others, to statistical examination of components and to quantification (Freeman and Merriam 1956:465).

Wiora (1975:19–25) also tries to classify comparative studies through the history of ethnomusicology, dividing them into eight "centers or directions": (1) the holistically comparative Berlin school of Hornbostel and Sachs, (2) the somewhat more biologically oriented Vienna school of R. Lach and W. Graf, (3) European folk music scholarship, (4) comparative study of Jewish and Christian liturgies, (5) scholarship involving comparisons of closely neighboring areas, (6) American research concentrating on musical areas, (7) comparative study of European classical and folk music, and (8) comparative study of national styles of art music in Europe.

Thus, despite the lack of attention to method, there are a number of clearly separable kinds of study making use of comparison. And there are works that function as guides. The analytical systems of Kolinski (e.g. 1956, 1959, 1961, 1965a and b) provide frameworks for the comparison of repertories in accordance with individual elements of music such as scale, melodic movement, rhythm, and tempo. Hornbostel, in establishing a method of describing musical styles, also provides such a framework, and was followed in this by some of his students, in particular George Herzog (e.g. 1936a). Bartók's approach to analysis of Eastern European folk song (e.g. 1931, 1935, 1959–) provides guidelines for comparison as well, and so does the method for comparing English folk tunes developed by Bayard (e.g. 1950, 1954) and Bronson (1959, 1959–72) and analyzed by Shapiro

(1975). The voluminous work dealing with classification of folk songs in one repertory, beginning early in the century (Koller 1902–3 and I. Krohn 1902–3) and continuing through several decades (e.g. Hustvedt 1936, Bayard 1942, Herzog 1950, Elschekova 1966) is likewise a cornerstone among the methodological guides to comparative study. The importance of comparing Afro-American repertories in various parts of the New World with each other and with the folk music of whites has been particularly striking in the history of ethnomusicology, as indicated in the publications of Herskovits (1945), R. Waterman (1952), Merriam (1955b), and Jackson (1943). There are, further, many more models, including the large literature on geographic distribution of styles and on classification of instruments (Hornbostel and Sachs 1914). And of course there is cantometrics.

THE OPPOSITION

Ethnomusicologists seem not to have become very much involved in the epistemology of comparison and rarely ask whether it is possible to deal interculturally with music without, in some sense, systematically carrying out comparative study. Yet the importance of the question is suggested by the ubiquitous discussion of the identity of the field, with the presence or absence of comparative components as a major criterion. Some assert that ethnomusicology comprises the study of music or musical culture outside the investigator's own purview. The identity of investigators vis-à-vis their subject matter is here a major factor, and the fact that it should be accorded such significance is epistemologically significant. In several publications Mantle Hood (1963a:233–34, 1971:349) maintains that comparison is not a primary goal of the field and cannot, at the present time or perhaps for a long time in the future, be carried out properly. Even so, he states that the American (or European) ethnomusicologist, "because of *who* he is, is capable of insights and evaluations which no Javanese, even with training . . . in Western methods, could ever duplicate" (1961:374). While this statement shows Hood to be perhaps of two minds, not insistent on refraining from comparative study, the view of ethnomusicology as essentially comparative is questioned by scholars and musicians the world over. It is the opinion of many non-European scholars who concentrate on their own musical traditions that only the "insider" is truly qualified for scholarship and, by implication, that comparison is not truly possible.

The many criticisms of comparative work revolve about the difficulty of comparing cultures of which one has varying kinds and degrees of understanding, personal contact, data, and the problem of knowing any culture or music in sufficient depth and breadth to carry out meaningful comparison. There is fear of unwarranted conclusions. There is the allegation that the purpose of comparison is to make value judgments, detrimental to those whose music is being compared. One is in awe of the complexity of musical systems, which itself can make them inherently incomparable. There is suspicion of the quantitative techniques inevitably used in comparative study, and the belief that in a field devoted to this kind of work data gathering will be prejudicial in favor of materials that lend themselves to comparison. Let's look at a few of these objections.

Are musics indeed comparable? In a widely quoted statement John Blacking suggests that superficial similarities may not be worth noting. To find the same intervals in the scales of two cultures, he contends, may be of no interest at all if these intervals have different meanings in the two systems. Well and good, if one is also concerned at the moment about meanings. The argument sounds weaker when Blacking gives its opposite number: "Statistical analyses may show that the music of two cultures is very different but analysis . . . may reveal that they have essentially the same meaning, which has been translated into the different 'languages' of the two cultures" (1966:218). The latter finding would seem to be highly significant and interesting, but how would one ever come up with it if one had not made the comparison in the first place? What Blacking is objecting to is the drawing of unwarranted conclusions, and he seems to have in mind certain studies that go no further than making a statistical comparison. The prescription would seem to be not avoidance of comparative study but more and better comparative study.

Western traditional harmony has become a major component of the modernized sector of traditional music in twentieth-century sub-Saharan Africa and the Middle East. A comparison yields the broad conclusion that Africans do better with it, that is, conform more closely to European practices. If one can assign a broad meaning to the use of harmony in the two cultures, it is, grossly speaking, the same: a major musical symbol of modernization. The fact that the Africans use it differently and, in Western terms, better than Middle Easterners may tell us something about the relative compatibility of the two sets of systems. Considering the long-standing use of other harmonic systems in parts of Africa, it may also show something about the effect of one harmonic system on the adoption of another and also about the role of successful (in Africa) versus unsuccessful (in the Middle East) Christian missionary efforts, and many other things (see R. Waterman 1948, 1952).

The fact that a number of small, isolated cultures around the world share certain scalar and formal patterns in their songs may tell us something about the melodic patterning of the earliest music (Wiora 1956). This is not to suggest that these patterns have identical meanings in all of these cultures. The fact that they do *not* share singing style, for example, and that music has greatly different uses and functions in these societies, may suggest that they have diverged, for reasons we cannot understand, continuing to use old scalar and formal patterns. Or, with an evolutionist view, we may take it that as the meaning of music and the nature of societies changed and developed, singing style was modified accordingly, while other aspects of music were selected to remain stable. One may compare structures, or meanings, or both, but what is being compared should be specified and conclusions should not be confused.

Mantle Hood, quoted above, chastises early scholars for rushing into comparing what was not yet individually understood. Though not unalterably opposed to comparative study, he seems to expect an almost unattainable degree of intimacy with a musical system in its own terms before comparison can be carried out. On the face of it, this viewpoint can be easily accepted, but one may push it too far. The issue confronting a commentator on this objection is epistemological: is the essence of a musical system best studied in its own terms, or is it more accurately viewed through a comparative prism? For example, at an elementary level, in teaching a survey course on musical cultures of the world, is an instructor likely to be successful if dealing simply with a group of musics, one by one, without reference to each other, finally summarizing them in a comparative way; or be more successful if dealing with several at a time, exploring, for all, first the tone material, then the singing style, then rhythm, and so on? Teachers of ethnomusicology have no agreement on this point, although probably the former approach is more common. But, echoing the view of his teacher Jaap Kunst, who maintained that ethnomusicology was no more comparative than other fields, Mantle Hood has put his finger on a major problem.

The question of comparability of musics—and, for that matter, of components of musics such as tune variants—is closely related to the political and social relationships between field investigators and informants, between Western scholars and those of third world nations. The growing skepticism of comparison goes hand in hand with a viewpoint characteristic of some scholars from these areas, its basis the deep conviction that a musical system can be properly understood only by its own people, a conviction also bearing on the nature of fieldwork and indeed the essence of ethnomusicology. I doubt that anyone actually believes that comparison is totally unacceptable. Rather, one objects to the way in which it has been, or threatens to be, carried out. Thus, for example, if ethnomusicology is the study of music outside one's culture, it can hardly be taken seriously, for the definition seems like an excuse for superficiality. And it is undignified for anyone to study a musical system if the purpose is *only* to compare it to others.

On the issue of dignity, one may ask whether, in making comparison, one is looking for differences or similarities. In simply making a comparison, the ethnomusicologist would appear to be neutral. But, examining the conclusions that have been drawn, one quickly realizes that they are based on similarities—among musics, among genres and pieces—for producing something meaningful that one can publish. Identifying historical strata, as was done by Curt Sachs for instruments (1929, 1940), establishing musical areas (Merriam 1959, Nettl 1954b), tracing influences of Middle Eastern music on Southern European folk musics, identifying tune relationships among Spain, England, and Hungary (Wiora 1953)—these are conclusions, justified or not, that could hardly have come about if the scholars at work had not found similarities persuasive enough to lead them at least to tentative conclusions. Whatever differences they found seem to have played a very small role. So the suspicion has foundation: comparativists are impressed by similarity, and seek it out.

So the musically sophisticated Arapaho Indian may be put off by the idea that the white ethnomusicologist is interested in his music not because it means something important in Arapaho culture or to the world of music, but because he hopes to draw conclusions from comparing it to Cheyenne, Comanche, Shoshone music. The conscientious comparativist can perhaps reply by saying, "Of course your music is valuable, and there are those among us who study it in terms of its value. And you should study it in that way yourself. But in the end, we can perhaps tell you something about it that will interest you if you allow us to engage in comparative study, something about your relationship to other peoples, something about your history. Even if you feel that all ethnomusicologists in the end wish only to do comparative work, you must realize that they consider this kind of musical study only one of many kinds in which human beings can and should engage." If ethnomusicologists are determined to be mainly comparative, they should stop acting as if all non-Western music belonged to them alone for good and all.

A major purpose of comparative study has always been an understanding of history. We compare musics to see how they have developed, whether they have a common origin, and so on (Wiora 1975:81–90). What we conclude will always be conjecture. Whether it is worth doing or whether, as John Blacking says, speculative history is a complete waste of effort (1973: 56) depends on the value one places on historical knowledge. If an understanding of history is accorded enormous importance, then any way in which one can gain insight, however tentative, in situations lacking solid verifiable data, is worth much effort. If it is a matter of only secondary or, as Blacking puts it, "encyclopedic" interest, then one is better off devoting one's energy to other pursuits, for even a great deal of effort will indeed produce only the most tentative results.

A related objection comes typically from students of the complex classical musics of Asia. They accept the ethnomusicologist's comparative approach to tribal and folk musics, simple and inferior systems (Daniélou 1973:28–33). But greater dignity must be accorded to classical systems, because they are complex and therefore closer to unique. Western scholars should treat these classical systems as they have dealt with European classical music, which has not, it is felt, been the object of *primarily* comparative study. Thus it is sometimes put.

This objection can be countered in two ways. Of course we espouse the value of classical musics in Asia. But if knowledge of non-Western musics and the admonitions of Asian musicians are supposed to rid us of the kind of prejudice that always places Western music and its values at the top, then we should not substitute for it a feeling that classical music systems in general—those of India, China, Japan, Indonesia, the Middle East, and Europe—constitute a musical elite. The old line would still be there, only moved over a few inches. If any musics are worthy of more than merely comparative study, then all are. And if comparative study is a major component of understanding tribal and folk musics, it can be so also for more complex systems, the work admittedly becoming more difficult. As we have said before, at some point of conceptualization all musics are equal. Beyond that, a careful look at the historiography of Western music indicates that comparison, among regions of Europe, periods of history, composers, pieces, is clearly a major activity. In historical musicology, as in ethnomusicology, one would wish for better development of comparative method.

A COMPARATIVE METHOD?

Comparative study pervades the academy. We have comparative anatomy, comparative psychology, linguistics, law, religion, all found as terms in encyclopedias, as titles of courses and books. In all cases separate systems, usually defined as belonging to different populations, cultures, or societies, are somehow compared. It seems that scholars are attracted more by similarities than differences, trying to draw conclusions regarding function and history from them. There have been some attempts to draw together the many venues and uses of the concept of comparison (Warwick and Osherson 1973), and there are even departments of comparative study in some universities, with the implication that this represents a particular disciplinary focus. The idea that comparative study is circumscribed by particular methods and limitations which go beyond the subject matter of an established discipline seems to be widely accepted. Thus Myrdal (in Warwick and Osherson 1973:98) implies that comparison must precede detailed examination of a phenomenon in its own terms, stating that "generalizations about reality, and their organization within an abstract framework of presumed interrelations, precede specification and verification." But if there is such a thing as a general "comparative method," valid for many fields, it is perhaps no more than a manifestation of Merriam's very general admonition that "the approach must be cautious, that like things must be compared, that the comparisons must have some bearing upon a particular problem and be an integral part of the research design" (1964:53).

And yet the comparative approach seems in each discipline to have had a specific, and in many cases unique, purpose. The general purpose of comparative psychology is simply to ascertain the similarities and differences in behavioral organization among living beings, with a large variety of specific aims. Comparative law, while encompassing historical and anthropological interests, seems to have as its major aim the articulation of various legal systems and the improvement of the world's legal security, in the character of an applied field. Comparative literature deals with themes and motifs of literary content across linguistic boundaries, while linguists have reserved the name "comparative method" for something quite specific, a method of reconstructing earlier language or earlier stages in language by structurally comparing similar words, with identical or related meanings, in different languages and dialects.

As we have said before, there is in ethnomusicology no such thing as *a* comparative method. Linguists engage in comparison for other purposes such as the establishment of cognitive systems or the solution of problems in the interrelationship of language and culture, but *the* comparative method tries to establish the history of genetic language relationships. In ethnomusicology the purpose of comparison is or perhaps the major and even first purpose of comparative musicology was also to contribute to an understanding of history. Linguists have established a clear-cut method, and its results are generally accepted by the profession and the public at large. The existence of proto-Germanic, proto-Indo-European, proto-Algonquian is not seriously questioned, although these languages are simply constructs (Anttila 1972:65–66). There has been no similar comparative method to deal with the reconstruction of musical forms. While comparison of widely separated cultures, or of variants of a song in a restricted area, has provided insights analogous to those of the comparative linguist, their significance is not agreed upon and often denied. Ethnomusicologists have rarely tried to adopt the methods of comparative and historical linguistics directly, and Gilbert Chase's suggestion that "the term 'comparative musicology' should be revived . . . but as it is used in linguistics . . ." (Brook and others 1972: 219) may fall on deaf ears. Comparison in ethnomusicology has been more a combination of attitude (e.g. "a comparative approach provides insight") with a group of techniques used *ad hoc* to deal with specific problems.

But if no single comparative method has been accepted, there are approaches that have, by implication, tried to claim such a title. They are methods that have been widely used, in a variety of cultures, by a group of scholars with divergent aims. None of them has had sufficient force to be adopted as the central methodology of the field for a long period. And yet the analytical approach of Hornbostel, that of Bartók, the frameworks of Kolinski, and the various approaches to stating geographic distribution of styles all seem at one point or another to have been informally considered as filling this role.

If there is a recent approach that seems to be considered by some as a candidate for being *the* comparative method of ethnomusicology, it is Alan Lomax's cantometrics (1959, 1961, 1968, 1975). It provides a system of describing musical style within a comparative framework, already discussed, but also a theory according to which intercultural comparison illuminates a central problem, the relationship of musical style to culture type.

While its main value seems to me to be its system of describing singing style, Lomax and his staff have carried out specific comparisons, largely for the purpose of identifying cultural determinants of musical style. Among the musics compared are those of large culture areas (e.g. American Indian, sub-Saharan Africa, the Pacific Islands, Australia, Europe, the "Old High Cultures" of Asia) and of culture groups that contrast in some significant way, as in the fundamentals of social and political organization, type of subsistence economy, and child-rearing. Of course, the matching of culture types and musical styles is a venerable habit in ethnomusicology; M. Schneider (1957:12–14) asserted that hunters, gatherers, and agriculturists have different styles of music, and Sachs (1938b:31–33) tried to distinguish patriarchal and matriarchal peoples. Lomax differs from them in large measure by his use of a formal technique for comparison.

Rather than having a comparative method, ethnomusicology continues to use the concept of comparison in a large variety of ways. Several of the kinds of studies mentioned by Lewis for anthropology find their analogues in ethnomusicology. But one that seems hardly to be found is the "restudy," exemplified by the classic study of a village in Mexico first by Robert Redfield (1930) and then by Lewis himself (1951), a type of approach used in several instances in the history of anthropology during the 1950s and 1960s. In ethnomusicology comparisons of past and present in one culture are usually based on widely divergent sorts of data, for example, modern field research as against the description of early travelers (see e.g. Nettl 1967c and Merriam 1967a). Comparison of one village at different times was, however, made by Merriam (1977b). Comparisons of past and present, or of recent and distant past, are implicit in many of the historical studies carried out by scholars in Asian art music. But these studies usually do not make explicit comparisons, certainly not systematic ones, and if they were to do so, these comparisons would have to be limited to a few special areas of music and musical culture, since the fieldwork of the present and the historical records of the past usually speak to entirely different matters.

While almost all of the work touched upon in this chapter involved the comparison of musics because musical styles lend themselves to statistical analysis, there is a trend, exemplified by the rather formal comparison of Ibo and Hausa musicians by David Ames (1973a), to provide comparisons of cultures in terms of musical behavior aside from the sounds that are produced. It is also evident in Lomax's work, as his parameters include aspects of the social roles and relationships of musicians. Another recent trend is the use of explicit comparisons within a repertory or a single musical culture to identify norms and deviations. Studies of the range of performances and improvisations over one model in Persian music by several authors, and even the range of performances over the model by a single musician in Arabic music, in jazz, and in African music, may be mentioned as examples (see Nettl and Foltin 1972, Massoudieh 1968, Wilkens 1967, Owens 1974, Nettl and Riddle 1974).

Some recent publications foresee a bright future for comparative study. John Blacking, often skeptical, nevertheless acknowledges its uses and feels that its problems may be solved by such concepts as the relationship of "deep structures" and "surface structures," borrowed again from linguistics. We need, he says, "a unitary method of musical analysis which can . . . be applied to *all* music," and which takes into account and explains sound itself and musical behavior as well (1971:93). A number of attempts to develop such a method have been made and are described in Chapter 8. Only when a satisfactory one is established, Blacking implies, will we be in a position to make acceptable comparisons, which are our ultimate technique (1972: 108). Wiora (1975), who does not simply equate comparative study with ethnomusicology, nevertheless shows dozens of examples successfully carried out. Porter (1977) seems to consider a renewed interest in comparative work as the last, best hope for research in European folk music. And, as Kolinski (1971:160) says, the avoidance or indefinite postponement of the comparison of musics "deprives the discipline of an essential tool in its quest for a deeper insight into the infinite multifariousness of the universe of music."

Chapter 6

I Can't Say a Thing Until I've Seen the Score

A DIFFICULT AND INTRICATE TASK

Western urban society has a special view of music. We may say that a folk singer deviates from the way a song is "written" when we really mean from the particular form in which he has learned it. We use the term "writing music" broadly, substituting it for "composing," whether notation is involved or not. We think of a piece of music as existing in its truest form on a piece of paper. The academics among us can hardly conceive of discussing music without knowledge of a single, authoritative, visible version. "I can't say a thing until I've seen the score," the critic may say upon hearing a new piece; it is surprising that he does not normally say about a new score, "I can't say a thing until I've heard it." Dealing with the written music is the classical musician's ideal. "Can you read music?" is the question used to separate musical sheep from goats, to establish minimum musical competence.

I am making a bit of fun of a segment of Western society for being so tied to notation. It equates composing with writing and accepts the creation of music on paper even when the composer can barely imagine its sound until he has heard it, of music which contains devices that can only be appreciated by the eye. Given that in all societies music is created and transmitted entirely or largely aurally, the culture of Western classical music seems to represent a serious departure from the norm. Of course I do not wish to berate but, rather, to point up this major characteristic of Western academic musical culture precisely because of its impact on ethnomusicology. Concerned with a study of music that lives largely in oral tradition, ethnomusicologists have spent a great deal of their energy finding ways of reducing it to visual form. Like the critic, the ethnomusicologist faced with a recording tends to throw up his hands and say, "I can't say a thing until I've written it down." And so, having given some thought to the definition of music, to the ways in which music comes into existence, and to ways in which we can view the world of music—as a universal phenomenon, as a group of separable musical systems, and as a large quantity of phenomena that can be understood only by comparing them with each other—we turn to an intensely practical issue, the ethnomusicologist's need to reduce sound from recordings to visual form.

This is accomplished with a process known as transcription, widely discussed in the general literature of ethnomusicology, as in the comprehensive survey by Doris Stockmann (1979). While this literature shows the concept to be in some ways complex and overlapping with others such as description and analysis, it is most widely interpreted to mean the reduction of sound to standard Western notation. Looking at the matter more broadly, transcription may include other notation systems such as those developed for a variety of purposes in Asian societies (see Kaufmann 1967, Malm 1959:261–75), and certain ones developed especially for ethnomusicological study (e.g. Koetting 1970). Beyond this, transcription includes graphs and other ways of presenting data provided by automatic devices. All of these systems tell us, on the one hand, how a musical performance changes from one moment to the next but, on the other, what the characteristics are that endure throughout a piece or a song, such as a tone system, a way of using the voice, etc. Thus the concept of transcription might well also include general characterizations of singing style or descriptions of the musical vocabulary on which the composer of a piece draws.

Only with difficulty can transcription be separated from description and analysis of music, techniques that normally both precede and follow it. It is often regarded as the central and most difficult task of the ethnomusicologist, competence in which distinguishes him from other kinds of scholars. In transcription, the ethnomusicologist presents him or herself as a kind of superperson, able to control and make sense of a plethora of previously inexplicable sound with a set of extremely demanding techniques. Thus, Kunst: "The transcription of exotic phonograms is one of the most difficult and intricate tasks which ethnomusicological research has ever put before its devotees" (Kunst 1959:37). Bartók: "We should never tire of improving and changing our methods of work in order to accomplish this task as well as is humanly possible" (Bartók and Lord 1951:20). Merriam: It is assumed that the ethnomusicologist "has available to him accurate methods of transcribing music sound to paper, but this is a question that is far from resolved" (1964:57). Hood, in whose general book on ethnomusicology transcription is one of the fundamental concerns, also dwells on the need for accuracy: "The process must begin with the most specific and detailed transcription possible" (1971:320). All agree: transcription is enormously difficult, and one must strive continually to prove oneself competent and to improve competence.

It is not only difficult, but some seem to consider it hopeless. Sachs: ". . . even the most painstaking method will not give us ultimate satisfaction. No musical script can ever be a faithful mirror of music . . ." (1962:30–31). Estreicher, as summarized by McCollester (1960:132): "The ideal goal of a musical transcription then cannot be realized because it seeks to find a visual equivalent to an oral phenomenon. . . ." Seeger: "A hazard of writing music lies in an assumption that the full auditory parameter of music is or can be represented by a partial visual parameter . . ." (1958a:184). But these somewhat handwringing caveats in the general discussions of ethnomusicology contrast with the typical study of a specific culture or repertory that includes transcriptions, imperfect and arrived at with difficulty, and provides matter-of-fact explanations of the procedures used. It's hard, but one does the best one can.

Until well into the 1950s the ability to transcribe was viewed as the basic and perhaps even diagnostic skill of the ethnomusicologist, and many still regard this ability as essential. My own training in fact began thus: I approached my teacher, George Herzog, about specializing in what was then still called comparative musicology and, after a sentence or two of congratulation or condolence, he told me that I must first learn to transcribe, asked me to come to his office to get some material (then available on acetate discs, in the pre-tape era), and put me to work. And for a year or so I did little but transcribe. Hood (1971:50–55) relates a similar experience in his initial studies with Jaap Kunst. Like the student of unwritten languages at that time whose major activity was the collection of phonetic transcription of texts, and like the scholar of Renaissance music who transcribed earlier into modern notation as the daily bread, the ethnomusicologist for long was in the first instance a transcriber of music. The first task of the field was thought by some to be the transcription of all available recordings.

The history of transcribing in a nutshell: in the nineteenth century the idea of preserving disappearing musics dominated. The first decades of the twentieth century saw concentration on establishing standard methods of objectively stating on paper what happens in sound, for the purpose of providing a way to describe and analyze (see Abraham and Hornbostel 1909–10). Toward the middle of the century there appeared attempts to increase this objectivity by drawing on acoustic and electronic machinery to do the work of humans. After 1955 there was increasing diversification of methods of transcription, of ways in which transcription was used as a part of a larger research design. In the 1970s the art is characterized by a tendency to use transcription for the purpose of solving specific problems, each one generating a particular kind of transcription. The last twenty years have also seen interest in the theory and methodology of transcribing.

Several issues have been manifesting themselves throughout this history: (1) the contrast between prescriptive and descriptive notation; (2) the nature of the unit of musical thought, song or piece, that is being transcribed; (3) the relationship of transcription as the description by the outsider to notation as a way of expressing the culture's own understanding of its music; (4) the roles of humans and machines; and (5) transcription as a unified technique for the field as against the development of special techniques for providing special insights.

SEEGER'S DICHOTOMY

In one of the most influential pieces of writing on the subject Charles Seeger (1958) identified two purposes of musical notation: one provides a blueprint for the performer, and the other records in writing what has actually occurred in sound. Let us see how they differ. Ludolf Parisius (see Weber-Kellermann 1957:1–23), an exemplary collector of the middle of the nineteenth century, wrote down hundreds of song texts and some 200 melodies of Altmark, his native area in central Germany, mainly in order to preserve a repertory that was quickly going out of existence. "Whoever wishes to collect from the mouth of the folk ought to hurry; folk songs are disappearing one after the other," he wrote in 1857 (ibid. p. 7); and so he did. But he produced collections whose purpose, like that of others of his time, is not completely clear. Following the trends of the time, Parisius wished somehow to make his collection part of the intellectual mainstream, and he was therefore mainly interested in the songs as artifacts and not so much as results of the process of oral tradition in the folk community. He corrected and improved some of the texts and combined versions into archetypes, and he notated the tunes quickly, thus unable to give attention to singing style, ornamentation, metric irregularities. What was to be done with these songs? Presumably they could be read and even sung by those who wished directly to experience the folk culture of Altmark. The idea of contributing to a major corpus of song for comparative study or for the understanding of a special regional musical style was probably not yet in the air. There was little doubt in the minds of the collectors of the time that this kind of notation would give the reader a realistic idea of textual and musical style, and if one could sing the song from his written version, one could also understand it. This collection is both prescriptive and descriptive.

In the middle of the nineteenth century, when close analysis of music was not yet developed, the issue of this distinction had not arisen. After all, in dealing with the folk music of his own culture, Parisius (like many nineteenth-century collectors) was transcribing material in a style known to him before his field experience, and presumably known to the typical reader. Perhaps one of the fundamental truths in the use of transcription was already clear to him: whether prescriptive or descriptive, whether intended for performance or analysis, a transcription gives readers an accurate idea of the specific sound of a song only if they already know generally the kind of sound to be expected and are already acquainted with the style. Otherwise, it serves only as a vehicle for abstract perception of style characteristics. Depending, of course, on the context in which they are produced, many transcriptions serve prescriptive and descriptive purposes equally.

One cannot always tell by looking at a transcription whether its purpose is one or the other.

On the surface, an ethnomusicologist simply sits down with a tape recorder (at one time it was with a disc, harder to use but adequate, or a cylinder; earlier yet, with an informant and possibly with only the memory of a piece once heard) and writes down what he or she hears or remembers. But, in fact, attitude and conception determine much of what is done. Two different transcriptions of the same piece do not simply indicate varying competence. Differences in the purpose of the task at hand, in the conception of what constitutes a piece of music, may play a greater role. The distinction between prescriptive and descriptive notation was Seeger's terminology for music written in order to be performed and music to be analyzed. But there is an obvious correlate. It is "insiders" who write music to be performed, and they write it in a particular way. Typically, outsiders start by writing everything they hear, which turns out to be impossible. Some have tried, like Bartók in his incredibly detailed transcriptions of Eastern European folk songs (e.g. Bartók 1935, Bartók and Lord 1951), but of course even he did not have symbols for many aspects of singing style. Even so, it is hard to make head or tail of his notations because of their immense detail. On the other hand, the writer of a prescriptive notation normally includes only what is needed by a native who knows the style. In order to learn a new mazurka by Chopin, one must read his notes with an aural knowledge of how Chopin is supposed to sound. The simple notation systems of Asian nations tell only what the musician needs to know about a piece; they do not describe the style. But a descriptive notation tries in fact to provide a thorough and objective description of a piece, similar to that of the phonetician describing the details of speech. Thus Seeger might also have named his two kinds of notation "emic" and "etic," or perhaps "cultural" and "analytical."

Some years after Seeger, Mantle Hood (1971:90) proposed three "solutions" to the general problems of transcription. One depends on the notation systems of non-Western societies, a second on the mechanical or electronic melograph, and a third includes dance and movement notation with the notation of sound. The first appears to be in essence prescriptive, and the other two, descriptive. The first is the notation of the culture's insider, the others are or can be the work of outsiders. For Hood, the three approaches appear to be different solutions of the same problem, but I would suggest also that they result from different aims.

Transcription has ordinarily meant notation that distinguishes temporal segments in a piece, one phrase from another, one note from the next. But the need to characterize, to transcribe, as it were, those elements of a performance found throughout the entire piece has always been recognized as well. Thus even some of the earliest transcribers typically include verbal remarks about tempo, dynamics, and singing style. This type of statement is regarded not as transcription but as analysis or description. The transcriber is thought to divide music into style elements, which are *de*scribed, and musical content, which is *tran*scribed. Just as the content of pieces has been recognized through the availability of first recordings and then melographic devices as increasingly a complex of many elements, the number of generally present, abstracted musical traits pervading a piece has also increased. Thus the cantometrics method (Lomax 1968), thirteen of whose thirty-seven parameters could be included in a description of singing style, is most readily regarded as an analytical tool, but its "profiles" of individual pieces should also be regarded as a kind of transcription (see Figure 2). A person trained in cantometrics can look at such a profile and get a sense of the sound of the music, just as one can from a perusal of a conventional notation. Like the songs of Parisius, cantometrics is descriptive but potentially also prescriptive. A singer with the simplest notation, if trained to read a cantometrics profile, should theoretically be able to give the tune the right singing style. The difference between descriptive and prescriptive notation, insightful as it appears, is not always as clear as Seeger implies.

THE PIECE AND THE PERFORMANCE

While folk music dominated in the nineteenth century, notation of music from cultures foreign to the transcriber's experience was, of course, carried out as well, though in much smaller quantity. Here the main purpose seems to have been not preservation of a repertory or the desire to have the transcriptions performed by European readers but mainly to provide a certain kind of hard evidence of the existence of the music. If, before the days of recording, music was conventionally thought to exist perhaps almost exclusively on paper, a piece of writing about music was hardly complete without reference to this written form. The transcription was evidence that the music really existed, and that the transcriber had really heard it. But the notation was not of great help to the reader of the accompanying commentary, hardly giving the visual version of the total sound of a music. But then, it is hard, from the vantage point of one accustomed to recordings, to step into the shoes of a scholar of music in the days before recordings.

You can get the feel of these shoes from one of the early classics of ethnomusicology, Carl Stumpf's article about Bella Coola Indian songs (1886). Having heard a group of Indians on a tour singing in Halle, Germany, he made arrangements to spend several hours with one of the singers. In the description of his experience of transcribing from live performance, he tells that he very quickly came to the conclusions that the work was difficult and that many earlier transcriptions were perhaps done hurriedly and unreliably. Those now used to tape will gain some insight from his procedure. Lacking recordings that could simply be repeated, he asked his informant to sing each song many times while he notated. He first listened all the way through and got a sense of the total structure, then notated only the main pitches, transposing the song to C, and then began to fill in other pitches and the rhythm (1886:406–7). He included considerations of tempo and dynamics, and noted major departures from the standard Western tempered scale. Even in those early days he was aware of the fact that performances especially elicited might differ from those in a proper cultural context.

Stumpf is clear in his intentions. He wishes to present data, to describe it but not to theorize about it (1886:425); his transcriptions are explicitly descriptive. And they look very much like later transcriptions done from recordings, for example, those of Frances Densmore or George Herzog. But in substance they are different. Inevitably, as much as his informant may have tried to repeat each song precisely, Stumpf's transcription is a combination of several renditions, a kind of archetype; Densmore and Herzog, and most others later, provided notations of individual renditions. Stumpf's transcription claims to tell you what the song itself is like; scholars using recorders tell you what happened on a particular occasion. It is easy to dismiss Stumpf's transcriptions as inadequate for this reason, simply giving him due credit for having done his best in his time. But a case can be made for both types of transcription. The pervasive problem of ethnomusicology, the difference between the insider's and the outsider's view, is again back to plague (or guide) us.

Stumpf (and I am citing him mainly as an example of the scholars transcribing before the advent of recording) gives us not the singer's certified conception of the essence of the piece but the closest thing to it, a kind of average of several performances, a statement of what happens most frequently in a group of closely related variants of a song. The difference is mainly theoretical; no doubt the variants, individually transcribed, might hardly look different to us. Yet, in giving us a sense of "the" song as a concept in a culture, or in the total musical experience of a singer, Stumpf goes beyond the transcriber of a recorded version.

After Stumpf, scholars such as Hornbostel worked mainly on the problem of purely descriptive notation. The idea of providing a notation that gives the essence of a piece as manifested in many performances was abandoned, a movement intensified by the efforts of the champions of mechanical means. With the exception of some transcribers of folk music of their own culture, most scholars of the twentieth century used increasingly sophisticated descriptive notation. But during this same period ethnomusicologists also felt a growing need to view each music from the inside, in its own terms, and it is perhaps strange that this need was not in part met by transcriptions claiming to give "the piece" or "the song" as a unit of musical thought in a particular culture, rather than as a statement of an individual performance. The idea of presenting a notation whose purpose is clearly not prescriptive, but which also takes the approach of Stumpf, not of necessity but from conviction, can nevertheless be found in recent literature. "The musical transcriptions represent the generalized norms of the children's songs," says Blacking in his classic book on Venda children's songs (1967: 35). "No excuse need be made for the omission of these details, as this is a study of the children's *songs,* and not of the numerous *ways* [emphasis mine] in which Venda children sing the same songs." To Blacking there is a difference between the song and its many renditions, and he insists that the distinction is relevant to the presentation of transcriptions. But this approach is clearly exceptional in a period emphasizing description of the performance.

PHONETICS AND PHONEMICS

One of the factors contributing to the prescriptive-descriptive and performance-piece dichotomies is the need, in a truly satisfying description of a performance, to provide a great deal (and by the standards of some, enormous amounts) of detail. The prescription, on the other hand, need provide only what the informed performer or his scholarly surrogate requires to distinguish one piece from another; there is much that can be taken for granted. Given that standard Western notation is essentially prescriptive, its use in description requires the addition of symbols for types of events not found in Western music, and also for details that need not be stated in the prescription for a piece in a style you already know. This distinction has sometimes been compared to that of phonetics and phonemics in linguistics (Bloomfield 1951:127–38, Anttila 1972:207–8). Phonetics deals with the actual sounds produced, phonemics organizes them into a system with a limited number of significantly distinctive units, from which, for example, an alphabetic orthography can be derived. A descriptive musical notation ideally gives all musical sounds and all distinctions; a "phonemic" transcription groups those that are random or predictable variants so as to provide a list of significant units. These might comprise, for example, a limited number of pitches or note lengths that allow a performer to render a piece or a scholar to understand at a glance its character and structure. (Or do we ethnomusicologists, looking at transcriptions, inevitably hum under our breaths?) But the phonetic-phonemic analogy has limitations. For one thing, linguists seem to have begun with phonetics and to have moved in the direction of increasingly sophisticated ways of stating phonemic systems. Ethnomusicological transcription has moved in the phonetic direction from something like a phonemic beginning. Perhaps this results from the fact that prescription and phonemics (in music) are mainly the purview of the cultural "insider," and ethnomusicology has been practiced mainly by outsiders. While one can say that written language is rather definitely prescriptive or descriptive, musical notation in fact is usually a balance of phonetic and phonemic elements—it is not exclusively one or the other.

The first attempt to establish a general method and set of techniques for transcribing was made by Abraham and Hornbostel (1909–10), and included a set of special symbols for aspects of sound not normally notated in Western music. Hornbostel was, after all, the first to try to transcribe large amounts of music from many cultures. But after him, in the period 1930–50, before automatic devices had been developed, a number of scholars, among them Bela Bartók, George Herzog, and Frances Densmore, greatly influenced the development of detailed, descriptive transcription. While their work can clearly be classed as "phonetic," they vary in the extent of the phonemic component.

A look at the transcriptions of all three quickly indicates greater degree of detail and less regularity in comparison with the nineteenth-century work of Parisius and Stumpf. Bartók in particular abounds with grace notes, with small notes symbolic of sounds barely intoned, along with the large notes written normally (e.g. Bartók 1935). He gives variants departing from the main notation appearing in the various stanzas of the song by bracketed numbers. Herzog (e.g. 1936a) is more interested in rhythm and structure, using bar lines to divide phrases, shortened bar lines for rhythmic subdivision, his notation indicating an awareness of the close interaction of rhythm and form. Where no metric superstructure can be discerned, formal devices such as repetition of rhythmic motifs, rests, or contours may give a sense of rhythmic structure, and Herzog's transcriptions show that he did a good deal of analytical work before proceeding to write. It seems likely that these two scholars differed in their approaches in part because they dealt with music to which they had different kinds of relationship. Bartók, suffused with the styles of Balkan folk song, wanted to preserve, but to preserve everything he heard, moving doggedly through the song from the first note to the last, measure by measure. Herzog, using transcription as a way of discovering a style unknown to him, followed a technique of getting a general sense of the structure, then putting down the pitches, gradually getting to the rhythm.

Frances Densmore (e.g. 1913, 1918), who transcribed more American Indian melodies than anyone else, indicates yet a different approach. If Bartók and Herzog used the transcription process as a way of avoiding the constraints of Western musical thought, as with the use of special modificatory signs, she seems rather to have used it as a way of associating Indian music with the Western. Instead of eliminating the concept of Western-style meter as irrelevant in American Indian music and using formal devices to shed light on rhythmic phenomena, she shows, by frequent changes of meter, the complexity of Indian rhythms when compared to the Western.

One of the most instructive publications on transcription resulted from a symposium on the subject held by the Society for Ethnomusicology in 1963. Four scholars, Robert Garfias, George List, Willard Rhodes, and Mieczyslaw Kolinski, were asked to transcribe the same piece and then to compare the results (Symposium 1964). It may seem curious that such a comparative project was not undertaken until some seven decades after the first transcriptions based on recordings had been made. But the art of transcription had always been regarded as a very personal one; to many scholars, the emotional flavor of publishing transcriptions seems almost to have been like that of composition. And yet, one has normally assumed that transcriptions, once published, are "correct" or "right." To accuse someone of incorrect transcription is still tantamount to denying total competence. Possibly for this reason, the examination of transcriptions in publications or reviews has usually been avoided. The 1963 symposium was intended to shed light on problems of transcription, not to produce a competition. The recording used by the four, a Bushman song with musical bow recorded by Nicholas England, shows the transcriptions to have occasional mistakes, but these are modest and easily forgiven, and in any case do no damage to the general understanding of the song that the transcription provides. But while the four transcriptions do not differ greatly in their approaches from the notations of Bartók, Herzog, and Densmore made some thirty years earlier, nor greatly from each other, the differences they exhibit do illustrate approaches to the process, and the interaction of phonetic and phonemic components. Figure 1 illustrates the four transcriptions at the symposium.

The music of the musical bow is comprised of two simultaneous pitches, a fundamental and an overtone produced by manipulation of the resonator. The fundamental produces one or more overtones but can itself be predicted from the overtone. Kolinski and Rhodes faithfully produce both tones, giving the reader accustomed to Western notation an idea of the total sound, a phonetic notation, but one that rather gives the impression of standard Western notation, which is usually prescriptive. But List and Garfias give only the overtones, a phonemic device since the readers can fill in the fundamental. The basic metric scheme is stated differently by Rhodes and List. List also provides two forms of the vocal line, giving two different rhythmic interpretations, one correlating the melody with that of the musical bow accompaniment, the other based on the dynamics and phrasing of the vocal line itself.

Garfias avoids a Western bias in establishing the tone system by using the five lines of the staff to represent adjacent notes in a scale of the song rather than nodes along the diatonic scale. Using horizontal lines instead of notes, he by implication attacks the sanctity of the "note." From the beginning, aural transcription has used Western notation because of its breakdown of musical structure into often abstract units represented by notes. Graph notation and melographic devices readily dispel this assumption; a graph, once drawn, cannot easily be retranscribed into notes. The concept of the articulated note, with beginning and end, works well for certain musics, and Garfias properly uses it to represent the repeated strokes of the musical

Figure 1. Examples of transcriptions from the SEM Symposium on Transcription and Analysis (from *Ethnomusicology* 8 (1964):274).

bow. In other kinds of music, perhaps most singing, notes are useful prescriptive devices, but they are not particularly descriptive. Lines may be much more appropriate, providing opportunities to show glides and other ornaments. Indeed, there may be in certain cultures segments of greater significance than those that we label as the "notes." Aural transcription need not depend exclusively on Western notation, nor need scales be shown exclusively on the Western staff. If we recognize notes as abstractions, the door is open for using other and often more appropriate abstractions as well. If the four scholars in the transcription symposium had set out to make phonetic, strictly descriptive transcriptions, these might well have been more alike than they in fact turned out to be. It is in matters of interpretation, in establishing the phonemics of the system, that they differ.

HUMANS VERSUS MACHINES

Should transcription be carried out by humans, with their human ears, or should one rely on mechanical help? In a sense, the history of transcription moves from the human to the mechanical, but actually there has been a continuing struggle between the two approaches. The human component continues with unabated strength. Doris Stockmann (1979), in the most comprehensive account of the problems, history, and bibliography of transcription, concentrates on it as if it were bound to remain dominant. Charles Seeger, one of the most powerful proponents of automatic devices, in his closing comments on the 1963 transcription symposium, admitted the continued usefulness of Western notation and transcription by ear: "Best for the present and for the foreseeable future must be, I think, a combination of the two techniques" (Symposium 1964:277). The struggle has some parallels to the conflict between humanistic and scientific approaches to scholarship.

The classic date of its beginning is 1928, when Milton Metfessel, using a stroboscope, photographing its oscillations, and superimposing a graph against the photograph, produced a publication with graph notations (Metfessel 1928). As a matter of fact, using a broader interpretation, recording and mechanical instruments provided something related to transcription even earlier. But even Metfessel had few serious followers until the 1940s, when melographic devices began to be developed in various nations, and at that point one suddenly feels great enthusiasm on the part of many scholars for what they hope will be a final solution of sorts for the problems of the ethnomusicologist's central activity. Thus Seeger, in reviewing Dahlback's study of Norwegian folk song (1958), the first to present large quantities of melographic transcriptions, heralds a new age: "From now on, field collection and study of musics of whatever era . . . and of whatever idiom . . . cannot afford to ignore the means and methods of the . . . present work. Thus a new era of ethnomusicology has been entered" (Seeger 1960b:42).

Some of the new devices made no attempts to provide complete transcriptions of performances, remaining limited to one or several elements. Thus Bose (1952) tried to show differences in singing style between black and white American singers, Obata and Kobayashi (1937) concentrated on a device for recording pitch, and Jones (1954, 1959) produced a transcription device for the complex percussion rhythms in West Africa. List (1963b) carried out spectrographic analysis to distinguish speech from song and other intermediate categories of sound-making, while Födermayr (1971) and Graf (1966, 1972) used sonagraphic analysis to distinguish various kinds of singing style and other sounds in and associated with music. Three others, developed at UCLA by Seeger (1953b), in Norway by Gurvin and Dahlback (Dahlback 1958), and in Israel (Cohen and Katz 1968), have actually been those most widely used for transcription as of whole pieces.

"Widely" may be an overstatement. It is actually surprising to see that graph notations, generally admitted to exhibit less Western bias and thus be more conducive to both the elimination of ethnocentrism and the development of comparative method, have been used so little in a period emphasizing these values. Ethnomusicologists as a whole continue to remain untrained in reading them and unable to derive from them directly some sense of musical sound and structure. There have been relatively few publications based on melographic transcriptions, and there has actually been widespread resistance. Thus Kunst: "It is possible, by applying a mechanical-visual method of sound-registration . . . to carry the exactitude of the transcription to a point where one cannot see the wood for the trees . . ." (1959:39). Herzog: "The profusion of detailed visual data . . . will have to be re-translated into musical reality and musical sense" (1957:73). The International Folk Music Council: ". . . notation tending to mathematical exactitude must necessarily . . . entail the use of signs intelligble only to the specialists" (1952). List: "The inescapable conclusion is that the capability of the human ear should not be underestimated" (1974b:375–76). And Jairazbhoy, while accepting mechanical devices as useful for many things: ". . . there is, and perhaps always will be, a large gap between what an automatic transcriber would 'hear' and what an experienced listener of a particular musical idiom might 'hear'" (1977:269).

What are the bases for resisting something that should appear, to any right-minded individual, an incredibly useful device, one that would drive away human error and cultural bias and save labor to boot? Briefly: (1) We have an excessive association of music and notation; thus Herzog seems to equate a conventional Western notation with musical sense and musical reality. We cannot quite remove ourselves from this concept of urban Western academic music culture. (2) Ethnomusicologists, most of us believe, must be able to *hear* music, not merely to analyze, and reliance on automatic devices deprives them of a way of giving evidence of their competence. List

(1974b), in assessing the reliability of aural transcription, emphasizes the value of teaching this skill to students. (3) Ethnomusicologists are emotionally tied to the sound of music and thus get much of the pleasure of their work from transcribing. Furthermore, having made a transcription gives them a certain sense of direct ownership and control over the music that they have laboriously reduced to notation. (4) Although transcription is supposed to be descriptive notation, it nevertheless, in the corner of the scholar's mind, is something that is potentially prescriptive. At the very least, someone can look at the notation and, humming under one's breath, get at least something out of it, a general sense of how the music sounds. To the Western ethnomusicologist, Western notation makes the music seem like "real music." (5) Just as Western notation may omit significant distinctions in the music, automatic transcription cannot distinguish what is significant from what is not, what is actually heard from what the member of a culture does not choose to hear. It does not provide the possibility of interpreting the sound as a particular culture would interpret it.

These may not be good reasons, and yet even Hood, who has done more than anyone to further automatic transcription, admits the widespread service rendered by Western notation. But in the long run, he feels, transcription by ear will have to go. "The fact that some of us are determined to solve the problem . . . will one day result in the abandonment of this ethnocentric crutch" (1971:90). Still, it continues to be used, while automatic transcription has not provided the volumes of songs and pieces of the sort that have always been produced by Western notation. And yet, beyond reducing specific sounds to graphs, melographs have taught us to view music in a new light. The heuristic value of the Israel melograph is discussed by Cohen and Katz (1968), appearing to have taught the authors that "even the measurement of all the intervals occurring in the performance of a particular song can be misleading if the concept of interval is that of a fixed size" (1968:164). It is a device that would "give a picture of the stylistic elements which take place 'between the notes.'" Indeed, the ear can hear attack and decay of tones, vibrati, glissandos, and interval differences. The point that Cohen and Katz seem to be making is that the melograph, in questioning the basic assumption of the note as a unit of music, points out to us something of which, because of the constraints of Western notation, we are usually not aware. As suggested already by Herzog (1936a:286), tones are convenient but sometimes misleading abstractions.

An important contribution of the melograph is thus to help us to hear objectively. Having had certain things pointed out by inspection of a melographic notation, the scholar can then go on to trust the ear. It almost seems that ethnomusicologists are the victims of an analogue of the Whorfian hypothesis, according to which thought is regulated by the structure of language; musical hearing on the part of Westerners may be profoundly affected by the characteristics of Western notation. It may be a major role of a melograph to liberate us from this constraint.

THE LATEST NEWS

In the 1960s and 1970s transcribing has added a new role. Transcription as a record to be used for all purposes of perception, description, and analysis replacing sound recording is being gradually abandoned because melographic and other techniques have shown just how incredibly complex a group of musical sounds can be. On the other hand, the wide availability of records makes transcriptions less necessary. While the typical ethnomusicologist of the 1930s would have said, "Let's get this piece down in notation, then we will see what it is like," the scholar of the 1960s was more likely to say, "Now we've listened to this piece (and to many like it) carefully and know in general what they are like, so let's transcribe some of them in order to get better insight into ornamentation."

This trend parallels, in research at large, the abandonment of the general description of the musical style of a culture as the norm of research design, and its replacement by studies that seek to solve more specialized problems. One such problem is the analysis of nonmetric music, in which rhythm and duration cannot adequately be represented by traditional note values. A promising approach is the presentation of notation in a time-space continuum, each line of music, for example, representing ten seconds (Nettl 1972a), or each inch, one second of performance (Tsuge 1974). Touma (1968) provides two transcriptions of the same Arabic nonmetric material, a second-per-second notation using Western note values as approximations and lines indicating length of notes within a framework of spaces representing seconds. On the other hand, the study of metrically precise materials may require other approaches. Koetting (1970), dealing with West African drumming, uses a kind of graph notation that avoids reference to pitch but distinguishes types of strokes and sounds and amounts of elapsed time between strokes, in what he calls a "time unit box system." These are a few examples of the many devices for solving special problems outside the framework of Western music.

Melographic analysis, as well, has been used for the solution of special problems. In one issue of the *UCLA Selected Reports* (vol. 2, no. 1, 1974) devoted entirely to melographic studies, one finds such titles as "Vibrato as a Function of Modal Practice in Qur'an Chant . . . ," "The Vocal Ornament *Takiyah* in Persian Music," and "Vocal Tones in Traditional Thai Music." Each of these studies is based on a small amount of music, as little as a few seconds, and in most cases the purpose was to analyze rather minute differences within or among pieces. The kinds of findings one may expect in this type of study are illustrated by those of Caton (1974:46) on a type of vocal ornament, the Persian *Takiyah:* It is "distinctly simpler in tone quality than the melody notes." Its loudness is determined by the accentuation of its syllable. It is more distinct from its melodic environment in folk music than in classical music and religious chant.

Although the value of such findings may depend, in the end, on the degree to which they are significant in the culture, one of the issues may be the degree to which the kind of distinctions that Caton draws can be heard by the human ear. There is the typical dilemma: If the distinctions can be made by the ear, why does one need the melograph? And if not, are we justified in assigning significance to them? Perhaps the melograph serves to draw our aural attention to certain musical events, or perhaps its contribution is more in the realm of psychology, psycho-acoustics, and physiology than in the study of music in culture. This is not to cast doubt on the validity of the conclusions; rather, we have not always made clear to ourselves just what the role of melographic transcriptions may be.

If one had tried to predict in 1960 what might be written twenty years later, one would perhaps have included a much larger proportion of automatic transcription, acceptance of the push toward more detailed and more comprehensive transcriptional statements with the use of highly sophisticated techniques, and the relegation of aural transcription to an essentially educational role. This has not turned out to be the configuration of events. The special value of aural transcription continues to be emphasized, while automatic transcription is valuable for the solution of special problems. But new approaches to ethnomusicological fieldwork, particularly the emphasis on participant-observer methods involving even performance, give human transcribers greater hope that they can provide truly "insider's" transcriptions. They hope to do this not by first making a comprehensive phonetic reduction that is then, by analysis, reduced to a phonemic one but, rather, by depending on their first-hand authority. Western notation is being adopted by musical cultures throughout the world, modified to account for diversity, a reasonably adequate prescriptive system; this is leading to a kind of vindication of Western notation for purposes of transcription.

We are thus likely to see the continued use of Western notation and of the human transcriber, who will be aided, but not replaced, by special techniques and technologies such as variable speed controls and loop repeaters (Jairazbhoy and Balyoz 1977). And we are likely to see the continued expansion of the concept of transcription combined with various analytical methods. Thus we will be faced on the one hand with transcriptions that give us only part of the musical picture, be it ornamentation, singing style, or melodic contour, but give it in enormous detail; we may, on the other extreme, come to view abstractions such as formulas (AAB (bb) A or AA^5A^5A) as a particular kind of transcription as well, having admitted that the Western concept of the note is equally an abstraction.

Since about 1960, statements about the purposes and methods of transcription and its relationship to analysis (e.g. Hopkins 1966, List 1963c, Rouget and Schwarz 1970, Hood 1971, Jairazbhoy 1977) have again come to the fore. Attempts to establish universal notation systems applicable to modern composition as well as ethnomusicology establish a new link (Wenker 1970, Cole 1974). After a period of almost exclusive attention to the development of automatic transcription, scholars have again begun writing about the value of aural transcription. The ethnomusicologist with field experience and a participant's understanding of a music can well compete with the machines. Jairazbhoy (1977:270), comparing human work with automatic devices, maintains that for certain purposes "aural transcription by a trained ethnomusicologist . . . may be far more meaningful." The amount of transcribing and the role of transcription in the career of the typical ethnomusicologist have declined. But for better or worse, the ethnomusicologist continues to deal with music mainly in its visual form.

Chapter 7

In the Speech Mode

THE ANALYSIS CLASS

You return from the "field," and two months later arrives a trunk full of tapes. You have been spending your time asking questions, recording performances, day by day putting your informants and teachers through their paces. Now the express company delivers the central product of your work. You look at a rather vast pile of little boxes, make a quick count, and find that you have some 60 hours of music, some 500 separate songs and pieces, and it dawns on you dramatically, perhaps for the first time, that one of your jobs will be to say in words and with symbols just what this music is like. You may have to transcribe it and, before doing so, to work out a description for yourself; or you may say to yourself, "I'll just doggedly transcribe five pieces a day, and be done in three months." After transcription, you will come face to face with one of our monumental issues, how to analyze and finally describe a large body of music.

It's a problem that has been faced, more or less in the way it was just described, by hundreds of scholars and graduate students. In a more general way it has been faced by most musicologists. One would be exceptionally presumptuous to propose a specific, generally applicable solution, or even to survey and discuss all of the vast literature that speaks to it. My purpose here will be to ferret out a few of the major intellectual issues, and to refer selectively to a small portion of an immense body of literature.

We must begin with reference to some issues that are by now familiar, the interface between universal and culture-specific, between insider's and outsider's view, between comprehensive method and technique that speaks to special problems. Questions pop out at us from all directions. Can one establish a way of viewing music that will work for all imaginable musics? Is description necessary or can music not somehow speak for itself? What, indeed, is the difference between analysis and description? Should there be a single procedure for analyzing music, a sort of paradigm of ethnomusicology? Or can one safely rely on the characteristics of each music to guide one, or on the way in which a society conceives of its own musical structure? Or again, should one act the scientist, able to produce replicable statements, or should analysis be much more a matter of personal interpretation? Can one scholar, in a reasonable amount of time, make a comprehensive description of a music, saying concisely everything worth saying? Or must one perforce concentrate on those aspects of music that are relevant to the solution of a particular problem? These questions face the scholar working with music alone, but they will crop up again, slightly modified, when we turn to the study of music in culture. All of these problems in the end boil down to one identified long ago by Charles Seeger, repeatedly discussed by him, and again clarified in one of his last works (1977b:16–30). It is the problem of using language, or, as Seeger would put it, the "speech mode of communication," for discourse about music, a related but totally different form of communication. Although it is hard to imagine practical alternatives, there is no doubt that the first and most general difficulty of analysis and description of music results from our need to integrate them in a way of thinking that is substantially conditioned by the characteristics of language and its particular way of using time.

Most teachers, and certainly most students, take all this for granted, and so it seems best, keeping Seeger's caution in mind, to move to more everyday matters. Let me for a moment look back to 1950, my days of undergraduate study. Ethnomusicology was very different from its present state. Perhaps one can get some insight into the special nature of ethnomusicological analysis by studying its relationship to the way in which it was taught, to the way in which the analysis of Western music was approached.

Let me reconstruct a day. I attended a class in fourth-semester music theory. We spent our time distinguishing German, French, and Italian sixth chords, and as I look back at the earlier semesters of theory classes, I realize that almost all of the time had been spent on chords, very little on melody and rhythm. Certainly this represents much of the training that American and European scholars experienced until perhaps the most recent generations. I then went to a class in "Analysis of Form," where we looked at broad outlines, finding highly abstracted general principles that could be shown to govern the genesis and development of a piece lasting twenty minutes.

Later I went to a class called (logically, for the period in Western history in which it was taught) "Folk and Primitive Music," taught by my revered professor George Herzog, and listened to an American Indian song. Our teacher took it apart, beginning with something called "scale," on which he spent much time; going on to something called "rhythm," with which we all had a hard time; then saying a few words about the curious way in which the singers used their voices; and finally attempting to divide the song into phrases and assigning to each a letter in order to show similarities and differences.

How very different were the approaches to Western and to Indian music in these classes! I ask myself whether they were due to differences among the musical systems, or whether they suggest that there is a fundamental difference between the way in which a culture looks at its own and another music. The concepts of analysis and description most widely used in ethnomusicology would appear laughable when applied to Western art music, not because they are intrinsically inapplicable but because the purposes and the traditions of scholarship differ. One would think that the study—description and analysis—of a concept called music would have as its basis a set of assumptions applicable to all music. But the approaches to analysis for Western and non-Western music actually have quite separate though interrelated histories. Quite beyond this, as Blum (1975) has pointed out in detail, musicological analysis is itself a product of a particular social context and a special, culturally determined, set of values. To write the history of analytical thought in ethnomusicology is a task that cannot possibly be attempted here or by myself. Looking at a few samples, milestones as it were, can provide a taste of this history.

HORNBOSTEL'S PARADIGM

"Music is the universal language of mankind," said Longfellow, and while we know he was wrong, ethnomusicologists have often seemed to believe that there ought to be one universal way of looking at music and explaining its structure. Not preoccupied with the universality of music, much of their analytical work nevertheless rests on the assumption that there is enough common to all musics, and also enough about music that everyone will wish to understand, however diverse the sounds, that one approach can apply to all. The idea of establishing a single, universally applicable system is squarely in the mainstream of ethnomusicological research throughout most of its past history. Inevitably, one would expect analytical systems applicable to an incredibly diverse set of musics to take on the character of systems of classification. In other words, the concept of music would be divided into components along some lines, and for each of these components a broad but finite number of possible ratings would be developed, so that each component of each music would be somehow placed in its relationship to others, on a graph or a table showing degrees of similarity or difference.

The concept of classifying entire musics as well as individual pieces of musical creation is an important one in ethnomusicology and concerns analysis in general but also the more specialized study of genetic relationship among individual pieces, as well as practical matters such as deciding in what order to put the 700 songs in some published collection or other. But here we need to be concerned only with that aspect of musical classification that involves the placing of a musical repertory within a framework of world music. Interestingly, while the classification of the tunes within a musical repertory occupied some scholars early on, the idea of providing some way of classifying musical repertories at large came to the forefront later. The history of the universalist approach to analysis moves gradually from narration to typology. The scholars of the period to about 1940 did not formally classify musics, but their approaches, coming from a comparative perspective, had elements of a classificatory system. Viewing the world of music as a set of finite possibilities, they established a universalist approach as the mainstream of analytical tradition.

In selecting for discussion the work of a few scholars who have made major contributions to this tradition, the logical one to begin with is E. M. von Hornbostel (sometimes publishing jointly with Otto Abraham). Through a long series of publications Hornbostel tried to deal with a large number of musical repertories, each sampled rather modestly (see e.g. Hornbostel 1906, Abraham and Hornbostel 1903, 1906). Not having done the fieldwork and having little beyond a few cylinder recordings at his disposal, he perhaps perforce developed a way of dealing with all musics in essentially the same way, and this characteristic as well as the more specific traits of his method are evident in the work of some of his students and further even of their academic progeny.

What may strike the reader of Hornbostel's analyses first is his great emphasis on the melodic aspects of the music, particularly on what he calls scales. Enumeration of tones, and the relationship of the tones to a not always thoroughly defined topic, and, beyond that, the specific intervalic distances are what he speaks to most frequently and immediately. Throughout his work there is evidence of a feeling of urgency to establish a theoretical framework that, while often unarticulated, must surely exist for the creation of melodic material. Thus in Abraham and Hornbostel's study of songs of the Thompson River Indians (1906) we find a detailed accounting of numbers of pentatonic, tetratonic, and tritonic scales, an attempt to indicate frequency of intervals calculated to quarter tones, and indications of relative emphasis on different tones in order to establish a hierarchically defined tonality. The same is true in the study of Tunisian melodies (1906), while the short article on the music of "Neu-Mecklenburg" (1907) is devoted almost entirely to scalar matters. The distinction between "Materialleiter" (vocabulary of tones and intervals on which a composer may draw) and "Gebrauchsleiter" (tones used in a particular piece) illustrates his theoretical thinking (Hornbostel 1912).

Melodic movement and contour are dealt with more briefly. While the scale of each song is calculated and weighted, and statistical methods are brought in for comparative purposes, other aspects of the melodic process are characterized more briefly and generalized. The same is also true of rhythm, which is handled largely as a function of meter (although general statements about the relationship of components such as the vocal and drum rhythm are found); also of vocal style, which is briefly and informally characterized; and of form, which too is the subject of generalization although Hornbostel occasionally divided musical material into sections whose interrelationship is schematically indicated.

This characterization of Hornbostel's technique of analysis may not be quite fair, for he often went a good deal further. He was typically working in *terra incognita* and probably casting about for adequate ways of establishing a generally applicable method, and his publications are usually uncommonly insightful. Yet there remains the curious emphasis on scalar characteristics, outweighing all else. Considering the rather inadequate cylinder recordings with which Hornbostel had to work, scales were probably among the most difficult elements to perceive and describe. Rhythm might have been better, for amplitude and time elapsed between events are usually easier to observe in the presence of static. Overall formal design would be perhaps the element easiest to understand. But possibly Hornbostel felt that he needed to concentrate on those aspects of the music least obvious to the casual listener.

A more likely determinant of Hornbostel's approach, however, is the way in which the educated Western listener who focuses on the classical tradition thinks of music. The Western musician from the late nineteenth century into the middle of the twentieth was simply more interested in melody, in intervals, than in form and rhythm. Theory books and music dictionaries tilt heavily in that direction. We readily criticize singers for poor intonation, while the theoretical systems of the eighteenth century tried to establish proper division of the octave into intervals. A classic seminal publication, A. J. Ellis's relativistic statement about the coexistence of many musical scales (1885), established the primacy of melodic considerations in the early history of the field. Western musical thinking is of harmony, melody, scale, and pitch first. Indeed, even in the 1950s the novices to non-Western music whom I knew, like myself, were always first struck by the strangeness or similarity of tone systems in relationship to their own. So Hornbostel's emphasis on scale is a part of his own cultural background. This particular aspect of his approach—the tendency to deal statistically with scales and more generally with other components of music—became for a long time a paradigm of analysis. Hornbostel's own students refined but followed it, and those not as directly associated with him, from Frances Densmore to Alan Merriam, were obviously heavily influenced by it. And the emphasis on scale is still evident in recent studies, such as McLean's (1971) analysis of 651 Maori scales.

Hornbostel and his associates furthermore usually described each piece transcribed, then provided statistical and generalized commentary, and this two-fold approach—speak to each piece, and speak to the whole musical system as represented in the sample—became a widespread technique of presentation. But perhaps most important, Hornbostel tried to apply his approach, with variations as determined by the size of the corpus and the progressive stages in his thinking, to a variety of musics so large that one might well regard it as a sampling of world music.

HERZOG'S SYNTHESIS

George Herzog modified Hornbostel's standardized method, adding to it elements from Bartók's approach to form and bringing to bear his anthropological field experience, synthesizing several streams. Clearly his work grows out of Hornbostel's, but certain subtle shifts are evident. While recognizing the variety of the world's music, Herzog, like his teacher, tried to approach a number of musical styles in essentially the same way. In particular, he dealt with American Indian, Oceanian, and European folk musics. Where an articulated music theory exists, this standard method might not be adequate or for that matter needed, and perhaps as a result of this belief Herzog restricted his work to folk and tribal cultures. But he made it evident to me that he regarded this standardized approach with a limited sample almost as a necessary evil, something to do in the absence of a larger corpus, a native theory, a field method with which one could develop something more sophisticated. The method he taught and often used was an initial foray, after the basic transcription process had been completed, a way of introducing and saying something about a musical repertory in a style that could be understood by the ethnomusicological layman.

In his study of the music of the Yuman tribes (1928) Herzog follows Hornbostel in analyzing each song, but he does it more systematically and thoroughly, though devoting himself only to scale and overall form. In his general analytical discussion he devotes equal space to "manner of singing," interestingly placed first in his order; to tonality and melody; to rhythm, accompaniment, and form. The discussion of melody is generalized, less dependent on a statistical approach to scale than is Hornbostel's. The things that strike him as interesting and significant are singled out for special comment, probably a result of his understanding of the limitations of a small sample. The detailed discussion of the formal principles, the description of the "rise" form of the Yuman peoples in its various manifestations, is particularly significant because it heralds, in the history of ethnomusicological analysis, a gradually increasing emphasis on the way in which the composer works, moving from section to section. Hornbostel had worked mainly toward establishing the basic musical vocabulary on which the composer draws, and Herzog here deals with the way in which this vocabulary is handled over a span of musical time. In Herzog's dissertation (1936a) comparing Pueblo and Pima music we find the same approach, but also an attempt to establish song "types." While general statements regarding relative frequencies of scale, form, and typical rhythmic phenomena can serve to establish the character of a musical system within a world context, such a system is nevertheless comprised of a number of characteristic subdivisions, subsystems, each of which is worthy of the same statistical and generalizing treatment.

Implicitly Herzog here came face to face with a general problem in the presentation of ethnomusicological data, the identity of the unit that can be described. The question is whether such a unit is only the individual piece, or *the* music of a society, or whether there are musically self-contained groupings of pieces. It is certainly conceivable that in Herzog's terms all of the songs in a particular repertory could belong to only one type, all songs sharing scale, form, rhythmic character. But in his teaching Herzog regarded this as unlikely and urged students, after having analyzed the individual songs and generalized about the repertory at large, to look for subdivisions. He did not overtly theorize about a typical repertory structure, as suggested in Chapter 5, but of course he was aware that such a structure exists.

Herzog did not emphasize scalar material as much as did Hornbostel, and he did less with a quantitative approach. This implied questioning of statistical methods may result from his substantial field experience (which Hornbostel lacked), and from skepticism about the concrete appearance that such statements would give in what is bound to be a highly fluid corpus whose statistical abstractions are illusions. This interpretation of his reasoning seems supported by his treatment of the Ghost Dance songs in another major study focusing on the understanding of history through ethnomusicological research (1935a). Here Herzog deals mainly with material recorded by others, and with a closed corpus, the Ghost Dance songs having been largely abandoned by the time he came to study them. Interestingly, statistical statements are much more in evidence here, and, indeed, his conclusions depend largely on relative quantities.

The technique of providing an individual analysis of each song or piece together with a statistical survey is found in some important later works. In his thorough account of Flathead music Merriam (1967a) in tabular form and more detail does essentially what Herzog had also done. Merriam's grouping is less by musical type than by use of songs, and he makes much more use of formal statistics. In one of the exemplary studies of Anglo-American folk song Schinhan (1957) gives information about the tonality and structure of each song and, in an appendix, a statement of each scale with precise frequency of tones. In addition, tabular information on many aspects of style is provided for the repertory as a whole and for portions of it, separating "old ballads," Native American ballads, North Carolina ballads, etc. This technique to me seems to be an outgrowth of Hornbostel's paradigm as well.

If I am right in tracing the primacy of pitch organization in ethnomusicology to the Western musician's concern with this musical element, I am not able to explain the much less systematic way in which ethnomusicologists have dealt with the phenomenon of pitches heard simultaneously, and their configurations in space and time. Harmony, after all, is enormously important in most Western music, the hallmark of Western music to both Westerners and members of other societies. Ethnomusicologists have generally been cavalier in the treatment of this musical element, sometimes using the term "polyphony" to indicate any music in which one hears more than one pitch at a time, and using as subdivisions such concepts as harmony (emphasis on the relationship of simultaneous pitches), counterpoint (emphasis on the melodic progress of the voices or instruments performing together), heterophony (simultaneous variations of the same melody). Among the few suggesting a universal framework for analysis, Kolinski (1962) proposes a system for dealing with consonance and dissonance; M. Schneider (1934) compares musics in accordance with the degree to which the various voices use the same tonality; and Malm (1972) suggests adopting the concepts of homophony, heterophony, and disphony to indicate various kinds of relationship among voices. But a more or less generally accepted set of concepts analogous to those in the realm of scale, about which one can at least argue, has not appeared for this element of music—for which I can't even find a proper term!

KOLINSKI'S GRAND SCHEME

Like Hornbostel, Herzog sought to describe different musics in the same terms, providing a basis for comparison, but his statements are considerably less rigid, more generalized, indicating his perhaps greater appreciation of their potential weakness. His approach contrasts interestingly with that of Mieczyslaw Kolinski, a fellow student of his under Hornbostel. Kolinski tried to be considerably more rigorous and established frameworks for the classification of the musics of the world. In his work the issues of analysis and comparison overlap greatly. Hornbostel and Herzog were faced with musics, one at a time, that would be described in similar terms; for Kolinski, the job became to establish a system of analysis, or rather a network of systems, providing niches into which songs and then musics would be placed. His approach is therefore much closer to that of classification.

In 1978, after having published many articles that together state his system, Kolinski wrote that ". . . only when recognizing both the extent of the socio-cultural diversification and the nature of the psycho-physically rooted constraint, and only when utilizing methods of analysis developed through a cognition of these two vital factors, will one be able to approach objectively, comprehensively, and meaningfully the structure of the music of the world's peoples" (1978:242). This statement shows Kolinski's understanding of musical diversity but also his insistence that it can nevertheless be subjected to comparison through a single classificatory system, this system being a reflection of and determined by the outer limits of the mentioned constraints; it also reflects his interest in the *comprehensive* approach to the world's music. The article from which it is taken follows his publication of a number of articles dealing with the analysis of various components of music: melodic movement (1956, 1965a and b), tempo (1959), harmony (1962), scale (1961), and rhythm (1973). In most of these publications Kolinski states possibilities or options of which musicians and entire musical cultures may take advantage, and gives examples of how these options may have actually been used. Together they constitute a grand scheme for describing and comparing musics of the world.

In his "Classification of Tonal Structures" he established a series of 348 types of scalar and modal arrangements in accordance with number of tones and their interrelationships (Kolinski 1961:39–41). The scheme has some problems, not accounting for intervals that are incompatible with the chromatic scale, but it is a highly comprehensive system for such classification. To show its usefulness for comparative study, Kolinski tabulated the presence or absence but not the frequency of each of the 348 types among five repertories—Teton Sioux, Papago, Suriname, Dahomey, and English-Appalachian. Similarly, a number of melody types become a system within which one can plot the distribution of materials in actual repertories (Kolinski 1956).

Kolinski's methods require painstaking work, but they lend themselves to easy decision-making. Contrary to the cantometric system developed by Lomax, they do not require special training in order for one analyst to make his work compatible with that of another. All he requires is transcriptions that he can trust and a conventional Western-style musical background.

Among the difficulties inherent in Kolinski's style of analysis and comparison is the basic problem of "translatability" of cultures. It emerges particularly in his work on tempo (Kolinski 1959), an element of music which one might expect to be very readily quantifiable and comparable. Kolinski's method of describing tempo essentially involves the average number of note articulations per minute, along with various refinements such as standard deviation. But the concept of "musical speed" seems to vary from culture to culture, and the actual number of notes per minute may not really be an indicator. Indeed, even within Western classical music, at least according to the conventional conceptualization of most musicians, the tempo in a set of variations by Mozart may remain constant, despite the more rapidly moving last variation with its characteristically quick thirty-second-note passages. Kolinski's system, criticized in detail by Christensen (1960), is objective, but it may not be compatible with the concepts of any of the cultures whose music is being studied.

Perhaps Kolinski's most ambitious scheme involves the analysis of melodic movement. In the final version of his study of this musical element

(1965b) he provides a complex classification of melodic structures using a number of criteria: degree of recurrence of a motif; dominant, initial, and final direction of movement; and concepts taken from visual representation such as "standing, hanging, tangential, overlapping, distant, and including." The system is complicated in a number of ways, such as the possibility of connecting several categories of movement, each present in a motif of about three to eight notes, and the introduction of the concept of "indirect" ascents and descents. Kolinski provides over 200 examples of different kinds of melodic movement. Throughout, certain kinds appear to be common, others rare, in a broad sampling. In contrast to his work with scales, in which there is a finite number of possibilities, Kolinski does not limit the number of kinds of things that can happen in melodic movement. But he does limit the number of types of units, instead allowing their kinds of combinations to be infinite. But again, he tries to provide a system in which any music can be accommodated—or any music in which the concept of "tone" has any meaning. Kolinski's approaches were not widely followed and his methods rarely developed further, but in the area of melodic movement he has a successor, Charles Adams (1976), who provides a yet much more intricate system.

It is interesting to see that, like Hornbostel and Herzog, and like typical Western music theorists, Kolinski is much more tentative when dealing with rhythm than with melodic phenomena. In his major publication on this subject (1973) he develops broad categories—isometric and heterometric, that is, with tendency to have measures of equal or unequal length; superimposed on this are the concepts of "commetric" and "contrametric," which involve the degree to which audible accents support or contradict a preconceived metric structure. Here he only gives the beginning of a classification but again suggests that there is a finite group of classes within which one could place all musics, defining rhythm as "organized duration" and meter as "organized pulsation functioning as a framework for rhythmic design" (1973:499). This definition, he says, is interculturally applicable. He goes on to imply that one should class musics along continua "ranging on the one hand from most simple to extremely complex metro-rhythmic patterns, and on the other hand from a strict rigidity of durational and pulse values to a highly flexible rubato style" (1978:241), and to suggest that the "extensive latitude between strongly commetric and highly contrametric structures" (1978:241) could provide one way of placing the musics of the world along a rhythmic scale.

The relative neglect of rhythm in the early decades of ethnomusicology may have resulted in a tendency, later on, to deal with it in more culture-specific ways than has been true of melody. Description of rhythmic structure in recent literature tends to be based on native theory, whether articulated or not, and so the ways in which scholars of Asian Indian, African, and Japanese music talk about rhythm differ from each other much more than do discussions of scale and melody in these cultures (see e.g. Kauffman 1980, Koetting 1970, Deva 1974, Malm 1959).

Kolinski's work shows a belief that the possibilities of musical creation are limited and can be divided into classes, and that one way of describing the world's musics is to find for each the appropriate classificatory niche, not necessarily related to a class as perceived by the owners of the music. Kolinski was surely aware of the importance of studying each culture on its own terms, but found it necessary to short-circuit this approach in the interest of comparison, doing so on the basis of evidence from perceptual and Gestalt psychology (1978:230, 235–39).

CANTOMETRICS AND COWS

We have had occasion several times to refer to another, more recent approach to the description of world music in a single system, the rather controversial method called cantometrics. By its nature it would appear almost to be an outgrowth of certain of Kolinski's work, but as a matter of fact the developer of this method, Alan Lomax, makes little mention of Kolinski in his publications (see Lomax 1959, 1962, 1968). Having cited it as a tool for comparison, we now return to examine it as a strictly analytical procedure. Its purpose is simply "to provide descriptive techniques for the speedy characterization and classification" of musical style (Lomax 1968:8; see Figure 2). The idea of a single system for describing all music, informally established by Hornbostel and amplified by Herzog, then pushed in the direction of classificatory schemes by Kolinski, is here more rigidly formalized. Hornbostel and Herzog provided a way of describing musics by pointing out certain characteristics in a given proportion of emphasis, about each of a specific group of aspects of music. Lomax provides a diagram which can be produced on a single page and on which the characterization, or profile, of a music is given, the result, of course, of a complex procedure. With musical sound divided into thirty-seven parameters, any musical piece can be rated as to the presence, strength, or force of each of these parameters. Averages of the pieces in a repertory can then be established, giving a characterization for each music.

Cantometrics has been severely taken to task for many shortcomings. The parameters are unevenly distributed; some are clearly single components that are readily measured, but others are really groups of components not easily distinguished. "Range," the distance between highest and lowest tone, and "register" or tessitura are in the former category. "Rasp," an extraneous noise that obscures the clear articulation of pitch, or "basic musical organization of the voice part" are harder to define. Recordings are not equally applicable to the method. Thus, for example, the analyst is expected to determine how loudly a singer is singing, something that cannot readily be determined from a record and that a singer is likely to vary with

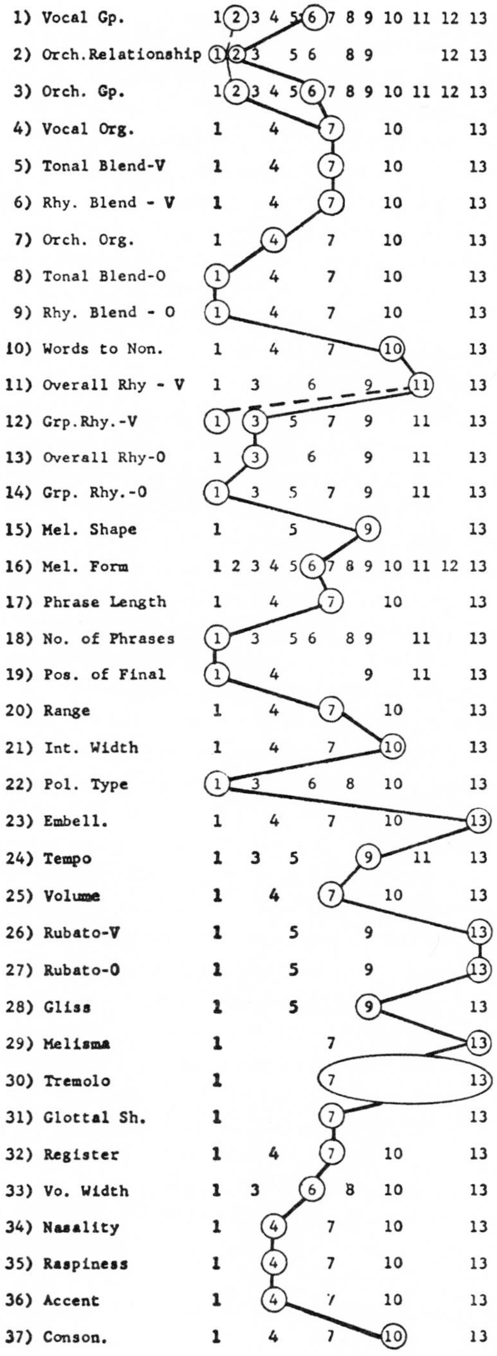

Figure 2. Example of cantometric analysis: Modal profile for North American Indian music (from Lomax 1968:86).

the presence or absence of a microphone. Criticisms of this sort could be applied to a good many of the parameters.

In order to carry out cantometric analysis, one must undergo special training. But despite an elaborate set of training tapes that Lomax has published in order to allow students outside his own staff to learn the method (1976), I have found it difficult to achieve agreement on the ratings from a homogeneous group of fairly experienced students. Beyond this, Lomax's implied belief that a folk culture normally produces a homogeneous musical style which can be deduced from a small sample may also be questioned (E. Henry 1976).

But the cantometric system deserves great credit for having moved vigorously in a direction previously uncharted: the description of singing style and of the nature of musical sound in general. Several of Lomax's parameters involve components of music in the realm of what is usually called "performance practice," which are either neglected or described only impressionistically in earlier literature: vocal width or tension, glissando, glottal shake, tremulo, rasp, volume, pitch level, vocal blend, degree of accentuation of stressed tones. In this respect cantometrics provides the beginnings of a more comprehensive system for describing music in a large number of the aspects of its sound, as well as a classificatory scheme for rating a piece or a music in many respects. The profiles provide descriptions, and comparison of the profiles provides at least a suggestion of degrees of similarity and difference among the world's musics. Lomax's work has not been carried further by many scholars, but attention to singing style has become a component of the field to a much larger degree since the invention of several melographic devices. It has been particularly carried forward by scholars working in Vienna (see Födermayr 1971) and at UCLA (see the special issue of *Selected Reports in Ethnomusicology,* vol. 2, no. 1, 1974).

The approaches I have briefly described are important in the history of ethnomusicology, but by no means are they the only ones that have been followed, although they seem to me to constitute the mainstream of history. These approaches are, as it were, music-specific, deriving from Western thinking about music, from the history of Western music theory. But there are also some systems of analysis that approach music—and all music is again implied—from the viewpoint of other disciplines, particularly semiotics and linguistics.

Given that there are many different approaches to analysis, do they really tell us different things? Marcia Herndon, in a rather significant if controversial article entitled "Analysis: The Herding of Sacred Cows," tried to find out. As an introduction to the presentation of a new method of her own, Herndon (1974) analyzes and/or describes one piece of music, a song from Madagascar, providing eight separate descriptions, each based on the approach given in a major text or study (some mentioned above), classifying the approaches themselves. Herndon may be taken to task for misinterpreting and in some cases parodying the approaches to description of music taken by various earlier scholars. But she does provide what is perhaps the only extant attempt to compare analytical models by applying each to the same piece of music. She then goes on to propose a further method, departing from the traditions I have described above, and, characteristically of the 1970s, based on analytical models developed by linguistics and semiotics. She regards it as clearly superior to the earlier ones, but due to lack of paper and the fact that her analysis is based on a piece which she knows only from transcription, she is forced to present a simplified version of her own approach. Yet it strikes the reader as extremely difficult to emulate and I must confess to having tried to encourage students to use her method, but with no success. Herndon's criticisms of the earlier approaches are often well taken. Yet she was able to apply them to a new piece herself, while on the other hand it is evidently very difficult for someone to do this very thing with her approach.

In all justice, we must admit that the same problem is encountered by those trying to use some of the other suggested semiotic and linguistic models (e.g. Boilès 1967, 1973b; Nattiez 1971, 1975; Chenoweth and Bee 1971), touched on in Chapter 16. These linguistic models dominated for a time and are now again in decline, but the style of thought required by them leaves its mark.

What has happened to the effort of ethnomusicology to establish comprehensive, all-encompassing ways of describing a variety of musics for the purpose of comparison? Those most easily applied are also the least satisfactory because they simply give little information. As the music-specific characterizations by Hornbostel and Herzog, and for that matter Lomax, are replaced by the semiotics of Nattiez and Boilès and others, the methods become more and more complex; in a sense they give more information but are harder to read, lend themselves less easily to comparison, and are more difficult to apply by someone who did not originate them. Despite the universalist intention, they turn out to be culture-specific, or at best scholar-specific. One must conclude that for a system of analysis that is universally applicable and that makes possible the comparison not only of pieces within a repertory but of musics of the world, some kind of classificatory scheme is still the most adequate.

The description of musics by ethnomusicologists and their accounts of procedures fill volumes; yet these are not really used very much. Authors refer to each other constantly but rarely to the analytical statements. The kinds of things that we still continue to find significant about most of the world's music are the things we can, more or less, establish rather quickly through listening. Trying out the procedures Hornbostel, Herzog, Kolinski, and Lomax have developed quite likely will result in intangible and subliminal insights, but probably beyond that only confirmation of what is already evident from hearing.

It is all rather frustrating. We can trace our problems to the antithesis between attempts to provide universally applicable analytical models and the long-standing realization that music is not a universal language but a group of related or unrelated systems. The obvious alternative to universal systems is to analyze and describe each music in terms that are applicable to it alone. There seem to be three distinct avenues. (1) Our description is derived from the way in which its own culture describes the music, or if, as is more usual, specific descriptions are not available, the way it appears to perceive, classify, and conceptualize it. (2) It is derived from those features of the music that appear to the analyst to be particularly significant or interesting; thus the analysis satisfies the criterion that it should give the analysts and their readers fresh insight. (3) The analysis is established in order to solve a specific problem derived from historical, anthropological, or psychological inquiry. These three approaches are not unrelated to those described in our chapter on transcription.

Why should one describe and analyze music in the first place? In order to be able to talk and write about it, I suppose. Here is the crux of the issue about which Charles Seeger has so frequently regaled and even harangued his colleagues. We continue asking whether one can really talk about music, whether one must find a meta-language, and whether it is all related to our tendency to want visual representation—notation, description, play-by-play accounting—of music (and of everything else that is not already speech). It is interesting, therefore, that Seeger himself, despite misgivings about dealing with music in his "speech mode," was also one of the first to write comprehensively on the methodology of dealing with a music (1953a).

THE INSIDER SPEAKS

If we analyze music in a system derived from the way in which the culture that produced the music analyzes or presents it, it stands to reason that we are likely to come closer to perceiving how members of that society hear their music. Many recent scholars, such as Blacking (e.g. in 1970b) and Daniélou (1966), have suggested that such an approach is the only one that makes sense. For cultures with a detailed, articulated theory such as India, this can easily be done, but for others such as the American Indians, it may require intermediate steps such as the formulation of a music theory from texts of some sort. Many scholars have taken it for granted that they should present the musical systems they have uncovered in the field in the terms their teachers used to present it to them. We can distinguish two ways of going about this. In most societies people do not talk much technically about their music; even when analytical statements are made, there is not always much of a consensus. Thus, when asking various musicians in Iran to analyze one performance on record, I found divergence on not only the details ("Is he now playing this, or is it still that?") but also on the approaches

("Should one be looking for these components of music, or should we rather talk about those?"). This will be no news to the American and European music theorist; musicians seem always to agree more upon what one should do in composition and performance than on ways of conceptualizing and justifying what they have done.

Acknowledging this characteristic, we may be content to describe music precisely as the culture does, or would; or we could use the culture's own approach to go further, establishing a new system of description that nevertheless is derived from and continues to be compatible with what would be done by the informants.

Let me explain what I mean by giving a somewhat simple-minded example from my own experience in Iran. Iranian musicians teach the *radif,* the body of music that is memorized and then used as the basis for improvisation and composition (see Zonis 1973:69–92, and Nettl 1978b for detailed description). They label its sections *(dastgāhs)* and their subdivisions *(gushehs)* clearly, although there is some disagreement on terminology and in determining which *gushehs* properly belong in a particular *dastgāh,* and although there is much overlapping in this complex set of materials. Musicians then are willing to analyze certain performances which are divided by the player or singer into sections, and to state upon which section of the *radif* a portion of an improvised performance is based. An ethnomusicologist who has studied with Iranian musicians can analyze such sectioned performances in this manner but cannot be sure, on account of the lack of complete consensus, that the analysis will be accepted by every Persian master. This is the kind of analysis in which the ethnomusicologist does what the musicians of the culture do.

But one can also go further. There are, for example, performances that masters of the *radif* are not willing to analyze in this fashion. They may make several kinds of statements about such performances: the musician does not know the *radif;* he is purposely and expertly mixing materials from several sources; he is simply playing *āvāz* (nonmetric improvisation) in a *dastgāh* in general, not taking account of the differences among the sections within the *dastgāh* given in the *radif.* The first approach mentioned here would simply report these anomalies, and perhaps point out the difference between sectioned and other performances and refer to the fact that it seems to be readily recognized by Iranians.

The second approach (followed in Nettl 1972a) would take these unsectioned performances and, with the use of motivic analysis, determine almost second by second on which part of the *radif* each short bit is based. Instead of accepting the statement that a five-minute segment is simply "*āvāz* of the *dastgāh* of *shur,*" one could determine that it is comprised of materials from three *gushehs* (e.g. *salmak, golriz,* and *shahnāz)* and makes fleeting reference to three other *gushehs.* Now, when in my experience Persian musicians were confronted with analysis of this sort, they pronounced it correct but found the information only mildly interesting, and not really particularly relevant. I had tried to take their way of looking at their own music further, and had managed to avoid violating their way of approaching the analysis, but I had gone further than they were willing to go, had divided their concepts into units smaller than those they were willing to use. I had given myself some insights into how the music is put together but, on the other hand, I could no longer claim simply to be presenting the system as it presents itself.

Blacking's distinguished study of Venda children's songs (1967) likewise uses a society's own musical perception to construct a description that goes beyond the culture's own way of describing itself. He uses this technique to show the materials within the adult repertory upon which the children's songs are based, something the Venda know but do not articulate. He deals with the music on the Venda's own terms but does things the Venda themselves would not do, things that he, however, would also not do in the same way were he dealing with another repertory and another culture. The history of analysis in Western music has similar trends. The highly influential Schenkerian system is essentially based on classical and early nineteenth-century German and Austrian music, and does not work as well, at least without considerable modification, for other kinds. It uses the general conceptual framework of the musicians of that period and the way it is interpreted by later musicians who regard themselves as part of this tradition. But it also goes further, showing within this framework what its practitioners could accept but would not do on their own, and would likely consider only mildly interesting or irrelevant. (For an example, see Salzer 1952.)

NAHAWAND AND THE SONGS OF ISHI

The teacher of analysis asks, "What is it that strikes you about this piece?" Bartók's (1931) analyses of Hungarian folk music include a great deal of attention to the configuration of cadential tones; he compares the tones within a scale on which the various lines of a melody end. By contrast, the transcriptions of Anglo-American folk ballads published by Sharp (1932), Bronson (1959–72), and Schinhan (1957) are accompanied by descriptions, for each song, of scale and mode. Bartók also had interest in the relationship of lines ("form" or "structure"), but the students of Anglo-American folk song cited paid little attention to this, or for that matter to rhythm, which Bartók studies mainly in relation to the rhythmic patterns of the poems. Why analyze Hungarian and English folk songs so differently? Both are European, monophonic, largely pentatonic, have a lot in common. The answer must lie partly in the supposition that each style has certain parameters which are striking to the Western-trained scholar who therefore gives attention selectively.

Now, we can hardly debate whether there is something inherently interesting in Anglo-American modes and uninteresting in the overall form. But there is a reason why, beyond the general Western preoccupation with pitch, Sharp's, Bronson's and Schinhan's attention was drawn to scales and modes. The search for a connection between folk music and medieval music, particularly chant, was long a major focus of folk song scholarship—perhaps on the assumption that, once established, the relationship would legitimize folk song research. What was known about medieval music at the time was substantially in the domain of the melodic, and the medieval classification system of music began with the modes. Thus it seemed appropriate to do the same with folk music. In the case of Bartók, the aim was not to show relationship to medieval Western liturgical music or art music but, rather, to establish a group of types that could then be placed in some kind of historical order, a group of strata, as it were; also to determine a way of comparing Hungarian folk music with that of other Finno-Ugric peoples to which it may be historically tied, and to other folk musics in southeastern Europe; and finally to find a way of placing various melodies in some kind of musically logical order in a large collection. And Bartók was evidently struck by the usefulness of certain parameters for satisfying these needs. Walter Wiora, in a limited illustrative anthology (1953) of European folk songs aiming at a demonstration of the unity of European folk music, emphasizes melodic contours that, to him, indicate genetic relationship of tunes found in various parts of Europe.

In each of these cases it seems that the scholars whose work I have used as examples were struck and attracted by a particular thing about the music with which they were concerned. They concentrated their analytical statements, making no attempts to say everything about their musics, nor to find a way of looking at the music that would also necessarily be applicable to other musics. Their approaches, therefore, are a combination of personal predilections and of the characteristics of the music in relation to their own musical and musicological backgrounds. This approach is not one specifically and systematically espoused in the ethnomusicological literature, and yet it is evident in a great many ethnomusicological publications, and while it may be going out of style, we must nevertheless mention it. It is widely and with confidence used in the analysis of Western art music.

In looking at the most recent publications in ethnomusicology, I find it difficult to escape the conclusion that the analytical work of the future will be specialized. Universal systems such as cantometrics may be developed, but their application is bound to help only with certain broad problems. To learn the analytical approach, overt or implied, of each culture can of course provide important insights. Practically all that we have learned about the classical music of India, for example, is based on the ways in which Indian musicians and traditional music scholars lay out the musical system. It will be necessary to devote considerable energy to each of a group of problems, culture-specific and specialized, and it will probably be necessary to find, for each, an analytical procedure that satisfies the need. Presumably it will be one susceptible at least to understanding by those not acquainted with the culture or the problem, and ideally it will not violate the culture's own way of conceiving its music. But special ways of dealing with individual situations must be found. The history of ethnomusicological analysis has moved in gingerly fashion and very gradually from universal "etic" to "emic" approaches; as implied in the discussion of the Iranian project above, it may next be moving to a combination. Let us look at situations in which a general comparative approach, the culture's own musical taxonomy, and the need to find a special method for the solution of a particular ethnomusicological problem had to be combined.

Two personal illustrations: I will try to analyze the procedure carried out after the fact, as it were. For the first (Nettl and Riddle 1974), the corpus is a group of sixteen recordings, all improvisations of one Arabic *maqam, Nahawand,* cast in the genre of *taqsim,* a nonmetric sort of improvisation in several sections, and performed by the Lebanese musician Jihad Racy within one year. The purpose was to see in what respects these sixteen improvisations are similar and how they differ; and to ascertain the range of difference, finding out what is typical or exceptional, and what is rare or evidently forbidden, or ubiquitous. No conclusion about the same musician's performance of other *maqams* is attempted. Using a general comparative approach, it was logical to divide the pieces into sections marked by pauses, useful because it is supported by the other approaches. Transcribing and examining the recordings in a broadly comparative fashion showed that the performer does more or less the same thing in his treatment of ornamentation and rhythm throughout the corpus. Because of the ubiquity, these parameters to a large degree determine the style and should, for other purposes, be dealt with in great detail, but not for the particular purpose here, which is to find the spread and distribution of elements whereby the performances differ.

By contrast, the way in which the performances seem to be most readily distinguished is by length, number, and temporal relationship of the sections. Along these lines, it was possible to distinguish three types of structure: (1) The *taqsim* consists of a number of minuscule or short sections followed by a single long one. (2) It is comprised of more or less regular alternation of a short section with one of medium or great length. (3) After an initial long section, it consists of a small group of short sections followed by one of medium length, and this sequence is repeated. This finding is the result of following the "What is it that strikes you" approach.

The other approach, "What is it that the culture — i.e. the performer — regards as significant for solving your problem," may also be followed. What the performer stressed verbally turned out to be the tendency to modulate within a *taqsim,* from the basic *maqam* to secondary ones, and to return, periodically and at the end, to the original. Analysis of this component yielded definite patterning but no clear distinction of types of performance, and a rather normal distribution: one *taqsim* modulated to no secondary *maqam;* two each modulated to only one, or to five; five performances modulated to two secondary *maqams;* and three each to three and four—something like a bell-shaped curve. A similar distribution was found for the total length of the performances and for the number of sections. It was thus in accordance with the solution of a specific problem that certain parameters were described and analyzed with great care, and others neglected.

In my second illustration a somewhat similar approach was necessary for describing the structure of the repertory of Ishi, the "last wild Indian," discovered in California in 1911 (Nettl 1965). We have a closed corpus and no informant. The problem is to identify the general character of the repertory and of its mainstream, to see in what respect it is similar to the repertories of other North American Indian groups, and, further, to see what general principles of composition may be identified. It is impossible to find out anything about the culture's own way of looking at musical structure, except to note that Ishi identified songs (as do many North American Indian peoples) by use, labeling them as gambling songs, doctor's songs, sweathouse songs, etc., and to realize that there seems to be no correlation of use types with types established through the outsider's analysis.

The procedure is two-fold. First, using techniques derived from the work of Hornbostel and Herzog, we make a generalized description of each song (i.e. scale, form, general rhythmic structure, singing style). The singing style is hardest to pin down because of the age and quality of the recordings, but it appears to be the same throughout the recordings. Rhythm is hard to deal with and turns out not to be susceptible to easy classification; that is, the general rhythmic structure, however hard to define, is more or less the same throughout the repertory. Scales vary from two to five tones with intervals extending from major thirds to minor seconds. Three tones seem to be the scalar norm. There is a variety of forms, but songs are extremely short and consist of from two to four sections. These are the *kinds* of statements made by Herzog (1928, 1936a), but of course he went further, and so would we if we wished to devote more space here to this example.

But once this general description is here, we proceed to the special problem and find that scales and forms, which vary considerably but lend themselves to grouping and typology, as well as their interrelationships, are the most useful for establishing mainstream-sidestream distribution and general principles. It is here that the problem determines analytical method. Let me describe in a bit of detail a process that was actually carried out very rapidly, through inspection. Having determined that form, in some way, is significant for solution of the problem, we must decide how to analyze it. On first blush, there are only short stanzas (four–seven seconds), which are repeated. If we divide them into large subdivisions, we usually find two halves (some of unequal size); if we go further, we find a total of four or five subdivisions, which in turn can frequently be grouped into two. It is the interrelationship of the smallest subdivisions that determines the general relationship of the halves, and it is then that we realize that the main structural principle of most of Ishi's songs is the statement of a musical idea which is repeated once, with variation. The second one varies the first in many ways: expansion, contraction, inversion, extension, internal repetition, substitution of one pitch for another in cadential position, etc. Now, there is correlation in Ishi's songs between this dominant form type and the tritonic scales. There are also a few other "minority" form types that correlate somewhat with the scales of more than three tones, and that are based upon formal principles also found in other North American Indian cultures. But attempts to match these correlations with rhythmic and other parameters do not yield what appears to be significant results or insights.

It is interesting to see that the major form type uses the same general principle that dominates the forms of Indian songs in other areas of North America, particularly the Plains and the eastern Pueblos, a form type sometimes called "incomplete repetition," in which a group of phrases is partially, and with variation, repeated: for example, AABCD BCD. Looking at only this one aspect of Ishi's songs, we can see the possibility of a significant relationship between them and those of the Plains and the Pueblos, although what it means is not of concern to us at the moment. To use Ishi's analytical view, the classing of songs by use, would have been impractical, and from what we know of other peoples with extremely short songs, we must guess that Ishi's people would also not have given articulate information on these forms. By the same token, some Plains Indians do not regard their songs as being basically in two unequal sections; rather, they tend to describe them in terms of two pairs of sections, the above cited arrangement being interpreted as A A BCD BCD. Comparing these repertories on the basis of the cultures' own approaches would not by itself have yielded insight into the relationship of the form types. On the other hand, adhering to a single universal method such as Kolinski's or Lomax's, without elaboration, would not have gone far enough to solve the particular problem of the relationship of the mainstream of Ishi's songs to Plains and Pueblo styles. To have followed the traditional approach of what strikes the listener as giving general insight into the music would probably have led one to attempts to measure the sizes of intervals, or in any of a number of other directions, but perhaps only by chance to the detailed examination of forms. From a combination of these approaches, however, there emerged a way of attacking one particular problem posed by this repertory.

Ethnomusicological literature consists substantially of descriptions and analyses, and gives the scholar little in the way of explicit theory for analysis, techniques, and methods. The general problems of analysis are discussed by few scholars and the analysis of a piece is discussed more than the description of an entire music. The theoreticians of analysis and the authors of specific analytical publications exhibit the tension, once again, between the insider's and the outsider's approach, and between culture-specific or music-specific and general or universal approaches. I suggest that they are best resolved if one establishes for each project or problem a special method or approach, avoiding any dogma, each time taking account of the cognitive system of the culture being investigated, and adding insight of the comparison-oriented ethnomusicologist. In this way we may finally succeed in dealing with music in the speech mode.

Chapter 8

The Most Indefatigable Tourists of the World

THE "TOP OF OLD SMOKY" EFFECT

In the world of music, one ordinarily does not just sing or play an instrument; in order for musical behavior to result in what may properly be considered music, one must ordinarily be singing or playing *something,* some kind of a unit of musical conceptualization that has identity, can be distinguished from other such units, and changes when it moves in space and time. We usually call such units "songs" or "pieces." Some of them move across national boundaries, rivers, mountain ranges, oceans, across language and culture areas, stimulating one of their earliest observers, Wilhelm Tappert (1890:5) to nominate them as "the most indefatigable tourists of the earth." Their very movement, their capacity for change while retaining integrity, justifies their existence as units in musicological conceptualization.

But the nature of the unit, the "something" that is performed, how it is distinguished from its fellows, is a major issue in ethnomusicology, a kind of counterpart to the nature of *a* music; like other major issues, it concerns the interface between general and culture-specific, between the outsider's and the insider's perception. Ethnomusicologists and historical musicologists have developed different practices and face different problems. To the music historian and to the Western academic musician, there is little controversy upon what constitutes a unit of music in the Western classical system; it is something we call "the piece," and it usually has a name (distinctive, as in "Prelude to the Afternoon of a Faun," or more general, as in "Symphony no. 7, in A major, Opus 92"), which is further associated with a composer. We have little disagreement even when a piece (such as "Don Giovanni") can actually be regarded as a group of units, because all concerned—composer, performers, scholars, the audience—regard these short, separate pieces as belonging together. The practice of using opus numbers, practically but also literally dividing the music of a composer into distinct *works,* supports the interpretation. In popular music the repertory is organized along the same lines, with names of pieces based on the verbal text and the work associated not so much with a composer but more often with a performer or group.

Ethnomusicologists do not have a single model, but when not dealing with a "classical" system, they tend to base their consideration on a paradigm developed for European folk music, whose repertories are better known in the West than those of tribal societies. The most standard conceptualization of folk music as music in oral tradition is derived in large measure from a different idea of what constitutes a "piece." It is the group of tunes derived from one original that, like the opus of classical music, theoretically represents a single if complex creative act. The simplest illustration shows a person composing a song that is then taught to others, who go on to change it, and eventually it is altered by innumerable singers, all possibly singing (or believing that they are singing) the same song in different ways. They create what is known as versions and variants, all of which, taken together, at least in the abstract, can be described as a single, isolated tune family. In a certain sense the variants are all simply performances of the same song, just as the many performances of Beethoven's "Waldstein Sonata" are variants of the same piece. We could agree that the difference among tunes in a tune family is greater than that found among the Beethoven performances, but perhaps this difference is one only of degree. So, indeed, we could say that *the* piece, the unit, in European folk music, is something that is once created plus all of the different ways in which it is performed.

Unfortunately, the model is ideal but only rarely real. Tunes that are strikingly similar may be related in several ways, and only if we could observe the live process could we determine the kind of relationship. Thus, for example, the person who creates a new tune may be imitating one he or she already knows. It is, of course, difficult for a scholar coming along after the fact to distinguish something created as a variant from something which is the result of imitation. Variants may come into existence as the result of forgetfulness or creative embellishment. But they do not come about only in the vacuum of a tune family but also under the influence of outside forces such as musical styles newly introduced or a foreign stylistic surrounding—occurring perhaps when a tune crosses an ethnic, linguistic, or national boundary. Further, a variant of a tune may take some of its content from another tune family, perhaps one line from an unrelated song. Beyond this, the historical sequence in folk song transmission may cause a complete turnover of musical content, to the extent that no folk taxonomy could be expected to account for it.

Let us look at the configuration of variants that constitute a unit, a family, and how they may differ. Bayard (1954) points out that in the life of a tune the second of two contrasting adjacent motifs, phrases, and even lines may be replaced by a repetition of the first; this occurred in the family he la-

Long Form

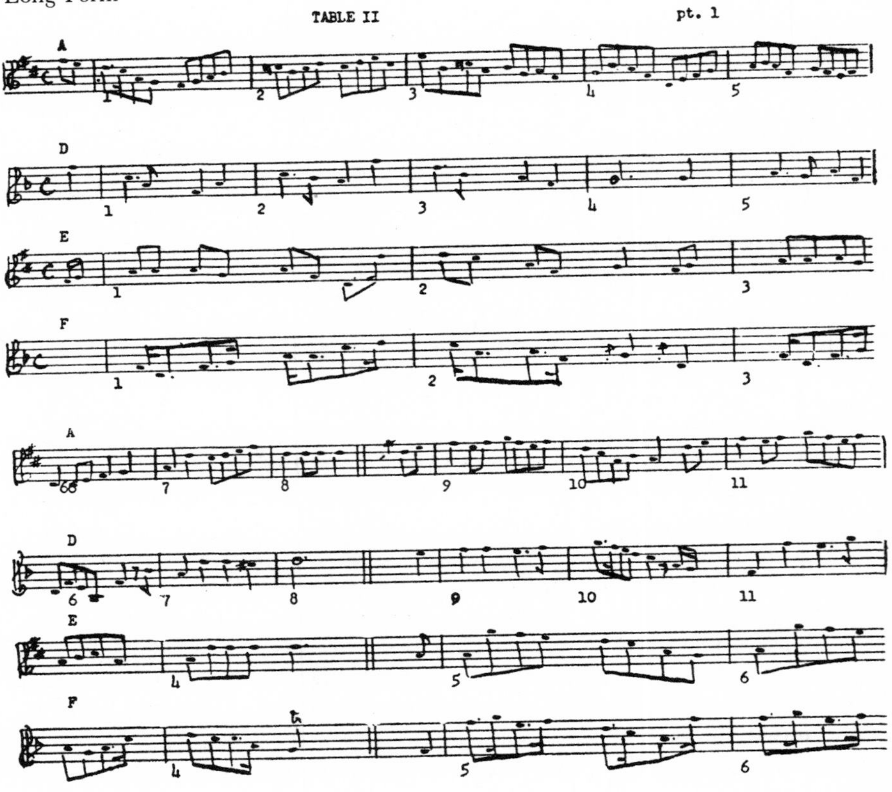

Short Form

Extended Short Form

Figure 3. Samples of the tune family "The Job of Journeywork" (from Bayard 1954:18–19, 22–25).

TABLE II

beled "Brave Donnelly." In more radical change, a song may lose a significant portion; this seems to have happened to one tune of a British-American broadside ballad, "The Pretty Mohea," whose second half, with few changes, appears as the country-and-western song "On Top of Old Smoky" (see Cox 1939:31–33). The relationship of the two seems clear, but we don't know whether it is accepted by the Appalachian folk community that sings (or sang) both. Yet this truncating process may be sufficiently common to allow us to nickname it "The 'Top of Old Smoky' Effect." In "Little Mohea" a tune with the form AABA seems to have changed to BABA. Bayard demonstrates this trend more dramatically in the tune family he calls "Job of Journeywork" (Figure 3). Here a tune with the structure ABCD seems to have changed to simply CD. In due time it seems to have added new material from an extraneous source, and then become CDEF. Very likely, if this process occurred in many songs, CDEF was in one case or another reduced to EFEF. We would have to admit that there is a clear genetic relationship between the two forms of the song, ABCD and EFEF. But they have no material in common, and coming on to the scene later, as is normal, we would have no way of identifying the two as relatives. And yet even these two are in a sense manifestations of the same piece.

If these tune families are indeed the equivalents of the pieces of classical music, their number and scope are very different. Bayard in various publications (e.g. 1953) suggests that the Anglo-American folk music repertory is comprised of forty or fifty such families, each of them a group of essentially similar tunes. The difficulty lies, of course, in equating similarity with genetic relationship. There are other ways of accounting for great similarity between tunes in even a large culture. List (1969a) examines a group of tunes including "Twinkle, Twinkle Little Star" and the "Hatiqva" from a number of European folk repertories, showing that they bear the kind of similarity one finds among the tunes of a family as clearly identified by Bayard (1954) and Bronson (1959), and as studied in detail by Charles Seeger (1966). He also argues that this represents the diffusion not of a tune (1979a:50) but rather of a "style." I would interpret this to mean that somehow a way of putting a song together rather than a song itself was taught and learned. List's tunes do not comprise something akin to the diverse performances of a Beethoven sonata but perhaps rather something like the concept of sonata, a genre, if you will. In order to decide whether List's approach is right for any one cultural situation, or whether an extension of Bayard's is more appropriate, one would have to solve two problems. First, one would have to be present when a new "variant" is composed and to see whether it is indeed viewed by its composer as a changed form of something he or she already knew. Second, one would have to find, for that culture, the line between content and style. Given the general rules of composition of which European folk song composers may avail themselves (and these composers may be in the folk community or not), one asks whether tunes having this degree of similarity can come about repeatedly. If so, then they share style, not content; if not, perhaps they share content as well, possibly differing in many aspects of style. The question remains: at what point is something new created, and how many such units of innovation does a musical repertory contain?

I PLAY IT THE SAME WAY EVERY TIME

In accepting the possibility that a musical system can be comprised of a small number of units of creation, such as forty in Anglo-American folk music, we are not making a value judgment of the degree of creativity. We are only trying to show how a tradition works. We may also look at some of the world's most complex music with this "tune family" approach. The Iranian classical system turns out to have a two-tiered structure. As already explained, its fundamental content is the *radif,* which is divided into twelve modes or *dastgāhs.* This is the basis of improvisation, and since each performance is based on one *dastgāh,* these *dastgāhs* could be viewed as the "parent tunes" of immense families in which each performance is a variant. But the *dastgāhs* are also the basis for composed pieces, by known composers, and these are somewhat like the pieces of Western classical music in belonging to several established genres (Pishdarāmad, Tasnif, Reng, for example). Like the improvised performances, they are also, in a sense, variants of the appropriate sections of the *radif.* But having a specific identity, a composer, and perhaps a name, and permitting less departure in performance, they themselves function as "parent tunes" to variants created in performance. Yet in some ways the performer of an improvisation believes himself to be doing in essence what he does when he plays a composed piece.

A curious system for a Western academic musician to understand. The *radif* itself contains the units of musical thought most specifically. If one wishes to know what, in essence, is the *dastgāh* of *Segāh,* the most obvious place to search is the memorized and today perhaps published and recorded section of a *radif* labeled as *Segāh.* But in a certain sense a *radif* is less music than the basis for making music. One way of stating the relationship is to say that musicians improvise upon the *radif,* and so we would find that the various performances based on *Segāh* may take from five to fifty minutes and differ enormously. But Iranian musicians do not necessarily think that they are using it as a basis and creating music upon it; they speak simply of performing the *dastgāh,* accepting the differences among performances but not acknowledging that it is these differences which are central to the musical system rather than the relationships among them. And so I was surprised to find that one musician, asked to play two performances of one *dastgāh* for me on two different occasions, wondered why I should wish to have these, and when I answered by pointing out the interest of the differences between the two, said pointedly, "No, I play it the same way every time." In the end, he acknowledged that he played "from the heart" and that each performance depended on his mood, but he wanted me to understand what was really important, that those things that were essential to the *dastgāh* were present in each performance. It was like saying, "Of course each time it is really 'Barbara Allen,'" or "When I play the Waldstein Sonata I always play the same notes."

In a sense, then, all performances of *Segāh* are alike in the way that all performances of the Waldstein are alike. We simply expect a wider spread, but then also assert that in Iranian music there are only a few basic units to which all performances can be reduced. If there are myriads of pieces in Western music, only forty tune families in the Anglo-American (Bayard 1953), and only twelve *dastgāhs* in Iran, then the fewer units there are, the greater and also further apart the number of the manifestations of each unit.

The study of a piece of music requires us to take a certain view of the total repertory from which it comes. A tune such as "Lord Randall" is really all of its variants, past and present, known and unknown, for the total identity of a piece is also its history. In the case of music in oral tradition, one is usually limited to extrapolating history from recent manifestations, and only in the rarest instances have brave souls tried to reconstruct parent versions from a comparison of the variants recently extant. Boilès (1973a) gives the melodic outline of a reconstructed parent tune for a group of songs related by text, without pretending that he has found all of the relatives. Bayard (1954) suggests that some processes have taken place but refrains from reconstruction. And yet, it seems worth the risk. After all, much of the knowledge we have about the way of life of European classical music comes from a comparison of versions and revisions by composers, and from tracing the history of the understanding of the piece by subsequent performers and audiences.

The songs and pieces we have been talking about have one thing in common: in their cultures they may be performed separately and individually. Their performance by themselves, outside a context, sometimes under protest, can normally be elicited by a fieldworker without (we would hope) total violation of the indigenous musical values. An informant in Appalachia would be willing to sing a song by itself, even in a recording studio; a Blackfoot Indian is normally prepared to perform a song once, even though he will say that it should be sung four times, and is willing to isolate it from the other songs to which it is normally attached in a ceremony. A Navajo singer will sing a song from a nine-day ceremony of which it is an integral part, even though in another sense the ceremony itself is the musical unit. An aria can be lifted out of an opera and sung. A unit marked off in this way has its own history, not necessarily shared with others from the same context.

There are also shorter sections, lines, motifs, rhythmic formulas, which are the constituent members of the songs or pieces. They cannot normally be reproduced separately by informants and, sung in isolation, they do not properly constitute music. But in analysis they too may be treated individually as units of musical thought that have variants, individual origins, and their own life stories. In the history of Western classical music scholars have been concerned with motifs that pass from composer to composer, usually inferring knowledge and conscious quotation from the relationship. Stating categorically and enthusiastically that "the melodies wander," Tappert (1890:5), one of the first to call attention to the phenomenon, lists and gives distribution of a number of motifs. Making no attempt at precision, he nevertheless shows that certain motifs are used by many composers and in the folk music of a substantial part of Central and Western Europe. Yet the compositions from which the motifs are taken may be only slightly or not at all related to each other. The similarity or identity resides in the motifs. Evidently they do or did travel, though perhaps they do not, as Tappert unequivocally asserts, frequently "cross violent rivers, traverse the Alps, cross oceans and nomadically pass through deserts." According to List (1979a), it was not a motif itself but a way of composing motifs that moved around.

Thus, for example, there appear to be certain lines that move from song to song in Czech folk music. They typically appear as the third line in a structure of AABA. The same line in much American popular music of the first half of the twentieth century, known as the "bridge," is also flexible in the same way. Similarly, certain musical and textual lines in North American Peyote song repertory appear in variant form in several songs, confirming the way in which some composers of Peyote songs describe one process of composition, saying that one can create a new song by singing to oneself songs one already knows, combining parts of several to make a new song. There are units of music that cannot be performed alone but nevertheless have some independence and a life of their own.

RELATIVES, FRIENDS, AND COMPATRIOTS

As a way of explaining the similarity of tunes and their history, the model of a tune family is attractive. We never have the complete genealogy. Instead, we have a group of tunes from one country or a related group of countries, and a theory of variant development. We observe that they have some similarity and would like to think that they are related in some way. But are they relatives, or just friends, or perhaps merely compatriots? Which of the three turns out in any one case to be the proper explanation depends on a number of factors. We are confronted here by one of the major issues of musicology and ethnomusicology, the measurement of similarity and difference, an issue to be discussed at greater length in

Chapter 9. But the difficulty of the situation was long ago illustrated by the judgment of an Arapaho friend and informant. In comparing two pairs of practically identical songs, he maintained that one was a set of variants, and the other, independent though similar songs. I was obviously not aware of the musical criteria he used, and supposed that very intimate knowledge of the music is necessary in order to make such judgment. Yet it is not just musical criteria that are involved. What are we to do when two songs of the Blackfoot Indians are clearly almost identical, fill the same function, are recognized by their singers as identical in sound, but are accorded separate status because they appeared in two separate visions?

A number of Czech songs, with humorous or light verbal content and probably of eighteenth- or nineteenth-century origin, usually sung by or for children, have the same general structure and very similar contours and configurations of the main notes. They are readily distinguished by the specific content of the words. Let me reconstruct, in parable form, a fictitious situation. We imagine that we were there when they came into existence, entering at a time when the repertory includes one song with the specified style and structure. In a village a light-hearted farmer who spends his evenings in the tavern and his Sunday afternoons with his children takes it upon himself to make up some new songs for the kids. He wants to teach them songs so that they can spend an hour singing together, and to amuse them he makes up some silly texts. First he takes the song he already knows and fits it with new words, changing the tune slightly to accommodate the fact that his new text has longer lines. This pleases the children, but as he continues the practice, they become bored with the same tune. He decides to make up new tunes but, being relatively unimaginative, he comes up with tunes that have the same structure and are hardly distinguishable from the first. He then begins systematically to take the old songs, making changes so that new ones will emerge, but he keeps ending up with tunes that differ only very slightly from the original one he knew, when he was simply revising it to make room for additional syllables. But of an evening at the tavern he hears songs from the city that are quite different, and one day he tries his hand at making up some words for children to one of the more sophisticated (and perhaps bawdy) tavern ballads. Unfortunately, the children won't try to learn it; it is too hard for one of them, and for another somehow uncomfortable because it goes too high. They beg the father for songs like those they already know, and he learns in no uncertain terms that if he is to make up new songs for the children, they must be acceptable. The children have rather specific and quite limited ideas of how children's songs should be, and so he continues his practice of making up new songs that sound like the old, learning to be careful not to step outside certain limits. Thus they won't accept songs with five lines, preferring four; they won't take minor or dorian, only major; the four lines must be alike, except the third, which is comprised of two similar sections, must in some way do the same thing twice.

This imaginary but perhaps realistically conceived folk composer has created variants, has also composed songs imitating the old, and has found that the stylistic limits within which the new songs can be composed are narrow and dictate to what extent he may innovate. Years later, when his repertory of children's songs is collected by a folklorist from Prague, the differences among the songs are minor, all sound like variants of the original, and the old man, his children now grown, no longer remembers how each one came about. He may say, "Yes, they are really all the same song," or more likely, "Well, they are all simply children's songs," and detailed perusal by a scholar from the university who knows hundreds of Czech folk songs indicates that they are all equally similar to each other.

So we see that a group of similar tunes can come about in various ways, and we may not often be sure to what degree the tune family interpretation is valid or how it is to be applied. All the Czech tunes in this little parable are in various ways derived from a single original, but the ways are indeed various. They are not closely related in the sense that a group of successive generations think they are singing the same song and simply making changes in it.

To illustrate further this intriguing matter of the unit of musical creativity, we should confront a set of tunes that have considerable similarity, coming from different countries. Let's look a bit more closely at one of the tune groups brought together in Wiora's (1953) anthology (Figure 4).

LADY ISABEL AND THE TOURISTS

They rather sound alike, these tunes under Wiora's group no. 70—they have four lines and an arc-shaped contour, similar but not identical scale configurations, and they coincide in the identity and location of structurally significant tones. In the relationships of their lines, however, there is diversity, from the progressive ABCD (Number 70g, Polish), to the reverting ABBA (Number 70f, Ukrainian), to the almost iterative AA(5)A(5)B (Number 70i, English), the second line simply a fifth upward transposition of the first. Comparing rhythms, we find even more variety. The Finnish song has quintuple meter, the Hungarian a parlando style, the Irish one has lilting dotted progressions, and the Ukrainian, alternation of two eighths and a quarter. The notations tell us nothing about the singing style, but we can imagine that there were different ways of using the voice. We ask ourselves why these tunes seem so similar, and why upon a closer look they have such great differences.

To carry this further, we must go a bit more deeply into the distinction between content and style, something already brought up in other contexts.

Figure 4. Tunes from a number of European countries showing possible relationship (from Wiora 1953:70–71).

The two concepts continue to be hard to disentangle, so let me try to explain the difference with a parallel from folklore. It is well known that a large number of folk tales and ballad stories are told throughout Europe and other parts of the world, in different ways and versions, but with recognizable features that make identification easy or at least possible. This kind of thinking is a standard part of the discipline of folklore, a method described by Thompson (1946, 1953). Aarne (1961) tried to make a comprehensive list of all of the story types found in the world's folklore, which is a bit like Bayard's statement about the forty or so tune families comprising Anglo-American folk music. Ivar Kemppinen (1954) assembled some 1,800 versions of a story that forms the text of a ballad sung in the English-speaking world as "Lady Isabel and the False Knight" or as "May Colvin," in Holland as "Heer Halewyin," and elsewhere under many titles. The story varies greatly but usually has the following features in common: the protagonist is in some way unusual (strange, foreign, rich, sometimes supernatural, even musically interesting in one form, claiming to be able to sing polyphonically in three voices). He attracts a rich young girl, daughter of his host, persuades her to elope, but then robs her and threatens to drown her. She somehow (through stealth, or his stupidity, or the fortuitous appearance of a relative or even intercession by the Virgin Mary) gets the better of him and kills him. This is the content. In style, the versions of the text differ as much among themselves as any group of folk songs from widely separated cultures. Some are short, telling the story briefly and only alluding to major events; others are extremely detailed. Some use formulas that reappear off and on, others are in unobstructed narrative. Some use dialogue. They are differentiated even by their use of different languages, forms of poetic meter, and rhyme scheme. These differences comprise style and hardly interfere with the content. The distinction is not easy, and there are borderline areas. Thus we may ask whether the difference between the villain as a supernatural figure in a culture accustomed to explaining the unusual by such references, and the knight as a strange-acting foreigner in a rationalist but xenophobic society, is a matter of content or style. Be that as it may, we know that in each culture area within Europe, people have a distinct way of narrating tales, including singing them, and of course a distinct language with its rules for setting words to music. But each of them is able to accommodate, in its style of verbal art, the content of the story of Lady Isabel.

In folklore, this may all be obvious. In music, separating the style from the content is much harder. The problem is moderated if from reliable account or observation one knows the specific history of a piece. But we rarely have this knowledge, and as we note that Wiora's tunes have something in common, we have trouble putting our finger on just what it is. We perceive differences, noting that the English tune shares characteristics of other English tunes that we know; the same is true of the Spanish, Hungarian,

Rumanian. We may, for the time being, have to be satisfied with the conclusion that we can perceive the likelihood of identity in content but cannot specifically define it and, thus dissatisfied, might be tempted to accept List's implication that it all amounts only to identity of style.

Assuming, however, that these songs have the same musical content and differ in style, we ask how they got distributed around Europe, and whether we can go beyond Tappert's generalized embrace of musical tourism. Musical content moves from one culture to another; we know this well even from non-Western cultures, from the diffusion of Peyote songs among dozens of North American Indian peoples in the last hundred years, of the Ghost Dance songs among Plains Indian peoples in a short decade after 1880, from the statements of Blackfoot Indians to the effect that this song came from the Cree, that one from the Cheyenne. Specific rhythms, with names, have been diffused among peoples of Nigeria and Ghana, and it is likely that units of musical thought of a much broader sort, the Indian ragas, sometimes came into the Indian classical system from Iran, the Arabic world, and Southeast Asia.

But the area in which most work by far has been done continues to be European and European-derived folk music. The extant explanations for the continent-wide distribution of musical content are only moderately satisfying. One, rather hoary, refers to a presumed unity, primordial and distant from Europe, of the Indo-European peoples who may have developed certain elements of culture, including some of the content of their folklore and music, before they fanned out geographically as well as linguistically. Considering that some Indo-European peoples seem to participate in only the most general sense, and that non-Indo-Europeans such as Hungarians and Finns share fully in the heritage of content, we should probably do no more than to mention it. A more plausible explanation is the spreading of tunes (which may later have become abstracted to tune types) by medieval minstrels who traveled far and wide, from court to court, singing and entertaining. That this process occurred is attested in detail by Salmen (1960), but of course we do not know to what extent tunes now extant and deemed similar were the long-range result of this other sort of musical tourism. The diffusion of style elements from country to neighboring country is easy to accept, but whether this is done by way of teaching tunes, musical content, or by in effect teaching style, as List suggests, a way of composing a tune, is not at all clear. Historians of European art music also face the problem posed by this distinction, but they are much more expert at tracing the history of themes and motifs, the spatial and temporal distribution of melodies such as the "Dies Irae" or the theme based on the name of Bach.

It may seem strange to the reader that an essay about the study of the individual piece of music within its repertory should be so concerned with the history, diffusion, and geographic distribution of songs. But in order to study a "piece," one must first determine what it is, and we have noted the many ways in which different cultures divide their world of music into units of musical thought. One way to isolate such units and to separate them from their accompanying stylistic superstructure is to trace them through their travels in space and time, something that requires attention to the relationship between content and style.

Chapter 9

A Note-for-Note Steal

MEASURING SIMILARITY AND DIFFERENCE

In our consideration of musical universals and of the world of music as a series of musics, of comparative study, and of the identity of repertories and of individual pieces, we have touched upon an underlying and frequently frustrating issue. Most of the research to which we have referred depends in one way or another on assessment or even measurement of degrees of similarity between musics and among their components. Actually, a vast proportion of musicology consists of statements that implicitly measure difference. The issue appears in the comparison of composers, of periods in a composer's life, of schools; it is basic to decisions about periodization in history and in establishing order on the musical map of the world. It appears even to be basic to the work of the music critic surveying his contemporary scene. In Western academic musical culture generally, someone wishing to evaluate a musical work or a style must understand and state the degree to which it is new and different from what came before.

Given the importance of measuring similarity and difference, it is surprising that musicologists have not developed some kind of a unit, perhaps nicknamed the "sim," to express them. (I am grateful to my colleague Lawrence Gushee for suggesting the term.) It would be delightful to be able to say that the difference between Blackfoot and Arapaho Indian music is one sim, and between Arapaho and Menominee, three; between West African and American Indian music, six sims, but between the African and the European, only four; or that Bach and Handel are separated by five, but Handel and Haydn, by seven. Statements of this general sort have surely been made, if often only by implication, but without an attempt at precision. The few studies attempting measurement and its expression are rather outside the mainstream.

Musicians may have intuitive ability to discern degrees of difference but their opinions on any one case often differ widely. Oscar Levant (1940:72) tells of an incident in which the film composer Erich Korngold, hearing Gershwin's "The Man I Love," declared that it was "a note for note steal" from "Tea for Two." Levant could see not the slightest resemblance between the two songs, and neither can I; Korngold's motive may have been to show that Gershwin had little originality as a composer. Clearly the two were not drinking the same musical tea, but even such an anecdote shows that the value placed on matters of difference may determine supposedly objective judgment.

Less dramatic but similar events seem to have occurred in the history of ethnomusicology. One involves the hearing, decades ago, of a group of American Indian songs from the North Pacific Coast by someone unacquainted with Indian music but knowledgeable about certain Buddhist chants of East Asia. This listener maintained that "an Indian song seems similar to a Buddhist chant for funeral services, used among the nomads of Mongolia" (Barbeau 1934:110, also 1962), and the remark was construed as evidence for the Asian origin of contemporary American Indian music. Ethnomusicologists may smile about this incident, assuring each other that such a bald generalization would be inconceivable today. The songs could not have been alike, they would say; the listener must have simply regarded the Indian music as incredibly exotic, and uncritically joined it to his knowledge of other exotica; they were alike in being very different from Western music; the listener misremembered the Mongolian song, heard years before the incident. And so on. Of course, it is quite possible for two musical systems with certain surface similarities (e.g. the most familiar kind of pentatonic scale, complex metric structure, vocal monophony) to create, by chance, two pieces that are substantially similar. To link two musical systems owing to the similarity of a single item from one to an item in another is surely unjustified, but the desire to do this reflects a typical tendency of ethnomusicologists, when comparing musics, to seek out similarities and to attach significance to them.

But if there is no standard technique for establishing degrees of similarity, there are certainly methods that, at least as a by-product, suggest ways in which one could proceed further. I should like to mention three, which have been touched on before very briefly, again in this context: the classification of tunes in a repertory, the study of genetic tune relationships, and the comparative study of repertories.

THE BEST METHOD . . .

The nineteenth century saw widespread collecting of European folk songs and the beginning of the publication of large, even vast collections intending to encompass total repertories of folk communities and nations. Collectors and publishers were faced with the problem of putting the songs in some kind of rational order. While some were content to group songs by overt use and cultural context or by content of the works, others wished to go further, finding typologies that would make it possible to locate tunes by their musical characteristics, or that would unite those tunes with genetic relationship. There ensued a broad literature dealing with the classification of folk tunes. The first milestone is a pair of publications that, among other things, may hold the record for length of title. The first, by Oswald Koller (1902–3), is entitled (in English translation) "The Best Method for the Lexical Ordering of Folk and Folk-like Songs," and classified 300 German tunes by assigning to each tone a number that indicated its distance in semitones from the tonic, using Arabic numerals for those above, Roman for those below. This is an adequate finding list if you know a tune precisely, but it will not necessarily locate a tune if you know even a close variant of it. For that reason Ilmari Krohn (1902–3) replied with an even longer title ("What [in fact] Is the Best Method for the Lexical Ordering of Folk and Folk-like Melodies According to Their Musical, Not Textual, Characteristics?"). He suggested a system that reduced each phrase of each song to a "Stich-Motif," a motivic abstraction, consisting of three notes, and subdividing the tunes first according to the initial note and its distance from the tonic, then the final, and then the "mid-point of melodic expression."

With these two publications begin two strands of intellectual history, one seeking to establish a simple finding list, and the other, classificatory systems in which truly musical or perhaps even genetic relationships can be identified. Krohn evidently came to regard his method as too subjective and thus not reliable for placing together the tunes that struck him, intuitively, as related, and went on to recommend a configuration of cadence notes of the four lines of his tunes as a more reliable diagnostic feature. As happened in this case, a more mechanical approach frequently either follows or is tested against the first-hand knowledge of the scholar. This seems to have been true in the work of Bartók (1931), who used a number of criteria of descending importance to order Hungarian folk songs: number of syllables per line in the text, configuration of cadence tones, and overall form. This curious order of criteria, which does assemble tunes that appear to be similar, could probably only be devised by someone who already knew which tunes were similar and could, *ex post facto,* identify the criteria that had led him to make the identification in the first place. The same configuration would evidently not work for other repertories, for example, English or German folk songs, for which other features such as melodic contour appear to be more relevant (Poladian 1942). Bartók's work in classification resulted, after his death in 1945, in a large body of scholarship (see Erdely 1965, Járdányi 1962, Elschekova 1966).

Working in another direction, Bronson pioneered the use of computers (in their earlier incarnation; 1949, 1950, 1951), deciding that aspects of melody—mode and contour—rather than rhythm, form, or for that matter singing style were the criteria that would enable him to put similar materials together. In other words, he sought to assemble tunes which exhibited similarity in certain parameters, believing (correctly for his Anglo-American repertory) that these remained more constant in the life of a song and its variants. Like his predecessors, he does not state specific degrees of similarity, but he implies clearly that there is at least a vague line separating similarity from difference, or sufficient from insufficient similarity, to enable him to make judgments regarding relationships. In most of the classification schemes there is the implication that tunes falling close together by examination of particular criteria are more likely to be related than those farther apart in the list. There is perhaps even the unspoken belief that adjacent tunes represent the smallest available degree of differentiation and thus perhaps something like a standard unit for measuring degrees. This approach might conceivably be the foundation for a way of measuring that is culture-specific, providing for each culture an emic statement of the minimal unit of difference necessary to set apart discernible variants of a tune.

In the history of classification of tunes, further work with computers has moved us to more complex statements made with more precision, but still specific measurement of degree of difference is normally implied rather than stated. Classification has continued to gain in importance among scholars of European folk music but has not found a very receptive climate in research dealing with other areas of the world. The conclusion of the latest literature is that each repertory must determine its own system, based on criteria specific to it (Elschek and Stockmann 1969, Elschek 1977, Stockmann and Steszewski 1973).

ALL IN THE FAMILY

Although classifying a repertory and establishing genetic relationships among its components would seem to be different kinds of work with different aims, we have seen that the two are closely associated. As already stated, the concept of tune families is widely used or alluded to in the literature, but only a few specific studies exist, and we return again briefly to Bayard's (1954) classic description of two families and Wiora's presentation of groups of similar tunes from a variety of European cultures (Wiora 1953). While both have brought together tunes with certain similarities from a broader yet stylistically limited repertory, it is important to note that to do so they have weighted their criteria, concentrating on aspects of melody, especially contour and the correspondence of main tones. In dealing with several dozen tunes in the group he labels "The Job of Journeywork" (1954:17–28), Bayard has drawn on his wide knowledge of the Anglo-American folk song repertory in order to identify a distinct set of similar tunes (see Figure 3). He has not used song titles, texts, or geographic distribution, only the musical characteristics. Dividing these songs or versions into three groups, he makes a convincing case for a history, already described in Chapter 8, in which a tune first existed in several versions of one original form. Some of these versions lost their first halves, producing a second, short form, of which a number eventually added more material at the end, making a third, "extended short" form.

Now, all of this grouping is done by informal measurement of similarity. In making it, Bayard has clearly taken into account only certain features. Meter and mode are not criteria; the members of his tune family share a wide variety of metric schemes and modal configurations with the rest of the repertory. Nor are the broadest outlines of melodic contour criteria but, rather, the details of melodic movement; all of the related tunes have several distinctive phrases, motifs, or measures in common. The overall forms, shared with the repertory, are used as criteria on some level, but only in the formal relationships of a few short bits does this group of tunes show itself to be unique.

One may accuse Bayard of potentially prejudicial weighting of criteria. Thus, in certain respects, versions A and D of the long form of "The Job of Journeywork" are significantly similar; but in others, each might be closer to songs outside the tune family. The purpose here is not to attack Bayard's conclusions; one cannot imagine a case better argued. But let me try the role of devil's advocate. Bayard was obviously trying to compare, to measure similarity and difference, for a certain purpose—to identify genetically related tunes—and this he does convincingly. Whether one can as readily accept his historic analysis of the three forms is theoretically less certain. Thus one version of the "long" form (F) and one of the "short" (J) look more similar, if the total length is disregarded, than do E and F (both long forms). Clearly, total overall structure has been an overriding criterion in separating the two "forms," in comparison to specific melodic detail. Thus, while Bayard measures degrees of similarity and difference among a large number of tunes, he does so with the use of criteria selected because they are likely to produce certain desired results. Whether it is ever useful or even possible to avoid weighting criteria remains to be seen, but it does not appear to be so in the establishment of tune families in the Anglo-American repertory.

A similar study to Bayard's, its results given mainly through example, is the one by Wiora, already mentioned in Chapter 8 (Wiora 1953). Wiora gives us two groups of tunes (pp. 48–49 and 50–51, from which Figure 4 is quoted). In the first, twelve tunes from a number of European countries for which he postulates some kind of relationship share, in fact, detailed melodic contours in the first two of four phrases, while the third and fourth phrases differ considerably. In rhythm they vary greatly, and several modal structures are represented. In overall contour they are alike, and all have the general progressive form ABCD. The second group is equally homogeneous, despite greater difference in form. But if the two groups are intermingled, in some respects, such as contour, they might easily form one group. Measuring contour gives us one grouping, and measuring form, another. Even so, Wiora's grouping strikes me as acceptable, perhaps for the following reason. Evidently Wiora, like Bayard, has weighted his criteria, but in a way in which I and probably others in his culture weight them. His statement can be labeled as "emic" because he is a member of the society that, broadly speaking, owns this music. One cannot count on the same consensus in working with songs outside one's own culture. It is perhaps for this reason that Western scholars have succeeded more readily in finding acceptable genetic groupings for European folk music, for in a certain sense they can act as both scholars and informants.

A QUESTION OF BOUNDARIES

The question of degree of difference and similarity is at the base of some of the most fundamental work of historical musicology and ethnomusicology, the basic paradigm of mapping the world's music in time and space, stating most broadly what goes with what. Having tried to show that one of the fundamental assumptions of the field is that the world consists of discrete musics, we need again to stress that the main difficulty in identifying these units and drawing boundaries among them involves measurement of similarity.

In historical musicology the issue looms behind some of the basic facts a student is asked to learn in a music history course. The concern with style, the division of history into periods, the attempts to establish "central" and "peripheral" styles in eras such as the Renaissance and the nineteenth century (Reese 1954, Einstein 1947a), and the division of a composer's work, like the early, middle, and late periods of Beethoven—all depend on the seldom articulated assumption that one can take such things as three pieces of music or three repertories and show that two are similar and in turn different from the third.

For example, Renaissance and Baroque are usually presented as highly differentiated periods. In his classic book on the Baroque era Manfred Bukofzer (1947:16–17) draws distinctions between their styles on the basis of eleven major criteria, these revolving mainly about relationships between instrumental and vocal music, harmony, general characterizations of rhythm, counterpoint, and melody. Though this is a large complement of parameters in the context of music-historical literature, many other elements such as singing style, sound, ornamentation, and vast numbers of detail in melody, rhythm, and orchestration are not mentioned. If the two periods were to turn out to be indistinguishable according to these unused criteria, one might argue that they should not really be separated. Bukofzer goes on to distinguish three phases of the Baroque period, pointing out the great differences between the early and late Baroque, between Monteverdi and Bach, Peri and Handel. There seems little doubt that the music of Monteverdi is really more similar to that of the late Renaissance than to Bach's, and that his place in the Baroque era has to be based on minor distinctions from late Renaissance, distinctions derived from a small number of heavily weighted criteria. In part the distinction is an "emic" one, though followed by scholars working "etically." Around 1600 a number of musical thinkers insisted that something radically new was taking place, and this lead was subsequently followed by historians. If this example is characteristic, judgments of musical similarity have usually been made by historians selecting certain criteria for special attention; they work a bit like the students of tune families.

It is somewhat similar in drawing musical maps, establishing musical areas. In a now quite ancient attempt to do this for North American cultures (Nettl 1954a), I accepted as units or "musics" what had been presented as tribal repertories in standard publications of the time. Practically all repertories shared some characteristics in a majority or a large plurality of their songs—pentatonic scales, monophonic texture, percussive accompaniment. It was found, as well, that some traits were present in several styles, but to varying degrees. Few traits were found to be present exclusively in a severely limited area. Thus these tribal repertories were essentially similar. They could be grouped into areas only by the varying predominance of certain traits. Pentatonic scales, for example, comprised the vast majority of scales in the East and only a plurality (about 40 percent) on the Plains. On the other hand, imitative polyphony is present in a very few songs in the East but almost completely absent elsewhere. Such rather undramatic factors allow the separation of the East from other relatively similar style areas.

Granted, one statement that may be made on the basis of these findings is that North American Indian music is fundamentally a unit, and that the areas within it are only slightly different. But the question of precise measurement remains, and we have no standard way of expressing the rather obvious observation that in American Indian cultures the eastern and Plains styles are close, and the style of the Navajo and Apache substantially more removed from both, but all of them rather alike when compared to West African music. Can we say and prove that Renaissance and Baroque music are further apart in style than any of these?

A FEW BITES OF THE BULLET

There are so many who have given approximations and implications, and so few who have bitten the bullet. But there are a few scholars who, usually as by-products of other quests, have presented something approximating inch and foot. Let us look briefly at some of their work, all the while wondering why throngs have not followed in their footsteps.

An early example is Melville Herskovits's (1945) rating of Africanisms in the music and other cultural domains of various Negro populations in the New World. There are five degrees of similarity, described only as "very, quite, somewhat, a little," and "absent" or with a trace. One notes from Herskovits's table (1945:14) that music is generally more African than other domains. Indeed, Herskovits assigns the "very African" rating to the musics of Guiana, Haiti, most of African-derived Brazilian cultures, and parts of Trinidad and Jamaica; the rest, including even the northern United States, is "quite African." The musical distinctions are thus limited to two categories, and one wonders about Herskovits's unwillingness to separate, say, Cuba from the United States. But it is interesting to see that in all of these cultures music is the most African domain, that folklore and magic follow, that religion is less African, and technology and economic life, least. Herskovits may have missed an opportunity afforded by the fact that the music lends itself readily to being divided into elements and is capable of being quantified, but he is a pioneer in making comparative statements among musical repertories of an area, and among domains of culture, using a generalized African model as a base. He went well beyond the completely general and often sentimentalized way of putting it that dominated earlier writing.

It will be no surprise that some other pioneering attempts came, so to speak, out of Herskovits's shop. One of the most formidable, in its later effect on studies of music under cultural change (though the author had no thought of being formidable), is Richard Waterman's comparison of African, Afro-American, and European musics (1952) made for the purpose of showing why an African-derived music would flourish in a Western cultural context. Waterman simply says that African and Western musics have a number of common features, leaving to implication their mutually greater difference from other large bodies of music. Merriam (1955), a student of both Herskovits and Waterman, takes the matter a step further, bringing in North American Indian music, which, he asserts, is further from and less similar to either African or European than they are to each other.

The approach to measuring similarities among such large bodies of music is continued by Lomax in his often-mentioned cantometrics project (1968:80–105). His measurements may be questioned but they often confirm what is widely assumed, despite his weighting of the criteria in favor of those involving performance practice and singing style. For instance, Oceania is internally less homogeneous than Africa, which turns out to be highly unified but lacks the perfect homogeneity of Europe, a bit curious since Lomax elsewhere (1959) makes sharp distinctions among some European areas.

Lomax's use of formal statistics was preceded by less sophisticated and comprehensive studies, some of which can again be traced to Herskovits's influence. Although one may cite Densmore (1929b) and Kolinski (1936) as partial models, Freeman's and Merriam's (1956) work stands out as a rigorously controlled study of the interval frequencies of two Afro-American repertories, songs of the Ketu cult of Brazil and the Rada cult of Trinidad. The "discriminant function" technique was used to state differences and to determine the degree to which a newly analyzed song has a chance of being in one or the other repertory. The authors go to great lengths to show how different or similar these song groups are to each other, grasping firmly the nettle of this particular issue.

Formal statistics is also used by Keil (1966), a sometime student of Merriam's, in dealing with a completely different problem, the degree to which a number of musics are perceived as being different from each other by a group of American students. Using the semantic differential technique of psychology, this study compares four Indian ragas and selections of jazz and Bach. The results reflect not broad stylistic differences but perception along several specified continuums, e.g. flexible to rigid, warm to cool. I mention this study here because it, too, is an early attempt to measure comparatively the difference among musics, at least as perceived by a specific group of listeners.

One would expect that studies of tune families such as those of Bayard would go in for statements of degrees of similarity, but these are at best present by implication. Moreover, the question of simple similarity and difference is sometimes obscured by the question of genetic relationship. Further, the analyst's assessment of similarity may well differ from that of the informant. In a study that tries to take into account similarity, relationship, and the folk evaluation, Goertzen (1979) attempted to measure similarity among versions and variants of the North American fiddle tune "Billy in the Low Ground," according to criteria that are revealed and weighted within the performance of fiddle tunes. The nature of repetitions of each strain makes clear what sorts of difference are considered significant by the performers. For instance, rhythms are varied at will while overall contour is varied only slightly, and diagnostic tones not at all. Replicating Bayard's findings, Goertzen shows that if two tunes differ drastically in the rhythms employed but are otherwise much alike, they are regarded by informants to be much more "similar" than two tunes identical only in rhythm.

The question of measuring degrees of musical similarity and difference and associating this to genetic relationship is one of the most vexing in musicology and ethnomusicology. It is always with us, but those who have bitten the bullet and gone on record with some kind of even very rudimentary technique have not been widely followed. Among them, typically, are scholars with a background in anthropology, presumably impressed by the fact that musicians have developed ways of dividing their materials into elements that can be handled quantitatively. If we could increase the sophistication and precision of measuring similarity, and if we could also distinguish simple similarity from genetic relationship, many of the outstanding problems of analysis, description, and comparison would no doubt fade away.

The Study of Music in Culture

Chapter 10

Music and "That Complex Whole"

ANTHROPOLOGISTS AND MUSICOLOGISTS

A substantial body of ethnomusicologists consider themselves foremost to be students of music as related to culture. For the moment, let us not argue whether in this respect they should be distinguished from other musicologists, or for that matter how one defines culture, or whether the studies produced by ethnomusicologists actually deal in some way with culture as a concept. If indeed there is no ethnomusicologist who would not agree that his or her work should somehow relate music to culture, and each music to its own culture, the question is whether the relationship is the primary concern.

At various times I have been told that this or that scholar is more interested in the "cultural side of things," while another is interested in the "musical matters." Clearly, this distinction is a practical one if not one of principle. Alan Merriam has argued that ethnomusicology is the study of "music *in* culture," and later suggested that this definition did not go far enough, that it is the study of music *as* culture (1977a:202, 204). This is quite different, at least in flavor and emphasis, from the concept of ethnomusicology as the study of music, "not only in terms of itself but also in relation to its cultural context" (Hood, in Apel 1969:298). The differences among these three levels of relationship are blurred, hard to separate with sharp lines. The approach most widely used, best labeled "music in its cultural context," might include fieldworkers who study tabla in Delhi, spending most of their time taking lessons and practicing but also learning as much as they can about Indian culture, trying to approach their work in a manner sensitive to Indian cultural values. It would also include those who collect folk music, trying to learn for each song where it is normally performed and why, the singer's opinion of it, and so on, nevertheless focusing on the song. Studying music *in* culture would imply a holistic view of culture as an organic unit, and descriptively assigning to music a unitary role, ascertained in field research. The "music *as* culture" approach moves one further in that direction, implying that one takes up a theory of the nature of culture and applies it to music. Each approach has its disciplinary home base. If "music in cultural context" is standard musicology, the study of music in culture may be carried on with conventional methods of history and ethnography, while Merriam's study of music as culture, a term recently taken up by others (Herndon and McLeod 1980), is an anthropological specialty. Many disciplines deal with culture, but anthropologists are different in their view of it as a single thing, a system with interlocking and interrelating parts.

The concept of culture has itself been a major issue in anthropology. There are hundreds of formulations. However, the basic chord was struck early in the history of this discipline, as E. B. Tylor (1871:1:1) noted the interrelationship of domains, defining culture as "that complex whole which includes knowledge, belief, art, morals, law, custom, and any other capacities or habits acquired by man as a member of society." While differing enormously in their ways of studying and perceiving culture, anthropologists have not, it seems to me, departed so very much from this formulation. The study of music *as* culture would require the integration of music and its concepts and its attendant behavior and indeed, all musical life, into this kind of a model of culture. Let me illustrate a bit further these three ways of going at the music/culture relationship, using odds and ends of the kind of information that typically would have appeared in an initial foray into musical life in Teheran of ca. 1968.

Conclusions drawn from the "study of music in its cultural context" approach might provide the following kind of information: classical music is performed in concerts, at garden parties, and at small men's gatherings. Musicians have low status and are sometimes members of minorities. Folk music in rural Iran is performed by specialists, each devoted mainly to one repertory and one kind of social occasion such as weddings. The names of instruments, how they are made, who owns them, would be given. We would learn that the modes of Persian music are accorded certain characteristics such as aggression, affection, contemplation. We would hear how people learn music. This would amount mainly to the details of ethnography regarding the production, performance, and experience of music.

The study of music *in* culture would have a different emphasis, going into greater depth with a view differently flavored. It might tell us that among various activities in which Iranians engage, music is one whose hearing occupies a good deal of time, but that people feel somewhat guilty about this fact and deny it. It might compare the attitude toward music on the part of traditional and Westernized Iranians, or the techniques of music teaching with the teaching of other skills. The study of music *as* culture would make an attempt to seize the general nature of Iranian culture and show how music accommodates its structure. It might identify certain central values of Iranian society such as hierarchy or individualism and show how these are reflected (or perhaps violated) in musical conceptualization, behavior, and sound.

That these three approaches appeared successively in the history of ethnomusicology is an indication of the way in which ethnomusicology follows anthropological theory, though often lagging behind by a number of years. They are successive in another way, as the second approach usually depends on data generated by the first, and the third, by the information derived in the second. They are not easily distinguished, their overlapping is obvious, and perhaps they exhibit only a continuum. They are also basic to a historic conflict within our field. Anthropologically oriented ethnomusicologists, feeling perhaps that anthropologists somehow own the concept of culture, argue that they have put culture back into the study of music. General musicologists, historians, and humanists may maintain that they have always been students of music in culture, but to them music is primary and culture a less specific concept. The same conflict, incidentally, is found as well within the music profession. Musicology is the study of people who are involved with music, so music theorists or practicing academic musicians have been known to say, while they themselves study the music directly (and think themselves at times better persons for it). Beyond this, socio-musicologists, psycho-musicologists, sociologists of music all have different ideas of whose task it is—or better, who may be permitted—to study music in culture and how it should be done.

The issue, then, is not whether there is a cultural concern in ethnomusicology but what should be the role of the concept of culture. Behind it are accusations of past neglect and of misinterpretation. But, taking a very broad definition of culture—human knowledge agreed upon by some definable group of people—it is unfair to maintain that the general musicologists have not paid attention to it as a context and receptacle for music. They have not been very technical or systematic in their treatment of culture, but ignored it they have not. A brief look at the works of a few prominent historians as a sample may illustrate.

Some of the earliest histories of Western music, works which pre-date the formal establishment of musicology, are hardly histories of music as such. Burney (1776–89), perhaps the most prominent before 1900, reads rather like social history with emphasis on music. A century later the more scholarly and academic work by Ambros (1862), the first man to hold a university chair specifically in musicology, could well be read as cultural history, or history of ideas, arts, philosophy, with special attention given to music. Toward the end of the nineteenth century the field of musicology began to develop as an independent discipline. Perhaps the leading figure among the scholars of that time was Guido Adler, whom we have already met as the author of a highly influential formulation of the field and its subdivisions (Adler 1885). His emphasis on the direct study of music and musical style, often referred to as "style criticism," was probably motivated by his desire to see the discipline recognized as a separate entity, but he seems also to have taken the study of music in culture for granted. His outline of musicology as a discipline with various subdivisions is replete with references to "Hilfswissenschaften" deriving from other, more established humanistic areas, particularly history. To be sure, anthropology and sociology are not among them for obvious historical reasons, although a subfield called "Musikologie," devoted to the study of non-Western music, is to serve ethnological ends. This article is the first in the initial volume of the first professional periodical devoted to musicology and edited by himself, and it may be an indication of Adler's interest that the second article is a lengthy piece on ancient Indian Vedic sacrifices by the Handel scholar F. Chrysander (1885), devoted largely to the cultural context of music.

It is true that after the turn of the century many if not most musicologists turned to the study of the musical artifact, more or less separated from its cultural context, although it may be debated whether this was a matter of ideology or convenience. And yet some of the outstanding scholars in the field nevertheless continued to devote much of their attention to context. Thus Alfred Einstein's book on nineteenth-century music (1947a) has six initial chapters on the place of music in nineteenth-century culture. Walter Wiora (1965b), in his attempt to show the history of world music as something encompassing mainly four periods, depends on cultural typology for his framework. Knepler (1961) devotes most of his book on nineteenth-century music to the interpretation of musical events, including the broadly Western, the national, and the personal, in the light of a Marxist view of culture and history. One could give many more examples, but these perhaps suffice to remind us that musicologists dealing with European music have not neglected the cultural context.

Whether the students of culture, anthropologists, have given consideration to music as a domain of culture is an instructive if not totally relevant question. The typical American anthropologist has been much more inclined to deal with visual and verbal art than with music. As a small sample, the large general though introductory works on anthropology by Harris (1971), Hoebel (1949), and A. L. Kroeber (1948) barely mention music but devote some substantial attention to visual art. Similarly, the major histories of anthropological scholarship (e.g. Harris 1968, Lowie 1937, Honigmann 1976, Voget 1975, Naroll and Cohen 1973, Manners and Kaplan 1968) avoid mention of music. The existence of ethnomusicology seems to be passively accepted by American anthropologists, but on the whole they are unwilling to include it actively in their purview. It remained to scholars interested primarily in music to point out that musical studies can make important contributions to anthropological theory (Merriam 1955b), and to present the relatively central role, sometimes overstated just a bit, of music research in the development of particular methodologies of anthropology such as that of the German diffusionist school of the early twentieth century (A. Schneider 1976).

It seems that music in Western culture is generally regarded as a symbol of happiness, but I am not inclined to write off this curious omission of music to unhappiness of the members of the anthropological profession. Rather, it may illustrate something else about the way Western urban society conceives of music. It is an art treated rather like science; only the professional can understand it properly. The fruits of music, like science, are enjoyed daily by practically all of the population, but the academic musical establishment has made the lay public feel that without understanding the technicalities of musical construction, without knowledge of notation and theory, one cannot properly comprehend or deal with music. This perhaps accounts for the shyness of the anthropologist.

Interestingly, this attitude toward non-Western music is reflected in the publications of even many of those anthropologists who have a thorough understanding of Western classical music. For example, Oscar Lewis, a great anthropologist but also a distinguished amateur opera singer, did not in any detail deal with music in his works on the Blackfoot Indians, Latin American peoples, and Indian villagers. Claude Lévi-Strauss, who devotes, one might almost say, a major book to music (1969), organizing his work in accordance with the forms of Western classical music, avoids analyzing musical behavior among the South American Indians whose other arts, closely allied to music, are the main subjects of his work. Evidence perhaps for the conclusion that even the interculturally relativistic scholar cannot shed the skin of his own culture.

FOUR MODELS

Anthropological literature is full of discussions about the nature of culture, full of theory about the concept of culture. Frequent shifts in emphasis seem to be typical, but in using the culture concept for ethnomusicological analysis, approaches both early and recent appear to be effective, and I wish now to examine a few of them briefly in the context of the music/culture relationship. The "study of music in its cultural context" approach seems not to pose major theoretical problems, although one should not make light of the problems of data gathering, sampling, and interpretation. The study of music in or as culture, on the other hand, requires a conception of culture, and a conception of music for juxtaposition; so it is with these two segments of our tripartite continuum that we are now involved.

Since about 1950 the various conceptions of culture seem to have moved from something static and subject occasionally to change to something in which change is the norm. The words "culture change" appear with greater frequency in the more recent literature. The matter is still an issue. One may argue that nature is incapable of repeating itself precisely and that therefore constant change must be characteristic. But one may also respond that an observer is incapable of perceiving a complex phenomenon except in its static form, change being a rapid succession of stable states, and that therefore if one espouses the conception of culture as something constantly changing, one can deal with it only as an abstraction. Ethnomusicologists have followed anthropologists in gradually increasing their interest in musical change, having begun with a model of music that is static at least for the purposes of analysis. Most approaches to the study of music in culture use a static conception of culture. Music in or as culture implies a relationship, and what we are about is the examination of views of this relationship. In all cases there is at least the implication of influence of one on the other, normally of culture on music, or of a time sequence, normally of music following culture. Here are four approaches for the ethnomusicologist.

(1) A large number of ethnomusicological publications follow an enumerative approach to showing the relationship. It is based on the proposition that culture consists of a large number of separate components, interrelated to be sure, but a group of more or less separable domains. These include politics, religion, economy, each of which can be further broken down into components such as, say, public and private religion; rituals associated with birth, marriage, puberty, death; scriptures, prayers, interpretations, sermons; and so on. The essence of this approach, used in anthropology by Boas (Lowie 1937:152) and some of his followers, is the desire to study each culture and each of the components individually, with no prior overall model or hypothesis about its workings. The emphasis is on the diversity of the culture artifacts and the variety of their histories.

Music in culture can also be viewed thus, the proposition then being that each aspect of culture has its own special relationship to music, and that the appropriate picture of music is one in which the roles and functions of individual items of musical concept, behavior, and sound are enumerated and explained separately. Thus an enumerative view of the musical culture of the contemporary Blackfoot Indians would tell us that there are many events at which music is heard: powwows, a major intertribal celebration in the summer, performances for tourists on and off the reservation, gambling games, small dances sponsored by local businesses, a pageant, reconstructions of older religious and social rituals. It would indicate that musical interests coincide with the division of the population into full-blooded and mixed ancestry. It would state that there are some fifty men known as "singers" who perform most and who are loosely organized into some five singing groups, but that there are another dozen men who know old ceremonial songs no longer sung. It would indicate that an average singer knows between one and two hundred songs. It might well present this information in outline form, tying it, *ad hoc,* to other domains of the culture, but eschew the formulation of a theory of music in culture that depends on a single intellectual thrust.

It is, of course, not usually enough to enumerate details in a study of the way in which music can be viewed as an aspect of culture. One of the main problems of the ethnographer of musical life is to find a way of organizing a vast body of diverse bits of information. The establishment of typologies that can serve as templates for comparative description is a major task of ethnomusicology. In the 1970s considerable attention has been focused on the musical event as the main node of musical life. Thus Kaemmer (1980) proposes a set of relationships among the various roles involved in the realization of a musical event, listing five types of "music-complexes": individualistic, communal, contractual, sponsored, and commercial. As he indicates for the Shona people of Zimbabwe, any or all of these complex-types may be found in one society. But it may also be possible to show that one society is dominated by a particular type. This sort of classification is the outgrowth of simpler and more generally accepted typologies such as the folk-popular-art music continuum and the distinctions between sacred and secular, public and private, professional and amateur.

(2) Another way of looking at the music/culture relationship is to see what music does, what it contributes to the complex whole of culture. Several approaches to the study of music in culture derive from the functionalist or structural-functionalist view of culture made famous by Malinowski and Radcliffe-Brown. One is rather simple, asserting, as Radcliffe-Brown suggests (1952:195; see also Harris 1968:527), that culture is like a human or animal organism, with parts or organs interrelating and contributing something to the whole. The interrelationships and interdependencies of the organs are paralleled by the same kinds of relationships among the domains of culture. Music is one of these, and (like perhaps the liver?) makes a single main contribution and others of a less crucial nature. One may conclude that music, in all societies, fills a particular role, or assert, by contrast, that it has, in each society, a particular function not shared with other societies (the liver of social organisms everywhere; or perhaps the liver here, the stomach there, the nose elsewhere). Merriam suggests a number of basic functions of music in general (1964:219–27), a statement sufficiently vital to require more discussion in Chapter 12. But he illustrates a kind of universalist approach to the issue of musical function. Archer (1964a), one of many to try their hands at a variety of derived approaches, uses the principles of ecology to analyze the relationship of music to other domains.

At the same time, the idea that in each society music has a major function seems more attractive. In Western culture it has to be entertainment. Among the traditional Blackfoot it seems to have been validation of ritual behavior (Nettl 1967c:153); among the people of Yirkalla, enculturation (R. Waterman 1956:41). In upper-caste Hindu society it may be a way of making the connection between religious values and everyday life, and for the Havasupai, of warding off dangers of the dark and maintaining what is of value in society (Hinton, personal communication 1968). Boilès (1978), deriving from this manner of thought, relates specific musical activities to a large variety of ritual occasions in many cultures. If the culture-specific functional approach is preferable to the universalistic, this may show that the diversity of human behavior is easier to understand and analyze than its unity.

(3) A second kind of functionalist approach involves the hypothesis that there is for each culture a core or center, a basic idea or set of ideas, whose nature determines the character of the other domains, including music. The types of this core include broad characterizations, such as those suggested by Ruth Benedict (1934)—the Apollonian Pueblo Indians, the Dionysian Plains peoples, the paranoid Dobu Islanders—and range from control of energy by Leslie White (Kaplan and Manners 1972:45; R. Adams 1975:11) and technology (Harris 1968:662) to social structure (Radcliffe-Brown 1958) and a set of values or ideology (Kaplan and Manners 1972:112–15). Logically, it would seem that the types of centers would proceed causally from control of energy to technology, and on to social structure and values. It is difficult to disagree with White that control of energy is basic, and that from it flows technology, and hard to disagree with Harris that technology evokes social structure.

From the musicologist's point of view, however, the question might be whether one should regard the core of culture as simply the kind and degree of control of energy that a people have developed, or whether one gains more insight by, for example, expanding this core to include technology or, further, the resultant social structure and the values to which it gives rise. The point is that one can say little about the way in which control of energy is inevitably accompanied by a kind of musical culture. Adding technology would enable us, for example, to speak to the differential development of musical instruments. Thus the existence of stone tools alone allows the development of bone flutes and musical bows, the invention of pottery adds kettle drums and clay percussion instruments, and the development of metalwork makes possible the construction of brass gongs. Modern industrial technology provides the opportunity for highly standardized instruments. Beyond instruments, development of complex architecture gives us theaters and concert halls, electronics, the possibility of precise reproduction and unchanged repetition of performances. And so on to hundreds of other examples.

But the specifics of musical culture, to be seen as culture and to be explained in terms of their intercultural differences, require a broader culture center. For example, social structure determines such things as the division of labor, providing opportunity for musical specialization. Even so, the mere existence of specialized musicians does not tell us much about the kind of music they produce. Social structure may also tell us much about the kind of interrelationship among musicians, in and outside of performance, and speak to such matters as the equal or hierarchical arrangement of parts in an ensemble, the blending or individual articulation of voices, the kinds of vocal and instrumental timbre preferred.

But in order to establish a clear framework for the study of music in culture, the culture center as core ought perhaps to be expanded further to include certain fundamental values or an ideology, for these might provide the most fruitful opportunity for studying in great detail the relationship between the nature of culture and society and the nature of musical style, concepts, and behavior.

The extraction of values from the conglomeration of statements and forms of behavior that a culture provides is no small matter. Characterizations of cultures, brief, distilled, and abstracted, are not numerous, and when they appear, they are often sharply criticized by those who regard the whole thing as too complex and who question the mutual translatability of culture systems into broad frameworks. Nevertheless, to the ethnomusicologist who needs a succinct characterization in order to tie to it the complex of musical systems, these few statements are attractive and insightful. Widely cited, because of its use for the interpretation of musical values, is Kluckhohn's formula for formalism as a central value of the Navajo approach to life, its function being "to maintain orderliness in those sectors of life which are little subject to human control" (McAllester 1954: 88). The now classic characterizations by Ruth Benedict suggest ways in which musical behavior and musical style can be tied to a culture core.

Let me again give in a bit more detail an example from Iranian classical music. We have seen that urban Iranian society maintains and balances certain values. The stress between equality, a basic Islamic tenet, and hierarchy, a principle of actual social and political structure, is reflected in the structure of the system of Persian classical music, which is based on a group of pieces collectively called the *radif.* They are presented initially as equal, equally capable of being the basis of improvisation and composition, but under the surface there emerges a carefully structured hierarchy of musical units whose relative importance is determined by various criteria. The countervailing value of individualism in the society is reflected in the centrality of musical improvisation and the prestige of music that departs from norms. The related value of surprise is reflected in the centrality and prestige of musically surprising elements, from modulatory devices in the modes to the rhythmic unpredictability of nonmetric improvisations. The value of precedence in socially informal situations, and of introductory behavior and personnel in more formal situations, is reflected in the differential positions of the important portions in learning materials and in formal concerts (Nettl 1978b).

What ethnomusicologists need is a way of establishing central values of cultures, expressed in such a way that their distinctiveness becomes clear, but also so that comparisons among cultures are possible. This is the task of the student of culture, and only when completed can we study music as culture by showing its relationship to the core of values. On the other hand, characterizations of musical systems, extracting from them their own core of central values, could be suggestive to the anthropologist.

(4) A fourth model, subsumed in part under the foregoing three but yet worthy of special mention, envisions a line of relationships leading from a major value of a culture to music. This model uses Merriam's tripartite model of music (Merriam 1964:33), but in contrast to Merriam's further interpretation that these three parts—concept, behavior, and sound—all interrelate equally, it proposes that the part of the model closest to the central conception of culture is the "concept" part of music. Thus the line moves from culture core to music concept, on to musical behavior, finally to music sound, clearly related but hard to pin down. Let me give an unelaborated example: Islamic culture places relatively low value on music, in theory forbidding it. Thus one *conception* of music in the major Islamic cultures is that it is something low in the scale of values. The *behavioral* result is low status of the professional musician and higher status of the informed amateur, and associated ideas of freedom of the latter. This leads to improvisation as the form of musical behavior of greatest prestige and cultural centrality. The musical style or *sound* is the result of musical choices made within an essentially improvisatory system.

THREE STRESSES

If there are many ways of viewing the music/culture relationship, there are also issues that cut across them. Although we will have occasion to refer to them repeatedly as they appear to affect many of the issues in this volume, I should like to mention three of them here. They have already put in their appearances: (1) the emic-etic dichotomy, (2) determinist versus functionalist approaches, and (3) the comparativist/particularist controversy.

(1) One may look at culture, at music, at music-as-culture from the viewpoint of a member of the society being studied or from the viewpoint of the analyst. It's perhaps the most basic of all ethnomusicological issues. The emic-etic dichotomy comes from linguistics, a field in which it was at first relatively simple to conceptualize, if not always to handle. Thus the common linguistic illustration: unaspirated and aspirated "p" can mean different things in Indian languages, and words distinguished only by that difference are different words. In English we can predict that initial "p" followed by a vowel is aspirated, medial "p" will be unaspirated, and if we reverse them (popp^{h}a instead of p^{h}oppa), we will at worst be speaking with an accent. Aspiration of "p" is phonemic in Hindi, not in English. In English the difference is "etic" but not "emic." Speakers can recognize it but do not regard it as significant.

Translated to cultural studies and to theoretical discourse, this distinction is a bit different. The crucial interface between investigator and informant is summarized thus by Harris (1968:575): "Etic statements are verified when independent observers using similar operations agree that a given event has occurred." On the other hand (Harris 1968:571), "emic statements refer to systems whose . . . things are built up out of contrast and discriminations significant, meaningful, real, accurate [to] the actors themselves."

Music as culture? The Flathead (Merriam 1967a:3–24) "emically" regard music as something that comes about by dreaming, from supernatural visions, from other tribes. The American ethnomusicologist "etically" makes bold to say that the dreamers compose. Again, the Blackfoot maintain that two songs have in a sense been created if two men have visions in which they learn songs, even if the songs are identical. The "etic" view would label the two products as one song. More subtly: the Iranian music aficionado will maintain that only performers A and B know the basic material necessary for proper performance, while performers C and D are totally ignorant of it. The accompanying "etic" statement is likely to recognize the greater knowledge of A and B but find that C and D also know the material, if not quite as well.

No need to belabor. If we are to construct a detailed but broad picture of the music of a society as culture, we must decide which route we are taking at any one time, but eventually we will probably find it necessary to follow both and to discover a way of reconciling them. If the routes are distinct, we will come to realize that informants can make both "emic" and "etic" statements. Thus, faced with the assertion (backed by hearing the recordings) that two songs he had sung sounded identical, my Arapaho friend William Shakespeare said, "Yes, they do sound alike, but they are two songs." The point is, of course, to discover what it is about the way a culture works, in its core, that causes its practitioners to make certain kinds of conceptual, behavioral, and acoustic distinctions in their music.

(2) We have touched on the way in which culture, as a whole, affects or determines music. An essentially historic process, it can be analyzed in two ways. A strictly functionalist view would propose that while a central core of culture is responsible for the shape and nature of what could be called the outer organs (the biological model) or the definitely less important superstructure (the Marxist model), the interaction is constant. The effect of the core of values on musical behavior is more or less immediate. A determinist view would lengthen the time span. A society might, for instance, develop a certain way of harnessing energy, then gradually develop a system of technology that takes advantage of it. Eventually there would emerge changes in the social structure that in turn would impose certain values most clearly evident in religion, philosophy, and law. These values would eventually come to affect the arts and other aspects of lifestyle. The time from the first stage to the last could be a matter of centuries. The difference between the functionalist and the determinist conception can be interpreted as a difference between the immediate and the gradual.

Now, of course, these are theoretical constructs that at best suggest ways of looking at music as culture. One is hard put to find examples that illustrate or totally negate either view. But let us look quickly at the function of the so-called "new" music in Western society, the kind of music stemming from the work of such composers as Webern, Cage, Stockhausen. Looking at it functionally, one might perceive the following characteristics of contemporary Western society: (a) highly developed technology, particularly in electronics; (b) fragmentation of society into many groups, determined by wealth, ethnic descent, age; (c) standardization of work habits and of products but a decline of interest in the standardization of ethical and moral systems agreed upon by all; (d) emphasis on personal ownership of products and their quantity. The new music depends on sophisticated electronic technology and is composed of a large number of styles that can hardly be subsumed under a single system of comprehension, drawing on other musics in and outside the society. It is a music that expects at times precise repetition from performance to performance, giving the most exacting directions to players and using instruments like tape recorders in "live" performance. But it may also give unprecedented latitude to the performer, and yet the individuality of the composer and the association between a composer and "his" or "her" pieces are stressed. This music system is a direct function of the culture that produces it, as it contributes to the general character of the culture; or so one might argue.

In the alternative interpretation, we may say that the perfection of electronics after World War II, resulting from a particularly efficient way of using and transforming energy, makes necessary a vast array of professional specializations. This development reinforces the emphasis on personal property, already present, and results in the development of a fragmented social structure accompanied by the ready possibility of instant communication through the mass media. Such a society, one could assert, is bound to give rise to the kind of music called "new" in the 1960s and 1970s.

(3) Many have sought theories to help explain music as culture in all societies. Theories abound, but a method of systematic description is another matter. The theoretical approaches most widely used are derived from functionalist, evolutionist, and Marxist modes of thought, and when they have provided universalist theories, it has been on bases derived from single and most often Western cultures. The typical ethnomusicologists' statements about the relationship of music and culture are based on the way in which the major cultures they have studied work and can be explained. Such statements have often failed to stand up under comparative scrutiny.

On the other hand, some have insisted that we must find for each culture an approach that is particularist, drawn from its special character. We have heard this song before, and in our consideration of comparison of musics as sound noted that systems that make possible a view of all musics in relation to each other are widely developed, while the culture-specific approach, with much to recommend it, is not. In the study of music as culture, however, systems that draw similar lines for all societies and make comparison possible are hardly commonplace. Comparative statements about musical conceptualization in relationship to culture type are exceedingly rare. There is a marked contrast between the publications of ethnomusicological fieldworkers such as Merriam, McAllester, and Blacking, who draw the picture of musical culture on the basis of specific ethnography, and those of the scholars most involved with the study of Western culture (Weber 1921, Blaukopf 1951), whose world view, while recognizing cultural differences, springs from a general view of humanity with Western culture at the center.

FIVE STUDIES

The student of music in culture must at least implicitly take a theoretical stance and come to terms with the stresses here described in abstract. A greater task yet is the organization of musical ethnography, the discovery of a systematic way of comprehending the enormous number of ideas, activities, and events that comprise musical life in their relationship to the totality of a people's culture. Each author has a distinct way; there is much less consistency than in the description of musical sound. I should like to present some approaches by quickly characterizing five publications.

Ames and King (1971) provide what purports to be simply a glossary of terms and expressions used by the Hausa of northern Nigeria in talking about music and musical culture. Actually, this work can be viewed as a description of musical culture, using the vocabulary and thus generally the categories that the Hausa themselves use, therefore providing essentially an emic picture of the niche music occupies in the culture. It is a classified glossary. The authors first divide the subject into five broad areas, using their own taxonomy: instruments, professional performers, patrons of music, occasions on which music is performed, and music performance. Within each category some subdivisions, as that of instruments into the traditional categories of Hornbostel and Sachs (1914) (idiophones, membranophones, chordophones, aerophones), are imposed from outside, while others, such as the division of performance into categories distinguished by social context as well as musical style, are provided by the Hausa: proclamation, ululation, challenges, acclamation. The authors' way of taking musical concepts and fitting them, as it were, into the culture, is to examine each term that is used somehow in connection with music. It turns out that in Hausa culture the degree of integration is great; very few words are specific to music and the vast majority are terms normally used in nonmusical contexts but also applicable to music. This is common but not universal. The academic language of classical music in English was at one time much more music-specific, using loan words from Italian (allegro, andante), or words whose meaning is primarily musical (concert), and others with a specific musical meaning quite separate from their denotation in other domains (note, beat). This in itself may tell us something about the differences in the place of music in the two societies. In the case of Ames and King there is an overarching taxonomy imposed for comparative purposes, but within it appears clearly the folk taxonomy of the Hausa and its principles. One way to study music in culture is to use language as a mediator.

A very different approach is used by Merriam in his detailed study of the Flathead Indians (1967a). Following in some measure his tripartite model of music, he divides the first part, whose main thrust is the presentation of music in culture, into chapters that deal mainly with concepts and others that discuss behavior. Chapters on "The Sources of Music" and "Ideas of Music and Musicianship" mainly concern concept; "Sound Instruments" and "The Uses of Music" (subdivided into some categories recognized by the Flathead) comprise behavior. While a brief glossary of terms is appended, there is no attempt here to use the Flathead language as the point of departure. Rather, observations combined with the recording of statements by Merriam's own and earlier informants, elicited through questions about music from discussion presumably in English, are the main source. The overall organization is Merriam's to a much greater extent than it is the Flatheads', although Merriam does take the folk taxonomy into account at various points.

Surprisingly, what is less clear here than in Ames and King (1971) is the way in which music functions within, or is a part of, Flathead culture. The concepts of music and the ways in which people behave "musically" are described in exemplary detail. But other questions, such as the reflection of Flathead values in musical ideas, or how music relates to other domains of culture, are not frequently touched upon. It is interesting to see that even one of the most outstanding publications coming from the "anthropology of music" approach to ethnomusicology concentrates on the music, broadly conceived, and deals with music holistically, but less than Merriam might later have wished with music as culture.

Neuman's (1977) study of hereditary musical specialists in North India illustrates an examination of the relationship, in a number of specific ways, of a social and a musical system. For example, Neuman compares the hierarchical structure of performance, divided into various levels of soloist's and accompanist's roles, with the structure of the hierarchical social organization, supporting the parallel with the finding that soloists and accompanists are drawn from separate social lineages. The desire, probably of recent origin, of North Indian accompanists to become soloists is related to the coming of greater social mobility. Musicians become soloists by affecting the social appurtenances of the system within which the soloists normally live, such as officially recognized "gharanas" or schools of musicianship, which are also lineages. Neuman thus concludes that "the two phenomena are crucially interlinked" and "both affect and are affected by the changing character of the soloist-accompanist relationship" (1977:233).

Neuman does not try to state the central value system of North Indian society but concentrates on one social value in the lives of groups of people who are particularly concerned with music, the groups from which musicians are drawn; nor does he try to establish the totality of musical values but concentrates on a particular one whose understanding would have to precede a more detailed accounting of the technicalities of music. By thus limiting himself, he is able to interrelate one aspect of the central core of culture, social structure, with musical concepts, behavior, and sound.

McAllester's *Enemy Way Music* (1954), sometimes regarded as a classic study because it is among the first to deal explicitly with musical and cultural values in a non-Western society, examines the musical content of a Navajo Indian ceremony. Devoting only some twenty pages to the discussion, he manages to describe and comment upon a group of central values of Navajo culture, focusing on the perception of danger that comes through misuse of anything, including music, and further dividing values into aesthetic, existential, and normative. Examples are self-expression, quiet, humor, provincialism, formalism, and individualism. The differential treatment of these values—it is difficult to distinguish the degree to which each is aesthetic, normative, or existential—may be debated. But what is of special interest is McAllester's implied conclusion that while cultural values are reflected in music, this reflection appears in musical behavior and in attitudes toward music, and only secondarily if at all in the structure of the music. If I may venture to interpret his words, to McAllester it is concept and behavior that reflect culture, and if one is to study music as culture, one does so primarily through these components of music and much less through sound. His study supports the linear model suggested above.

While the studies just described are by scholars with a substantial interest in anthropology, the fifth example, Malm's (1959) general book on Japanese music, makes no pretense of being a contribution to that field or indeed to concentrate on music as or in culture. More than the other works discussed here, it purports to be about music, but Malm makes it clear that an understanding of the music must rest on at least some understanding of Japanese culture, past and present. For example, in his section on koto music, he first gives a detailed cultural and historical context of this instrument and its music. There follows an account of the history of the instrument, not purely organological but also mentioning persons, events and occasions, places, literary sources, myths, characterizations of the Japanese historiography, schools of musicians and the basis on which they are formed, and relationships to social classes, repertories, and other instruments. He goes on to a discussion of teaching techniques and their relationship to musical and social structure, and finally moves on to the contemporary instrument and its music, again laying stress on the social context. Thus it is an unusually good illustration of the "music in its cultural context" type of study, but it provides sufficient ethnographic data so that one could easily derive from it a more technically anthropological study.

Returning to the thoughts at the beginning of this chapter, Malm's book shows that a scholar working in the first instance as a musicologist may frequently make contributions that are compatible with and contribute greatly to the more specifically anthropologically oriented works described here. It is anthropologists who have given the greatest impetus in recent years to the study of music as part of "that complex whole." But the distance between the ethnomusicologists who come from anthropology and those who come from a background of a more strictly musical nature is hardly as great as it is sometimes made out to be.

Chapter 11

Music Hath Charms

BEND A KNOTTED OAK

Much of the literature on the study of music in culture involves the ways in which humans use music, which is therefore said to carry out certain functions in human society, and so we wish here to develop the subject of Chapter 10 a bit further in that direction. It is perhaps too general a statement to say that people everywhere have *used* music to *do* certain things, and at the same time that they thought that music was capable of *doing* something to *them.* The early literature of ethnomusicology often dwells on the presumption that in simple prehistoric, folk, or tribal cultures people use music to accomplish certain ends, and that therefore this music is *functional.* Herzog (1950:1034) cautiously says that "folk song is often said to be more functional in its use or application than cultivated poetry or music." The widespread acceptance of this view a few decades ago is also illustrated by a statement of Marius Schneider's (1957:2), whose opinions usually differed greatly from Herzog's, to the effect that "to a much greater extent than art music, [primitive music] is bound up with everyday life and with many special factors: psychological, sociological, religious, symbolic, and linguistic." The implication is that songs used to accompany turning points in a person's life and the course of the year are more "functional" than pieces used for performance in concerts, a work song more functional than "The Messiah." The focus on this special characteristic of folk and tribal music is no doubt related to the ethnomusicologist's need to justify the concern with simple, unsophisticated, and—in the academic musician's athletic view of music—inferior products.

But when Congreve said, "Music hath charms to soothe the savage breast, to soften rocks, or bend a knotted oak," he probably did not mean folk music. If modern American academic tradition, depending on misspelling as a major creative force, often finds music soothing the savage beast instead, it refers to the various settings of the Orpheus myth and "The

Magic Flute," all hardly folk music. It depends how one defines use and functionality, and ethnomusicology, gradually discarding the distinction between "folk" and "art," has come to admit that the concept of function is applicable to all music.

It stands to reason. If we make note of the fact that most of the songs of the Blackfoot Indians were used as parts of religious ceremonies, to accompany social dances, and to keep gamblers from revealing the location of a hidden object, we must also admit that religious services in eighteenth-century Leipzig or twentieth-century New York were and are hardly conceivable without music, that social events such as dances and parties in modern America are inevitably musical events of a sort, that a proper football game has a marching band in the half-time, and a baseball game, at least a hugely amplified electric organ swelling to glorify the Mudville team's home run. One may reply that this is true, to be sure, but the real difference between the simpler cultures and the more cultivated ones is that the latter also have events such as concerts, whose purpose is mainly musical, and at which their best music is exhibited. Yet, without itself being changed, a Blackfoot Sun Dance might well be viewed by an outside observer primarily as a musical event rather than a religious one, were it not for the fact that the Blackfoot themselves accord religion the primary role. By contrast, if many American concert-goers were to be honest with themselves, they would classify and analyze concerts as social events, as their typical program structures, their obligatory forms of dress, their standard length, the ever-present intermission, printed programs, etc., etc., usually correspond to social requirements. But one could also consider concerts as secular rituals. Again, we often accord to art music an edifying, educational role, believing that things of value can be learned from hearing Bach and Mozart. But it is also said that the function of music among the people of Yirkalla is essentially educational, and that they, like the Plains Indians, learned their culture gradually, symbolizing each step with appropriate music. Many other cultures conform to this pattern. Indeed, if we teach our children to go to concerts in order to learn important values in their own culture, we are doing what the technologically much simpler people of Yirkalla and the Plains did with their music: use it to teach people the important things about their own culture.

These are just a few examples, and more could easily be given to show the usefulness of leaving human cultures undivided when it comes to looking at the functions of music. Ethnomusicologists probably agree that people everywhere use music to accomplish something. The old issue, whether music in certain types of cultures was used more for certain kinds of things, has been submerged by a concern for ways of looking at these uses. The major issues appear to have been the difference between uses and functions, and the difference between the function of music in human society at large as opposed to the function of music in the individual societies, and beyond that, the specific function of individual segments of repertories, styles, types of music, pieces.

RESPONSE TO APM

The early literature of ethnomusicology deals with the concepts of use and function as if they were more or less the same. Later, in a very direct statement on the subject, Alan P. Merriam (1964:209–28) rather definitively distinguishes them: "When we speak of the uses of music, we are referring to the ways in which music is employed in human society, to the habitual practice or customary exercise of music either as a thing in itself or in conjunction with other activities" (1964:210). But, "Music is *used* in certain situations and becomes a part of them, but it may or may not also have a deeper *function*" (ibid.). Using the work of S. Nadel and following widely accepted definitions suggested by Ralph Linton, Merriam takes function to mean the "specific effectiveness of [music] whereby it fulfills the requirement of the situation, that is, answers a purpose objectively defined; this is the equation of function with purpose" (1964:218). Merriam goes on to list ten "major and over-all functions, as opposed to uses, of music" (1964:219): emotional expression, aesthetic enjoyment, entertainment, communication, symbolic representation, physical response, enforcing conformity to social norms, validation of social institutions and religious rituals, contribution to the continuity and stability of culture, contribution to the integration of society.

A formidable list. "To soothe the savage breast" is perhaps hidden in it. Without being able to do better, I must confess to a bit of uneasiness. The line between uses and functions is clear when we observe that a particular Plains Indian song is *used* to accompany a Grass Dance but has the *function* of contributing to the integration of society. But it is not always so, for in the case of entertainment, use and function may be identical. Then too, Merriam's list, intended to characterize music, is not specific to music but could apply to all of the arts, though admittedly to different degrees, and possibly to other activities not normally classed as arts (although they might well be), such as religious ritual and speech.

But music is different from the other arts. More than any, it is a product of human ingenuity alone. It is the most distant from nature, not normally speaking directly of or reproducing visually what the artist sees. It is likewise the most distant from the rest of culture. Unlike the other arts, it rarely depicts or deals directly with what humans do or think. Of the many domains of culture, music would perhaps seem to be one of the least necessary; yet we know of no culture that does not have it. Should one therefore not be able to articulate for it a unique function?

As a matter of fact, the function of music in culture and distinguishing function and use have not really been a major issue in ethnomusicological literature for some time. In the early stages of ethnomusicology it somehow seemed necessary to point out that one was interested in the way music was used. The idea of identifying use/function was almost tantamount to the idea of studying music in its cultural context. At one point ethnomusicologists were informally divided into musicians and functionalists, but except for matters of emphasis and approach this issue has long been settled. Even so, the term "function" remained around looking for takers, and adherents of anthropological functionalism took it on as something to be carefully separated from "use" and from other aspects of the study of music in culture. Uses can be easily listed, and such a listing does not arouse theoretical controversy. We simply do it. At the same time the idea that we must find major, overriding functions for music seems to have come to a dead end. Shall we try a bit of resurrection?

Merriam's ten functions could be regarded, as a group, as a substitute for this kind of statement, but the list is broad and diverse. Several of his group—symbolic representation, conformity to norms, continuity, stability, cultural integration—can be combined into the statement that music functions as the symbolic expression of the main values, patterns, or themes of a culture. Music as a symbol is a subject for Chapter 15, but it may be instructive to refer to Susanne Langer's description of music as an "unconsummated symbol, a significant form without conventional significance" (1942:195). There seems to be a relationship between the specifically unconsummated nature of musical symbolism and the concept of a relationship of general structural principles and of overall and ubiquitous characteristics of singing style (in contrast to the specific musical content of a piece of music) to major characteristics and values of a culture. In other words, if we are to be specific about the way in which music reflects the values of a culture, we can do so best by dealing with those aspects of music that are constantly present in its musical repertory. Clearly, then, there is a line between the function of all music in a given society or population group and the functions of individual genres, styles, pieces.

We turn again to the comparative approach. Let us assume that all peoples use music for performing certain functions, and that there are various things that music can do. We're not sure to what extent these functions are exclusive to music, or can actually be performed by music, but believe that cultures differ in this respect. Merriam's list of ten can be a template for distinguishing societies from one another. By way of an exercise, we could start by trying to establish a typology of cultures, for juxtaposition to dominant functions or group of functions of music. I give you a highly idiosyncratic characterization of cultures: industrialized, developing, and preindustrialized; heterogeneous and homogeneous; isolated and interacting; established and besieged. Now, from a perusal of literature but, more important, from personal field experience and in some cases using myself as an informant, I should like to compare several cultures that can be characterized, according to my major distinctions, as follows:

1. Flathead Indians in the twentieth century (using Merriam 1967a)—developing, homogeneous, interacting, besieged.

2. Blackfoot Indians in the eighteenth century, extrapolated from literature and informants' descriptions—preindustrialized, homogeneous, isolated, established.

3. A midwestern college town, USA, based on observation—industrialized, heterogeneous, interacting, established.

4. The "intellectual" community of Prague, Czechoslovakia, 1920–40, based on personal observation and family records—industrialized, homogeneous, interacting, established.

5. Teheran, ca. 1960–70, based on field observation—developing, heterogeneous, interacting, besieged.

6. Rural Appalachia, early twentieth century, based on literature and some statements of older informants—developing, homogeneous, somewhat isolated, besieged.

Using Merriam's ten functions but excluding that of communication, which I, like Merriam (1964:223), find difficult to assess, let us set them against the cultures mentioned. Taking a deep breath, and aware of the "comic relief" character of such broad generalizations, I present Figure 5 as a tabular statement of functions and a subjective rating of the importance of each in these six cultures, expressed in a scale from 5 (important) to 1 (unimportant). The results may seem intriguing but, of course, it must be stressed that this table is intended to do no more than to suggest that a comparison of cultures along these lines could be constructive.

This table ought to be accompanied by voluminous explanations, but for lack of space I shall skip over them and hope that the reader will accept the evaluations for the sake of argument. The point to be made is that the six cultures can be grouped in accordance with the rough typology given above. Thus in the literate societies the function of aesthetic enjoyment ranks high, as does entertainment. Those cultures in which music enjoys high status use it considerably for emotional expression. Physical response appears to be low in those cultures in which personal expression is inhibited. The function of music as entertainment is lowest in tribal societies with predominantly religious music. Validation of ritual is highest in rural, lowest in urban cultures. Music as an activity that contributes to the integration of society appears highest in cultures "under siege," that is, confronted by imminent change as a result of forced contact with other cultures.

Having agonized a good deal over these ratings, I proceeded, by way of doodling, to add up the numbers. Interestingly, it turns out that two cultures, Teheran and Appalachia, yielded lower totals than the others. Does this mean that their music is less functional? Well, it may be that it fulfills its

	Flathead	Blackfoot	Midwestern town	Prague intellectuals, 1935	Teheran	Appalachia, pre-1940
Emotional expression	4	4	4	5	3	3
Aesthetic enjoyment	2	2	5	5	3	3
Entertainment	4	1	5	4	4	3
Symbolic representation	5	4	5	5	4	3
Physical response	4	5	4	2	2	2
Conformity to social norms	4	4	4	5	3	3
Validation of social institutions and religious rituals	4	5	3	2	2	4
Stability and continuity of culture	5	5	3	4	3	4
Integration of society	5	3	4	4	5	4
Totals	37	33	37	36	29	29

Figure 5. Subjective measurement of the strength of Merriam's functions in a selection of musical cultures.

function less strongly in these two than in the other societies, something conceivably explained by their relatively smaller emphasis on music and the fact that their music is or was practiced under the shadow of disapproval.

In contrast to Merriam, several authors who share a broad acquaintance with a number of musical cultures seem to converge in their belief that music has one principal function. Blacking (1973) continually stresses the belief that "there ought to be a relationship between patterns of human organization and the patterns of sound produced as a result of human interaction" (1973:26). Lomax maintains that the principal discovery of his analysis of world music is "that a culture's favorite song style reflects and reinforces the kind of behavior essential to its main subsistence effort and to its central and controlling social institutions" (1968:133). But greater descriptive complexity is also espoused by anthropologists, as illustrated by Royce's (1977: 83–84) description of the task facing the anthropologist of dance: "A multiplicity of functions tends to be the rule rather than the exception. Functions may be regarded as either overt or covert and either manifest or latent . . . any dance event, moreover, may have multiple functions at both levels." It is interesting to see this recent publication dealing with the anthropology of dance making a statement somewhat parallel to Merriam's, written over a decade earlier, and to note that it concerns itself with an issue that ethnomusicologists seemed to have more or less abandoned in its explicit form. But, if pushed to the wall, we are still forced to say that "music hath charms," that it does the inexplicable, but that, as Merriam concludes, it "is clearly indispensible to the proper promulgation of the activities that constitute a society" (1964:227).

THE COIN

Ethnomusicologists may do well to develop theoretical models for concretely analyzing and describing a culture's use of music, using again the interface between comparative and culture-specific. Examination of the literature would provide a large number of approaches, but instead of following it or dealing with its history, let me suggest two views or models, labeling them for convenience the "pyramid" and the "coin." All of this involves more the comparison of theoretical constructs than the establishment of verifiable fact. Borrowing from Burling (1964), we admit that it is more "hocus-pocus" than "God's truth."

The pyramid model has layers: a base, a tip, and something in between. The base is comprised of the overt uses of music, the activities that music accompanies, the many things that informants will tell you are associated with music, what they tell you music does, what they use music to do, or the things one sees music doing on the surface. In any one society there are literally hundreds of these: entertainment, accompaniment of ritual, dance, concerts, military marching, and so on. In the middle there is increased abstraction of these uses. Here perhaps one might place Merriam's ten functions. Eventually, near the top, there is a statement of single, overriding, major function for any one society. One might here include statements such as McAllester's to the effect that in Navaho culture "many of the usual functions of music . . . are subordinated to an all-important function of supernatural control" (1954:88), or Merriam's, that among the Flathead Indians music functions "as a means for expressing the fact that they remain Flathead no matter what changes in their ways of life have occurred" (1967a: 158). At the top of the pyramid there is a single, overriding function of music for all humanity under which all others are subsumed. The top and the bottom are ideals. We may look for a way to articulate with extreme precision *the* unique function of music, but it is probably beyond us; and we will never get *all* uses of music onto one list.

The second model takes into account the differences between "emic" and "etic," perhaps more aptly called the people's and the anthropologist's analyses, and subsumed under my slogan of "two sides of a coin." The contrast and possible conflict between these two views, impinging on all ethnomusicological problems related to field research, must be faced here as well. Merriam (1964:209–10) speaks to it, appearing to believe that an accounting of the uses of music strikes more closely to the culture's own expression of itself. "Music may be used in a given society in a certain way, and this may be expressed directly as a part of folk evaluation. The function, however, may be something quite different as assessed through analytical evaluations stemming from the folk evaluation." The extremes of these stances seem out of reach. Ethnomusicologists, claiming to be empirical scholars, always use the culture's own analysis or evaluation at least to a degree. Nor can they eliminate their own cultural background completely.

Which side of the coin is up? One is tempted to associate the uses-functions dichotomy with the emic-etic distinction, but correlations end up being unclear. In certain respects Merriam's view lends itself to extrapolation of uses as emic, functions as etic. But this contradicts some of the other implications of the emic-etic contrast. "Etic" is the down-to-earth, the detailed description of specific events observed; "emic" is the generalization and structuring of the "etic." Thus, in one sense, phonetics involves actual sounds made by people speaking; phonemics structures them in abstract units that indicate functions used, identified, but not always easily stated by the speakers. On the other hand, it is phonemic distinctions that native speakers use to teach foreigners their language, create alphabets, keep linguistic categories separate, while phonetics is a highly complex characterization of sounds and their physical bases, and "native speakers" don't really know what to do with this kind of knowledge.

Emics and etics are related to the insider-outsider continuum, but the categories are not congruent and the partial abandonment of emic-etic in anthropology has to do with this problem. In field research it turns out that informants are quite capable of making "etic" statements, that is, of describing their own culture in "objective" ways that do not give the culture's primary evaluations. Thus, if the theory (i.e. emics) of Persian classical music is that an improvisor does not repeat himself, Persian musicians are nevertheless quite aware of the fact that repetition occurs. The "emic" statement may be an expression of the ideal, and the real is presented by the culture itself in subordinate, "etic" statements.

Despite the weaknesses of emic-etic analysis, it seems useful to present a model along these lines, but in order to avoid confusion, it seems advisable to speak simply of the culture's and the analyst's statements. If I may subject you, dear reader, once more to a brief, very compressed comparative exercise intended to show approaches rather than definitive facts and interpretations, let me try the coin and the pyramid: first the coin, applied to urban Western society, as viewed through the eyes of the academic profession. For lack of readily available informants, I must again act the part of informant as well as the outside analyst. These are some of the *kinds* of statements subsumed under each of the categories.

Analyst's statement of uses: Music is associated with a plethora of activities. Mostly it is used for listening, with the audience passive and the degree to which it pays attention varying greatly. Rituals of all sorts are accompanied by music, which is also used as background sound for many types of activity. Here we might present a list of all the activities that involve music, from concert, church, parade, football game, to obligatory background (in the case of teenagers, foreground at least in terms of volume) at parties, in supermarkets, on elevators, for traveling in cars.

Analyst's statement of functions: From the items on Merriam's list, entertainment seems most prominent. Emotional expression and group or subgroup integration are also factors.

Culture's statement of uses: Music must be available for listening most of the time. It is something one must hear daily. Almost no activity can properly be pursued without the presence of music. It is an indispensable flavoring that makes other activities or inactivity tolerable.

Culture's statement of functions: Music does something to a person, something not done by anything else; nothing can be substituted for it. As McAllester (1971:380) suggests, music transforms experience, a major function of Western music. We do not consider music to have a single main function except for being music, but we feel we cannot live without it. To my culture group, indeed, "music hath charms."

These simple statements are, I believe, supported by the more learned literature of the sociology of Western music, and they may be at least in some measure acceptable to my fellow informants, but I repeat that the purpose is not to be definitive about Western musical culture but to illustrate the model. Whether it works, is explanatory, is a question left to the reader. Clearly the culture's statements approach articulation of the ideal, so here, emic perhaps represents ideal while etic is real. For contrast, we attempt to make similar sorts of statements about the Flathead Indians, extracting them from Merriam's *Ethnomusicology of the Flathead Indians* (1967a).

Analyst's statement of uses: Merriam notes repeatedly the tendency to regard music as something concrete, not abstract. In a large section on "the uses of music" (pp. 55–122) he describes a large number of activities with which music is associated. Confronted with this amount of ethnographic data, it is difficult to escape the conclusion that the uses of music in Flathead culture are mainly to accompany other activities, perhaps in order to validate them as done in a properly Flathead fashion. The fact that the various uses of music correlate roughly with stylistic subdivisions of the repertory supports this interpretation. Music is used to accompany activities (pp. 316–22).

Analyst's statement of functions: We cite Merriam's view that the function of Flathead music in recent times, dominated by change largely brought about through the coming of Western culture and of white people to the environment, is to contribute importantly to the continuity and stability of culture and further the integration of society. This statement refers, of course, to traditional Flathead culture in earlier times. A clue is given by Merriam's extended discussion of "man and the supernatural world" (pp. 2–19): "For the Flathead, the most important single fact about music and its relationship to the total world is its origin in the supernatural sphere" (p. 3), suggesting that music had the same function vis-à-vis different worlds in recent and earlier times.

Music supports tribal integrity when many peoples, whites and other Indian tribes, because of the onset of modernization and Westernization, come into a position of influencing the Flathead. In earlier times music established the relationship between Flathead and other forces such as the supernatural, also supporting tribal identity but doing so by mediating between the tribe and the cosmos. The analogy may be far-fetched, but if it is heuristically valuable, it shows the usefulness of separating the analyst's interpretation from that of the culture.

Culture's statement of uses: According to Merriam (p. 55), the Flathead acknowledge approximately forty kinds of songs, labeled by use. The culture's statement of uses has to be almost identical to that of the analyst, something not surprising in this case, given Merriam's assertion that uses may be expressed directly through folk evaluation, while this may not be so for function (1964:209–10). We may wish to add from Merriam's ethnography the observation that the most important use is in connection with power obtained from the guardian spirits (1967a:55).

Culture's statement of function: It is difficult to find such a statement in Merriam's study, but we should consider his suggestion of "why people make music." Indeed, in eliciting a statement about main or single functions of music from informants not accustomed to discussing such matters in the abstract, one would be tempted to direct questions to this point. The informant who gave the clearest answer, according to Merriam (pp. 27–28), said that "people sang because they were poor and the songs helped them." Music is seen as something that functions as an aid, particularly in times of crisis, a statement quite far from the analyst's interpretation of music as contributing to tribal identity and integration. Perhaps this was felt to be the help most needed. The Flathead idea of music as "help" associates it with other activities that can be carried out properly only with music. In Herzog's terms, Flathead music appears more "functional" than Western music. In contrast, the urban American informant would perhaps respond to the same question by saying that he likes music, or that it itself does something ("turns me on" or "relaxes me"), while the concept of helping would probably be subordinate.

THE PYRAMID

In contrast to the coin model, the pyramid avoids confronting the difference between the analyst's and the culture's interpretations. The analyst's interpretation, which in the coin model is justified as a device for comparative study, is replaced in the pyramid by the overarching view that music is an expression or reflection or direct result of a central cultural core. Uses and functions are presented not as contrasting halves of a dichotomy but, rather, as the opposite ends of a continuum that moves from the absolutely down-to-earth and factual to the most vitally interpretive and thus perhaps unprovable. Let me continue the exercise, using data from the city of Teheran.

We must take a large number of musical styles, types, and genres into account: the most traditional Iranian, including some folk music of rural origin as well as the classical music originating in the courts, as well as religious and ceremonial material, and popular music distributed mainly through mass media, using styles that mix traditional, Western, and other non-Iranian elements in various ways. This list is a combination of Iranian and Western taxonomies of the music, historical categories, geographical venues, from a large and complex community. We ought to add to the complexity by including Western music also heard in Teheran, but for the purposes of this exercise we deal only with categories accepted by Teheranis as Iranian music. The "present" is ca. 1970.

Overt uses: Most music is used for listening and entertainment. There are relatively few concerts but many musical occasions in night clubs and music halls whose patrons listen and watch but rarely, as a matter of fact, dance. Radio listening is common, more among adults and less among children than is the case in the United States. Records are readily available, and some listening takes place in lightly ritualized formats: parties, concerts, music halls each patronized by members of one occupation group. The records have a use beyond simple entertainment, contributing to solidarity of special groups and allegiance to a particular view of Iranian culture. Beyond this there is religious chanting, which is not regarded as belonging properly to the sphere of music. Music is used to accompany traditional gymnastic exercises, dance performances as well as social dancing, military activity, public ceremonial events such as parades of labor guilds, and as background for poetry readings. Needless to say, it is impossible to list all, but they correspond moderately well to those of Western urban culture and not well to those of the Flathead. In Herzog's terms, Iranian music would have to be regarded as not highly functional. Most activities can be carried out without music and people do not seem to feel that music must be heard daily, frequently, constantly, as do many in the United States. That one could even consider the "outlawing of music" in 1979 is a case in point.

Abstracted uses: If we apply Merriam's list of ten general functions, we find all of them relevant to Teheran, but would have to emphasize particularly those of entertainment, symbolic representation (both by presence and absence of music), as well as contributions to religious ritual, continuity and stability of culture, and integration of society. But since many kinds of music are involved, it is *diversity* in religious observance, *change* as well as continuity of culture, and integration of a number of *subcultures* that are the first-line functions of music. Different repertories within the culture can be interpreted as having specific functions. The religious music, chanting the Koran, calls to prayer, are in this case not ways of communicating with God but, rather, devices to remind humans of their religious duty. The music accompanying "lascivious" dancing in traditional night clubs has as its use the facilitation of dance. But beyond that, it functions as a force mediating between the human observer and the forbidden; it throws a cloak of formality over an otherwise unacceptable situation, a function of music noted as well for African cultures by Rhodes (1962) and for American folk culture by Greenway (1953) and others. The modernized and partially Westernized popular music had a function of symbolizing the process of Westernization; years later, when Westernization came under a special sort of fire, it was this kind of music that was first and foremost singled out for proscription.

Let me digress and point to a contrasting situation in South America. Anthony Seeger provides a parallel illustration of abstracted musical uses or overt functions among the Suya of Brazil (1979). Examining two genres of song very different in style and use, he concludes that the function of *akia* involves "the intention of the singer to be heard as an individual by certain female relatives," while the *ngere* functions as a way "of expressing the existence and unity of name-based ceremonial groups . . ." (1979:391). But the overt use of the music is ritualistic, and these functions do not emerge until uses are analyzed and interpreted. From a further analysis of this level of functionality there might emerge a single, more culture-specific function of music. Seeger gives more than a hint: musical events actually create aspects of the social organization, in this case, dualism (p. 392). If generalized, this would be a far cry from Teheran, where one can hardly claim that music has a dominant effect over other aspects of culture. Perhaps this has to do with the value of music, low in Teheran and high, Seeger maintains, among the Suya.

Top of the pyramid: Time to show my colors. The function of music in human society, what music ultimately does, is to control humanity's relationship to the supernatural, mediating between people and other beings, and to support the integrity of individual social groups. It does this by expressing the relevant central values of culture in abstracted form. If we accept this, we find a kind of interdependence between the highest two layers of the pyramid model that does not exist among the other layers. In each culture music will function to express a particular set of values in a particular way.

If we continue to analyze a musical culture along these lines, the first problem is, of course, to identify the central cultural values. We can hardly speak to this problem here in detail, but a good deal of ethnomusicological and anthropological literature provides specific guidance. Returning to Merriam's description of the Flathead, one may well interpret one of their main values in twentieth-century American society to be the survival of Flathead society, and his statement of the major function of music, which (restated) is to express the fact that they are and always will be Flathead regardless of changes in their lives, could clearly be an expression of the value concept as I am using it. Indeed, the music sound expresses the value in abstract form: there is no way in which one could, even for a second, confuse Flathead music with Western music. Are there other domains of Flathead culture about which one could say as much?

Music can abstract and distill the relatively unclear and obscure character of culture. Lomax characterizes cultural values in terms of the ways in which people interrelate. The value of equality among the Pygmies of Zaire, of hierarchy in the empires of Asia, have musical analogues. The kinds of relationship between political leadership and the governed population, extending from informal chieftainship through one and then several levels of control inside and outside the community, all appear to be expressed in relationships between leader and chorus in group singing (1968: 155–59). There is only momentary musical leadership in Pygmy song, while the imperial and autocratic cultures (according to Lomax) of South and West Asia stress solo singing. But then, some political leadership must always be present even among the Pygmies, whereas the people in the Ottoman empire did occasionally have something to say even to their distant emperor. Thus one might suggest that the antiphonal performance of music in the folk religion of India is closer to the Indian soul, or that the great development of solo music results from the Indian proclivity for contemplation of the self. Extending Lomax's viewpoint, however, the point would have to be made that in the music the *ideal* values of political structure are expressed almost constantly, and it is in this sense that the music abstracts and distills.

The ability of music to abstract values helps us in returning to Teheran, where we ask how the music of its society functions to mediate between humans and the supernatural, and to help integrate society. As in the vast majority of religious systems, music in Islam is a ceremonial device, a way of formalizing a religious statement. We must deal with the fact that this "music" is not classed as music, which has low esteem in the society. Much has been published about the Muslim attitude toward music, so let me add yet another hypothesis. Islam is characterized by its insistence that humans may pray, speak directly, to God, without mediation. Understanding the importance of music as a mediator in other religious systems, adherents of Islam give it a role of low importance because, for them, this kind of mediation is not needed. A special device for addressing the supernatural—a priest or a music—is not really necessary. It is nevertheless there, but technically not recognized as music.

The role of music in integrating as complex a society as that of Teheran is evident in a number of ways. On the one hand, it served in the 1960s as a unifying device for the nation, bringing together its diverse elements and setting it off from its Arabic and Turkish neighbors. Society did this by emphasizing a classical system that is intended to be perfect, to which nothing need or may be added, a symbol of the perfect society being claimed by the elite of Teheran. At the same time various rural traditions were brought together in the mass media, and the whole thing underlaid by elements of Western music that were symbolic rather than musically functional. But since society was comprised of many rather distinct groups, there flourished a number of interrelated but separate musical systems, some of them distinguished by their degree of Westernization. Many social groups identified themselves with a particular music. But for the nation at large I suggest that the classical tradition in particular expresses some specific shared social values.

The main difficulty of the top of the pyramid turns out again to be the conflict between observer and observed. I think I see what it is that music does for Teheran society, but musicians as well as others in Iran do not find much to which they can respond in direct questioning. They are, for instance, more concerned with liking or disliking music and its various subtypes. They sometimes exhibit a certain guilty tendency to defend their liking of music, and as individuals or as members of particular groups of the population—Sufis, the Westernized elite, members of minorities such as Armenians and Jews—they use their identification with music as a way of underscoring individualism or specialness. When asked what it is that music does, Iranians would surely not say directly that it reflects their social and cultural values, although it is said by educated informants that the classical music is particularly Persian, tied to the culture and the soil, while the popular music shows how Iranians can and do interact with other cultures and take from them what they need to become modern. If music functions for the people of Teheran, as I believe it does for all societies, as a force for religion and social integration, it certainly does so in a peculiar and unique way. The very top of the pyramid is an abstraction, and the concrete data below it again put more weight on cultural diversity than on universals. To Iranians, the statement "Music hath charms" would mean something quite different from what it means to Americans or Europeans. But in the end, even they might agree with its implications.

Chapter 12

In the Beginning

MYTHOLOGY IS WRONG

"Mythology is wrong," writes Curt Sachs, startling the reader in the first sentence of a history of music. "Music is not the merciful gift of benevolent gods or heroes. . . . And wrong, so far, are all the many theories presented on a more or less scientific basis. . . . Were they true, some of the most primitive survivors of early mankind would have preserved a warbling style of song, or love songs, or signal-like melodies, or rhythmical teamwork with rhythmical work songs. Which they hardly have" (Sachs 1948:1). And so, in a brief paragraph, the venerable Sachs wipes out a large body of literature of a mainly speculative sort and affirms the specific responsibility of the ethnomusicologist, because of his knowledge of the world's extant musics, for establishing how music came about and the form it first took among humans.

Sachs was, of course, not the first. Two of the earliest books dealing generally with the musics of tribal societies had the word "Anfänge" (beginnings) in their titles, and even they deal mainly not with the origin itself but, rather, with what the authors presume to be the earliest stages of music. The question of actual origins was more typically the subject of other kinds of authors, earlier, a group less acquainted with the musics of the world. Towering figures in their fields, they included Herbert Spencer the pioneering social scientist, Richard Wagner the composer, and the economist Carl Buecher. Sachs clearly did not take their theories seriously, applauding instead those who would study the world's simplest contemporary musical cultures in order to ascertain the earliest stage of music.

It is somehow anomalous to find that ethnomusicologists often present themselves as students of the present and yet are almost automatically the recipients of questions about the most distant past. They develop special techniques for observing change as it occurs, for describing musical systems and cultures that they can experience directly, and they have sometimes identified themselves as the synchronic counterparts to the diachronic historians. But if cocktail parties begin with questions about the musicality of Indians and Japanese, they inevitably turn to ultimate origins. In the view of the general public, ethnomusicologists are also the prehistorians of music.

The literature on the so-called origins of music tends often to confuse issues that are actually separable, failing to distinguish the point of origin and what follows immediately, or music from nonmusic. The question of defining music is particularly, again, at issue. Hockett (as cited in Anttila 1972: 26) gives a group of characteristics of animal communication, pointing out that only certain ones of them are specific to human speech. While it has long been recognized that animals (including anthropoids) communicate, sometimes with the use of sound, it is nevertheless possible to separate human speech from the rest and to come to a definition that applies to all human languages. Universal features emanating from this definition are used in the literature on the origin of language (Stam 1976, Anttila 1972:26–28, P. Lieberman 1975). Language has an underlying "deep structure" that is related to the genetically established ability of all humans to learn it.

Defining the universals of music is harder than establishing those of language. But assuming that they can agree on what constitutes music, if not adequately articulate a definition, musicologists may be a bit better off than linguists when it comes to finding a bridge between origins and the present. All languages are more or less equally complex, and also about equally removed from the origins of language, a subject linguists tend now to approach by reference to psychology, primatology, paleontology, physiology, all involving study of the brain, rather than by attempting historical reconstruction. All musics also have a certain minimum degree of complexity, but there are differences, and we can perhaps use those among contemporary and recent musics to help us in reconstruction.

In doing so, we should try to distinguish three questions: (1) Why did music originate? (2) What was the actual process by which music was first put into existence? (3) What was the nature of the original or first or earliest musical products? The issue of origins shows the ethnomusicologist at his most speculative, and many have lost interest in the question for precisely that reason. They feel that the matter is hopeless and are inclined to throw in the towel. Why not turn our energy to more easily soluble problems? I would argue, if there is any justification for dealing with the matter of origins at all, that it resides in the relative importance of understanding history. Whether it is worth trying to find out something about the likely origins of music depends on the degree to which one regards historical knowledge, even of the most tenuous sort, as worth having.

According to Barnett, in his anthropological classic on innovation, "when innovation takes place, there is an intimate linkage or fusion of two or more elements that have not been previously joined in just this fashion" (1953:

181). Humans, he implies, cannot create culture from scratch; they use building blocks already present, combining and recombining them. If we imagine a point at which music was something new, we would do well to view it as a unique fusion of elements that were already present in human culture. Most origin theories of music argue along these lines. Music, the classic writers on the subject assert, grew out of materials already present: animal cries, speech, rhythmic activity. By the same token, if we are to imagine that music came into existence by becoming a system of organized sound, it must have done so with the use of sounds already known and recognized by humans.

Following along these lines, we may imagine that there was probably at some point in human or prehuman history a kind of communication that embodied certain characteristics of what we now regard as music. But in the view of the society that used it, it was not music, and probably it would not normally be regarded as such today. Perhaps it did not sound like what we think is music, not sharing the traits that the musics of today's vastly divergent world nevertheless share. Possibly it was also not distinguished from something else that was or became language. At any rate, somehow music was brought into existence.

Actually, many of the world's societies today have some thought of how or why music came about. The genesis myth of the Blackfoot gives a "why," though not a "how"; music was given to humans by the culture hero in order to help them with their problems (see e.g. Grinnell 1920). Or again, according to one South American Indian people, music was given by supernatural beings in order to establish an orderly society (Smith 1971). Mythology, even that of Indians, may be wrong, and the study of culture history via archeology does not go back far enough to tell us why music was invented. The only thing that may give us a clue is the study of musical universals, indicating whether there is anything that all humans do with their music, something so ubiquitous among the far-flung peoples that it makes sense for us to believe that they have always done so. The literature of ethnomusicology provides several statements of this sort.

There are theories relating the origins of music to vocal communication, deriving it from various special forms of speech. Among the more generally credible hypotheses is that of Carl Stumpf, to the effect that humans somehow developed music in order to increase the efficiency of vocal communication over long distances. Stumpf recognized the tendency for sustained pitches to carry farther than the ordinary speaking voice (1911; Nadel 1930:537), and perhaps indeed the need on the part of humans to call to each other over long distances led to the occasional use of a kind of vocal sound that has in common with music the sustained pitch. Sustained pitches, held long enough so that they can be reproduced rather precisely by the hearer and even give rise to performances in unison, are a major characteristic of practically all known musics. But Stumpf's guess tells us why humans developed a kind of communication that may sound like music without showing how it came to be music. To provide a credible bridge, something about the function of music as it now exists would have to be included. Following Stumpf's theory, we would have to believe that vocal long-distance communication led to such paramusical phenomena as drum and horn signaling of tone languages, a practice widespread in Africa and elsewhere but nowhere claimed to be primordial or to precede music. The fact that vocal music is so universally associated with words, and that everywhere humans sing what they also might speak, suggests that speech and song were at one time even more closely related than today.

This hypothesis is probably more attractive than the one suggested by Carl Buecher (1902; see esp. p. 364), that humans discovered the efficiency of rhythmic labor and developed music in order to facilitate it. As it happens, rhythmic work by groups to the sound of work songs or percussive accompaniment is actually not widespread. But the close association of dance with music everywhere makes the idea of rhythm and physical movement as generative forces of music tentatively credible.

Confining ourselves to the "why" and leaving out entirely the "how," we are drawn to a suggestion of Nadel's. Noting the close association in all cultures between music and religion, as well as the tendency to render the most serious and formal aspects of rituals musically, he hypothesizes the beginnings of music as a result of a need for establishing a particular way of communicating with the supernatural, a way sharing certain major characteristics of speech, the ordinary human communication, and yet readily distinct from it (1930:538–44). How it was that someone hit upon vocal music as a way to satisfy this need is a question we can hardly touch. Presumably something must have already been available from which music could be built—conceivably the mating calls thought by Darwin to be the first music, the use of calls for long-distance communication, the recognition that heightened or emotional speech sounded different from ordinary talk. This speculation leads to the belief that the ability to learn singing may not have been far removed. The specific and reasonably sharp distinction between speaking and singing must at some point have occurred, and, following Nadel's suggestion, it may have been made in order to distinguish human and supernatural ways of communicating.

Of course we will never know. But it is intriguing to note the many instances in mythology that ascribe the origin of music to the need for communicating with or within the supernatural. Leanne Hinton reports (1967–68) for Havasupai mythology that before there were humans, the supernatural beings communicated by singing. For the Blackfoot, a main supernatural presence is singing on the part of the nonhuman guardian spirit who appears in visions. In myths of various cultures (Laade 1975) music is the language of the supernatural, but the spirits give music to humans as a way of approaching the unearthly. Such myths serve to explain the world of the society that tells them, but they may recapitulate symbolically what humans actually did and why they invented music. Sachs notwithstanding, mythology may not be all wrong.

THE MOMENT OF INVENTION

These may be some reasonably credible suggestions of why music came into existence. But if we can suggest reasons for the invention of music and its conceptualization as something distinctive, we certainly have hardly any idea as to the process by which it was created. We have the same problem dealing with invention at large: we are at a loss to describe process. Confronted with the creation of something new, a technology, a work of art, we can often see why it came about, see needs and contexts that made it possible or necessary. We can also identify its early stages, describe a primitive steam engine, the sketches of a painting, or the notebooks of Beethoven. But how one moves from conditions that make creation possible to the stage at which the product exists in preliminary, primitive form is perhaps the most difficult thing on which to put one's finger.

We can use the traditional method of looking at change through a series of successive, static frames. If we don't know how music changes, we can perhaps describe the waystations of change. For example, we can ascertain that at one moment a folk song exists in form A; in the next frame an interval of the scale has been filled in at the beginning of the song, resulting in form B; next the cadence of the song also adds a new filler tone for form C. At that point change has taken place, and we see something about its working. Another artificial illustration: a five-stanza song consists of five lines, ABCDE. In the next stage its first and last stanzas are sung with lines CDE only; in the third all five stanzas except the third use the abbreviated form CDE; and finally only CDE is sung. One might suggest that between stages 2 and 3, the change from one form to the other has been made. Stage 2 is predominantly ABCDE; stage 3, predominantly CDE with the ABCDE clearly an exception.

Let us now imagine such frames in the prehistory of music, referring to an origin theory suggesting that humans at one time had a kind of communication which shared elements of language and music. Sounds were made, but the distinctive features of vowels and consonants, now regarded as a hallmark of language, were not used (Nettl 1956b:136). Pitch, length, and stress were present, but the technique of sustaining pitch, now universally essential to the concept of music, appeared only coincidentally. We can postulate a point at which one group of sounds appeared in two variants, one in which two contrastive vowels were heard, remembered, and repeated, and another in which two contrastive pitches were similarly held, imagining that this kind of event was in fact (no doubt repeated and varied many, many times) the point of origin of music. But I dare go no further than to make this speculative suggestion.

Most of the literature concerned with the origins problem comes from relatively early times in the history of ethnomusicology. But in the 1970s the anthropological study of universals, some of it concerned with the origins of language (see e.g. Stam 1976, P. Lieberman 1975), as well as research in the psychology of music and other forms of communication on an intercultural basis (e.g. Osgood and others 1975), brought it back. Blacking (1973:55, 58) speaks to the issue, wishing to avoid what he calls evolutionist approaches, which reconstruct historical sequences. "The origins of music that concern me are those which are to be found in the psychology and in the cultural and social environment of its creators, in the assembly of processes that generate the pattern of sound" (1973:58). What is proposed, it seems, is one of two processes. In a certain sense each separate act of musical creation is a kind of origination, and one can find out things of general validity about the origin of music as expressed in each such act, extrapolating from these findings some general principles that help to illuminate the earlier, ultimate origins. Blacking may also be suggesting that human behavior is sufficiently unified and historically stable that psychological insights themselves can tell us about early man.

In either case Blacking seems to suggest substituting one kind of speculation for another which he criticizes (1973:56). What justly seems to bother him most about the older theories of the origin of music is statements made in a vacuum about the reactions of early humans to their environment, reactions that are presumed to have led to the development of music. He also decries the tendency to try to reconstruct stages in a "world history of music" (1973:55). Whether one agrees with Blacking or tries despite all problems to gain insight from extrapolation, it must be clear that what one is doing is indeed speculating. It is supremely dangerous to transform these speculations, willy-nilly, into established fact. Beyond this, however, I am forced to conclude that the old origin theories probably tell us as much about the origin of music as do the more recent, psychologically oriented approaches.

There is no doubt, as Blacking says, that "each style has its own history, and its present state represents only one stage in its own development" (1973:56). But it is hard to believe that music was invented, if you will, many, many times, each "style" going back in an unbroken line to an act of invention, in a vast number of separate processes. It seems to me to make more sense to believe that music—definitional caveats aside—was invented, originated, created once or a few times, and that all present musical styles ultimately, each through its own separate stages, derived from one of these points of origin. Parenthetically, the older origin theories are not completely unilineal. Although he does not go as far as Blacking, and also does not claim to provide an origin theory per se, Sachs proposes two ways that music has come about, from speech and from emotion, calling the resulting styles logogenic and pathogenic (1943:41) and later referring to tumbling strains and one-step melodies as two strands of the oldest music (1962:49–59).

There need be no conflict. Once invented, music must have quickly or gradually become differentiated, each group of people developing it in order to satisfy their social, psychological, aesthetic needs, in accordance with their technology, and as a result of contact with other human groups. Each music has its own history, and in the sense that all go back to, and are in time equally removed from, the point of music's origin, all have a history equally long. They took different courses, some changing more quickly than others. Blacking is, of course, right; we cannot simply class musics in accordance with certain stages through which all must pass. Yet history is always somewhat speculative; one can establish facts, but assessment of their relationships and their significance is always in part a matter of interpretation. The study of the origins of music is a legitimate part of ethnomusicological inquiry.

THE FIRST MUSIC?

The issue is the documentation of age in music. If all music had been written down, then the oldest source would obviously be the oldest piece. Recent research has uncovered what seems to be the oldest extant musical notation, a Babylonian (more specifically Hurrian) clay tablet from circa 1400 B.C. (see e.g. Stauder 1967, Wulstan 1971) that gives in cuneiform writing the notation and the text of a love song as well as several lines indicating how the music is to be read. An attempt to realize a modern notational transcription into sound, made by Richard Crocker in 1975 and broadcast over national television, indicated that it was a rather extended, complex song. While this may indeed be the oldest known piece, it is almost surely not the oldest kind of music extant. Oral tradition, with all of its vagaries, has probably preserved older styles, though perhaps not older songs. Ethnomusicologists also deny that the Hurrian song represents the oldest music on the basis of the assumption that the earliest music must have been simple, and with the belief that some of those things that are ubiquitous in the world's music today were present as characteristics of the oldest music. While there is much criticism of such hypotheses as immutable laws, there is considerable agreement, if not on what the first music was like, then upon which extant music is closest to that archaic stage.

A number of scholars (e.g. Wiora 1956, 1965b; Stumpf 1911; Sachs 1943, 1961) have concerned themselves in various ways with identifying the world's earliest music, but collectively agree that there is an extractable oldest stratum present in the music of the twentieth century. This stratum, thought to precede even the ubiquitous and presumably archaic pentatonic system (see Tran Van Khê 1977), has the following characteristics: (1) It is a style of music that comprises most of the repertory of certain technologically simple and relatively isolated tribal societies, but it is also found as a minority repertory in the music of many if not most other societies. (2) Where it comprises a minority of a repertory, it is characteristically associated with particular social contexts, including the songs of children, of games (including those of adults), of old and often abandoned rituals still present in vestige; it may also include songs told in stories. (3) The songs of this music are short, usually consisting of one or two phrases which are repeated many times with or without variation. (4) Its scales are comprised of two to four tones usually separated by major seconds and minor thirds. (5) It is prevailingly or exclusively vocal.

The tribal cultures whose repertories are largely or entirely in this simplest style include, for example, the Vedda of Sri Lanka, whose music was described by the psychologist Wertheimer (1909/10), peoples of Micronesia (Herzog 1936c), and certain North and South American Indian peoples including the Yahi, the people of Ishi. As mentioned, many other cultures also have *some* songs in this style, and it is further to be noted that some of the characteristics of these simplest musics are among the features of music acquired earliest in children. One might expect this latter fact to be corroborative evidence for a prehistory of world music, but musical development in infancy is scarcely understood, and the fact that there are data only for children in Western culture weakens this line of argument.

Speculative reconstruction gives the following, perhaps credible, picture. A once universal, simple musical style was expanded in most of the world's societies, three-tone scales extended or filled in, brief songs replaced by others with four or more musical lines, repetition replaced by systematic variation. In most societies some of the archaic songs continued to be sung, and new songs in their mold were composed, but they were pushed into a remote corner of the repertory for noncentral uses. Interestingly, we find a parallel phenomenon among instruments. The world's simplest—e.g. rattles, the bull-roarer, flutes without finger holes—were central in the ritual life of certain tribal societies; in others, where the instrumentarium grew and developed, these simple instruments remained in existence but were relegated to less significant areas of life, becoming toys, or accompanied rituals whose function came to be merely antiquarian.

It seems a reasonable hypothesis. But aside from the lack of concrete evidence, it can be criticized on a number of bases. For example, those societies whose music is entirely in this archaic style so far as scales and forms are concerned seem otherwise to have little in common musically. The tritonic songs of Polynesia, with their sharply marked rhythms repeating the central tone, are rhythmically very different from the more evenly sung songs of the Vedda. Singing styles may differ greatly. We find only scalar content, general structure, and vocal monophony as common features. And so, more than describing the earliest human music, the hypothesis may tell us something important about ethnomusicology. A field that grew out of nineteenth-century Western classical music practices, it started out sophisticated in melodic and formal considerations, relatively naive in theoretical thought about rhythm, which has no basic unit analogous to the "tone." But if such a unit were found, it might well point to a different group of repertories as the world's simplest musics. While musicologists who engage in studies of comparative complexity at least come close to agreeing that the number of tones in a scale and the number of units in a musical form have something to do with relative simplicity and complexity of scales and structures, they have no hypothesis for a similar calibration of the rhythmic component. They do not know whether a strong, repetitive metric structure is to be regarded as primitive or as the crowning achievement of a long evolution, whether they should count note values and regard the apparent lack of organization of a structure that has many sixteenths, eighths, fourths, dots, and fermatas as simple or, instead, accord simplicity to an endless repetition of quarter notes. Consideration of singing style would yield similar dilemmas.

These questions seem not to have been addressed in the literature. Thus hypotheses about the earliest human music can be made only on the basis of a portion of the evidence available. If we accept the possibility that those cultures—Vedda, Yahi, Oceanians—that participate in the "simplest styles" and have little else have somehow kept a musical style that is close to the earliest music of humans, we ought also to guess at reasons for this curious state of affairs. These cultures are not greatly different from others; they are not "primitive" except in the technical sense of nonliteracy, something shared with other peoples who have much more complex music. Their languages are as complex structurally as the average, and so also are their social and religious systems. Can it really be that they got stuck in an early stage of musical development and were unable to go beyond it?

Ability can hardly be an issue. A possible explanation is the decision, for reasons unknown, to refrain from making changes in music, an extreme kind of musical conservatism. Again, it is difficult to believe in the face of greater change in other domains of culture over long or short periods of time. One would expect the forces that impel a culture to change its political, religious, and social system also to affect music. Yet, because of the close association of music with religion and its tendency to be used as an emblem of social and cultural identity and integrity, we must at least admit the possibility that some peoples singled out music for this special kind of conservative treatment.

But perhaps a more credible hypothesis involves the ways in which musical systems, once created, tend to expand. We can discuss the issue only by presenting a very simple model. If most systems developed from short, repeated forms with two or three tones by expanding outwardly, this would mean that tetrachords would gradually be expanded to pentachords, or be replicated to make a diatonic scale; that a single line of music simply repeated would gradually become two, three, eventually four contrasted lines; or that the repetition would evolve into systematic variation, including transposition. It would mean that simultaneous singing of a tune by two persons would gradually change to a systematic heterophony, or to parallel singing at various intervals, or to canonic imitation, as chance errors became institutionalized and accepted. Gradually, forms with vast numbers of components and interrelationships would have developed, ragas and operas.

In the case of a few cultures, however, there may have been inward expansion. Rather than adding tones outside the original scale, the intervals may have been filled in. Instead of adding lines to make longer forms, the internal interrelationships within a line were exhausted. Thus, for example, many songs of the Yahi are comprised of two half-lines, one a variation of the other, but there are many kinds of relationship between the two, including plain variation of a tone here and there, inversion, expansion, contraction, melodic sequence, and more.

The origin of music is obscure, and many ethnomusicologists have read it out of the purview of their field. But since the only even remotely reliable guide to the origins of music is the plethora of contemporary and recent musics known to us, the issue is too important to be left exclusively to others.

Chapter 13

The Continuity of Change

WHAT HAPPENED AND WHAT HAPPENS

A cliché about musical scholarship once divided scholars into historical musicologists, for whom music changes, and ethnomusicologists, whose emphasis is on what remains constant. The historians, it was thought, compare musical cultures at various points in their history, trace origins and antecedents and temporal relationships among repertories, pieces, composers, schools of musicians. Ethnomusicologists, seeing music as something which does not change, or in which change is an incidental, disturbing, exceptional, polluting factor, make synchronic comparisons. All this despite the widespread belief in ethnomusicology as a field that holds on to disappearing traditions and may in the end tell us the origins of music. A look at the ethnomusicological literature shows that nothing is really further from the truth. Well, almost nothing. There are surely ethnomusicologists who concentrate on procedures of musical analysis, or those who relate musical structure to social structure, musical styles to culture type, without explicit consideration of change. At one time there were even those who believed in almost absolute stability of the musical cultures of non-Western societies, stability only occasionally disturbed by devastating and sweeping changes brought about by conquests by stronger societies, particularly those of European origin.

A very great deal of ethnomusicological literature is concerned somehow with the fact that things do happen and that, in one way or another, happening implies change. If indeed one can distinguish, in their attitude toward change, between the historical musicologist and the ethnomusicologist, it may be this: historical musicologists wish to know what actually happened; ethnomusicologists, what (typically or normally) "happens." Although divided by a set of conceptual and methodological issues (see Dahlhaus 1977), historians in essence discover particular events and their relationships. There is among ethnomusicologists also a standard historical tradition, particularly in the study of Asian high cultures with written records going back for centuries (e.g. Harich-Schneider 1973, Malm 1959). Following trends in the field of general history and making use of a combination of oral transmission and documentation, this standard traditional approach to history has also become a major factor in research in African music (see e.g. Wachsmann 1971a). But for the most part, the approaches of ethnomusicologists to history, largely because of the lack of data but also because of the nomothetic tendencies of the social sciences, concern the processes of change more than the content of change.

This kind of a statement may be seen as a major offense to the self-respect of historians of European music, certain of whom are also deeply concerned with process. No offense intended. The past views of history and the various ways of interpreting change are certainly issues in the literature of historical musicology (see e.g. Allen 1939, Dahlhaus 1977). We can throw away all disciplinary labels and admit that all of us want to learn about the past, its connection with the present and the future. It seems to me that in order for the course of human music to be understood, music scholars will have to engage in several activities, seriatim or simultaneously: (1) development of some kind of theoretical perspective regarding the nature of the search, the relative significance of various kinds of data, the relationship of a source (manuscript or conquering neighbor) to the artwork, the artist, a repertory of works, a "style," a society; (2) gathering of data and development of specific, particularistic conclusions on individual cultures, periods, etc.; (3) generalization of the conclusions to culture-wide and then universal processes; and (4) prediction. Historians and ethnomusicologists both have addressed themselves to the first, although often by implication, and with a large variety of conclusions. Those who call themselves historical musicologists have perfected approaches to the second and rather made a specialty of it, although in limited venues of activity; ethnomusicologists have also engaged in it, but not nearly as well. The third of my series seems so far to have been carried out mainly by those who call themselves ethnomusicologists and, to a smaller degree, sociologists of music dealing with Western musical cultures. The fourth, dealing with the future, has been left to the future.

A glance at Brook (1972), a book of essays on the current state of musicology, illustrates the de facto division of labor. Essays by Blume, Lesure, Lowinsky, Landon, a highly distinguished group of historians, concentrate on the specific problems of particular repertories and source types. Those of Nketia, Hood, Chase, Harrison (all in this case specifically espousing an ethnomusicological viewpoint) speak to the question of generalizing about the structure and significance of events. And yet the distinction is not a sharp line. Duckles (in Brook 1972:39) gives seven generating forces that in the eighteenth and nineteenth centuries led in one way or another to the study of music history. Along with some giving a traditionally historical impetus, as chant reform and the custodial role of collectors, librarians, and bibliographers, he also lists forces pointing toward ethnomusicology, such as "the discovery of world music" and "the discovery of national song." Coming from the same nineteenth-century roots, it seems that the two groups of scholars in the twentieth have simply jumped into the stream at different points.

There is a good deal of ethnomusicological work that laments change, tries to ignore it, to preserve what appears to have changed least or not at all. But the most sophisticated thinkers have all along been aware that ethnomusicologists must take change into account because it is always there, and that they have a special stake in the understanding of history. Indeed, if there is anything really stable in the musics of the world, it is the constant existence of change. The one thing that perhaps unites all musicological endeavor—and possibly all humanistic and social disciplines—is the need to understand this constant of humanity.

To a considerable degree, the differences between the ethnomusicologist's approach to change and that of the typical music historian result from the former's association with the social sciences. Theoretical thinking about history and change in ethnomusicology is found most frequently in the writings of those most aware of anthropological thought. The early works by figures such as Curt Sachs and E. M. von Hornbostel were mightily influenced by the German diffusionist school of anthropology (A. Schneider 1976), and later scholars critical of this school, such as Merriam (1964:307–8), continue to emphasize the need for a study of musical change in the context of anthropological thought. Some of the most important analytical statements about change in recent literature come from the pens of anthropologically oriented scholars such as Blacking (1978) and Lomax (1968).

The approaches of anthropology and historical musicology may seem worlds apart, and yet they share a major thrust. In both cases emphasis is upon change of an entire system of interconnected units and materials, in the case of one, something called "culture," the descendant of Tylor's "complex whole," and in the other, "musical style," a term denoting a "musical system," using it as a concept symbolic of all the things that go into *a* music or a musical culture.

Cultural anthropology specializes in the concept of culture as a unit, as something one can view holistically, leaving aside the differences among its domains, worrying as little as possible about irregularities. Thus, in theoretically discussing culture change, anthropologists seem to brush aside the fact that in a given society religion changes more slowly than technology, or that a particular individual was "way ahead of his time," or for that matter that different cultures in their individual components change in completely different ways. They do this not out of ignorance of the details but because of their interest in the unity of culture and in the insights one may gain from this broad view. Thus Murdock (1956) generalizes about culture change, identifying innovation, social acceptance, selective elimination, and integration as a universal sequence. He is speaking of regularities, surely aware of the procrustean bed that would have to be created were one to apply this to each instance of change within a culture. Steward, even in denying that all societies go through the same changes (1955:14) and proposing a system of "multilinear evolution" as a way of explaining culture change in a comparative context, deals only with those limited parallels of form, function, and sequence that have validity for cultures as a whole, ignoring local variation. Sahlins (1960) contrasts "general evolution," the tendency for cultural evolution to yield progressively higher levels of organization and complexity, with "specific evolution," the tendency for each culture type to adapt to its specific total environment. The variety of these examples illustrates the ways in which anthropology tends to deal with culture change as a unit.

Historians of Western music usually engage in studies dealing with the particular, but the implications often direct the reader to wider generalization about the history of musical style. Historians are clearly aware of the fact that a form type such as the sonata may change, or a practice such as that of modulation, or indeed the way in which a piece is performed. But there is the implication that each finding of this sort contributes to the understanding of change in style, by which is meant the aggregate of generally accepted ways of composing music and perhaps of performing it. In some of the most respected writings dealing broadly with musical change (e.g. Meyer 1967:104–33, "Varieties of Style Change"; Szabolcsi 1965; Bukofzer 1947), there is continual emphasis on the idea of a musical system that moves, changes, regardless of the individual diversity of its parts. Music historians normally define music by practices, not, say, by the use of specific pieces of musical content such as melodies. The fact that a melody such as "Dies Irae" or a folk song such as "Malbrough s'en va-t-en guerre" is used widely in one decade and not in the next is at best a minor point of consideration, but the fact that most works in one century are composed for a small ensemble, and in the next for large orchestra, is of greater import. Again, the fact that in one century the typical composer wrote many pieces and in the next, far fewer, is not a major consideration, but the resulting increase in complexity or diversity might well be. So, for the music historian the holistic notion of "style" as both the essence of and also the major symbol of a music (and the definition of musical change as change in style) seems to me to be related to the anthropologist's interest in culture change as a whole. In a certain sense the concept of culture (the particular way in which societies take care of their needs) is analogous to the concept of musical style (the particular way in which societies go about making music).

Ethnomusicology seems at least sometimes to make a contribution to both fields. It does not have the large body of data available to the anthropologist working with cultural histories and comprehensive ethnographies, nor the depth of the historian's sources. Its studies of musical change have therefore had to be, on the one hand, vastly more generalized, as in the speculative extrapolation of the first human music from a comparison of recent sources, or highly specific, as in the case of musical autobiographies of living persons. The literature of ethnomusicology comprises a larger variety of approaches than is found typically in historical musicology and, on the other hand, work that divides the musical domain into a larger variety and number of components than one encounters in the anthropological study of other domains of culture. It is a matter of emphasis. Ethnomusicologists usually approach musical change on the one hand with much attention to method, and on the other, with single case studies used (often prematurely, I'm afraid) as the basis for generalization. They have little hope of finding out comprehensively what happened in history and so have usually been content to present models of the kinds or types of things that happen in the course of musical change, in different situations.

FROM ABSOLUTE TO INCIDENTAL

Typically, ethnomusicology studies the musical culture of a society through observation of the present. In a world that is constantly changing, the problem is to get a sense of organization from the bits and pieces in a musical system that undergo change. We can continue to use the concepts of content and style. Thus: A piece of music such as a song or a tune family may change. So may the normal construction of a type of piece, as in the way in which the procedure of varying a theme in a set of variations changes from the time of Bach to that of Elgar. Quite separately, this can occur in the distribution of style elements. Thus one can imagine the total repertory of a tribal group having prevailingly scale type A, with scale type B in a minority, and then the positions of prominence reversed in a later period—all this without necessary change in the inventory of the songs. But quite aside from all this, one must also be aware of changes in musical conceptualization and behavior, in the uses and functions of music, which are usually but not necessarily accompanied by changes in musical sound. The point is that musical change, viewed broadly, is a highly complex phenomenon. In order to organize the picture a bit, let us look at several types or perhaps levels of change, all of them assuming the continuity in some element against which change in others can be gauged. (See also Blacking 1978, Nettl 1958a, Sachs 1962, Bose 1966, and Merriam 1964 for examples of other approaches to the classification of musical change.)

1) For the case of the most complete kind of change, a population that shares and maintains one musical system abandons it for another. There seem to be few examples, for even those societies that have moved from a traditional to a totally Western form of music have kept some small vestige of the earlier practice. Certain groups of Australian aborigines may have experienced something close to this kind of musical change, been forced,

upon moving from tribal lands to cities, to experience abandonment of the older tradition and complete substitution of another, Western-based system of music. In the most extreme form this is one end of the continuum. There is change but no continuity.

2) Radical change in a system of music whose new form can definitely still be traced in some way to the old is more easily illustrated. There is not only a constant population but also at least some stable element of the music to establish the continuity. In Europe the change from the essentially tonal music of Strauss and Mahler to the tonally quite different music of Schoenberg and Webern is perhaps illustrative. Here elements with continuity abound—orchestras, the chromatic tempered scale, others—but the difference is easily perceived by even lay members of Western musical society. Non-Western illustrations may be the change from traditional West African to Hispanic-influenced Caribbean music among black slave populations in the New World, or the change from traditional Great Basin styles to the Plains style among the Shoshone in the nineteenth century.

3) A great many publications in ethnomusicology contrast elements of continuity in a culture with elements of change. Titles beginning "Continuity and Change . . ." are a cliché. But within a musical system a certain amount of change may be and probably is part of its essence. Most societies expect of their artists a minimum of innovation, and some demand a great deal. In contemporary urban Western society, composers are valued if they depart from the norm very considerably (staying, of course, within certain limits that define the music system, or departing from these only in very exceptional cases). Doing something "new" is in itself good, and doing something that has been done before is bad, even if it is done well. But even in societies that do not value innovation as greatly, a certain amount of change is needed. New songs must be produced, new variants of songs passed on in oral tradition are needed, and a singer may be expected to change his rendition of a folk song throughout his life. The absolutely static is inconceivable and it seems a safe hypothesis that every musical system has inherent in it a certain amount of constant change which is one of its core elements, required simply to hold the system intact and to keep it from becoming an artificially preserved museum (but see Meyer 1967:134–232 for detailed discussion of this issue). Exceptions may occur, as in rapidly Westernizing Asian societies of the mid-twentieth century, which try to keep a musical tradition going by isolating it from its earlier social context and attempting artificially to preserve it unchanged. Yet change is the norm, hence "the continuity of change" in our title.

4) In musical artifacts such as songs, or in song types, groups, repertories, a certain amount of allowable individual variation may not even be perceived as change. A folk song may be sung differently by a singer on various occasions, each performance representing a change from the past, but the artifact remains an unchanged unit of musical thought. This type of

change is distinguished from no. 3 above by its lack of direction. It is part of the system if it is accepted, and not if it is regarded as an error. To summarize: we distinguish substitution of one system of music for another; radical change of a system; gradual, normal change; and allowable variation.

These four types of change may occur in all societies, but surely to varying degrees. And yet, we can distinguish the death of a tradition and its replacement by another from the maintenance of a tradition in which change is a normal state of affairs. Various kinds of change in the nature of the musical unit, in its stylistic superstructure, in the demise of units and their replacement by others, are expected. Radical change is rare, change that occurs within a system, normal. A musical system itself embodies change, but a population rarely substitutes a system.

THE PRESENCE AND ABSENCE OF CHANGE

We are tempted to ask why music changes at all, but if change is the norm in culture and in music, we should rather ask the opposite question, that is, taking all of the mentioned possibilities into account, whether there are cultures or social conditions in which music does not change or in which change is greatly inhibited. What would conceivably cause such exceptions to the norm? The literature of ethnomusicology does not generalize to this question very much, but we may perhaps enumerate a group of widespread implications: (1) Musical change is absent or exceedingly slow in societies with a minimum of technology. Some technology is needed for the making of instruments, for the establishment of social contexts that foster musical events. A degree of division of labor, rudimentary perhaps, makes possible the personal variation that leads eventually to change. It has been widely assumed, in many cases probably correctly, that the technologically simplest tribal and folk cultures experience little musical change. (2) Musical change may be slow in societies in which the musical system has, through previous change, been adapted to the social system with a certain degree of perfection and thus need not adapt further, assuming musical change as adaptive strategy to a relatively unchanging cultural context. Examples? The unity of sub-Saharan music in the face of great cultural differences might be a case in point. (3) It is likely that musical systems experience a certain ebb and flow in the degree to which they change. Accepting a cyclic interpretation of history, we may find a music to be temporarily in a state of stability, waiting for the rather convulsive changes that must come as the cycles progress. European music history has been interpreted in such cycles of 150 years. (4) A music may resist change if it is associated mainly or exclusively with a particular domain of culture that changes less readily than do most activities. Religion is the most obvious example, and religious music seems in many societies to change less readily than the secular.

Let us also look at the other extreme, seeking instances in which music changes very quickly and dramatically. The most obvious example is the twentieth century, throughout the world. We may here have a special, exceptional situation, and deal with it in Chapter 27. But the cultivated and popular musics of Western culture have recently changed in many ways: (a) The "musical language" itself has been changed; perhaps more properly, beginning shortly after 1900 a new language was added, one with different central features such as a new type of harmony displacing that of the so-called functional system. (b) New technology of all sorts, from amplification to the generation of music through electronic means, has been introduced. (c) Types of sounds, such as white noise, incredibly small intervals, industrial and animal noises, have been introduced and accepted into the musical system. (d) Social contexts, audiences, groups of participants have changed greatly. In particular, music as a live performance has been replaced by recorded reproduction. Music historians like Walter Wiora (1965b) have ascribed a special character to the twentieth century, in Western culture, and this may indeed also be a special problem for ethnomusicology. Non-Western cultures have also changed rapidly in their musical sound and behavior, becoming substantially influenced by Western culture and by Western music and musical thought.

Taking the twentieth century as an exemplar of a time in which music changes very rapidly, we ask what are the conditions of culture that made this possible or necessary. The reader can surely supply the list, but I'll also make a stab at it. Parenthetically, it may be noted that some of these characteristics could conceivably also encourage stability as well as change.

A selection of characteristics of twentieth-century world culture (circa 1950–70): (a) Enormously complex technology, and a widespread assumption that the further development of technology, qualitative and quantitative, is a good thing in itself. (b) The possibility of immediate contact between almost any two persons in the world, whatever their national or societal base, contact which can be established through sound, and thus the derived possibility of imparting almost any available musical sound to almost anyone via the so-called mass media. (c) Widespread cultural and particularly religious relativism; and on the other hand, religious homogenization through the spread of Christianity (and secondarily of Islam), the mixture of these and other religions into nonexclusive units. (d) Allegiance to nation-states that usually supersede older culture units and that are composed of population groups once linguistically and culturally diverse. (e) Political and economic domination of the world by a limited number of major centers. (f) Large-scale migration, though not of entire culture units. (g) Establishment of a small number of widely used international languages, such as English. Now, one might argue that at least some of these characteristics would propel us toward cultural and musical stability. The possibility of recording music is in itself almost by definition a stabilizing force, for the record doesn't change while in some respects all live music must. Even so, the above list characterizes a period of very rapid change in world music. We can test the hypothesis by seeking similar traits in other cultures also experiencing rapid musical change. Again, a few examples must suffice, for while we know the twentieth century reasonably well, as it is ours, we have little data and must live with conjecture for other periods in Europe and, even more, for non-Western cultures. We therefore cannot speak to the question in an all-encompassing sense, but can at best find important individual events that might be indicators of other kinds of exceptional change. For example, it is believed that important changes in the music of India took place in the period roughly between 1500 and 1650.

This is the period after the conversion of much of the Indian population to Islam, when, very broadly speaking, Islam settled itself and developed (Rawlinson 1952:281–82). Only a small fragment of what really happened in Indian music at the time is known, but what we do know appears to involve mainly the classical music of the courts and the musical theory emanating from it. Historians of Indian music appear confident that music progressed in various ways through the solidification of theoretical systems, and by expanding its horizons through the increased influence from the Middle East by way of instruments, performance in form patterns, and theory. A large number of foreign musicians brought their art—different and excellent—to the subcontinent. In some ways we can tie this to cultural conditions that we also identified as characteristics of the otherwise so unique twentieth century. Let me speculate. Development of technology by import from the Middle East and Europe, especially in the realm of arms, seems to have been a considerable factor in this period. Communication grew because of travel and from the increase of political contact arising out of the coming of Islam from the Middle East and Central Asia and, gradually, the establishment of a major empire, that of the Moghuls. Whether relativism became a feature is hard to say, but the ascendancy of a new religion and the need for adherents of Islam and traditional religions to coexist and confront each other seems perhaps to be a related phenomenon. The establishment of a nation-state, the empire, and the spread of a widely used language, Persian, are further cases in point. In the India of this period there is a situation not completely unlike that of the twentieth-century world (see Neuman 1980, Jairazbhoy 1971:18–21, Deva 1974:27, etc.).

Our understanding of change in the past—and it must be of the past if we are to eliminate the special factor of direct contact with Western culture—in nonliterate societies is extremely limited. But trying a bit of reconstruction, let us see what can be known and conjectured of the Plains Indians before about 1800 A.D., noting conditions parallel to some of those characterizing the modern world. It is difficult to know when things happened in the history of the Plains Indians, but we know at least that certain things did happen. At some point, probably in the period between 1000 and 1500, a number of peoples from diverse areas collected in the western Plains. The diverse origin is attested by the diversity of languages: Siouxan in the case of the Dakota and Crow; Algonquian in that of the Arapaho, Blackfoot, and Cheyenne; Kiowa (a language family of its own) and Uto-Aztecan for the Comanche. In the course of the eighteenth century a number of significant and related changes took place. A relatively unified buffalo-hunt-oriented culture developed after horses had been introduced (indirectly, from the West). The Sun Dance, the large public ceremony probably radiating from the peoples of the central Plains (possibly the Arapaho), seems to have developed in response to the need for tribes to separate into bands for the winter but to unite in the summer. Partial dependence on agriculture was given up, and a sign language was developed for intertribal communication as travel began to be widespread, related to the nomadic lifestyle adopted in part because of the horse. (Among the many items of literature supporting these statements, see e.g. Ewers 1958, Driver 1961.) Relatively dramatic changes thus seem to have taken place, and we have in a microcosm evidence of some of the characteristics of twentieth-century world culture: (1) technology, suddenly improved by the introduction of the horse and other indirect acquisitions from the whites; (2) increased intertribal communication; (3) a unified religious system overlying more individual tribal traditions; (4) no nation-states, but a unified culture that led to tribal allegiances and intertribal languages such as the sign language and the widespread use of Dakota and, eventually, of English.

The evidence is extremely scanty, but there is a bit of indication that rapid musical change accompanied or immediately followed. The geographic distribution of the so-called Plains musical style indicates rather recent origin, at least in the "classical" Plains culture, where it developed its extreme characteristics. Distribution also suggests a diffusion to outlying areas, the eastern woodlands, the prairie tribes, and certain Salish and Great Basin peoples such as the Flathead and the Shoshone. Merriam particularly notes the Plains-like character of Flathead music and culture despite the Salish background (1967b:155). The overlay of Plains music in the Flathead repertory, contrary to the homogeneous style of the coast Salish, appears to be recent, as does the introduction of the Plains style in the previously simpler and homogeneous Basin repertory.

Again, it seems likely that rapid or at least substantial change in music and its surrounding social events occurred with, or perhaps followed, the development of technology, communication, widespread standardization along with knowledge and tolerance of diversity. But of course this highly generalized and speculative discussion is intended to do nothing more than to suggest to the reader the possibility that certain kinds of cultural situations seem to be accompanied by large-scale change, and others by virtual absence of change.

Historians of Western music often seem to believe that musical change is first and foremost to be explained in terms of the behavior of music and its tendency, because of its special character, to develop in certain directions. It's a view not often espoused by ethnomusicologists, but it is an undeniable fact that music sometimes changes in ways which cannot be explained by parallels to cultural or social change. We must admit that music sometimes follows its own laws, changing while other domains remain stable, or conservative in the face of cultural change. This again is an extremely broad topic, and I can deal with it only by way of a brief foray, suggesting one way in which music occupies a special place among the domains of culture.

The role of music as opposing the broad sweep of a culture has been spoken to by various authors, particularly for Africa (e.g. Tracey 1954: 237, Merriam 1954, Blacking 1978:22, Coplan in Nettl 1978a:108–9). One may say in song what one is not permitted to say in speech. In prerevolutionary Iran as well, criticism of the government and the secret police was sometimes voiced in song, a tradition with precedents in the revolutionary movements of the first decades of this century (Caton 1979). There are related phenomena. Minorities kept in national seclusion may be permitted musical prominence. A hierarchical political system may be reflected in the hierarchy of a musical ensemble, but unhappiness with the system may be expressed in singing style (see Lomax 1962:442–43) and, as in the Middle East, the widespread ascription of sadness as the dominant emotion of music. Stated very simply, music may do for society what other domains of a culture fail to do—provide relief from everyday sameness, a way of communicating with the supernatural when other forms of communication are directed to humans, a kind of luxury among necessities. It stands to reason, then, that if musical change is normally to be seen within a context of culture change, it may also occur outside this general scope. Music may be an antidote, an expression of anticulture.

A particular role of music, as we have said, may be to symbolize in distilled and abstract form the character and values of a culture. As an object specifically treated as a symbol, it would have to remain in essence static except for periods of rapid and radical change, like a flag, which symbolizes political unity, remaining unchanged despite governmental and political unrest until an especially drastic change forces its replacement by another flag. If indeed music changes in ways different from the constant change of culture, this may also result from the close association with religion, tending to give conservation a special value. Music as a form of communication with the unchanging supernatural as compared with the everchanging human may require reasonable stability, in contrast, for example, to a system of commerce or of warfare.

If there is a special dynamic of specifically musical change, perhaps the most plausible reason involves the systemic nature of music. A musical system may seek a kind of equilibrium in which the close interrelationship of the components plays a major role. Change in one parameter is likely to require or encourage changes in others. Thus addition of Western harmony in Middle Eastern music appears to strengthen the prominence of those modes that lend themselves to harmonization in major or minor, even when they are performed by a traditional ensemble. The change from solo performance to group may require adjustments in intonational or improvisational patterns and values. The various components of music must work together, and humans who make music try to find structures in which they are compatible. Having found such a way, people are not quick to accept change in the nature of the system, instead substituting constant internal change. And the better a musical system accommodates the need for the elements to interrelate, the more it will remain stable, and perhaps the more it will also permit and require changes *within* the system. Indeed, thinking of Western, Asian Indian, and African musics as examples, we may hypothesize that some of the most successful musical systems in terms of widespread acceptance, respect accorded in their own societies, overall stability, and demands made upon and fulfilled by musicians may be the ones in which the elements interact most perfectly.

PATTERNS, DIRECTIONS, REGULARITIES

We will have occasion to deal with various aspects of musical change in Chapters 14 (on oral transmission), 17 (the determinants of musical style), and 27 (on the special nature of the twentieth century). Having made some idiosyncratic suggestions, I feel it necessary to see whether there is much that most ethnomusicologists have come to believe about change in general. There are no results of polls or official statements of position, but on the basis of some prominent publications let me try to give a summary.

While we have been speaking of music as if it were an independent organism, it is important to be clear that we are talking about changes in behavior and practice of humans. Blacking reminds us that we are dealing with "decisions made by individuals about music-making and music on the basis of their experiences of music and attitudes to it in different social contexts" (1978:12). Merriam points out, in discussing change, that "no two people behave in exactly the same way in any given situation and thus there always exists an almost infinite series of deviations from the norms of society" (1964:308). Such statements would almost parallel those of the most particularist historians, refusing to recognize patterns outside the individual.

But ethnomusicologists (including Merriam and Blacking) are interested in regularities. It is their understanding of the important role of individuals as well as the complexity of music and the sheer quantity of data that has kept them from adopting a single theory of change, and from a specifically nomothetic approach. One way of seeing these regularities is to recognize the distinction between change brought about by a society from its own internal resources, and that which comes about as a result of intercultural contact. We hardly know of cultures that have not been exposed to others, and most research deals with "external" change. Merriam distinguishes the two, asserting that ethnomusicology "needs a theory of change that will apply to both internal and to external factors" (1964:307; see also Nettl 1958a). Such a general theory might view the phenomenon of musical change as the result of a balance, suggested above, between stability and continuity (the latter being "change" of the "internal" sort) and disturbances brought about by outside contact. Internal change may normally follow certain patterns established in a culture and thus be in some measure predictable on the basis of its own conception of music, of change, its technology and social structure. The results of outside contact would be subject to more variables but perhaps predictable in part from types of intercultural relationships.

Curt Sachs's statement about musical change in his last book (1962) parallels Merriam's distinction between internal and external. He identifies three fundamental types, "culture graft," "progress," and "simple change." Interpreting and expanding his brief statement, I suggest that progress is change in the direction of an objective or final goal, and this definition is Sachs's way of pointing out that there are regularities of change in any music. "Simple change" seems to be his way of identifying allowable variation, while "culture graft" distinguishes what results from intercultural contact. In these and other authors' statements there is often the implication that a society, left alone, will develop music in a particular way, in a direction. Several have been suggested.

The most common belief is that music increases in complexity, adding tones to scales, sections to forms, notes to chords. Certainly some societies have followed this direction, if not constantly then generally; the precise way in which the increased complexity is manifest varies, and thus suggests the usefulness of an approach such as Steward's "multilinear evolution." Ethnomusicologists are inclined to believe this, I think, but they are disturbed by the lack of clear-cut evidence. So many musics have been affected by external contact to a really significant degree that one can hardly find examples of undisturbed "internal" change. But there may be a core of data sufficient to allow us to believe that while increased complexity is one of several things that frequently occur, we cannot tolerate this process as an immutable law of human musical behavior.

A more difficult concept that takes into account the broad differences between major groups of cultures is related. Max Weber (1958) and his follower Kurt Blaukopf (1951, 1970) distinguish Western music (which in the past few centuries changed greatly) from most non-Western (which they regard as more static) with the argument that Western culture, and its musics, proceeded in the direction of certain "ideals." Weber's work, an incomplete fragment, is today mainly of historical interest. But Weber's theory that music changes in directions determined by social and economic developments, and, in the case of Western culture, also in the direction of increased rationalization particularly of the organization of pitch, is surely relevant to ethnomusicology. It was his belief that Western society, because it ceased to accord mainly "practical" uses to music, increasingly "rationalized" or intellectualized its system by strengthening its theoretical basis (Blaukopf 1970:162–63). One may question the special kind of uniqueness that Weber accords to Western music, but ethnomusicologists have generally tended to distinguish complex societies, with their "art" music and their professional musicians and theorists, in which music changes at least with deliberate speed, from the very simplest, in which musical change is thought to have been exceedingly slow.

In an earlier work Sachs (1946) proposed that change is frequently a function of the tendency of societies to react against the past, that people are driven, after a given amount of time, to reverse the direction of what they have been doing, creating something contrastive. Sachs here seems to follow the work of Lorenz (1928), who suggested a rather precise periodization of European art music in terms of thirty-year segments. Sachs points out that counterpoint dominates in the late Middle Ages, is replaced by more emphasis on melody and harmonic integration, but then reasserts itself in the late Baroque and again in the late nineteenth century. Classic is followed by Romantic, cerebral by emotional, lyrical by dramatic, even complex by somewhat simpler. The literature contains suggestions of other regularities. Oral tradition may produce simplification of a piece. Culture change is followed inevitably by musical change. Periods move from primitive beginnings to classicism to decadence. Musical concepts and behavior change more readily than music sound. In a related thought Blacking (1978:21–23) suggests patterns based on biological processes.

Most studies of musical change in ethnomusicology have, however, involved intercultural contact. While some specific instances are discussed in other chapters, we should say in summary that the determinants of change are thought to include the following: (1) the quality of the relationship—political, economic, demographic—between the societies affected; (2) the degree of compatibility between the cultures in contact and between the musical systems; and (3) a perhaps untestable aesthetic criterion, the degree to which a musical system is integrated, that is, constitutes a successful combination of interlocking components (Nettl 1956b:133).

From all of this we can see that there have been many attempts to generalize about change but no generally accepted theory. The recent literature about the concept of change shows a good deal of dissatisfaction. Blacking (1978) has suggested an approach to a "comprehensive and definitive study of musical change," including synchronic, diachronic, and biological approaches. But the best one may expect at this point, it seems to me, is a theory that would be enumerative, pointing out a group of regularities and patterns stemming from a variety of circumstances and contexts. We know there are components which change, that there are reasons for change, typical directions, internal and external factors. It would seem that one possibility is to view the process of change as depending on equilibrium among various factors. Let me try to state it as a hypothesis.

In the life of a music some components always change while others do not. When style changes, content tends to remain, and vice versa. Where pieces themselves change, they are not often abandoned to be replaced by others, while rapid turnover in a repertory accompanies the avoidance of change of the individual pieces. Improvisation over a model, each performance signifying change of some sort, causes the model itself to remain constant. Where performance practice does not permit much change in a given piece, new pieces are more frequently created than where a performance style requires departure from a norm. Innovation and variation balance each other. Radical change and the kind of gradual, allowable, intrasystemic change that is always with us each claims its due, to different but balanced degrees. The hypothesis remains to be tested.

I once asked my teacher of Persian music how long a particular practice had been extant. "We have always done that," he replied. "Always?" I asked, "You mean, for the last 200 years, for example?" "Of course not," he replied; "nobody knows what was going on 200 years ago." I had not penetrated his sense of change, of history. So far, ethnomusicologists have concentrated on their own perception of musical change, learning little about the perception of musical continuity and change in the various societies of the world. This too remains one of the most significant tasks.

Chapter 14

Das Volk dichtet

RECORDED, PRINTED, WRITTEN, ORAL

For a long time in the history of ethnomusicology, the differences between oral and written transmission loomed as a major definitional paradigm. Some authors, like George List (1979b), actually saw ethnomusicology as the study of music in oral tradition, and folk music, one of its diagnostic repertories, was broadly defined as handed down by word of mouth (Herzog 1950:1032). A sharp line was drawn between the two kinds of tradition. But occasionally attempts were made to refine the concept. "Oral" was sometimes changed to "aural"; people learned not so much what was said or sung to them but what they heard. The concept of memory was suggested as a major factor. And early on, already, some of the most prominent figures in the field pointed out that the matter was not so simple.

In an article actually entitled "Oral Tradition in Music," Charles Seeger (1950) suggested that what was interesting about oral tradition was not so much that it was radically different as a way of teaching and learning from the written, but the relationship between the two. Thus, at a time when a dichotomy between them seemed widespread in scholarly thought, he showed the two to be inextricably connected. When the typical student of art music had barely become aware of the impact of oral tradition on the creation of a folk song whose existence was a mass of variants, Seeger delineated the basic difference between the historian's and the ethnomusicologist's conception of a "piece." In a period when we began to rejoice at the prospect that the proliferation of sound recordings would help us in the understanding of oral traditions, he already foresaw the impact that the development and dissemination of recordings would have on the very existence of oral traditions.

About the same time Curt Sachs (1948:378) suggested that in regard to the essentials of transmission there are four kinds of musical culture, dominated by oral, written, printed, and recorded forms. These could even represent a chronological order (see Blaukopf 1979:80), though one valid only for Western civilization, but for analytical purposes they are also a continuum of relationships, from close to distant, among composer, performer, and listener.

There is little literature about the differences among these four kinds of transmission, although the role of the record has received some attention (see e.g. Gronow 1963), and not much about transmission per se. A good deal of what there is comes from the unexpected quarter of history, where it has been particularly prominent in African studies (see e.g. Vansina 1965). Historians have seen oral tradition as a way of supplementing or sometimes replacing written or printed sources, particularly in cultures with unwritten languages but also in materials coming from sources of so-called oral history. They are concerned about the degree to which it can provide reliable data and facts. This concern is rarely shared by ethnomusicologists, although Hood (1959), in a study of Javanese music, discusses the maintenance of certain principles in an oral tradition that are necessary to hold a musical system intact. But most students of folk music have been more interested in what might be called the unreliability of oral tradition, seeing it as a force for change. In studying the way in which a piece develops variants, they have marveled not at the consistency of tradition but at the differences and, in fact, suspected the presence of written versions when confronted with standardization. Like students of folklore generally, they saw in the very unreliability of oral tradition the creative force of the community, developing for its tendency to proliferate within a strict set of guidelines the label "communal re-creation" (Barry 1933), a term derived from an earlier belief in the creation of songs and tales by the folk community at large, called "communal creation."

In the long history of folk music research there is a close relationship between the definition of folklore as orally transmitted and of folk song as anonymously composed. There is a difference, both in the process and as a subject for research, between a song composed and written down by an individual and then passed on orally, and another composed without the availability of writing. But in both cases one of the early questions for scholars has been whether folk songs (and by implication other music in oral tradition) are created by individuals or by the "folk" (see Barry 1914).

The most naive version of the concept of communal creation, of a primordial group of villagers somehow composing in concert, was never taken very seriously. An American pioneer of folk song research, Phillips Barry (1934), points out that German thinkers associated with it, such as the Brothers Grimm and Ludwig Uhland, did not hold this belief. Yet the conception of creation by *the* people, encapsulated in the heraldic declaration "das Volk dichtet," is not totally without significance. Oral tradition operates as a constraining, limiting, directing force much more than writing.

The limitations of human memory (see Treitler 1974:344–46), the rules of the folk aesthetic, the constraints of patterns already established—these do much to shape a musical repertory that, after all, must consist of pieces accepted and learned by members of a community, thus contrasting with a tradition in which music may be composed and then played only once, or never, or recorded only by the creator. Oral transmission is a concept worth looking at in a list of ethnomusicological issues.

But in doing so, we encounter complexities even before we begin. Taking Sachs's model, written tradition is closer to the oral than is printed tradition. Where writing alone is available, it will develop variant forms through the vagaries of scribes, their creativity, errors, forgetfulness, laziness even, more readily than one which has printing. Learning aurally from a series of live performances is different from the repeated hearing of a recording. As usual, the world's cultures exhibit wide variety in the differences of aural learning. Here insistence on precise learning inhibits creation of variants; elsewhere one is almost required to make change in a performance. Similar pieces may be regarded as variants here, identities there, imitations in a third culture, and easily separable units in a fourth. Oral tradition today is supplemented with Western notation in Iran, with a unique musical shorthand in India, by the cassette recorder among Plains Indians.

The general literature on oral transmission is actually based on a small number of repertories. For example, Lord's (1965) highly influential book deals with Yugoslav epic poetry; Cutter (1976) and Treitler (1974, 1975), with Christian liturgical chant; Hood, with Java. Barry, Bayard, and Bronson have developed the concept as it works in Anglo-American folk music, Wiora in German song and Europe generally. The conventional wisdom is based mainly on knowledge of European and American folk music. Let me try, by asking a few broad and fundamental questions, to see what has been established about the process of oral transmission and about the nature of the musical repertories, as a group, that live entirely in oral tradition.

SOME FUNDAMENTAL QUESTIONS

What is it that changes in oral transmission, and what remains the same? We deal with a large variety of phenomena and a broad range of behavior. Returning to my distinction between "content" and "style," in order for a piece to be transmitted intact, its content must remain while its style may change. Bearing in mind the special definitions of these terms, some musics have a great deal of content and little that can be called style. The Samaritans of Israel ca. 1970, we are told (A. Herzog, personal communication), were extremely anxious to keep their liturgical tradition intact, permitting no changes, a statement also true of the Navajo (McAllester 1954:64–65). Such cultures provide little opportunity for stylistic variation or change;

everything in their music is essential content. By contrast, the classical music of Iran, consisting of memorized pieces used as the basis of improvisation, permits enormous variation in performance but insists on a small but significant core of stability symbolized by the statement that one does not improvise upon a mode but "performs" it (Nettl 1972a:11–13). The content of English folk music seems to reside substantially in its melodic contour (see e.g. Poladian 1942), and of Hungarian, perhaps in configurations of cadential tones (Bartók 1931:6–8). But however defined, when a piece is transmitted, style changes, content remains.

What is it that is actually transmitted? On the surface, we think of discrete compositions, songs, pieces, and no doubt these are the major units. But there are alternative approaches. One may think of a repertory as consisting of a vocabulary of units, perhaps melodic or rhythmic motifs, lines of music accompanying lines of poetry, cadential formulas, chords or chord sequences. We could study the process of transmission by noting how a repertory keeps these units intact, and how they are combined and recombined into larger units that are acceptable to the culture as performances. The smallest units of content may be the principal units of transmission (see Treitler 1975; Lord 1965, Chapters 3 and 4).

At the other end of the spectrum: while a culture creates, forgets, creates anew, and internally changes a repertory of musical content such as songs, with some turnover, it also transmits to itself (and perhaps very slowly changes) the stylistic superstructure. For example, the northern Plains Indians have probably for centuries acquired songs, composing them in dreams or learning them from other tribes, new ones replacing forgotten ones. We can also observe by taking a broad overview of their music that features of performance practice such as singing style, intonation, style of drumming, range of melodies, have been handed down more or less intact but yet undergone changes in certain directions.

There is, furthermore, more to the question of transmission than the teaching and learning of music as a function of interpersonal relations. Transmission of a sort occurs also within the experience of one human being. The way in which a musician—concert pianist or tribal singer—changes and perhaps develops a conception and therefore a performance of a piece in the course of his or her life is surely a type of transmission and, in just about all cases (classical, popular, folk), specifically aural transmission. James Porter (1976), in describing the stages of a song in one folk singer's experience, shows that the history of such a song can be interpreted as contributing to the way in which a tune family develops in oral tradition, as otherwise represented by a chain of singers each with his or her variant.

What do we know about changes in form that take place when a music moves from oral to written tradition? We have few cases where this, simply and precisely, has happened, and in such instances we must cope also with other changes: for example, the Westernization of musical life, the introduction of Western music, the changing importance of mass media. Let me again illustrate from the classical music of Iran, into which notation began to be introduced before 1900, but which in 1970 was still prevailingly oral. The basic material, the *radif,* has now been notated and is frequently learned from written versions. In earlier times, we are told, each teacher developed his own version of the *radif.* This is still to some extent the case, but three major versions that have been published—by Abolhassan Saba in a fashion that incorporates non-*radif* material as well, in pure but extended fashion by Musa Ma'aroufi (Barkechli 1963), and less extensively by Mahmoud Karimi (Massoudieh 1978)—seem to dominate instruction. We can only guess at the effects, having few recordings that go back beyond 1960, but statements by older musicians as well as comparison of typical with more conservative performances may give some insights. Recent performances are more standardized in the material used and in length. Given many other kinds of changes in attitude, this standardization and the many other changes in music are difficult to relate to notation alone.

The introduction of notation may have allowed Persian music to survive, and the fact that it could actually be notated made it possible for its practitioners to hold their heads up in the face of encroaching Western musical culture. But gone is the reverence with which a student had formerly held his master's *radif,* which he had learned a bit at a time because contemplation of its miniature details was deemed essential, and for which he depended on the not always forthcoming good will of the teacher. After all, a musician can now learn the material quickly, looking up forgotten passages and controlling the pace of learning. He need no longer associate himself with a special school. Musicians sometimes feel free to depart from what is, after all, only another written musical artifact, not something to be revered and treasured above other music. On the other hand, in conjunction with other appurtenances of Western musical culture, notation has on the whole permitted Persian music to develop a broader scope and style, but at the center of its practice is a core comprising possibly the majority of performances, which are similar to each other and thus represent a narrowing of the tradition. We would say, then, that perhaps the form of the music (using the concept in its broadest sense) has not changed, but its distribution within what is formally possible has changed from broad and equally distributed to broad but now concentrated at the center. Similar kinds of observations can no doubt be made for other societies, but one can assess the role of the introduction of notation only in the context of the introduction of other aspects of Western academic musical culture.

Do oral and aural transmission and oral creation affect the forms of pieces and repertories? No doubt they must, but we have no theory to explain how. As a start, let me distinguish between the *creation* of pieces without notation and the *transmission* of pieces that may or may not have been composed with notation. We cannot take for granted that all pieces which have been notated by their composers were created specifically with the use of notation. Surely they could have been worked out in the composer's mind, so to speak, entirely without paper. So we are faced with several possible processes along with intermediate forms: pieces composed without notation and also transmitted orally probably account for the majority of musical artifacts in the world. In dramatic contrast, there are pieces composed with the use of notation—*Augenmusik* (music for the eyes) in the most extreme sense—and then performed only with the most exact use of the notes, by musicians who wish to follow the composer's instructions precisely and may indeed have little idea in advance of what sounds will emerge. But we also have music written by a composer and then passed on by oral tradition, something obviously true of much popular music. To it we should add music in which the writing of words is partially a musically mnemonic device. In the case of certain jazz traditions, we have music whose content is written and passed on orally by the composer but whose style is transmitted through recordings. And we have music composed aurally, in the mind of the musician (a Mozart or a Schubert?), but then handed down entirely through written tradition.

Elsewhere (Nettl 1956d) I have suggested that certain structural limitations are necessary if a piece is to be transmitted aurally. Dividing music into elements, I hypothesize the need for some of these to remain simple, repetitive, stable, so that others may vary. There is probably some point beyond which it is impossible for any sizable population of musicians to remember material. If these limitations are not observed in the original composition, they will be instituted through the process of communal re-creation. Recurring events or sign posts such as motifs or rhythmic patterns, conciseness of form, brevity, or systematic variation may, as it were, hold an aurally transmitted piece intact. This is probably true even in the complex pieces of South Indian classical music, such as the *kritis,* occupying as much as ten minutes, as the function of their repetitive, variational, and cumulative elements of form, I would venture to guess, is to make oral transmission possible.

There is a widely accepted generalization that a piece transmitted orally changes slowly but constantly. This is more a belief than a finding supported by data. There are few studies, but work such as the mentioned one of Porter (1976), who examines the successive versions of a song performed by one singer over a period of years, some attempts to re-record older American Indian songs after decades, the retrospective studies of European folk music by Bayard and Wiora, all indicate that we may be on the right track. No doubt, however, the particular view that a society has of change and the nature of music plays a greater role than any general law of human behavior.

FOUR KINDS OF HISTORY

To what extent does the way in which music is transmitted determine the overall shape of a repertory? Or, conversely, can one examine the structure of a repertory, the interrelationships among its units of content and style, and get some insights into the way it transmits itself, as a unit and as a group of separable units? Let me suggest a typology applicable to both pieces and repertories, in the belief that this could be a starting point for a comparative study of transmission.

Beginning with the microcosm, the piece and its history, let me propose that there are types of histories, four kinds of things that a piece, once composed, may experience. In Type I it may be carried on without change, more or less intact. In Type II it may be transmitted and changed, but only in a single version or one direction, so that it continues differently from its original but without the proliferation of variants. In Type III it may experience the kind of transmission that produces many variants, some of them eventually abandoned and forgotten, others becoming stable once differentiated, others again changing constantly. In all three of these types the history of the composition is essentially self-contained, all forms derived specifically from the original creation. A fourth type is similar to Type III, developing within the family principle but borrowing materials from other, unrelated compositions. Figure 6 illustrates.

It is important to bear in mind that this typology is speculative and hypothetical, a model which sets forth extreme cases. The literature shows amply that the family type, Type III, really does exist, and we have seen evidence of the existence of Type IV in the wandering lines of Czech folk songs and American Indian Peyote songs, the "bridge" in the third line of many popular songs and hymns (see also Olsvai 1963 for Hungarian examples). In its extreme form Type I may be totally absent, but something close to it occurs in the written, printed, and recorded traditions of modern urban culture, where pieces in particularly prominent performance versions may set something close to an absolute standard. Societies such as the Navajo or the western Pueblos may come close to this model in oral tradition. Type II must for the moment remain entirely hypothetical, but conceivably the liturgy of the Samaritans, known to have changed and yet the subject of laborious standardization, could serve as an illustration. The first two types may not exist in pure form; just because we find a tune without known relatives does not mean that we have a solid example. Translated into generalized tendencies, however, these four types of history may have credibility.

The other side of the coin, however, is also always there. For example, in what appears to us to be a family of Type III, with all variants directly derived from the parent, it is conceivable that the performers do not recognize derivation at all, ascribing each variant to separate creation.

An example from the Blackfoot, who compose songs by learning them in

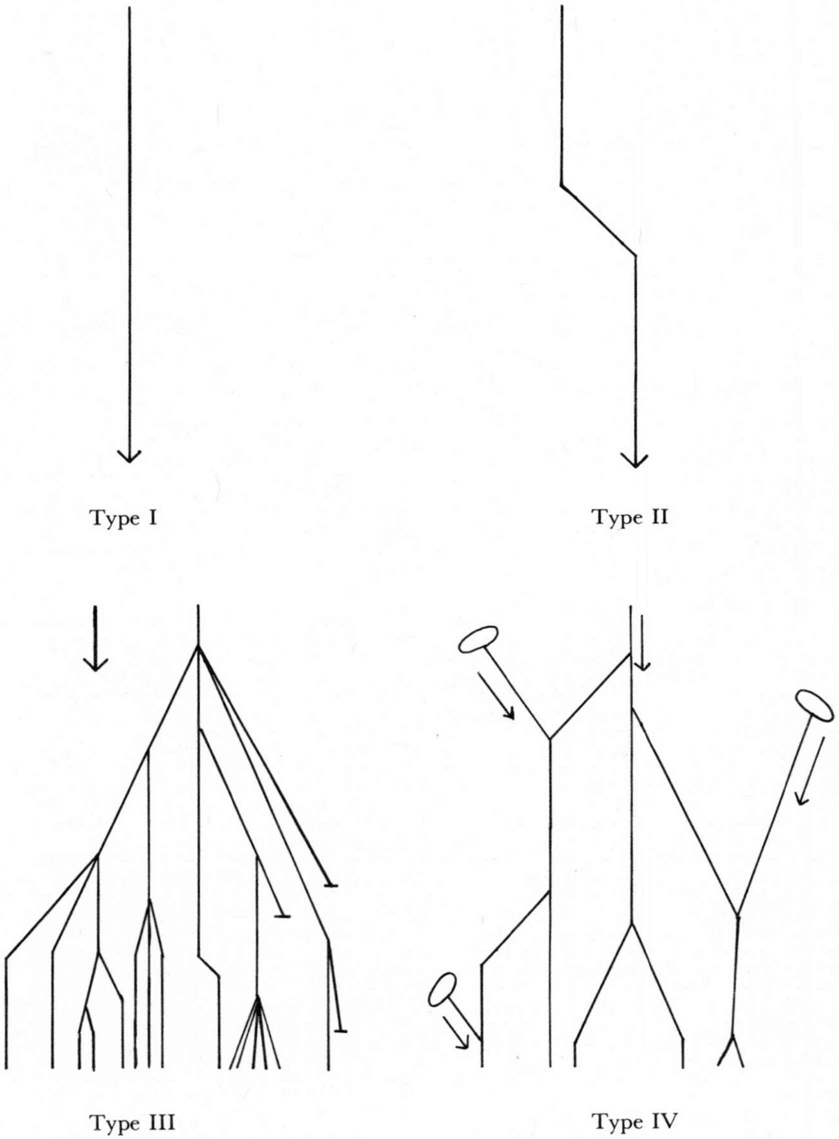

Figure 6. Types of song histories.

visions: each who had a vision was likely to receive songs from his guardian spirit. Many of the songs thus learned by different individuals, albeit perhaps from the same guardian spirit, may to the objective outsider be quite identical. Given the difficulty of understanding the criteria by which Blackfoot people differentiate songs, it seems possible that the very act of separate creation that the two songs undergo may be enough to give them status as separate units of musical thought, quite in opposition to our observation, shared incidentally by the Blackfoot who hears recordings, that they are almost identical. This is quite different from the already cited Iranian example, in which a performer claimed to play a piece identically each time, despite the fact that to any outside observer the performances would sound completely different, having in common only certain motifs and scalar patterns. Javanese Matjapat songs may be an even more extreme example (Kartomi 1973:159–60). The two sides of the coin may be very much opposite sides.

Having set forth four hypothetical kinds of history that a composition may experience, we next move to see whether entire traditions or repertories can also be thus classified. There is no doubt that a typical repertory exhibits a mixture of at least some of the types of compositional history, but it might be possible to find for each a dominant type. But first let me introduce another variable, the density of a repertory and the associated dynamics of change.

By density, I mean the degree to which separate units of a repertory are similar, whether or not genetically related. Or, putting it another way, how close or how far apart, musically, the units, pieces, songs, may be from each other. To illustrate the concept, let us imagine two tune families whose internal relationship has been proved by observation of the process, beginning with the composition of the parent tune. One family develops variants, versions, and forms that in the aggregate are very different from each other, and there may be considerable difference between one variant and its closest neighbor. This family would be lacking in density and could be called, for lack of a better term, sparse. Ultimately, the classification of a family as sparse would depend on the classifier's having a complete knowledge of all of its members, and this is, of course, only theoretically or experimentally possible. The other, dense, tune family has variants that are very similar to each other, and its closest neighbor-variants are almost identical.

This leads to other considerations. It is possible for a family to be dense, that is, to have a vast number of variants covering a great many points that are musically far apart in terms of any of a large number of components. But it would also be possible to find a sparse family that, because of the small number of its constituent variants, still covers, musically speaking, the same ground. A tune family may also be broad or narrow, depending on the specifically musical distance between the variants exhibiting the greatest difference. Bayard, in the study to which I have referred in Chapters 8 and

9 (1954), has illustrated these two types admirably; his "Brave Donnelly" is dense, and his "Job of Journeywork," relatively sparse and yet much more extensive and broad than "Donnelly."

Now, the same kind of thinking may be extended to an entire repertory, which may be dense or sparse and also broad or narrow, the two coordinates not necessarily correlating. Impressionistically speaking, with examples for which I have no more evidence than some first-hand acquaintance, I would say that twentieth-century Western art music is a broad repertory, and eighteenth-century Italian music, less broad but quite dense. Blackfoot Indian music of the nineteenth century, from what we now know of it, was probably broad and dense, at least compared to Blackfoot music of the more recent past, which is much less broad but equally dense. The English and Czech folk song repertories are probably more or less equally broad, but the English repertory seems to me to be denser and perhaps also larger. This mode of thought should some day lead to a way of comparing musics in accordance with the mentioned criteria; at any rate, it seems useful to consider a repertory from this point of view, realizing that the internal interrelationships tell us something about the way in which it comes about and grows.

An analogous concept is historical density, that is, the rate at which a piece or a repertory changes. We can simply call this component the dynamics of the tradition, but here even more the lack of documentation stands in the way. Still, the reconstructions of evolutionists, classifiers, and tune-family proponents may help us in this area. For example, while one song may change very quickly, another might undergo the same changes but with the process requiring much more time. The dynamic distinction is relevant to my model Types II, III, and IV. Type I, of course, does not change at all.

Let me return for a moment to the relative dynamics of oral and written tradition. Looking at the literature of ethnomusicology at large, one finds two contrasting implications: written traditions change slowly because they are able to hold on to their artifacts in a way not possible for oral ones, for these are thought to change almost involuntarily, as a result of faulty memory, the mentioned limitations, and the like. On the other hand, it is thought that oral traditions change slowly because the simplicity of their cultural context makes them inert, while written traditions, because of the very sophistication of their apparatus and even because there is a notation system, move quickly (see Herzog 1950:1033, Hood 1959:201). Within the history of a written tradition the speed varies, as in Western art music, in which the rate of change seems gradually to have accelerated, though with much variation and many tempi rubati. And the interaction among live performance, notation, and recording probably provides a template for a large group of tradition types.

THE PROOF OF THE PUDDING?

The concepts presented are suggested as a model. But are they in any way practical? Let us by way of an exercise make a superficial comparison of some repertories, classing them as proposed. Too little is known to make this more than a speculative exercise, but we may hope that with more knowledge one could proceed more seriously along these lines.

First, the contemporary musical culture of the Blackfoot and perhaps other northern Plains Indians. I shall consider primarily the social dances, which have wide intertribal currency. Their songs are very similar to each other, their forms are standardized, they are composed, so informants say, in considerable numbers, as their existence on a large number of LP records testifies. Most of them do not remain in the repertory very long and do not undergo much change. Many of the songs seem to belong to Type II, the sort that does not diversify but experiences some change. Some songs would readily fit into Type III (but this is not common) and Type IV, borrowing from extant song (somewhat more common). Thus the repertory cannot easily be classed as being dominated by one type of transmission. Density is considerable, as implied above, and the dynamic component indicates considerable speed, a rapid rate of turnover. Now, many "new" songs may, on the observer's side of the coin, simply be variants of existing ones, so perhaps the statement of rapid dynamic should be changed to reflect this observation (Nettl 1967c:141–60, 1968:192–207).

The Blackfoot people about 1967 themselves seemed to have a view rather like that of the outside observer, but there are differences. They did not appear to feel that songs change very much, seemed rather to regard each song as especially created and remaining essentially unchanged. Similar tunes were regarded as separate units. Thus their view might differ from my analysis in that they would consider many songs as belonging to the unchanging Type I. Some informants agreed that their songs are quite similar to each other and that two songs may indeed sound practically alike. And they said that turnover is quick, but believed that this had not been so in the past. They would presumably view themselves as a culture with an increasingly rapid-moving music history.

There is another repertory of current Blackfoot music, a body consisting of older religious music and associated material, a repertory whose songs, in contrast with these newer ones, are not shared with other Plains tribes (Nettl 1967c:304). It exists on older recordings of Blackfoot music and in the memories of older informants, but it is not widely performed. From scanty sources of information one might guess that this music lived to a large extent in the Type I tradition, that it was quite dense and also broad, and that it changed rather slowly, having far less turnover than the modern repertory.

As a contrast we look again at the Peyote songs. Quite different from the general repertories of the Plains Indians, they constitute in each Plains culture only a part of the musical repertory of the total population. Only some people participate, and Peyote music constitutes only a part of the individual's musical experience. On the other hand, it is intertribal, and groupings such as tune families may cross cultural, tribal, and linguistic boundaries. The idea that Peyote songs are made up from existing materials combining and recombining phrases from a limited vocabulary has been encountered here before. I once tried my hand at making a lexicon of musical lines found in a limited number of Kiowa and Arapaho Peyote songs, and must confess, except for the normal closing formula and several penultimate formulas to which the last four notes are attached, that I did not find a staggering number of such widely distributed lines, even if I liberally accepted variants. But the results were much more encouraging when I took into account only the rhythmic patterns of vocal phrases. Perhaps it is this rhythmic component, along with the accompanying syllable sequences, which constitutes the true content of this repertory.

On the other hand, one does not find large numbers of differentiated variants of individual Peyote songs or even of lines. I would conclude that this repertory belongs in large measure to Type I, the unchanging, single form—with modification, of course, and particularly with evidence of the process of Type IV, borrowing. It is interesting that the statements of Indian singers themselves imply that they regard this, in contrast to their other music such as the contemporary Blackfoot songs described above, as an essentially borrowing repertory. The Peyote song group is not as dense as that of the modern Plains songs, but more so than the older Plains music. Comparison between older and more recent recordings and among variants of the same song from different tribes would show this repertory as a slowly developing one with the songs themselves not changing very much, with material remaining in the repertory for long periods, and with little turnover. All of this is not easy to square, however, with the idea that here a tradition creates new songs by combining material from existing ones, and that its practitioners say so.

The body of music most studied for our purposes here is that of Anglo-American folk song. These songs—they play a role in their cultures related to that of Peyote songs, in that they occupy only a portion of the musical experience but are shared by a number of related culture units—live largely in the tune-family tradition, Type III, and in some cases they borrow material as in Type IV. The scope of this repertory is wider perhaps than that of the two Indian repertories mentioned but nevertheless not very broad. Considering the number of variants of some tune families available, it is quite dense, for the variants are similar and partake of a very limited number of modal, rhythmic, and formal types. The style is limited even when the content is not. It appears to be a rather rapidly moving repertory, with songs changing quickly, but the turnover of the songs is slow, and old material is retained while small amounts of new material are periodically introduced.

My last brief examples come from Iran. Here the concepts held in the culture seem to be quite different from those of the outside investigator. Let me compare the classical tradition of Teheran with one genre of folk music, the *chahārbeiti,* a four-line song form studied in Khorasan by Stephen Blum (Blum 1972, and in Nettl 1978a).

The Persian classical system has been amply described in these essays. In a sense the *radif* is the "content" of the music. Each of its parts or *gushehs* has variants, is in fact a small tune family. Each, at the same time, has organic and genetic relationships to other *gushehs* in its mode or *dastgāh* and to certain ones in other *dastgāhs.* Thus the entire *radif,* or large parts of it, could be analyzed as a single creation, a family, analogous to the Anglo-American tune family, with many internal interrelationships. The performances of each *gusheh,* though improvised, are in the aggregate also like a tune family, but extremely sparse. On the other hand, a performer produces, in the course of his career, a tightly knit, dense subgroup comprised of all of *his* performances of one *gusheh.* Each such tune family maintains only a few elements of content such as thematic and closing formulas to hold it together. The total group of performances or improvisations is a broad, sparse repertory, one that changes rapidly, while the *radif* itself changes only slightly. Here, then, we have two structures superimposed on one another, to be analyzed separately, exhibiting more or less contrastive behavior. The folk taxonomy, let me say very briefly and without discussion, seems indeed to be quite different from my analysis.

In certain portions of the Persian folk music culture of Khorasan, one may find a kind of microcosmic replication of what occurs in the classical music. The use of a small number of tunes to serve as musical vehicles for a vast number of texts is the basis of these repertories. The outsider perceives instantly, for example, that a great many of the tunes used for the genre *chahārbeiti* are very similar and, indeed, the Iranians refer to them collectively as *a* tune, *the chahārbeiti* tune (Blum 1974a:90). Of course this tune has variants, but these have not developed to exhibit broad differences; the outside listener has no trouble keeping them, so to speak, under one hat. This is true, generally speaking, of a number of other melodies and genres in the musical culture of Khorasan, where tradition may fit our Type I. Each tune family is dense and seems to move slowly through time, changing little. The entire repertory varies in density, the families remaining different from each other in several ways, exhibiting, incidentally, the influences of the many cultures that inhabit Khorasan.

These examples have been taken rather at random, and their classification is highly hypothetical, awaiting better methods of sampling and analysis. But ethnomusicology, concerned as it is with the musics of peoples, with total repertories, should work toward finding ways of comparing them as a whole. One of the major criteria of comparison ought to be the way in which the music is distributed within its repertory and how its units interrelate. An understanding of a music from this viewpoint is based in large measure on the way in which these units are transmitted, and on what in them changes and what remains.

It is indicative of the state of musicological thought that written tradition has been widely accepted as the normal form of transmission, if not of world music, then of what may usefully and effectively be studied. Given the available sources, this is an understandable thrust. Yet the approaches developed in ethnomusicology can underscore something already understood but rarely expounded, that oral (or more correctly, aural) transmission is the norm, that music everywhere uses this form of self-propagation, that in live or recorded form it almost always accompanies the written, and that it dominates the musical life of a society and the life of a piece of music.

Chapter 15

The Basic Unit of All Human Behavior and Civilization

THE THIRD RASOUMOVSKY

Interviewing a new student in the anthropology department, I asked for her view of what anthropologists do. Instead of giving the orthodox answer—to study humans—she told me that anthropologists study symbols. An unexpected definition, perhaps, but based on homework and on another startling statement by Leslie White, to the effect that "the symbol is the basic unit of all human behavior and civilization" (White 1949:22). When he wrote this, not many paid attention, but it is now widely believed that if humans are, as White said, distinguished by the fact that they use symbols, it is symbolism in the broadest sense that anthropology must be about. For the same reason, there are now scholars who believe that music, like other human works, can best be examined as a symbol and as a system of symbols.

It is a recent development. In the 1940s my father, a musicologist particularly interested in the Viennese classicists, brought to the attention of the family a curious book. By Arnold Schering, a man who had made major contributions to several branches of music history, it was an interpretation of many works by Beethoven as literal representations of classic works of literature. Entitled *Beethoven und die Dichtung* ("Beethoven and Literary Art," 1936), it interprets the Seventh Symphony as based on scenes from Goethe's *Wilhelm Meisters Lehrjahre,* the Kreutzer Sonata on Tasso's *Gerusalleme Liberata,* and the third Rasoumovsky Quartet, Op. 59, no. 3, on *Don Quixote.* The interpretations proceed in play-by-play fashion, motifs assigned specific meanings, instrumental melodies interpreted as settings of words.

Aside from the composer's well-known interest in literature, Schering gives no evidence that Beethoven used these works as models. What evidence he marshals is mainly internal, and thus the book was never taken very seriously by most Beethoven scholars. Today it has been relegated to the status of a curiosum resulting from the advanced age of a man whose scholarship had always been lauded as highly imaginative. My father eventually agreed, but for a time he regarded this book as important.

The desire to see in music something beyond itself has long been a significant strand of thought among lovers of Western classical music, especially of the last 200 years. The idea of great musical works having been conceived as symbols of great literary works appealed to some of these people, and it was rather with sorrow that one had to conclude that the association was Schering's alone, and probably not Beethoven's. But must Beethoven have consciously set out to write works based on specific literature in order for them to be accepted as symbols? The intention of the composer is important for an understanding of *his* life and work. But for an ethnomusicological view of Western musical culture, there are further considerations. Thus this incident underscores for me the importance of music as symbol, as a particular kind of symbol, in one sector of Western culture.

That Schering would try to make a case, and that it was believed by some, indicates one way in which musical symbols operate, and something of what we regard to be in the realm of the conceivable. If the association of Beethoven and Cervantes is not to be found in Beethoven's life, it may nevertheless become a valid association in the mind of the believing listener, and in other ways it might possibly provide a guide for understanding the musical work. The belief that motifs and melodies can symbolize specific events in a story is a major feature of Western musical thought. The fact that literary and musical works are perceived to have similar structural characteristics is indicative of some aspects of the role that the arts play in Western culture. What Schering did illustrates one way in which Western classical music culture conceives of musical symbolism. To repeat: the common-sense view is that Schering tried but failed. An ethnomusicologist, however, also wonders what it is about a musical culture that would make a scholar look at Beethoven in this way, and why his findings were accepted at least by some, and given up with reluctance.

If humans deal in symbols, the third Rasoumovsky Quartet must be a symbol. But of what? To one person it may signify musical greatness, and to another, stuffiness. To Schering, if not to Beethoven, it symbolized, in detail, *Don Quixote.* Perhaps it is just as significant to discover Schering's association as Beethoven's; what Beethoven may have "meant" could be construed as no more important than how Schering takes it for understanding humanity or Western culture. We may have to be content with saying that the quartet is a symbol, part of a complex set of symbols (i.e. culture), or itself a complex set of symbols.

Ethnomusicologists have approached the study of symbolism in a gingerly fashion, taking bites of the pie from different sides. As one might expect, they have been affected by music historians and by anthropologists, and mixed the influences. The anthropological literature dealing with culture as a set of symbols, large and impressive, is typically represented by a group of publications by Clifford Geertz (1971, 1973), Victor Turner (1974), Dan Sperber (1975), Mary Douglas (1966, 1970), Raymond Firth (1973), and particularly Claude Lévi-Strauss (1963, 1969, 1971, etc.). The work of linguists, philosophers, and structuralists dealing with literary art has also played a major role (see Sturrock 1979). Lévi-Strauss regards culture as "essentially a symbolic system or a configuration of symbolic systems" (Kaplan and Manners 1972:171), and to him it is the symbolic nature of human behavior, perceived in its structure, that makes it "culture" as distinguished from nature. But anthropologists are involved in the recognition of symbols (and of various related phenomena such as signs, similes, metaphors, master symbols, natural symbols, etc.—Firth 1973:57–71), and despite their widespread acceptance of the symbol as the basis of culture, a group calling themselves "symbolic" anthropologists seem to deal with symbols as a special phenomenon within culture. Thus Firth (1973) separates certain areas of life as special carriers of symbolism: food, hair, flags, giving and getting.

An alternative to studying symbolism by extracting symbols from a culture is to use language, the central symbolic code of humans, as a point of departure. I am speaking of a line of scholars known as "structural linguists," beginning with Ferdinand de Saussure, going on through Roman Jakobson and Zellig Harris, to Noam Chomsky, whose work led in part to that of the "structuralists" of a more general sort. The characteristic of the "structural" approach, it seems to me, is to study language, culture, or domains within culture as systems with structural principles that can be uncovered without reference to specific symbols or their objects, or to meaning, but with the underlying principle that human behavior is symbolic behavior. Thus, according to Sperber (Sturrock 1979:28), what Lévi-Strauss does is neither "to decipher symbols nor to describe the symbolic code." He is interested in "systems of relationships" (ibid. p. 30) that show how the human mind works. The connection with language may at times seem thin. But it may help to point out that the relationship between the structure or sound of a word and what it means is usually arbitrary, and that language is best analyzed through study of its internal interrelationships. This is what structuralists also say of culture, and it may be significant that anthropologists interested in symbolic studies have sometimes turned to music. Lévi-Strauss, especially, refers to music in many publications and is particularly noted for his use of musical forms as metaphoric titles of the sections in *The Raw and the Cooked* (1969), and for his analysis of Ravel's *Bolero* (1971; see also the analysis of his work in Hopkins 1977).

Musicologists have approached symbolism quite differently. For much of their history, following Hanslick's aesthetic and contradicting widely accepted concepts of the lay population, most of them have tended to avoid the subject. Recently they have become more sympathetic, sometimes basing their work on philosophers such as Cassirer (1944) and Langer (1942, 1953), who broadly interpret music as symbolic. Scholars such as Meyer (1956, 1967) and Cooke (1959) have argued the general relevance of symbolic studies for music. But mostly, musicology has dealt with one aspect of the symbolic universe, the attempts on the part of composers to signify specific, nonmusical facts, events, or artifacts through music, and the degree to which these can be discovered in a particular cultural, historic, or personal context. Contributing to the general theoretical picture, Schering (1941: 146) classified musical symbols, distinguishing between heuristic and concrete and trying his hand at the nomothetic ("everything which exceeds the normal tone range of the human voice is symbolic of the non-human, dark, sinister, demoniac"—1941:170). But others, rather than seeking laws, have looked for particular musical styles and repertories in which symbolism rises to the surface and dominates, such as the literature of the so-called *Affektenlehre* of the late seventeenth and early eighteenth centuries (Bukofzer 1947:388) and as suggested for the Renaissance by Lowinsky (1946; see also Brown 1976:80, 130).

Anthropology and historical musicology, in their approaches to symbolism, can perhaps be thus contrasted in their main thrusts: anthropologists try to find ways in which culture as a whole and at large can be viewed as a system of symbols. The existence of such systems is taken for granted, and the issue is how to use the concept of symbolism as a window to the special character of human culture. The music historian, however, seeks evidence of specific symbolic systems in particular repertories and is less concerned with generalized theory.

In ethnomusicology the symbol has a curious history. The concept draws together a number of otherwise separable ideas and methods. It is actually a short history, whose early theoretical statements come from the universalist aspects of German diffusionism (Danckert 1956; M. Schneider 1951). Nketia (1962) presents an early statement of the insider-outsider contrast. Merriam (1964) includes a chapter on "music as symbolic behavior" but finds himself able to draw on only a small amount of literature, devoting himself to relatively general studies of symbolism in philosophy, questioning whether the "theory of signs and symbols is truly applicable to music" (1964:234), and concluding that music does "function as a symbolic part of life, at least in the sense that it does represent other things" (ibid.). He proposes four ways in which this relationship is "manifest in human experience": (1) Art is symbolic in its conveyance of direct meanings. (2) Music is "reflective of emotion and meaning." (3) Music reflects other cultural behavior, organization, and values. (4) In a very general sense music may symbolize (Merriam phrases it as a question) human behavior in general.

Since Merriam's work of 1964, the literature of symbolic anthropology has grown enormously, and thus the term "symbol" and its relatives and derivatives have become commonplace in ethnomusicological literature. In the 1970s there seemed to be several areas in which the concept has been used: (1) Repertories, genres, types of music may within any given society have specific symbolic value. (2) Specific pieces of music, sections of pieces, devices, motifs, notes, tone colors, etc., may also have specific symbolic value within a given society. (3) Music, mainly symbolic or not, can best be understood if examined in the way in which other systems acknowledged to be symbolic, such as language, are examined. Repertories or groups of pieces in the first, units of musical thought in the second, and minimal components of the musical vocabulary in the third would be units to be studied or to form the bases of opposition for structural analysis.

To put it another way: some work in ethnomusicology looks for symbols in music, and some at music as a set of symbols. These two currents in the literature, widely separated at their beginnings, have come to approach each other, in parallel to anthropology and linguistics. The scholar seeking symbols in music deals with the issue in a culture-specific way, deriving particular systems such as ragas or program music from the nature of their culture. The school of musicological analysis that derives models and methods from linguistics conceives of the relationship of symbol and symbolized as less important than the structure of the system, and usually does not deal with the particular nature of the music analyzed and its relationship to the culture which produced it. From these currents, once only incidentally related, has come a closer union, clustered around concepts from semiotics, the science of signs, and from linguistics. The most ambitious statement of its position, a book by Nattiez (1971; see also 1972, 1973), deals with both the structural analysis and the cultural context of symbols.

SONG OF THE NIGHTINGALE

The stately theme near the end of "The Moldau" by Smetana clearly represents the river flowing past the ancient Bohemian castle, Vyšehrad. The marching band in the parade sends shivers up some spines. The sound of jazz used to remind people that they could break their routine, do the (at least slightly) illicit. Three kinds of musical symbol. Is it really the music that creates these effects, capable of meaning something other than itself? How, and to whom? Must the creator mean what the listener perceives? On the whole, ethnomusicology has eschewed the philosophical issues, but it has sometimes been concerned with defining symbol and symbolized when a society does not articulate such a definition or provides no consensus.

Bach may or may not have cared whether melodic movement that accompanies certain concepts, such as sharply rising melody for references to sky (Schering 1941:61), came to the awareness of his audience. One will ask whether the audience at any level understood the relationship, whether this kind of elaborate symbolism was lost on them, and what the significance of such a system was. The music historian is likely to treat the matter as a special accomplishment of Bach's, regardless of its role in Bach's society, and its significance would not be diminished if it were found to be absolutely idiosyncratic to Bach. Ethnomusicologists might admire Bach's genius, but their main interest would be in the degree to which this way of composing was shared and understood.

If we wish, therefore, to look at Persian classical music with a view to learning something about symbolism, we should study the way in which it is perceived as a symbol (in detail and as a whole) by the Iranian listener, and even by the Iranian who barely knows its sound and hardly ever listens to it. We must begin by pointing out that around 1970 this music existed largely in the city of Teheran, was performed at most by a couple of hundred musicians, had an audience of only a few thousand, but nevertheless was a symbol of something to many more. It was only one of many kinds of music to be heard in Teheran, there were many other styles and genres, Persian and foreign, and most people listened to, or consumed, several of these kinds of music and had opinions about others as well. One way of approaching this structure of styles in a symbolic context is to identify for each type of music a specific symbolic role. This is a view provided by the outsider-analyst, who may say that Western music in Iran is symbolic of the Westernized and industrialized sector of society, and of those aspects and values of the broadly shared culture that in the early 1970s were rapidly changing to a completely Western character—jet travel, Paris fashions, skyscrapers. Certain popular music, using orchestras of Western and of Middle Eastern origin—violins, santours, cellos, dombaks—may be symbolic of the mixture of Western and traditional elements in a vast number of everyday matters. Iranian classical music may appear as a symbol of the traditional and unchanging values of society, just as this particular music is thought to be unchanging.

Well, such an outsider's classificatory approach may be a useful initial orientation, but we next ask whether this kind of symbolism is in fact perceived by Iranians. The question begs for a very detailed exposition, but there is really very little data that can be provided to shed light on this complex problem. Outright interviewing of informants regarding questions of symbolism did not in my experience seem to be productive, and I must therefore depend on observations of musical behavior and on analysis of statements about music that were made for other purposes. The following considerations seem to support the above-listed contentions.

In a survey of attitudes about Persian classical music made among Teheranians more or less at random, it turned out that many individuals who did not know or listen to classical music had strong opinions about it, regarding it as a great art or as an obsolete artifact no longer consonant with the culture, something frivolous or something ponderous. But there was agreement on its peculiar Persian-ness, and its actually close relationship to Arabic and Turkish music was disregarded. Classical music was considered something above the regional limitations of folk music (seen as the music of smaller population groups), a kind of music representing the nation. It was also regarded as something old, tying the Islamic present to the pre-Islamic past. As already pointed out, detailed analysis of the *radif* shows that important cultural values or principles are reflected in its structure. To go into somewhat greater detail, the importance of a hierarchical structure in society, balanced by the need for direct contact with a source of power and guidance (once the Shah and later Khomeini, or the father of the extended family, the university president), can be shown as a dominating principle in the *radif,* which itself holds the position of central figure in relationship to performances derived from it. During a period of study with a master, the various portions of the *radif* were first presented as equal in importance, all equally capable of producing music, but gradually a hierarchy among the sections was unveiled, some parts emerging as more important than others. Importance correlates with position (what comes first is more important than what comes later), with exceptionality (those parts of a unit that depart from its typical scalar, melodic, or rhythmic structure are important), with size (longer sections are more important), and with the element of surprise (unexpected deviations from a scale are singled out for attention, and nonmetric sections, rhythmically unpredictable, have priority over more or even completely metric materials).

Similarly, individualism, another central cultural value, is reflected in the importance of the exceptional, as just mentioned; in the centrality of improvised music as compared to the composed; and in the theoretical absence of precise repetition. Another value, surprise, is reflected in similar ways. The position of what is important in social intercourse, the important coming first in informal situations but being preceded by introductory behavior or personnel in the more formal, is reflected in the precedence of what is important in the *radif,* something studied with one teacher and practiced in solitude, as compared to formal performance, where the material most closely based on the *radif* appears late and occupies less time.

Clearly, this is a personal interpretation, and its validity can only be established by analysis and logical argument. Nevertheless, it is interesting to see that other kinds of music in Iran do not share these values and characteristics to the same degree. In folk and popular music improvisation does not play the same central role; nor does the concept of hierarchy. Individualism of the sort exhibited by the accompanying system, the soloist a couple of notes ahead, is not present. Ensembles playing in unison, absent in the central parts of classical performance, dominate the popular music. Surprising tones are rare and metric structure gives rhythmic predictability.

The extraction of cultural values from a plethora of behavior patterns, particularly in a complex society, is a risky business. But those mentioned are evidently among the ones that seem to have been present in Iranian culture for a long time and, judging from changes that have taken place during the last thirty years, they seem to be consistent and shared by the traditional and modernized segments of society. Others, perhaps involving reactions to change, come and go. Of course the classical music is relatively constant while styles of popular music change rapidly.

The structure of the classical music system gives clues to the way it may reflect culture and act as a symbol of aspects of culture, but equally important is the Iranian musician's perception of this structure and his theories about it. These are not always realistic, but nevertheless may inform us about the society's perception of the relationship of music and culture. For example, there is the belief that the *radif* is perfect, contains all that can be included in a musical system, is all-encompassing of emotion and meaning, and cannot be changed; and that it is larger in its scope than Indian and Arabic music, systems objectively at least roughly equal in scope, something Iranian musicians know but do not accept. The integrity of the *radif* reflects the often stated belief in the wholeness of Iranian culture. The idea that it does not change reflects the abiding importance of certain cultural values, and the documentable fact that the *radif* is actually a recent restructuring of older materials which has changed a good deal since 1900 is typically ignored. In 1968 one said about classical music those things that one wished to be able to say about the culture of Iran.

Iranians themselves have a symbol for the classical music that shows its association with what is good, Iranian, and traditional. It is the nightingale, thought by Iranians to be particularly common in their nation, a bird which sings better than all others, which—very important—is thought not to repeat itself in song, a symbol of the ancient cultural treasures of Iran such as the poetry of the great literary figures of the late Middle Ages, or of Shiraz, a great cultural center, "city of roses and nightingales." It is a symbol in a particular sense, for it reflects idea and ideal. The theory that neither nightingales nor Iranian musicians repeat themselves ties music to central cultural values. Like the bird, the music is symbolic of the whole nation and all of its past.

Most of the world's societies find themselves in the twentieth century participating in two or more musics that can be rather easily distinguished, and the idea that each music functions as a symbol of particular aspects of a culture is a convenient approach to the study of one aspect of musical symbolism. In the culture of the northern Plains Indians during the 1960s, three kinds of music were distinguished by insiders and outsiders: older, traditional, tribal music; modernized intertribal or "pan-Indian" music; and Western music. The three had different values, the first as a symbol of the tribal past, to be remembered but placed in a kind of museum context; the second, of the need of Indian cultures to combine in order to assure cultural survival as Indians; and the third, of the modern facts of Indian life. Integration as a tribe, as an Indian people, and into the mainstream American environment are symbolized. The relationships seem obvious to an outsider, but they are also articulated by the culture's own interpretation of itself (Witmer 1973:86–90).

McFee (1972:92–102) follows a similar line of thought, dividing the Blackfoot population and its values into white- and Indian-oriented groups. For Indian culture he lists individualism, bravery, skill, wisdom, and generosity; for white orientation, self-dependence, acquisition, and work. The two groups overlap, but one can find some of the Indian-oriented values in traditional music and musical behavior. Individualism is evident in the need for each man, ideally, to learn his own songs in visions, and to develop a personal repertory of songs, perhaps also in the tendency for traditional music to be soloistic or, when performed by groups, to avoid a high degree of vocal blend. Bravery can conceivably be related to the practice of singing before a group, sometimes with improvised texts, in a ceremony replicating courage in physical conflict. Generosity is exhibited in the system of giving songs, the willingness to borrow from and give to other tribes. The three "white" values given by McFee can be associated with "white" music and with the modern Indian music used by the Blackfoot. The use of notation and the ownership of complex instruments such as pianos and electric guitars can in various ways be associated with all three. Composition (in contrast to acquisition of songs through visions) is related to self-dependence. The importance of size of repertory in the modern genres and the idea of rapid learning with the use of tape recorders are relevant to the value of acquisition. The practice of rehearsing and the conscious development of complex performance styles in the modern Indian music can be related to the value of work.

HE RIDES AN ELEPHANT AMONG THE HILLS AND VALLEYS

There is no intrinsic relationship between ascending melodic contour and going to heaven, but if this is the way a group of people agree to represent the Ascension, then a symbol has been created. Among the issues for ethnomusicology is the existence of interculturally valid, general or specific symbol systems. We have explored one possible symbolic universal, the association of styles or repertories with major divisions of a culture, and perhaps can go no further, so we now return to Schering's paradigm in order to see how symbol and symbolized are related within a given style or repertory, to what extent the association is abstract and to what degree based on more concrete factors.

The literature of ethnomusicology has not explored with very much sophistication the large number of cultures in which explicitly symbolic systems exist within restricted repertories. The most widely known such system is in Indian classical music, in which ragas are assigned nonmusical character. Associations range from season and time of day to attributes such as love, devotion, and aggression, to specific natural events such as fire and rain, and on to highly specialized images (also represented in icons) such as "a youth, wearing a red cloth . . . he rides an elephant among the hills and valleys, at night, singing heavenly songs . . ." (Deva 1974:21) for raga Deepak. The existence of the system is well documented. Among the questions not thoroughly understood is the degree to which listeners in general are or were aware of and affected by the association. One should discover how essential the symbolic system is to an understanding of the music, whether it is thoroughly believed by musicians or simply used as an explanatory device for laymen, much as teachers of music appreciation have sometimes explained the strictly musical difference between major and minor by associating it with the concepts of "happy" and "sad."

While the association of ragas with nonmusical things seems to have been well established in India at one time (though gradually lost on both audiences and musicians—Deva 1974:21), similar systems less widely accepted in their own cultures and less standardized exist or existed in the Middle East. The supposed extramusical character of the ancient Greek modes has been widely discussed and their traits—inspiration of enthusiasm for the Phrygian, sadness for the Mixolydian, etc.—attributed to interval sequences, range of scale, a particular type of music cast in a given tonality. We have little idea whether in Greece the Mixolydian music caused listeners to be sad and, if so, whether because of the characteristics of the mode; or whether other things about that music, cast by chance in the Mixolydian mode, associated it with sadness; or for that matter whether it simply made listeners aware that a quality of sadness was present, without in fact changing their mood. It's an issue that goes beyond symbolism, involving even music therapy, a subject only occasionally touched upon by ethnomusicologists (see Robertson-DeCarbo 1974, Densmore 1927), and yet an example of the direct practical use of a symbolic system.

Caron and Safvate (1966:59–98) give nonmusical characteristics of the *dastgāhs,* the units analogous to "modes," in Persian music. Thus the *dastgāh* of *Shur* expresses tenderness, love, pity, incites sadness but also consoles. *Segāh* represents sadness, chagrin, abandonment of hope, but *Chahārgāh,* which shares melodic motifs and many other details with *Segāh* though not the scalar interval sequence, gives the impression of strength. *Mahour* represents dignity and majesty. In my experience Iranian musicians, asked to identify such nonmusical traits, tend to agree, but with moderate enthusiasm, typically suggesting that these considerations are not important in their everyday thinking about music. They may also disagree with Caron and Safvate, and among themselves, about the specific nonmusical traits of the modes. Thus *Chahārgāh* is said by some to be profoundly moving, but by others, warlike. Some ascribe to *Dashti* a plaintive, moving quality; others maintain that it is happy. But there are further ramifications. Rather specific characterizations can be found: one musician described *Shur* as an old man looking back at his life, finding much sadness but philosophically accepting it. When asked for the reasons for this association, he connected *Shur's* meditative, poetic, somber character with his perception of the Iranian personality and the nature of Iranian history, varied but prevailingly sad. And with this special Persian-ness also was associated the great significance of *Shur,* the most important *dastgāh,* known indeed, because others are derived from it, as the "mother of *dastgāhs.*" The *dastgāh* of *Chahārgāh* is warlike because outside the classical system it is thought to be used for chanting heroic epic poetry; indeed, a good deal of the chanting of the text of the *Shāh-Nāmeh* by Ferdowsi, while not truly in *Chahārgāh,* coincides or is compatible with its scale. The components of the symbolic system feed into each other in a chicken-and-egg situation.

A complex thing to comprehend. Do the *dastgāhs* or ragas symbolize characteristics that can be abstracted in adjectives, or ideas about the aspect of culture with which they are associated, or are they simply related to uses and words of particular genres? We wish to know who in the consuming public shares in this system, and how much agreement there must be for us, as ethnomusicologists, to accept it as truly a part of the culture. Like music historians, ethnomusicologists seem to jump at the chance to find associations of such a qualitative sort between music and culture, and the tendency to accept them without taking these points into consideration may tell more about the cultural background of ethnomusicologists than about that of the music.

The concept of "program music" was developed in Western culture, and we are hardly in a position to say that other cultures also have it. Even the related phenomena vary enormously. The parallels between *dastgāhs* and the tone poems of Richard Strauss are modest at best. Australian aboriginals in Yirkalla use a different scale for ceremonial songs of each lineage, which, according to Richard Waterman (1956:46), permits them to be identified at a distance even when the words are indistinct. The association seems to be arbitrary, the relationship somewhat like that of the sound of a word to the content it symbolizes.

But in a way close to nineteenth-century Europe's, Chinese classical music has for some centuries featured a type of solo instrumental piece that is thought to represent images, scenes, objects, or even battles (Malm 1977: 159, 1969; F. Lieberman 1969), with titles such as "High Mountain, Flowing Stream," "Great Wave Washes the Sand," or "An Embroidered Purse." With a little effort the Western listener can empathize, but whether there are aspects of a piece that are definitive symbols of water, ornamental art, or mountains does not seem to be stated in Chinese literature. Yet the association does not seem arbitrary.

At the other end of the continuum are some love songs of the northern Plains Indians, which may also be played on the flute. Singers often end such songs with two short, high cries or calls, using indefinite pitches not related to the scale of the rest of the melody. When played on flutes, these songs end with short "cries" on the instrument, in this case of definite pitch, but using tones outside the scale already established. The vocal cries are symbolized—not merely imitated—on the flute because of their relationship to the scalar structure.

Symbolism of yet a different sort is found in the *mbira* ("thumb-piano") songs of the Shona people of Zimbabwe. The structure of a sung and played genre may be explained by reference to the life of the human body. Thus Abraham Maraire (1971) describes pieces played on the *nyunga-nyunga mbira* as beginning and ending on a basic pattern, for which the concept of a skeleton is used as metaphor. After this basic pattern is performed and repeated, the musician adds to it thematic material, varying it in many ways, fleshing it out, as it were, developing a more complex texture; then the elaboration is gradually dropped, the piece eventually returning to the simple basic pattern. The music is presented as a symbol of life (but simultaneously as a symbol of other things as well) or perhaps also of death. As the elaborations drop away, only the skeleton is left.

These are a few examples, and I have not even mentioned symbolism of instruments, musicians, musical occasions and rituals. There is almost no end to the number of ways in which we could illustrate the kinds of symbolic associations between music and something else in culture, the number of ways in which music can have meaning—and no end to the number of ways in which musical symbolism can be explored or interpreted (see N. Sachs 1975 for a synthesis of approaches).

AS THOUGH IT DID HAVE A LIFE OF ITS OWN

If all music is a system of symbols, one ought to be able to analyze it in a way similar to or derived from the accepted analysis of the intellectual grandfather of symbol systems, human language. Reasons for doing so present themselves: in order to integrate music among the various symbol systems in culture; to take advantage of the precise and rigorous methods of analysis developed by linguists and their elegant way of stating findings; in order to establish a comprehensive method of analysis valid for all musics; to explore a significant aspect of the music/culture relationship; in order to show how much music is like language; and to help in understanding the relationship between music and words in song.

The results so far are mixed. Linguistic and semiological approaches to music have stated ambitious goals and sometimes given the impression that they will save analysis of the musical artifact as well as the study of music in culture from the many pitfalls of the past. In fact, the publications in this realm have largely been devoted to case studies showing the usefulness of linguistic methods for the analysis of the specific musical piece. The methods go back to the work of Saussure, the godfather of symbolic studies, to Roman Jakobson, who developed structural concepts such as phonemics, and to Noam Chomsky, the culture hero of modern linguistics. Leaning on such powerful forebears, music scholars gingerly and sporadically attempted to make some sample studies in the pretransformational period, the phonemic procedures of the Prague school serving as models for stating distribution of musical segments (e.g. Nettl 1958b). In a seminal article Bright (1963) suggested a number of ways in which linguistics could help musicology. Later, transformational and generative grammar exerted great influence on a number of disciplines, and a series of musicological publications ensued. Among the early ones the most influential was Boilès's (1967) study of a ritual of the Tepehua people of Veracruz, treating motifs in songs (without words) as elements in a generative grammar. The fact that the Tepehua themselves are said to have agreed with his conclusions is impressive, as is the elegance of his statement. But Boilès's study at best deals with an exceptional situation in world music, as specific meanings appear to be assigned to the motifs, and the culture verbalizes the symbolic system.

Further attempts, sometimes less successful because Tepehua songs lend themselves to linguistics-derived analysis better than other music, are nevertheless varied and interesting. Blacking (1970a) deals with "deep" and "surface" structures in Venda music in a somewhat idiosyncratic way, using concepts developed by Chomsky. Cooper (1977) proposes a grammatical system through which the scales of Indian ragas can be derived. Theoretical considerations are at the heart of publications by Nattiez (1972) and Ruwet (1966, 1967). Chenoweth and Bee (1971) establish a grammar of melodic structure in New Guinea. Herndon (see Chapter 7) proposes a system of analysis that may be applied to any music, and tests it with an example from Malta (1974:251–58). The movement may have peaked in the large number of (largely unpublished) papers read at a meeting of the Society for Ethnomusicology in Toronto in 1972.

What are we to make of this recent development in ethnomusicology? On the one hand, it must be admitted that much of what has been done is in the realm of exercise. Influenced by linguistics, semiotics, and structuralism, the authors have been trying to find ways of stating what really goes on in a piece of music, going beyond the listing of characteristics and the repertory-specific statements of general principles developed in the theoretical system of Western music, by dealing with the structure of relationships. So far, despite the charisma of this aim, they have only rarely gained insights that could not have been provided by older and more conventional approaches or, indeed, by simple common-sense inspection.

Feld (1974), Kneif (1974), and Powers (1980) are among the most significant critics. Feld, speaking perhaps for others, seems to be asking, "Has it all been worthwhile?" The thorough-going revolution has not taken place. But contributions to the field have been made, even if no great leap forward has been achieved, and there have been valuable byproducts of the experimentation. In his critique Powers points out that the use of linguistic models adapted to music is only a stage in a long history of scholarship making use of comparisons between language and music, a history that includes early medieval music theorists and scholars of the German Renaissance and Baroque concerned with the relationship of music and rhetoric. In Europe, as well as other cultures, musicians and theorists have long used language as a model for explaining music and for teaching aspects of composition. Going far beyond modern linguistics and semiotics, Powers concludes that "language models for musical analysis used circumspectly can contribute fundamentally and not superficially to the musical disciplines, as they have more than once over the past millennium or so" (1980:55). One might add to Powers's history the large number of publications in the tradition of historical musicology dealing with the relationship of music and words in vocal compositions.

The analyses carried out with modern linguistic-derived methods are highly technical, and I shall refrain from any attempt to describe or summarize. One may debate the degree to which they have introduced rigor into a previously flabby activity, but as a group they have played an integrative role. They deal with Western and Asian classical music, European folk and non-Western tribal music. Their authors (I mention only a few) come from general musicology (Nattiez 1971, 1972, 1973; Powers 1980), linguistics (Ruwet 1966, 1975; Chandola 1970; Cooper 1977), anthropologically oriented ethnomusicology (Boilès 1967, 1973b; Herndon 1974), music theory (Lidov 1975), music-derived ethnomusicology (Chenoweth and Bee 1971), and anthropology (Springer 1956, Durbin 1971). A group of scholars from diverse traditions have joined in a loosely collective enterprise, itself an unusual event in the history of scholarship.

And the musical-semiotic literature has made its contribution to some of the familiar issues of ethnomusicology, in slightly disguised form. The typical member of this group hopes to build a universally valid procedure, but there is evidence that the greatest success has been achieved in certain instances particularly susceptible to linguistics-derived analysis. Powers (1980:37–38) insists on the "close resemblance between the way Indian classical music works and the way languages work," and adds that "few musics are as much like language as Indian music is." The universalist-particularist dichotomy shows up again, with a special twist. Music may be like language, and Powers stresses the "real insight available to musicology" (not just ethnomusicology) "from a knowledge of the study of languages." Culture is symbols, and language the key, but a key that works better for some languages or musics than others. In some cultures, Powers implies, music was constructed in a way similar to the structure of language; in others, rather differently, more influenced, one might guess, by dance, ritual, emotion, in what may be a residue of Curt Sachs's division of music into logogenic and pathogenic, word-born and emotion-born.

One of Steven Feld's main criticisms of linguistics-based analytical systems sounds a familiar trumpet: such analysis does not take into account the culture from which the music comes. Powers (1980:8) gently corrects: ". . . some music may sometimes be more efficiently interpreted by discussing it as though it did have a life of its own." Here perhaps is the old conflict of anthropology versus musicology again but, if so, it is interesting to see that most of those ethnomusicologists who try their hand at this game would incline to throw in their lot with the anthropologists. Perhaps here, too, semiotics et al. has given us a healthy mix, producing strange bedfellows but also a new kind of integration; the different camps are communicating, if not better, then more frequently.

But the publications to date, and the critiques of Feld and Powers, make it clear that uncritical attempts to use methods from linguistics at random on music often fail; the similarities between music and language are important, but the two differ in essence and at many levels. The players of the game have had to bend the system, and perhaps they did not bend it enough to provide musically useful results. The desire to cleave to linguistics, to approximate its exemplary rigor, may have overshadowed the musicological needs. But taking what is helpful—perhaps the concepts of phonemes and morphemes, transformation and generation, emic and etic—and leaving what is not, seems more hopeful than the insistence on analogy. In particular, specific and direct knowledge of musics and their underlying theory can temper the dangers of excessive linguistic enthusiasm (Powers 1980:55).

Feld also points out the degree to which structural linguistics outside a context of cultural study falls short of the aim of many linguists (1974:207). In the musical analogue the behavioral and conceptual components of Merriam's tripartite model are often ignored. Viewed thus, semiotic description of music falls squarely into the Western tradition of analysis; it does not directly take context into account. The criticism may be unfair. One must do one thing at a time, and the music historian who carefully analyzes the Beethoven quartet would probably be aghast at the suggestion that what he is doing at that moment is all that should ever be done, that this "pure" analysis should not later be combined with understanding of cultural and historical context. We can look at the Persian *radif* as an artifact that, as a whole or in its parts, can be analyzed as a symbolic system like language. We can also view it as a system that is broadly symbolic of the cultural system of which it is a part; further, that it is consciously used by its society as a symbol in the service of the culture. One of the major tasks is to find ways of combining these three pictures. Language may serve as a metaphor, and semiotics and linguistics, as inspiration. Perhaps we should expect no more.

Chapter 16

The Singing Map

AREAS, CIRCLES, CLUSTERS

If one listed the questions ethnomusicologists would wish to answer in the long run, the following two would no doubt be among them: What is the musical map of the world, that is, where are the significant musical phenomena found? And what can one do, from a mass of data limited to the contemporary, to reconstruct the history of world music? The second question has been frequently judged futile, but those who have tried to answer it have most commonly become preoccupied with the first. Fundamental statements of ethnomusicological fact have typically been presented in geographic terms; e.g., this instrument is found here and here; the music of this culture is like the music of this neighboring one or that rather distant one. Much attention has been devoted to methods of finding data about and presenting statements of the geographic distribution of music.

We wish to establish maps whose spaces and borders outline the distribution of traits, clusters of traits, partial or comprehensive musical systems. In drawing the singing map ethnomusicologists have mainly been inspired by three concepts developed in anthropology and folklore. The approach most clearly descriptive and found acceptable for the longest time is based on the so-called culture area concept, developed by American anthropologists and said by Driver (1961:12) to be "a convenient way of describing the ways of life of hundreds of peoples covering a whole continent or a larger part of the earth's surface." First used in 1895 (Harris 1968:374), it originated in the need to map and classify the large number of tribal groups of the Americas. On the surface the concept seems simple enough. A group of peoples living in contiguous distribution and having similar kinds of subsistence, use of energy, social organization, religion, arts, etc., would belong to one culture area. On the map the boundaries between culture areas appear rigid, but anthropologists recognized that they "are actually the approximate lines where two neighboring types of phenomena are present in equal amounts" (Driver 1961:13).

Culture areas have always been useful as purely classificatory devices. But it was probably inevitable that certain features of culture, such as the method of food production, would be stressed over others and weight the distributional statement. Moreover, it was quickly found that a group of societies assigned to the same culture area did not share in its culture type with equal intensity. For example, the Plains Indians of North America, a group of peoples with diverse origins as indicated by the variety of their linguistic stocks, shared in the Sun Dance as a major ceremonial occasion. But the Sun Dance was developed differentially, taking its most complex form from the Arapaho, in whose culture it was also most dominant. Thus, early on, anthropologists found themselves using the culture area concept as the basis for historical interpretation. Kroeber proposed the theory that a culture area has a center or "climax" in which the characteristic culture of the area is most developed; from this again grew the speculation that the main features of the area diffused from the center to the outlying, more marginal regions and continued until they met and merged with the diffusion of contrastive traits from a neighboring culture center. The use of the culture area concept developed among anthropologists who were concerned with American Indians and it worked best when applied to these peoples, who could be rather easily seen as a large number of small tribal groups. The idea of the culture area as an automatic guide to history was widely questioned (Harris 1968:375–77).

A related but also contrastive approach was that of the so-called German diffusionists, known because of its strong interest in historical interpretations as the "kulturhistorische Schule" (see Lowie 1937:171–95, Schmidt 1939). Comprised of research by such scholars as Leo Frobenius, Fritz Graebner, Wilhelm Schmidt, and to a large degree based on studies in Oceania and of physical artifacts, the concept developed in this school came to be known as "Kulturkreis," i.e. culture circle. Like the culture area concept, a culture circle is a statement that a number of peoples share a group of culture traits. These peoples need not be geographically contiguous, and since one society may have a number of trait clusters each of which is shared with a different group of peoples, it may be a part of several "Kulturkreise." At the root of the concept is the idea that humans are basically uninventive and thus extremely unlikely to develop the same thing more than once. So two societies, no matter how far apart, may be members of the same culture circle if they share one trait, but the likelihood of historical relationship increases if they share more than one. Now, since the diffusion of elements from various points to one culture must have occurred at different points in time, the various culture circles in which a society shares also represent strata in its history. The relatively dogmatic approach of this school of thinkers, and their insistence that all similarities of culture traits result from diffusion, eventually made their approach unacceptable to most anthropologists.

Referring to the distinction made in other chapters between musical content and musical style, we can draw an analogy here between music and culture. The culture area and Kulturkreis concepts involve the style of culture, perhaps drawing together societies that use the same way of organizing a pantheon while not requiring belief in specifically the same gods. They expect similarities in social organization but not in terminology, in the nature of story-telling events but not in the content of the stories. By contrast, the so-called historical-geographic method in folklore involves content. It traces the versions, variants, and forms of an artifact of folklore and shows the clustering of their distribution, basing on it conclusions about its history. Thus a particular story with characters and significant actions may be plotted on the map, but use in society, the length of narration, the narrative style itself are generally ignored. Developed by Scandinavian scholars (K. Krohn 1926), who in turn influenced a number of Americans (see Thompson 1946, W. Roberts 1958), and applied mainly to tales but also occasionally to ballad stories (Kemppinen 1954), the method compares versions by assessing their degree of similarity as well as the intensity of their geographic distribution. From the comparisons are developed archetypes of events and characters, and density as well as similarity are used to develop an archetype of the entire story, a key to its original form. So, through an elaborate method combining territory and quantity, a historical statement is made, giving an approximate sequence of events leading from the story in original or reconstructed form to its diffusion through its geographic area. In his classic history of the "Star-Husband" tale, a story of the marriage of two girls to stars followed by their successful escape, widespread among North American Indians, Stith Thompson (1953) shows that its origin is likely to have been in the Central Plains but that special characteristic forms developed later on the Northwest Coast while fragmentary versions developed on the outskirts of this area of distribution.

DRAWING THE MAP

Studying the geographic distribution of musical phenomena is generally more complex than the typical distributional study in cultural anthropology, where statements are often restricted to indicating that a given trait is present or absent in a culture unit. An element of culture can, of course, be broken into components for this purpose. For a particular type of string instrument, one could map the number of strings, the material from which the instrument is made, its shape, and so on (see e.g. Walin 1952). Going somewhat further, a similar study of musical style requires sensitivity, for it would have to be concerned with identifying relationships among forms that are not identical or similar, and with rejecting as unrelated some that may on the surface seem alike. As noted already in our consideration of similarity and difference (Chapter 9), one might need to decide which of various similar tunes are actually variants of one basic type, or whether two slightly different pentatonic scales are really subtypes of one form.

There is, moreover, the problem of deciding on geographic units to be used as a basis for statement, whether they should be determined by political affiliation, by language, by physical geography, whether smaller units such as villages should be considered, or perhaps even families, units that can often be studied most realistically. As in speech, each individual has his or her own musical idiolect and could even conceivably be considered as the minimal unit. But for practical purposes, the linguistic, cultural, natural, and political units encompassing homogeneous groups of people have had to serve. Several ways of making musical maps have been used.

The distribution of individual elements, components, or parameters of music, such as scale type or specific instrument, may be most easily treated. The literature provides many examples, among them Baumann's (1976) study of yodeling in Switzerland. Although geographic distribution is not his main purpose, he provides a map indicating yodeling types in a large number of Swiss locations, using towns and villages as the main units of reference. Lomax's cantometrics studies (e.g. 1968) give distributions of individual elements or parameters, using large culture areas as units; each of these can be the basis of separate charting, and Lomax makes much use of schematic maps.

Charting presence or absence of a trait yields information to the effect that culture A has rhythmic types X and Y, and culture B, types Y and Z, but of course we would wish also to indicate relative quantity. As pointed out, music lends itself rather well to being analyzed in this way, and in fact this is how one must proceed. There are few characteristics of music not found in a vast number of cultures, but in many of these they play an insignificant role. Giving mere presence and absence only establishes a capability realized. Statements of proportion are needed. Thus, when Collaer (1958:67), in one of the earliest publications dealing explicitly with the problem, proposed the desirability of mapping the distribution of the anhemitonic pentatonic scale, he must have had in mind some sort of quantitative approach, for compositions using such a scale are found in most cultures. A statement of the strength of this scale in each repertory would show that it is found in the vast majority of Cheremis songs, in about half of those of the Plains Indians, with some frequency in India, rather rarely in Iran. Sampling is a problem; even for some cultures for which there are many published and recorded pieces, these are sometimes from a single and perhaps exceptional corner of the repertory.

Since studies of the percentage of compositions in a repertory that contain a given trait are still not common, let me give a brief example, by no means definitive and here only generally illustrative. Based on small samples of varying reliability, it must be viewed as an example of method and of conceivable fact, and no more. It concerns a phenomenon in North American Indian music known as the "rise," identified and so designated by George Herzog (1928). In a song with nonstrophic structure, a short section is repeated at least twice, then followed by another bit of music at a slightly higher average pitch, followed, in turn, by the lower part. This alternation can continue for some time, but the lower section tends to appear more than once at a time, while the higher or "rise" section is less frequent. Herzog's description and terminology apply to the Yuman peoples, but somewhat similar forms are also found elsewhere.

The "rise" occurs in the music of a fairly large number of tribes along both coasts of the United States, given tribal locations when first discovered and disturbed by whites, and data published or recorded largely before 1960. It is strongest, occurring in over 50 percent of the songs, among several of the Yuman tribes of the Southwest, and among the Miwok, Pomo, Maidu, and Patwin of central California. In the repertories of the Northwest Coast Tsimshian and the southeastern Choctaw, it occurs in 20–30 percent of the songs; among the northeastern Penobscot and the northwestern Nootka, in 10–20 percent; and in the songs of the Kwakiutl as well as the southeastern Creek, Yuchi, and Tutelo, in less than 10 percent. Considering that most of the other peoples of the coasts are musically not well known, it would appear, provided the sample is reliable, that the rise has a center of distribution in the southwestern United States and thinning-out strength across the southern part of the country and up both coasts. This information might be interpreted in various ways but is in any case more valuable than a simple statement that these musics "have" the "rise."

While we could follow certain distinct musical features throughout the world and get one kind of picture or map, we might approach the entire problem of cartography from the point of individual compositions, pieces or songs. As already discussed in Chapter 8, our first problem would be to determine the identity of such a unit of musical creativity. Assuming that we can come up with an acceptable concept and a working definition, we would have to distinguish similarities genetically determined from others. From Wiora's presentation of tune types discussed in Chapters 8 and 9, it became obvious that distribution of musical style may actually be quite different from the distribution of compositions. Data for the distribution of the variants of songs or pieces, and for configurations or clusters of pieces, are available for much European folk music. For the rest of the world there is less, but there comes to mind one fine example, a study by Willard Rhodes (1958) of the opening song of the Peyote ceremony among several

Plains and southwestern United States tribes. The discovery of similar or almost identical tunes in the folk music of Hungarian and Cheremis (Kodály 1956:24–57)—and their absence among the Finns, who are linguistically close to the Cheremis—leads to questions about the relative behavior of music and other domains of culture. More detailed investigation of this kind would show whether a number of songs coincide in their geographic distribution and thus form areas, or whether each song has a unique distribution, and whether such areas coincide with those of style.

MUSICAL AREAS

Studies of the distribution of musical styles, of clusters of traits, or of the total configuration of elements have not been carried out as widely as one might expect, given the rather basic quality of this information for other kinds of study. A number of publications make general statements of distribution. Slobin (1976), for example, distinguished several subcultures in northern Afghanistan, stating their common characteristics as well as their differences. Merriam (1959:76–80) divided Africa into seven musical areas coinciding more or less with the culture areas established by Herskovits. McLean (1979), in a statistically and geographically sophisticated study, established musical areas for Oceania, separating musical structure from instruments, though the distribution of each shows broad correlation with the conventionally recognized culture areas. For instruments, McLean recognized Melanesia, Micronesia, the Central Pacific, and marginal eastern Polynesia; for structure, western Micronesia, Melanesia, the Central Pacific, western and eastern Polynesia. In a collection of American folk songs Lomax (1960) found areas largely on the basis of performance style but also by distribution of tunes and texts, specifying the North, the West, the southern mountains and backwoods, and the Negro South, and provided a map with quantification. Jones (1959, vol. 1) provides a map of types of harmony in sub-Saharan Africa, using as a basis the most prominent intervals between the voices (unison, thirds, fourths, and fifths), but no indication is given of the amount of such harmonic music in the various repertories or of possible overlapping distributions. Of course, while the presentation of maps is not widely practiced, the many comparative statements in ethnomusicological literature might readily lend themselves to representation in an atlas.

The most widespread attempts to establish musical areas involve the North American Indians. The popularity of the concept of musical areas then has to do with the importance of native North America in the development of the culture area concept, with the number of easily separable culture units, and with the relatively good sampling of available music. Then, too, examination quickly shows that each culture area does not simply have its own musical style, but that the results are more interesting. Herzog (1928, 1930) was probably the first to suggest the existence of areas and their usefulness for creating some order in the vast data, noting particularly that the singing and formal characteristics of the Yuman peoples of the Southwest differed from those of the rest of the continent. In a highly significant study Helen Roberts (1936) described the distribution of instruments and vocal styles. In view of the role that instruments played in the work of the German diffusionists, it is perhaps characteristic that she devotes more space to instruments than to the vocal styles, which, after all, account for most of the musical activity. It is interesting to see that her instrument areas differ somewhat from those of the vocal styles. The vocal areas are to a considerable extent based on culture areas, not on musical groupings of smaller culture units. She lists Eskimo; the Northwest Coast and the Western Plateau; California; the Southwest, the Plains, and the Eastern Plateau; the East and Southeast; and Mexico, which is hardly described for lack of data. I later published a more statistically oriented approach, revising Roberts (Nettl 1954), and dividing the area north of Mexico into six not always contiguous areas: Eskimo-Northwest Coast; California and the Yuman style; the Plains and the Pueblos; the Athabascans; the Great Basin; and the East and Southeast. Methodological problems revolved about the lack of sufficient data and its unevenness, the different degrees of nineteenth- and twentieth-century change, the difficulty of separating musical style from instruments and social context, and the need to work statistically because Indian musics have much in common and can only be distinguished by relative frequency of traits. The main problem, so common in comparative study, was the difficulty of measuring degrees of similarity.

On the whole, the areas were arrived at in a manner similar to that evidently used to establish culture areas by Wissler (1917), A. Kroeber (1947), and Driver (1961). A single, outstanding, striking trait that correlates roughly with a group of less concrete and perhaps more questionable isoglosses is the determining factor. In the culture areas the striking trait may be associated with contrasting aspects of life. Along the Northwest Coast it may be the Potlatch ceremony or a distinctive style in art; in the Plains, dependence on the buffalo. Similarly, the music areas are sometimes distinguished primarily by noncoordinate traits in music. One may be based on a trait present in it and not found elsewhere, although its distribution within the area may be uneven. Examples are the moderate complexity of drum rhythms for the Eskimo and Northwest Coast cultures, and of antiphonal and responsorial singing in the East. A musical area may, on the other hand, be based on the prevalance of a trait that is also found elsewhere with much less frequency. This is true of the California-Yuman area, characterized in large measure by the frequency of the "rise," which we also found extant but less prominent elsewhere. Again, an area may be determined by its style of voice production, something generally more typical of a whole repertory than other aspects of style. This is true of the Plains-Pueblo area, which is held together only loosely in other respects.

Later these areas were subjected to further scrutiny, and I found it necessary to take into account their varying homogeneity. Some are more convincing than others. The best ones seemed to be small and to coincide rather well with culture areas. Recognition of the rapid changes in musical style during the periods in which the studied repertories had developed—changes due to the forced movements of the Indian peoples, to intertribal contact, and to Westernization—all weakened the musical area concept. A later statement (Nettl 1969b) suggested four areas, two large and heterogeneous (Eskimo-Northwest Coast, and Plains-Pueblo-East) and two smaller, more homogeneous (Yuman-California-Navajo, and the Western Basin). A further refinement of method and conclusion, though not radically different, is made by Erickson (1969). At the 1980 meeting of the Society for Ethnomusicology the matter was again debated, and a hundred years after Baker's (1882) epochal first serious book on American Indian music, a basic question of this subject is still not settled.

The fact that the arrangement of Indian music areas has been successively changed, attacked, and modified does not dismiss the value of the musical area concept as a classificatory device; it only proves that areas are hard to establish. The same, indeed, was experienced by anthropologists, as may be noted in the gradual revision of the American Indian culture areas by Wissler, Kroeber, and Driver. At one point it was thought that culture areas could be regarded as units with separable histories, but in the end they served mainly as ways of creating order out of the chaos of ethnographic data. The same may be true of musical areas. Like culture areas, they may have centers and marginal regions, and sometimes the relationship between the two can give insight into the past. But the thought of establishing a set of musical areas for the world in the belief that this rather specialized concept would provide a key to prehistory and its laws is no longer taken seriously.

THE SINGING GLOBE

The issues in the history of ethnomusicology intersect; here in the context of cartography we meet up with old friends, the measurement of similarity, comparative method, and universals. Attempts to divide the globe into musical areas are uncommon but interesting because of basic assumptions and method. Let us look first at a few, Paul Collaer's map of musical zones (Collaer 1960), Lomax's presentation of nine major and fifty-seven smaller areas (1968:75–110) and his ten major singing styles (1959), and an ancient attempt to divide the world into three major style groups (Nettl

1956b:141–42). In each case the division of the world is made mainly on the basis of one or a few heavily weighted criteria. My own attempt (the Far East, North Asia, and the Americas; sub-Saharan Africa and Europe; India and the Middle East with North Africa) is based on harmony and scalar intervals, criteria normally prominent in the Westerner's perception of musical differences. The first area is pentatonic and heterophonic; the second, diatonic and harmonic; and the third, microtonally differentiated and monophonic. Collaer (1960:pl. 1) divides the world into several "zones musicales" based entirely on scalar structure, distinguishing "pre-pentatonic," "anhemitonic-pentatonic," "heptatonic," and others. Also an example of extreme generalization, the character of these areas is determined by knowledge of a small number of cultures. Further, the existence of a typical, central musical style for any large group of cultures is assumed. It is obvious, for instance, that Europe has seven-tone and five-tone scales in great quantity, and that seven-tone scales are found in China, although both schemes put Europe into the seven-tone and China into the pentatonic category. If one is to do anything about dividing the world along these lines, one must do so on the assumption that one can distinguish a central, majority style for any culture.

Using far more criteria, more sophisticated statistically, and showing a willingness to subdivide the world more closely, Lomax (1968) also requires the concept of centrality. A "favored song style" (1968:133) is diagnostic of each of fifty-seven areas. But while Collaer's zones are based entirely on a few musical criteria, Lomax establishes a group of naturally or culturally determined areas and then describes the musical style of each, testing its degree of internal homogeneity and its similarity to others. It is interesting to see that some of his areas are far more unified than others. Essentially, however, he describes the music of culture areas rather than providing musical areas.

In an earlier publication, however, Lomax (1959) divided the world into ten musical styles, largely on the basis of what is usually called performance practice. Separating styles that he labels American Indian, Pygmoid, African, Australian, Melanesian, Polynesian, Malayan, Eurasian, Old European, and Modern European, he grouped some styles in correlation with geographic or readily recognized culture areas. In others, however, he identifies styles that do not so correlate, among them the Eurasian, Old European, and Modern European, three varieties of European folk song to the first of which is also appended most of Asia. The distinctions among the European styles are insightful: the Eurasian is "high-pitched, often harsh and strident, delivered from a tight throat with great vocal tension" (1959:936). Old European is "relaxed . . . facial expression lively and animated . . . unornamented" (ibid.). The modern European style is hybrid, physically and musically between the other two. In his attempt to deal with the world, it is obvious that Lomax has had great experience in European folk music, and that his combination of most of Asia into a single area indicates less experience in this domain. But Lomax's ten major areas are probably the least unsatisfactory grouping of the musical globe.

A further theory of musical distribution appears in an unexpected place, an appendix to the history of melody by Bence Szabolcsi (1959), the Hungarian music historian. Szabolcsi dealt with the question of world musical geography more holistically than have most others. He did not confine himself to the presumably less volatile folk and tribal musics but considers classical systems as well. Relating musical styles to geographic factors such as river valleys and access to the sea, he saw the musical map as a combination of areas with boundaries and of a patchwork resulting from musical differences of locales with varying degrees of isolation. Generalizing about principles of musical distribution, he concluded: (1) Musical life is closely tied to the natural divisions of the earth. (2) Geographically "closed" areas preserve musical styles, while open ones favor change and exchange, providing a venue for the development of cultivated or classical systems. (3) The center standardizes and unifies materials developed throughout the area, while the margins develop and preserve diversity. (4) Diffusion of musical styles from the center is the typical process of music history; the longer a musical style exists, the further it becomes diffused. (5) The unity of archaic folk music styles is evidence of the most ancient intercultural contacts (Szabolcsi 1959:313). Here is a set of fundamental hypotheses on which one can build a cultural geography of music.

Szabolcsi gives these as a set of preliminary conclusions. Developed on the basis of musical data alone, they lead to a concept somewhat like the American culture area, which coincides, according to Kroeber (1947), with a natural area. Unity is at the center, the source of diffusion, and variety at the edges. As a matter of fact, the idea of a musical area with a strong center and a more diffuse outer circle can also be found in other interpretations of the geographic-stylistic structure of European art music. Reese (1954) in his survey of Renaissance music describes an area in which the "central musical language" of the Renaissance developed—France, Italy, the Low Countries. This was subsequently and gradually introduced to a peripheral area—Spain, Germany, England, and Eastern Europe.

Szabolcsi's as well as Kroeber's conceptualizations are related to older theories to the effect that normal cultural distribution comprises a progressive center and marginal survivals. Once widely used by folklorists, it is generally associated with the definition of folklore as "gesunkenes Kulturgut." Developed by German scholars of the nineteenth and early twentieth centuries such as Rochus von Liliencron and Hans Naumann (see Pulikowski 1933:167–68, Danckert 1939:9–12, Naumann 1921:4–6), the concept implies that folk songs, tales, riddles, and beliefs are remnants or imitations of practices developed at culture centers such as cities and courts, where they had been abandoned in favor of further developments and left to live as archaisms in the surrounding countryside. As a general theory of folklore, the concept has been abandoned; like other dogmas, it fails in universal application. But it may be often on the right track for description of the history of specific items. The hurdy-gurdy, once used at Western European courts and in churches, became after the Middle Ages largely a folk instrument, and some folk ballads now restricted to the folk community were once court entertainment.

THEY SING THE SONGS OF HOME

Indirectly, a concept like that of "gesunkenes Kulturgut" seems to have led to a major thrust in ethnomusicology, the comparative study of musical cultures in their original venues and in forms carried to distant lands by immigrants. Since the 1950s the music of immigrant enclaves has become a major field of study. Although there are early models (e.g. Schünemann 1923), a major breakthrough came with the realization that North America could be a major source for the collection of old English folk songs (see Sharp 1932:xxi), and from a contrastive discovery, that historical processes could be extrapolated and explained from the comparative study of African and Afro-American music (e.g. Herskovits 1945). Although many studies of immigrant musical behavior have involved the relationship of European folk music and its import to North America, other cultures have also been drawn in. Thus we find the tacit establishment of culture and music areas in which migrants play a major role, e.g. the area of British and British-derived populations of the world with a center in Britain and marginal populations in North America, Australia, and elsewhere, or a German area with marginal populations in Eastern Europe, the Americas, and even Israel. Although Szabolcsi's broad statement is intended to extend over long periods of history, one can note some of his processes in the shorter term as well, in the history of ethnic musics in such diverse spots as North America and Israel.

The study of immigrant musical culture is a geographic problem of sorts, involving relationship to the music of home countries and of host countries. A large body of knowledge has been built up about the folk music and folklore of non-English-speaking immigrant groups in the United States and Canada, producing hypotheses of typical immigrant musical behavior that reinforce hypotheses about stability as related to marginal survival of archaic culture traits, about the development of syncretic styles, and about the gradual modernization, Westernization, and linguistic and cultural Anglicization of older European musical traditions. Considerable work has also been done in Israel (see e.g. Katz 1968; Shiloah 1970; many studies by

E. Gerson-Kiwi; also Erdely 1964, 1979; Nettl 1967a; the "Canadian" issue of *Ethnomusicology,* vol. 16, no. 3, 1972). All of this is related to the body of literature about musical change as an aspect of culture change.

The music of immigrant groups is subject to many variables that in part determine the outcome. Relative size and selection of the immigrant group, motivation for immigration, the amount of contact later maintained with the original home, the degree of physical, cultural, and linguistic isolation and cohesion of immigrants in the host country, the cultural and musical differences and compatibilities of an immigrant culture in its relationship to the host culture, the attitudes of such a group toward diversity and change—all these obviously play a part. We can translate a few of these variables into practical questions of ethnomusicological relevance.

Was an entire musical repertory physically moved? Did the immigrants bring with them their musical specialists? Did they perhaps play a special, musically skilled role in the home country? Were they motivated to change their musical behavior, or would the maintenance of a musical tradition reinforce the maintenance of the whole cultural tradition? Would musical change symbolize acceptance of the host culture? Or would music be used to remind the population of its heritage while other forms of behavior conformed to that of the host culture?

All of these relationships bear strongly on as yet unarticulated theories of musical change in the context of culture change. We know enough to give examples of a few types of events: (1) Some cultures immigrate en masse and bring their music with them, using it as a pillar for the maintenance of tradition, pushing out of the fold those individuals who change in conformity to the musical and other behavior of the host country, if necessary holding the tradition intact at the expense of maintaining population. The Amish in various parts of North America are an example (see Hohmann 1959, Nettl 1957). (2) Other immigrant groups merge into the mainstream of the host culture and keep their traditional music, substantially unchanged, as a reminder of home, performed on specific occasions. Many Eastern and Southern European ethnic groups in the United States—Poles, Greeks, Arabic Christians—do this in a secular context; a few, such as immigrants from India via the West Indies, do so in a Hindu religious context (see H. Myers in Nettl 1976:127–30). (3) Some immigrant populations maintain their traditional music in most respects and strive, because of special skills brought with them and because of their musical prestige in the host country, to change its musical culture in the direction of their tradition. This may be an unusual situation, but one illustrated by urban Germans coming to the United States after 1848 and again by Central Europeans arriving in the 1930s. These examples may suffice to indicate the variety of behavior but also the possibility of establishing a typology. It appears that the musical behavior of indigenous minorities (e.g. American Indians) may often parallel the behavior of immigrant minorities; perhaps the minority status rather than the fact of immigration is the main factor in determining subsequent musical behavior and musical style. This may also be the case with Israeli Arabs as far as classical Arabic music is concerned.

The situation in Israel is particularly instructive because of the large amount of immigration from many diverse places and the number of active local scholars. In a number of ways the absorption of immigrant groups in Israel, allowing for their larger proportion and the greater speed, parallels the United States situation. Like American studies, most in Israel have concentrated on the ways in which the old traditions from Eastern Europe and from Jewish groups in the Islamic world have been preserved. Israel has been referred to as a nation in which the heritages of many other nations are at least temporarily kept intact, and the studies of Moroccan, Kurdish, Syrian, Yemenite, Iraqi, and other Jewish groups have been undertaken as much in order to find out what the musical culture of the homeland was and had been as to assess musical behavior after arrival in Israel. A number of interesting if tentative conclusions have emerged.

Immigrants to Israel from Arabic-speaking countries brought with them the music of two streams of musical culture: one comprised the traditional Hebrew liturgical music and its semireligious and secular correlates, the folk music specifically of the Jewish minority, sung in vernacular languages—Ladino, Turkish, Arabic, sometimes also Hebrew; the second, since Jews in Muslim societies often occupied a major role as musicians for the Islamic community, consisted of the mainstream traditional music of the home country (see e.g. Loeb 1972:4–6). In regard to the first, some communities, which remained relatively intact in Israel, although their repertories may have become impoverished, appear to have kept their heritage and even to have developed it further under the active stimulation of official Israeli cultural establishments. In respect to the latter, Arabic music itself, it is evident that the lack of a cohesive and numerous audience or of a patronage system has contributed to a great decline in frequency of performance, thus perhaps also of expertise (see Cohen 1971 and Shiloah 1974: 83 for contrastive views). Despite official efforts to the contrary, Jewish musicians of Arabic music seem to have diminished, a condition to which the desire to integrate into Israeli culture and the breaking of direct contact with the Arabic population of the homelands has also contributed. The folk music of Jewish immigrants from Eastern Europe who came well before World War II seems to have changed to a general "Israeli" style with texts relevant to the contemporary resident of Israel. These songs abandoned the dominant subjects of Eastern European rural life and adopted a musical style mixing East European and Balkan elements with certain characteristics of Middle Eastern music and with elements of modern Western European popular music. More recent immigrants, largely urban and exposed to modern Western popular and art music, have established close contact with Western musicians, participating in their tradition and its ongoing changes. It seems a reasonable hypothesis that traditional secular music has been kept alive more readily in communities that remained intact after immigration and in those that took up rural residence.

QUESTIONS OF SPACE AND TIME

If questions of marginal survivals and of the impact of immigration involve the interface of geography and history, the greatest impact from distribution studies on the ethnomusicological view of history came from the Kulturkreis school of German and Austrian diffusionists. Its role in ethnomusicology seems to have been greater than in anthropology itself, where it had a checkered career, where one sees it as a powerful but rather isolated group of scholars led by Fritz Graebner and Wilhelm Schmidt, working in the firm belief that they were discovering laws, first arousing the curiosity of the active and large group of Americans led by Franz Boas, then repelling them with their dogmatic approach. One finds them also being rather ignored by the French sociologists and structuralists and by the British social anthropologists, their work the subject of conflicting critiques of their espousal of unilinear cultural evolution and their nomothetic views of culture history. Some of the members were eventually blamed for a religious bias and then for supporting racist and political excesses. After World War II it was largely abandoned by anthropology. In ethnomusicology it had a more lasting role and became the basis for several specific theories of history, but it was widely criticized after World War II by those with an interest in anthropology and ignored by most others as wild-eyed fantasy. In the end, however, even some of the sharpest critics felt obliged to praise the broad knowledge and suggestiveness of the Kulturkreis school. Lowie (1937:177) respects the seriousness of their approach, Merriam (1964:289) believes that aspects of their method "remain to be well used in studying diffusion problems of more restricted scope" (than of the globe), and Wachsmann (1961:143) asserts in a discussion of Hornbostel and Sachs that German diffusionism was useful, at least as a working hypothesis.

In his extremely detailed account of the relationship between the Kulturkreis school and musical studies, Albrecht Schneider points out that some of the significance of this school could not have been achieved without the help of comparative musicology (1976:66). Some of the earliest Kulturkreis work, for example, is based on the mentioned studies of instrument distributions by Ankermann (1902), Wieschoff (1933), and of course Sachs and Hornbostel. Some other prominent figures in the history of ethnomusicology worked with Kulturkreis concepts—Marius Schneider, Werner Danckert, Walter Wiora. Merriam (1964) was attracted by the school's contribution to an understanding of instrument distributions and their historical implications, while A. Schneider (1976) finds several quite diverse strands of the history of musicological thought to be also part of the history of this school. Here are a few examples of the kinds of thinking that we are talking about. In all of it, however, it is important to remember that the basic uninventiveness of mankind, and the resulting assumption that any phenomenon is likely to have been invented only once and then diffused from its place of origin, are the points of departure.

Early in his career Curt Sachs proceeded to map the distribution of all musical instruments, a formidable task even for one with his comprehensive knowledge of the literature. In what was perhaps his most ambitious book (1929), he organized his findings in twenty-three areas, which he then placed in historical order on the basis of distributional criteria as well as technological level. For example, stratum no. 7 includes Polynesia and parts of South America, the whistling pot, double-row panpipes, and bone buzzers. Stratum no. 13 comprises Indonesia and East Africa and includes the "earliest metal instruments," various kinds of xylophones and board zithers. Stratum no. 18 extends from Indonesia to Madagascar, dates from about the first century A.D., and is characterized by the tube zither. Hornbostel (1933) used a similar approach to establish twelve instrument areas for Africa. Sachs later went on to simplify, combining most of his twenty-three strata into three groups (1940:63–64), but began to have doubts about the kind of detailed historical speculation in which he had engaged: "The geographic method, too, may prove fallacious. . . . Nevertheless, geographic criteria are safer than any other criteria . . ." (1940:63). Few today pay much attention to this work of Sachs's, but no one seems to have tried a better or more comprehensive statement. The data are solid; the historical interpretations remain in question, but not many have been contradicted outright.

The ways instruments are tuned have also been the subject of interpretations derived from the thinking of the Kulturkreis school. Some of Hornbostel's most prominent works (1910, 1911, 1927) involve the belief that panpipes were tuned with the use of a circle of fifths produced by overblowing. Instead of "pure" fifths of 702 cents (with 100 cents to the tempered semitone), the "blown" fifths were thought to comprise only 678 cents. Scales presumably derived from this interval were found on instruments in Melanesia and South America, giving rise to speculation about prehistoric connections. The theory turned out to have weaknesses, especially in the accuracy of measurement, and was "exploded" by Bukofzer (1937) among others, but historical relationship of Melanesian and South American panpipes remains a possibility. In related studies A. M. Jones (1964) tried to show the tunings of Indonesian and African xylophones to be similar and, with other factors, to point to a common origin of aspects of music style of the two areas. Jones was harshly criticized (Hood 1966) for methodological weaknesses, but the common origin of the two xylophone groups remains a possibility. In contrast to Sachs's instrument distribution, the data appear to be weak, but the historical conclusions remain to be considered.

One of the major tenets of the Kulturkreis school was a belief in a particular order of events in world history, linking subsistence and social structure (discussed in detail by Harris 1968:384–85). Although several stages and circles give the appearance of a complex picture, the belief in essence is that gathering cultures preceded and changed to hunting cultures, which added herding and cultivating activities, and from the combination of which sprang the high cultures. Based on logic as well as geography, this order of events was used for musical extrapolations by various scholars. Marius Schneider (1957:12–14), in considering tribal musics, correlates style with culture and adds chronology. Hunters have much shouting and little tonal definition; cultivators have an "arioso style . . .; the style is tonally regulated and form is rounded off" (1957:13). Pastoral cultures, says Schneider, occupy a middle position. Accepting the important role of women as cultivators (and following Schmidt's notion of the matriarchate as the dominant social structure when agriculture became the norm of food production), Schneider believes that where men are more influential, one finds predominance of meter and contrapuntal polyphony; where it is women, predominance of melody and harmony.

Here we have an evolutionary scheme, a group of predetermined stages, for music, to parallel the evolution of culture proposed by Schmidt. Schneider also used geographic areas in his major work (1934), a history of world polyphony. Stressing the tonal relationships among the voices, he finds four areas, noncontiguous in the Kulturkreis mold: (a) The area of variant-heterophony is sporadically distributed worldwide. (b) In Southeast Asia, Melanesia, and Micronesia one finds various kinds of voice relationships, with each voice holding to a different and unique tonal organization. (c) Characterized by but not limited to Polynesia, the third area exhibits more varied relationship among the voices. (d) Much of Africa is characterized by the tendency to homophony. More data would have allowed Schneider to extend these areas, but here we have an example of musical distributions arrived at essentially in the way in which the German diffusionists dealt with other culture traits.

Relationships between the Balkans, the region around the Black Sea, and Indonesia, resulting from a presumed migration ca. 800 B.C., were taken up by Jaap Kunst (1954), who noted similarities in several musical instruments and thus established something like a musical Kulturkreis of a rather early date. It has the traits expected in a culture circle, but the similarities are so modest and their basis, the presumed migration of the Tocharians (A. Schneider 1976:212–18), so hypothetical that little has been made of this finding. Werner Danckert, in his studies of European folk music, also made use of the Kulturkreis concept in the sense of noncontiguous distribution and the establishment of strata, dealing with styles as well as distribution of tunes and tune types, and also with aspects of musical culture such as symbolism, kinesics, and physical features of humans (A. Schneider 1979:23–27).

Evidently the thinking of German diffusionists had more lasting impact on ethnomusicological literature than have most other theoretical movements from cultural anthropology. It also influenced scholars who did not associate themselves directly with its theories. Thus Wiora, in one example among many from his pen, notes the common elements of the music of herdsmen in the Alps, Scandinavia, Mongolia, and Tibet (1975:84) without, however, claiming that these regions are part of a culture circle. Herzog's explanation of the fact that American Indian game and story songs usually contrast with other songs in their repertories but share an intertribal style because they are part of an archaic layer underlying later strata (1935b:33) sounds amazingly like a Kulturkreis statement, despite Herzog's personal disinclination to accept the school's axioms and methods. Indeed, if one removes the quality of dogma from Sachs's basic axioms but regards them as statements that express likelihood, tendency, regularity, one can hardly disagree with him when he writes: "The object or idea found in scattered regions of a certain district is older than an object found everywhere in the same area. [And] objects preserved only in remote valleys or islands are older than those used in the open Plains" (1940:62). The fact that music and instruments are relatively complex phenomena in human culture compared to certain implements or perhaps folk stories makes the insistence on a single point of origin relatively credible.

The musical map-makers have said much about style, much less about content. The historical-geographic method of folklorists was applied to tales and ballad stories but rarely to their musical equivalents, songs or tune types. We have looked at some of the difficulties (Chapter 8), and must conclude that the study of geographical distribution of musical content is in its infancy. There it may remain, for it depends considerably on the maintenance of culture groups in some degree of isolation and stability of locale. The coming of mass media to the world, increase in travel, publication, emigration have provided a basis for a completely new kind of music sharing among the peoples of the world. If musical map-making was ever close to being a hard science, it is no longer so if one uses contemporary data; if distributions on the map were ever good indicators of history, they are hardly so if one uses maps of recent distributions. It makes little sense to draw conclusions about remote history from a comparison of the musics found among Indian peoples living in Oklahoma, if one does not take into account that these peoples came from diverse reaches of the continent less than a hundred years ago. Future archeologists will find the remains of pianos distributed throughout the world, but they will surely realize that it is an instrument invented later than the xylophone. Geographic extrapolation may supplement other studies of history; if it is forced to replace them, our chances of making accurate guesses are modest.

And yet, ethnomusicology will probably remain a field in which much of the information is given in terms of "where." We will continue to wonder what it may mean when we find the same instrument in three isolated valleys in Europe and Asia, or the same sounding tune on three islands, thousands of miles apart, on the oceans of the world.

Chapter 17

It Was Bound to Happen

THE CENTRAL QUESTION

Let me recall for the reader another segment of that highly instructive genre of cultural expression, cocktail party conversation. Average American academics may not know much about the world's musical cultures, but they were quick to identify some of the most fundamental questions of my field, and they showed a variety of opinions about them. "You have certainly traveled a great deal," said an elderly gentleman, "and you've observed how the races of the world play on different instruments, sing with different scales, make all sorts of strange sounds which we can't understand. Do you ever ask yourself what it is that has caused them to be different?" "Oh, but it must be simply because there are such different races," broke in someone at his left. "I know it's not fashionable to say this today, but how could people looking as different as African Pygmies and Chinese not also do everything differently, including making music?" And the first: "But the musics you have heard aren't all that different, are they? After all, you seem to enjoy them all, you get something out of hearing them. Perhaps they were once linked. Isn't it true that the chants of some South Seas islanders are very much like those of the ancient Greeks? And didn't I read somewhere that African music is rather like that of the Middle Ages in Europe? Don't all cultures inevitably move through the same stages?"

"Well, yes, in a way," I began my response, but fortunately was quickly interrupted by a young, scholarly looking lady. "It just stands to reason that peoples who speak such different languages would develop very different kinds of singing. I've heard that in South Africa, the natives use strange-sounding clicks as if they were consonants, and Chinese is almost sung instead of spoken. They would just have to sing music in a very special way."

A portly gentleman expressed another viewpoint: "It's not just that they speak differently, they live differently. Can you imagine a small band of people who must spend all their time finding food for themselves developing a great kind of music like that of Bach? Or, since I'm speaking with you, Ravi Shankar? And also, I've read somewhere that there are tribes in which women have all the power; their music must certainly be different from ours because it is the women who determine how it will sound."

I was about to say, "I'm not so sure whether it is men or women who determine what goes on in any society," but the subject at hand obviously fascinated the little group, and so a sixth member felt compelled to chime in. "Can you imagine that our concert music would have turned out as it has if it hadn't been for Beethoven? In this age of ethnic groups and social forces, we seem to have forgotten that our lives are really shaped by the acts of great men and women."

It's easier to be an authority in a classroom than at a cocktail party. I would have had to say that indeed I had often wondered why different societies have different music, and whether it was by some law bound to happen that a group of people would develop a particular kind. But I didn't know such a law. Fortunately I was interrupted at that point by somebody's elaborate farewells, saved by the bell, as it were, from having to admit ignorance in what has long seemed to me to be the central question of ethnomusicology. But my friends had mentioned a number of the answers most widely cited, and also some of the ideas most rejected, of what it is that determines the nature of musical style.

I am not sure whether ethnomusicologists will agree that there can be a central question. Some of them might well give others. What is the function of music in human culture? What are the universals of music? And so on. But to me, it seems that the determinants of musical style are what we have all in the long run been after. The question, of course, needs immediately to be refined: not, why is music as it is, or how did this piece come to sound that way but, rather, what determined the stylistic character of the main body of music of a particular society? The question brings together various strands of ethnomusicological definition: comparative study of musics; the music of the world's peoples; the normally oral way of transmitting music; music as culture, because culture is what we share with all humans and with our group of humans. Perhaps because my central question has a certain sacredness, few have tried to give a comprehensive answer. It is sacred because we are all afraid of what would happen if we definitively knew the whole truth (or afraid of people who think they know the whole truth). Like members of a cult, we do but also don't want to know. And so we remain convinced that we can arrive only at partial answers, that we will never be able to give a comprehensive, detailed picture of the reasons for the particular and unbelievably complex pattern of ideas, behavior, and sound that constitutes the music of a people. Thus whenever someone publishes a hint to the effect that an answer is at hand, there ensues sharp and even bitter criticism.

Ethnomusicological literature rarely speaks directly to the question of determination. It focuses instead on relationships and usually avoids (properly enough) making the leap from relationship and correlation to causality. In the past several chapters we have had various occasions to note the relationship of musical style and content to the kind of culture a society has, to such things as technological level, intercultural contacts experienced, symbolic and value systems, attitudes toward stability and change, and more. The few statements dealing comprehensively if often implicitly with causality can be grouped in two categories, conveniently if simplistically labeled historical and synchronic. The historical orientation sees whatever music is to be examined mainly as a result of the past, implying that the preceding music has been developed and changed to produce the later or present form. This orientation has two strands. In the one, music is determined by more or less fortuitous and in any case unique configurations of events. In the other, history follows a predetermined sequence, modified (but not in its essence) by the vagaries of fate. The synchronic orientation extrapolates cause from relationships, seen at one time, to other domains of culture or nature. Neither approach excludes the other; I am only distinguishing emphases. In history, one cannot go far back without making wild guesses; in the present, the direction of causality is obscure.

Historians of European music have great concern for cause but take a particularistic approach. Even elementary texts are full of hypothetical statements involving relationship to what came before, musical and nonmusical. The music of Bach "grew out" of the music of his German predecessors, that of Schoenberg, "out of a need" to provide something contrastive to the exhausted harmonic procedures of the late nineteenth century. The characteristics of the Baroque are the result of tendencies developed in the Renaissance but also of a desire to do things differently. On the other hand, the Venetian concerto style has often been related to the peculiar architecture of the San Marco cathedral. Beethoven's unique role is in part a result of wide-ranging social and political changes of his time. Today's "new" music is traced to developments in electronic technology. The implication is twofold: musicians and their audiences experiment with what they have, moving in a new direction determined in large measure by directions already established. On the other hand, changes in society, general and particular, determine changes in music. The characteristic stance of the music historian seems to be a balance of social, aesthetic, and personal forces.

This kind of explanation does not speak to the intercultural aspect of the question. If ethnomusicologists were given a multiple-choice test, many would probably opt for the answer that says, "The most important factor in determining musical style is the nature of a people's culture." But they would perhaps do this with hesitation, and many might also check the "no opinion" box. Before turning to culture we ought to examine some factors outside the culture concept that have had a role in the ethnomusicological literature involving our central question.

GENES, INDIVIDUALS, SPEECH, AND THE WEATHER

Are there in a population biological factors that determine its musical style? Ethnomusicologists on the whole stay away from this question, fearing the undesirable connotations of racism but aware of the obvious importance of biology and genetics to understanding humanity. Blacking has courageously insisted on the role of biological considerations in ethnomusicology: "All musical behavior and action must be seen in the relation to their adaptive function in an evolutionary context, whether this is limited to their function within the adaptive mechanisms of different cultures, or extended to their function in biosocial evolution" (1978:31). He is right in pointing out the biological basis of all human behavior, reminding us that culture is in the end part of nature. But we can still distinguish between genetic equipment and physical environment (nature) and choices made by humans in dealing with these (culture).

Statements like Blacking's are rare. Since humans are very much alike, they all have music; so much for genetics. Beyond this, physical differences among population groups have rarely been regarded as factors in musical style. It is accepted that a member of any racial group can learn to do what one of another group can do, although indeed this statement does not speak to the possibility of general proclivities of any population. The fact that racial groups often constitute cultural units makes it hard to separate physical and social factors, as does the fact that the physical elements we use as racial criteria are themselves culturally determined. If a tall population has music different from its short neighbor tribe, we are unable to correlate this fact with a "tall people's" music that may characterize large individuals within a society. Extremely low singing, thought to be a feature of the tall Russians, is also found among shorter Tibetans and American Indians. No need to belabor; ethnomusicologists generally do not believe that the genetic apparatus determines a people's musical style. One reads statements about this or that society being particularly musical, but this can usually be related to cultural factors of value and function; anyway, most fieldworkers insist that "their" people are particularly musical.

But if Blacking's statement shows a renewed and sophisticated interest in biology, there was also an earlier time in the history of musicology when racial matters received much attention. During the Nazi period many books were written about "music and race," some purporting to show the—often undesirable—results of (a certain) heredity. It is hard to know whether authors of 1930–45 were taken very seriously, but the movement continued beyond 1945 in publications such as Moser's (1954), which discerns musical differences among the remnants of German tribal groups; Fritz Bose's (1952) attempts to show racial differences between black and white Americans by examining recordings of the same songs; or Marius Schneider's statement that "racial characteristics in music are easily detected when one actually hears a singer, but they cannot be described in words. Race shows itself by timbre, by the general rhythm of movement . . ." (1957:13). It is not clear whether Schneider wishes to separate out biological factors or uses the term "race" in a broad sense indicating a population group that shares a culture. The implication seems to be that singing style and body movement are determined by genes, but whether the music is polyphonic or uses quarter tones is a matter of culture. The most benevolent criticism of this position must revolve about the difficulty of separating race and culture in the practical situation.

There are no known racial differences in the human brain, and the music-producing organs do not differ significantly. Such matters as talent and perception are not well enough known to be tested interculturally or outside a cultural context. In any case, we do not know what aspects of musical ability, abstracted from musical activity, would show specific musical talent in an individual or a group. Of course the criteria of musicianship differ among societies and cannot be used in a universal comparison.

In his last book Curt Sachs, Schneider's contemporary, takes a definitive stand on the issue. "Most suspicious are we of the slippery and often criminally exploited concept of 'race.'. . . The word . . . has been so abused that it has become at once meaningless and too full of meaning" (1962:47–48). Most ethnomusicologists rightly follow Sachs in this respect, at least until the biological factors are more adequately separated from the cultural. But I must stress that I am cautioning against the acceptance of racial criteria as factors in determining the musical direction of individual cultures, not the recognition of biological factors in the musicality of humans (see Graf 1968).

The suggestion that topography or climate determine musical style may elicit a chuckle from humanists and social scientists. Is it conceivable that one could take seriously the correlation of monophonic and ornamented singing with the stark desert ecology of the Middle East, or the development of long ballads in Northern Europe with the need to remain indoors during long winters? And yet there are aspects of geography that appear to play a direct though secondary or contributing role. Grame (1962), for example, has suggested that in those parts of the world in which bamboo is found, there is a tendency to develop particular types of instruments. Somewhat more specific to musical style is Blacking's statement that the tempo of Venda music is related to the steady walking pace of the people, "thrust upon them by the mountainous environment" (1965:47). Blacking also relates the Venda's preference for circle dances to the mountains, which do not provide space for line dances. The neighboring Tsonga, he says, live in the flatlands, walk faster, and have music of more rapid tempo (ibid.). From such examples, however, one could hardly claim that an entire musical style is determined by geographic factors.

Beyond this, climate, availability of water, presence of seaports, types of raw material available for technology all play enormous roles in the formation of culture. If music derives from culture, these must also be underlying factors. Indeed, geographic determinism as a fundamental theory of culture was known to the ancient Greeks and continues to be a credible explanation. Kroeber's (1947) delineation of North American Indian culture areas, we will remember, coincides remarkably with natural areas. As Szabolcsi (1965) suggests, mountain dwellers may often preserve musical styles because they live in isolation, as do inhabitants of remote islands, while classical musics develop in accessible river valleys open to many influences and capable of supporting large populations. Yet in all of this music is not affected directly by geographic features but through the central core of culture.

The content of language is clearly related to culture, but it is hard to make the same case for linguistic structure. There is no evidence that a particular kind of grammar goes with a lifestyle, and the members of one language family may differ culturally as much from one another as do the Indo-European Bengalis and Swedes, the Algonquian Penobscot and Arapaho. Features such as initial stress, tone, or proportion of vowels seem not to be related to culture type. On the other hand, styles of speech, elements such as the amount of pitch variation, dynamic contrast, and various aspects of rhetoric are. Sociolinguists (e.g. Labov 1972) study and illustrate the relationship of the way in which a language's structure is used and the culture or subculture that it symbolizes.

But given the close association of music and language, one would expect to find some general relationships between the structure of a language and the music of its people (beyond those of a specific piece of vocal music). Again, the relationships are there but as minor contributing factors. The typical patterns of linguistic tone sequence in some African languages seem to affect the patterns of composing melodies (Waengler 1963, Nketia 1974: 77–88, Blacking 1967:166–68). The Czechs and Hungarians have languages in which utterances begin with stressed syllables and folk songs typically beginning with stressed beats. It is difficult to establish, in even these cases, that music was molded to fit the characteristics of language, that the structure of language determined musical style.

Western society conceives of itself as being determined by the thought and action of highly influential men and women. A glance at a library catalogue will confirm their importance. And yet the idea that certain individuals influence and determine the main musical style of a society because of their personal character and what they do *not* share with their fellows somehow goes against the grain of ethnomusicological tradition. The idiosyncratic genius who is of great interest to the typical musicologist, but whose work was never accepted by any sizable portion of his society, is rarely the object of ethnomusicological study. This somewhat unjustified neglect of the individual can be traced to another characteristic attitude, belief in the musical homogeneity of most of the world's cultures, which would have each informant giving the same facts, all members knowing the same repertory, and each person equally capable of producing new music. Of course this is at best an enormous oversimplification. Western culture was not the only one to have a Mozart or a Schoenberg, and there are studies of Asian art musics and even some of tribal societies that indicate the great effect of certain individuals in determining the course of music. Berliner (e.g. 1978: 3–7, 231–33) describes the special role of great masters of the mbira among the Shona, and Merriam (1967:140) asserts that the greatest changes in Flathead Indian music in recent times were caused by the missionary zeal of a tribesman who returned after years of absence to revive aspects of supposedly traditional musical life. The role of nonmusicians, such as the Paiute prophet Wovoka, who brought the Ghost Dance to the Plains Indians and with it a new musical style, must also be considered. But few ethnomusicologists would subscribe to a "genius" theory of history, believing that talented individuals who effected widely accepted change must have worked within a culturally valid system of values and rules. The world's cultures differ, of course, in appraisal of the role of great men and women. Some American Indian peoples, while ascribing the creation of songs to individuals, do not associate them with large-scale changes of style or determination of musical direction. But in some high cultures of Asia musical innovators are remembered through document and oral tradition, their roles perhaps exaggerated.

The individual is part of his culture but, as recognized by anthropologists since the 1930s in their studies of "culture and personality," is also its prisoner, as illustrated by Jules Henry in *Culture against Man* (1963). The exceptional person in music frequently tries to escape, and the history of music probably owes much to the conflict. The specific musical consequences are far beyond the scope of this foray. But there is something ironical in the picture of an ethnomusicologist who studies what a population group holds in common, but who often depends for the bulk of his data on the teachings of one person regarded as unusual in his or her society.

Biology, climate, geography, language, the talented individual—all play a part in determining the nature of a music. But in the end, the overriding determinant must be the special character of a culture. The way in which people live, relate to each other, see themselves in relation to their natural and human environment, control energy, and subsist, determine the kind of music they have. Although I have suggested that most ethnomusicologists agree with this assertion, it is more than anything else an article of faith. In this context we must again address the question of the concept of culture and the aspects of culture that play a role in determining musical style. We have touched in the past several chapters on a number of relationships that imply causality: social organization in the most general sense (Sachs); type of basic subsistence (M. Schneider); a set of values (McAllester); relationships among people in terms of power and sex (Lomax); and relationship to other cultures, stages in a predetermined evolution, culture as a group of diverse and uncoordinated concepts and objects, the core of culture as control of energy and division of labor, music as a domain of anti-culture. Most ethnomusicologists are not yet ready to pinpoint that part of culture which provides the main clue. And so, instead of trying to generalize further, let me recapitulate briefly two musics we have used widely for illustration, in order to see what can conceivably have determined their particular character.

WHY IS BLACKFOOT MUSIC . . . ?

Why is their singing so strange, I was asked after a talk about their musical culture. It's not, I defended. But, then, why do they sing as they do? (For a detailed description of the Blackfoot style, I refer the reader to several sources: Nettl 1967c, 1968; a record, *An Historical Album of Blackfoot Indian Music,* Folkways FE 34001; and several recordings of Blackfoot music on Canyon Records, 6095, 6132, 6133.) Physically, the North American Indians are a fairly unified group, but the Plains Indians, extending from the Blackfoot in the north to the Comanche in the south, are not particularly unified in comparison to other Indian groups. Yet Blackfoot music is very similar to that of other Plains tribes, and so we rule out racial factors. There is a closer relationship between the distribution of the Plains musical style and the physical environment of the high Plains. But while it is difficult to separate culture from ecology, Plains musical style is also found among peoples living in other areas (Merriam 1967:328–30) and has become a major component of the recently developed pan-Indian culture. Language also appears not to be a factor. While the minor musical differences among Blackfoot, Crow, and Comanche (members of three language families) may in part be related to differences in language and speech patterns, the main thrust of the musical style of these peoples is the same.

We come to cultural matters. The Blackfoot in recent times have been a hunting and gathering society in the western Plains, but there is evidence that they came from farther east and once enjoyed a different lifestyle possibly including some horticulture (Ewers 1958:6–7, Driver 1961:28). M. Schneider's description of the music of hunting cultures fits to a degree: It is "interspersed with much shouting, is formed from free speech-rhythms, and has little tonal definition" (1957:13). But Schneider's correlation of hunting with polyphony and with metric predomination over melody (ibid.) does not apply here at all. Melodic intervals are large and, as Sachs would expect, men have a distinctly dominant role, but this is true of many societies including those of the Middle East with their smaller intervals.

The core of traditional Blackfoot culture: based on human and animal energy, it had little social stratification, although the social organization was typically complex, revolving about the individual's association with nuclear family, band, various societies, other individuals who share the same guardian spirit, etc., all however within a rather informal framework. For all of this we can easily find close relationship to musical concepts, functions, behavior. But for considering musical style, one must look far and wide for correlation. The variety of social relationships is paralleled by a number of musical genres with stylistic boundaries that are blurred, reflecting conceivably the informal approach to life's rules. The lack of complex technology is reflected in the predominantly vocal music. In a more speculative vein, we could associate the great difference between Blackfoot singing and speaking styles to the supernatural association of music. We have already tried to relate some of the central values of Blackfoot culture as stated by McFee (1972:96–102)—individualism, bravery, generosity, wisdom—to aspects of music, but found success largely when considering musical conceptualization. We might be able to go further, but in the end, some of the most obvious musical traits cannot be related to a culture core, however defined. We would be unable to associate pentatonic scales with bravery, and heptatonic, with cowardice. Irregular metric units, descending melodic contour, binary forms in which the second half incompletely repeats the first, all leave us at a loss.

As Alan Lomax would lead us to expect, an aspect of culture that seems more likely to lend insight is the quality of interpersonal relationships, of which musical relationships may be illustrative. In Blackfoot culture there is a great difference in cultural role between men and women. In most respects human relationships are informal and easy. A person is associated with several groups. Political hierarchy is absent and authority temporary. People do cooperate and show little hostility to each other, but most actions are carried out by individuals while collaboration is not pervasive.

In Blackfoot music there are also substantial differences in men's and women's activities and repertories. The singing styles differ considerably. Informality is evident in many aspects of music, notably in the difference between theory and practice, stated rules and execution. Thus songs are said to be repeated four times, but recordings show great variation. The musical system is exhibited as a large body of separable songs, but in fact the difference between similar songs and sets of variants is not easily drawn. Songs have texts but may also be sung with newly created words or meaningless syllables. As a person is associated with several groups, a melody may be associated with several uses. Musical authority resides in part with song leaders who, however, hold musical power temporarily and informally. In a singing group there is a male leader whose tasks are mainly administrative. He also leads more performances than others, but the leadership role in a song's structure is confined to the beginning, after which others, again informally determined, hold roles of prominence. Singing in groups is common, but solo singing predominated in earlier times. A loose kind of musical cooperation is necessary, but singers make little attempt to blend voices and it is easy to hear the individual. Nonmembers of singing groups are welcome to "sit in," and a singer may perform with several groups though associated mainly with one.

This shows some relationships. Those elements of style that are most readily drawn in are the ones, conventionally called "performance practice," that are present constantly in musical performance whatever tone, rhythmic beat, or section of song is being sung. The general outlines of scale, meter, and form could not be easily related. But the central question, whether the relationships indicate cause, remains to be answered with certainty.

AND HOW COME IN IRAN . . . ?

In a survey of musics those of the Blackfoot and of Iran are worlds apart in style, even given some similarities such as monophony. The cultural differences are equally great. By comparing parallel situations we can again rule out race, language, and the character of the land as directly determining factors, and turn to aspects of culture as possible determinants of musical style.

In Iran, where one can easily distinguish classical, rural folk, and urban popular musics (and recognize other divisions), the following are illustrative. Certain aspects of performance practice such as the use of the voice are essentially the same in all repertories and strata. These exhibit at least some of the traits—tension, ornamentation, tightness, nasality, high pitch—associated by Lomax with a despotic social order, sexual repression, lack of concerted cooperation, traits perhaps typical of the culture at least in the past (Lomax 1959:933; see also Jacobs 1966 for examples of these characteristics in culture). But some features of musical style are found in the three main musical categories to varying degrees. A hierarchy of accompanying instruments in relationship to the leading solo is more pronounced in classical music. It is less evident in rural folk music, which has fewer accompanying strata and where the accompanying instruments are often in the hands of the soloist. In the popular music it is only occasionally found, though replaced by other kinds of relationship. Yet the hierarchical kind of accompanying structure is a close reflection of the social order at large.

There are various features of music generally restricted to one of the repertories; in our examination of symbolism we have discussed the concepts of hierarchy, individualism, surprise, and temporal precedence as characteristic of classical music and urban social behavior. By contrast, popular music featured acceptance and encouragement of variety and of outside influence, reflecting a heterogeneous culture under influence from others. Improvisation is present in rural music, but in the classical music it is set off from lower-prestige performance of precomposed materials, reflective of the importance of individualism and avoidance of long-range planning.

Again, it is aspects of performance practice and not the specific scalar or formal types that can be related to the characteristics of culture. We turn to language as an analogue. Specific phonetic and syntactic systems cannot easily be related to culture. No one knows why one language uses several velar fricatives and another none, why one has initial stress while in another stress is unpredictable, except that these features resulted from change of an earlier structure. But speaking quickly or slowly, with high or low pitch, with great or indistinct accentuation are features of language that can sometimes be related to a speaker's culture. Similarly in music, certain components, prominently including singing style and the relationship among performers in a group, as suggested in the cantometrics projects, seem in the main related rather directly to the nature of culture. Others, including scales and forms, are the development of earlier forms in directions determined by cultural values such as attitudes toward change, but their specific character cannot be traced. They appear to be an arbitrarily designed code. Again, we cannot automatically move from relationship to determination.

It would be ideal if there were a laboratory in which culture, nature, language could be manipulated to give us musical results. We have none. Peoples of similar origin living in diverse conditions—Africans and Europeans in the New World, overseas Indians, members of a variety of American Indian cultures finding themselves together in the ecology of the Plains—have been contemplated as the closest thing to a natural laboratory. But there are too many variables, and we have only a few partial theories of musical change. At this point the most promising hypothesis is that the style of each music is determined by a unique configuration of historical, geographic, and linguistic factors. But the kind of culture of which the music is part is surely the major determining force.

The Study of Music in the Field

Chapter 18

Come Back and See Me Next Tuesday

ARRIVAL

I have arrived in the "field." It turns out to be a little town in the northern Plains, hardly different on the surface from many other crossroads I've just driven through. When I stop at a filling station, a bit of a chill crawls up my neck: the attendant is an Indian, one of the people with whom I now wish to spend some months, whose music and musical culture I wish to study and describe. An old man with a tattered shirt, speaking English with a tiny bit of an accent. I'm here, I want to say to him, here because I want to learn what you know, because you have something to offer that is different from all I've learned before, because you live and think differently. This is a great moment for me: I have finally made it to the "field," and fate somehow selected you to be the one to introduce me. I am wondering how to say this, can't quite get up the nerve, and he says, "Three dollars, please; don't look like you need any oil," and starts attending to another customer. I drive on into the town, park at a sandwich shop. Several people sitting at the counter, white, Indian, maybe some in between? The waitress looks Indian but serves my hamburger like any midwestern waitress. All these people—there must be one with whom I could strike up a conversation. But of course the great significance of the occasion, so obvious to me, is nothing to them.

I turn to my neighbor, a man dressed like a road worker. "Nice day," he says. "Goin' to the mountains?" I clear my throat, getting ready my prepared speech about wanting to learn about Indian music, but before my thoughts collect sufficiently he has gone. I pay my check, begin a walk through the dreary village. Stop in a store or two, in a bar, at a bench where several old men are passing the time of day. Long ago I determined that this would be my town, and now I'm surrounded by my people, but they don't know it, and I don't know how to begin. Each time I reach a point at which I think I have found someone who will listen, to whom I can somehow make known these lofty wishes, needs, desires, I'm defeated, begin to fear that I'll never have the courage to reveal myself. When I do, they will laugh at me, a city dweller who should know better than lowering himself to learn something so useless as old Indian songs, a white man who aspires to study things an Indian had to spend a lifetime learning, one of the exploiters, or someone who could provide badly needed help if only he weren't involved with a frivolous subject like music. I begin to fear that I shall end up a hermit in this town, never meeting anyone with whom I can talk. Fear and anxiety. Several hours have passed and I have made no progress. I'm on the verge of turning around, leaving the town, giving up on these people. I have come to them, my "field," ready to give them energy and heart; they see me as just another white tourist, or perhaps they don't see me at all.

Where does one go in a strange town, lonely and despondent? The public library? A bar? I enter a barber shop; one can always use a haircut. The barber is Indian. "Just passing through?" he asks, and I blurt out, no, I would stay the summer. "Here?" he says, astonished. "Nobody spends a summer here if he don't have to." I'm doing research, I tell him self-consciously. "Research? Are you one of them anthropologists?" A bit of distaste evident in his voice. Well, no, but I'm interested in learning about Indian songs. "Oh, you ought to talk to one of them singers. There's one lives just two houses away, usually sits on the stoop. An old timer, knows a lot about the old days." Heart skips a beat: my chance, come after all. I pay, tip heavily, walk down the street. Just as the barber said: a ramshackle hut, probably just one room, old man sitting in front staring into space. I greet. "Got any cigarettes?" came the answer. I didn't. "Got a dollar so I can buy some?" Sure. "I hear you know a lot of the old songs of your people." "Naw, I don't know nothing. My brother, he knows a lot, lives fifty miles away, he'll be coming to see me in a week or some time." "Sure, I'd like to meet him. But I was told you know more than anybody in this town." "You want me to sing some songs on your tape recorder?" He seemed to have learned something about ethnomusicologists. "That's Indian work; I'll have to charge you a lot." I have some money, not much. "Well, you've got a car," he says. "Come back and see me next Tuesday, and bring your machine." He took a swig from a bottle of cheap bourbon. Dismissed.

Through this one conversation I felt that I had made my entry. I had suddenly become a fieldworker, graduated from my first role as outsider passing through town. By the next Tuesday I had actually met several men whom I could ask to work with me. Some were willing on the spot, others made it clear they wished nothing to do with me, most temporized and postponed. I told them that I had met Joe F., who had promised to help me, and some were impressed by that.

Tuesday I presented myself at Joe's hut. "I have to go to G. [a town forty miles east]," he said. Fortunately I knew what my next move should be, and so I spent that day taking Joe in my car, with four other members of his family, all of whom treated me rather like a chauffeur to whom one gave directions but otherwise didn't speak, attending to various bits of personal business. At the end I asked about recording some songs. "I don't have time today, but come back in a few days," I was told.

To make a long story short, it was another week before Joe consented to be interviewed more or less formally and to sing a few songs, in a weak voice, with a poor memory, for my machine. I learned less clumsy techniques, and after a few weeks Joe had become a friend with whom one could converse easily about anything. I joined his family on picnics, moved from outsider to observer to participant-observer. Why did he make me wait, come back twice? Some informants didn't, were ready on the spot, said they had time, which Joe in fact also had but wouldn't admit. Was it to teach me some respect for his way of doing things, to tell me that I couldn't just rush in, or to test whether I had more than a casual interest? I have since heard variants of "come back and see me next Tuesday" in other countries. Getting started in the field is actually a time of stress, the moment of entry sometimes one of great tension, self-searching, requiring courage, patience, wit. In this chapter we present some thoughts on the general nature of ethnomusicological fieldwork.

THE HALLMARK OF ANTHROPOLOGY

Others, of course, would have handled the matter more efficiently and given absolutely different explanations, reactions, feelings. This is probably the reason why ethnomusicological literature, which has a good bit to say about fieldwork as part of research design, ways of dealing with recording and filming machinery, general principles of intercultural relations, tells much less about the day-to-day personal relationships that are the heart of this kind of research. All subsequent research depends so heavily on fieldwork, but it is the most personal part of the job, the part that cannot really be taught, which each must learn on his own, finding ways of mediating between his personality with its strengths and weaknesses, confidence and timidity, and the individuals whose shared beliefs he will learn and interpret.

Anthropologists and folklorists who claim fieldwork as their activity par excellence have said more but, like ethnomusicologists, until recently they have rarely told in detail what happened in the field. One does not often find straightforward accounts of daily life and feelings in an exotic environment, such as the posthumously published diary of Malinowski (1967), a man often cited for his prowess as a fieldworker. Very occasionally are transcriptions of interviews or field notes provided (Slotkin 1952, Merriam 1969a). But like the little parable above, most publications dealing with fieldwork focus on the role of the informant, the person through whom the ethnographer learns a culture and whose moods, empathy, attitude toward a visitor, idiosyncratic ideas, genius for discovering the instructive, interest in looking at life in a structured fashion, all determine the quality of understanding that ensues. An anthropologist may begin by seeing informants as faceless representatives of a homogeneous mass, but the fallacy quickly becomes apparent and, as illustrated by the many warm and emotional essays in Casagrande's (1960) collection of portraits of "favorite" informants by outstanding scholars, special kinds of human relationship develop.

It is in the importance of fieldwork that anthropology and ethnomusicology are closest: it is the "hallmark" of both fields, something like a union card. Members of the profession are expected to have some fieldwork under their belts. Anthropology has typically functioned as the guide. Early on, theoretical statements on the strengths and limitations of fieldwork were made, though usually buried in ethnographies. Thus Malinowski (1935: 317) gives general impressions and advice: the anthropologist must not only observe but constantly interpret, structure, construct, relating isolated bits of data to each other; be highly self-critical, realizing that many approaches inevitably lead to false conclusions and dead ends; and be ready to start over. He found that byproducts of his main work often provided the most valuable insights and suggested that one subordinate but also impose one's self on the field. Malinowski insists that the culture concept plays a major role in the nature of the fieldwork, which "consists only and exclusively in the interpretation of the chaotic social reality, in subordinating it to general rule" (1954:238).

The variety of field techniques and methods in cultural anthropology is immense, comprising everything from biographical approaches to parallel interviews on the same subject with many informants, the collection of texts, questionnaires, outright participation, teamwork, and much more. Most of these have analogues in ethnomusicology. The proliferation of techniques required structuring, and in the last two or three decades a body of theoretical writing about fieldwork has emerged in anthropology. A major change in attitude was exhibited in the development of the so-called "new ethnography" of the 1960s (see e.g. Tyler 1969) explicitly displaying the contrast between insider and outsider views, to be elaborated in Chapter 19. An extended essay by Morris Freilich (1970) is illustrative of attempts to circumscribe the field. He divides fieldwork activities into fourteen areas, beginning with such mundane things as preparing a research proposal and finding funds, but concentrating on problems faced in the field. Informants see their culture in a special way, play particular roles in their societies, and have peculiar views of their roles in the quests of fieldworkers. Freilich divides them into three groups—traditionalist, operator, and speculator—and subdivides them further, in accordance with the ways in which they are willing to tackle problems of their culture as expressed in the fieldworker's questions (1970:572–73). He classifies kinds of information that may be gathered—public, confidential, secret, and private (p. 549)—weighs social and economic risks faced by both partners, and so proposes a formal theory of fieldwork.

Freilich's approach can be a valuable guide to the prospective fieldworker, and it can give the nonanthropologist a sense of the complexity of relationships that are involved. There also emerged some textbooks and guides. These do not so much tell you what to do but provide case studies as examples (see e.g. Wax 1971, Freilich 1977, Georges and Jones 1980). Ethnomusicologists and folklorists seem to need more practical information than anthropologists about techniques of recording, filming, video-taping, special problems of text-gathering. Karpeles (1958) provides an early attempt at suggesting standardization of techniques. Goldstein (1964) gives a detailed volume of advice, and there are many guides to making recordings, among the most thorough and thoughtful being Hood's book, *The Ethnomusicologist* (1971). In all of this literature the stress is on theory generally applicable and techniques suited to a particular situation. Occasionally there are also suggestions of generally applicable procedures. Powdermaker (1967), in one of the first books devoted specifically to the nature of fieldwork, suggests such fundamental steps as making a census, providing a sketch of the society to be studied before proceeding to more specialized tasks, ascertaining matters of tabu and etiquette.

That all this can be a difficult, frustrating, slow process is obvious; but again, realistic accounts of what was actually done in a particular situation have only recently begun to surface in anthropology (see Golde 1970, Spindler 1970, Foster and Kemper 1974, Dumont 1978). In ethnomusicology, by contrast, fieldwork as a theoretical concept does not often appear as a subject to be discussed out of a broader context of research design. Hood's book and Herndon and McLeod's text (1980) are exceptions, each devoting two insightful chapters to the problem, discussing concepts as well as giving specific advice. Hood, despite his attention to other matters and interesting accounts of personal experience, does seem to be mainly concerned with the gathering of recorded material.

In the second half of this century it has become more or less axiomatic that a researcher does his own fieldwork, and Merriam (1964), reflecting the view that separation is not really thinkable, discusses it as an aspect of research design and general theory. In his book he does not tell specifically what to do in the field and, for that matter, like most authors, avoids giving in detail what he himself did. In later works (1969a, 1977b) he comes closer to giving such an account; indeed, self-revelation may be becoming a trend, as indicated by the appearance of musical ethnographies with great attention to the activities and experiences of the fieldworker (e.g. Berliner 1978, Keil 1979). Also important in the last two decades is the growing concern with the ethical aspects of researchers' interrelationships with their informants and teachers (see Chapter 22 and, for a critical appraisal of the issue, Gourlay 1978).

THE HISTORY OF ETHNOMUSICOLOGY IS THE HISTORY OF FIELDWORK

As the main interest of ethnomusicology is in total musical systems, the question of sampling is crucial, and the selection and evaluation of informants are a major component of the way in which we sample a culture. How we see a culture depends on the kind of first-hand looking that we do. With this in mind, it seems appropriate to try to identify several approaches to ethnomusicological fieldwork, presenting them in a more or less chronological arrangement, providing a bare outline of their history. If these are stages, they certainly overlap. Each represents only part of a mainstream and omits the work of scholars who did not conform to prevailing trends, were ahead or behind, dealt with problems outside the field's main thrust. But in a sense the history of ethnomusicology is the history of approaches to fieldwork.

In the period between 1890 and 1930 research most characteristically concentrated on artifacts, i.e. songs or pieces, collected with some attention to cultural context and in small samplings. The recordings were often made by missionaries or ethnographers who would not ultimately do the analytical and interpretive work. For example, many studies made by Hornbostel, Stumpf, and their contemporaries are based on a dozen songs or two. The assumption was that a small sampling of songs would give one something approaching the musical universe of the culture, or at least its major characteristics. Emphasis was on "collecting," in the sense of plucking the pieces out of the culture for analysis and preservation elsewhere, something that sounds a bit like colonial exploitation. To be sure, at this time and earlier, Oriental musical cultures were studied by individuals who had the opportunity of extended residence and a large accumulation of more or less random musical experience. Among these were missionaries, travelers, colonial administrators, who produced some of the early classics—Fox-Strangways (1914) for India, Amiot (1779) for China, Villoteau (1809) for Egypt.

More or less simultaneously but extending further into the twentieth century is a type of fieldwork that, like the first, involved collection of artifacts, but with the intention of preserving and recording a total musical corpus. The word "preserve" is used advisedly; the scholars in this group tended to regard preservation to be a major function of their work. Large collections of European folk music came into existence. In the twentieth century the work of Béla Bartók, who collected songs from many Eastern European cultures in enormous quantity, is surely an outstanding exemplar. But the approach was also followed in some work with non-Western cultures, as Frances Densmore's early publications on Chippewa and Sioux music must be considered as attempts to record the total repertories of these cultures. At the same time more recent collecting projects with the same purpose are not uncommon, as for example the large collection of Cheremis songs published by the Hungarian scholars Vikár and Bereczki (1971).

There followed a more diversified approach characterized by (a) continued concentration on the recording of musical artifacts, (b) extended residence in one community, (c) greater sensitivity to the cultural context and study of music in culture, and (d) attempts to comprehend an entire musical system, usually emanating from a small community with little or no musical or verbal literacy, a tribal or folk culture. This type of work seems to have been most common from 1920 to about 1960, and the various field trips taken to parts of the southwestern United States by George Herzog may be illustrative of its early period. In 1927 Herzog spent several months with the Pima in Arizona. By later standards this stay of some eight weeks is brief, but close to 200 songs were recorded and much information regarding uses of music and its role in society was gathered, appended to the songs in Herzog's major publication on the subject (1936a) and presented elsewhere as well (1938). More extensive fieldwork, spread over several visits or residence of one or more years, characterizes the later portion of this stage. Hood came to regard a year as minimal. We may cite David McAllester's repeated visits to the Navajo, resulting in a series of publications by himself and some of his students that present the entire musical culture in pieces, present and describe the music itself, and speak to general problems of music in culture (see McAllester 1954, Frisbie 1967, Mitchell 1978, etc.).

All of these approaches cast the fieldworker in the role of observer, although he may at times have been an occasional participant. Emphasis on participation is characteristic of the fourth type of field venture. The fieldworker appears as a student of performance, even including the sensitive areas of improvisation and composition, more or less on the same terms as the native music student. Dating from the early 1950s and still very much in evidence, this development coincides with several other important events. Following World War II, it came at a time of increased opportunity for travel and thus of increased exposure of Westerners to the ancient and high civilizations of Asia. These cultures had developed systematic ways of teaching their music, sometimes in the process separating it from its cultural context. I do not suggest that other societies, such as American Indians or Australian aboriginals, lacked ways of teaching their music. But these were rarely distinct formal activities and could not as readily be separated from the ceremonial, religious, social, or enculturative functions of the music. Thus the entry of an American or European into the musical system as a student would probably depend more heavily upon his ability to enter the entire cultural system. In the case of India, Iran, Japan, and Java, music teaching was at least somewhat separable. One could go to India, study with an Indian vocalist, live in the Westernized section of society, and not be obliged to become thoroughly a participant in Indian culture (although indeed some such participation would be a desirable result).

Another factor was the rather sudden expansion of interest on the part of Western musicians in the Asian classical musics, an interest that had heretofore been nurtured only by a few with a decidedly historical orientation. The study of Asian and African performance techniques and practice was carried out by ethnomusicologists but also by others who had no interest in research but who wish simply to learn to play or sing. This cannot properly be called "ethnomusicology" any more than studying the 'cello can by itself be called historical musicology. There is certainly no reason to discourage such learning. But in the 1950s and 1960s the contrast between participant and observer in fieldwork was a major source of conflict in ethnomusicology, the one side being blamed for neglect of scholarly objectives and the other for lack of truly musical interest. Direct study of performance became, however, an extremely useful vehicle for understanding a musical system. Like that of our third stage, this kind of fieldwork involves extended residence in one community, and in a certain way it too is an attempt to comprehend the entire system, at least as seen, perceived, and taught by one full-fledged member of the musical culture. Typical of this approach is the work of those who studied in the UCLA program in ethnomusicology (see Hood 1957 and 1960 and, for analysis of a personal experience, Koning 1980). Also typical would be the work of Ella Zonis (1973), who for three years studied primarily at one institution in Teheran, the Conservatory of National Music, along with Iranian students, and who in her book presents the musical system essentially as presented by her teachers there.

A fifth stage differs from the rest in that there is no attempt to be comprehensive but, rather, to carry out a strictly limited project whose task it is to make a specialized contribution. It is nevertheless difficult to separate from the others, for even its characteristic project is usually in practice accompanied or preceded by a good deal of general ethnographic work and recording. As many of the world's musical cultures have become reasonably well known and broadly covered in the literature, the need for solving specialized problems emerged as a further stage of research.

An example of this type of study is the work of Jihad Racy in Egypt (Racy 1976), whose subject was the history of the record industry in Cairo and its impact on classical music early in the twentieth century. Much of this was conventionally historical, with printed and archival sources. But he also engaged in fieldwork, with a group of informants who were not musicians but rather collectors of old records, and with elderly individuals who could give first-hand accounts of musical life in the period involved. Somewhat more characteristic are the many studies dealing with specific cultural problems, such as Neuman's work (1980) concentrating on the background and social structure of classical music in Delhi. Musicians had to be interviewed primarily on matters not dealing with music per se. For other examples, making selective recordings such as performances of one piece by many, or improvisation on one model by one person at different times, provides a slice but not all of a musical system and yet solves problems of performance practice or improvisation. The vast number of attempts to study (and for that matter to record or film) one ritual, context, person, also fall into this broad category. Emphasis on a specific problem other than total comprehension via sampling, with a research design integrating fieldwork and subsequent analysis, is more typical of the period since 1960 than before.

INFORMANTS AND TEACHERS

Some disciplines in which fieldwork has a role—sociology, political science, economics—tend to depend for their data substantially on written sources such as constitutions, statistical abstracts, voting records, and on surveys such as questionnaires directed to large numbers of people. Anthropologists, folklorists (and ethnomusicologists) are typically distinguished by their belief that a (musical) culture can best be understood through intensive work with a relatively small number of its representatives. Known as informants, they should more appropriately be called teachers, for that is precisely what they are. Since ethnomusicologists do not usually deal with many individuals, they are involved in a more delicate sampling procedure than those scholars who attain statistical validity with larger samplings. The selection of informants is therefore a major issue, but I cannot presume to tell someone how to do it. Informants often select themselves; they appear in the fieldworker's life fortuitously, and one may have little choice. Even so, one must consider what is happening.

In working with the Blackfoot people, I was introduced to a man who was described as a singer. I did not ask further; he had been so designated in contrast to dozens of others who were not. I didn't care whether he was considered the best or the worst. I was grateful for anyone's help, and I assumed that he would be somehow representative of that part of the population who were titled "singers." I had it in mind to study the musical culture as it existed, was interested in the mainstream of musical experience, not in what was exceptionally good or, for that matter, bad. I valued most the contact with someone who would speak articulately, give me lots of information. I hoped he would in some way be typical, and thought I would later be able to put my hope to the test.

All of this hinged on the ethnomusicological interest in learning what actually happens in a society and not what the society would wish to happen, as it were, if each member had control over his or her experience. Although

I needed to know what the ideal was, I did not mainly want to study it. Unlike some of the early scholars, I no longer assumed that all informants in a simple society would tell me the same thing; I had discarded the idea of essential homogeneity. But I did believe, rightly or not, that among the fifty or so "singers" which the community turned out to have, perhaps half a dozen would be considered outstanding, another few barely adequate, and the majority simply good, in a sort of bell-shaped curve. This last group most interested me. The members of the society seemed to find my approach compatible, didn't feel that I should be concentrating only on the best.

Working later in Iran, I had the good fortune to find myself under the wing of a man who was highly distinguished as a musician though a bit controversial among his colleagues. He became my main teacher, and I learned the system through his presentation of it. Subsequently I spoke to other musicians, a majority of whom agreed that he represented the best their culture had to offer, while others considered him overrated and recommended other authorities, including themselves. The Plains Indians did this too, but the difference consisted in their insistence that I talk to people who, generally speaking, had it right, while the Iranians cared that I learn the system from someone who knew it extremely well, not just a run-of-the-mill musician.

In each case I was lucky to have stumbled on a way of operating that fitted the society's values. In each one might have taken an opposite approach, created friction, conceivably learning equally valuable though different things. There is not one right way; it's just that one must know what one is doing and, later, has done. We need to discern between ordinary experience and ideal, but the "ideal" musician may also know and do things completely outside the ken of the rest. My teacher in Iran was able to explain things about Persian music that might have been beyond the comprehension of others. Learning them was itself worthwhile, but I should also know whether they are things shared by only a few, the ordinary musician unaware of them. The question is worthy of Malinowski's admonition to create structure out of chaos: were these things I learned uniquely from my teacher properly part of the culture?

There are other ramifications of the informant selection process. For example, if it is important to be accepted in a community, and if this acceptance is enhanced by having a prestigious local "sponsor," one must decide whether such a person, regardless of other qualities, should become a key informant. One must decide to what extent one should depend on those who know things about older traditions but cannot participate, or how important it is to have a main informant who is an active participant in musical culture, depth of knowledge aside. We must deal with the self-selection tendencies of informants, realizing that those who do this may have ulterior motives and provide the advantage of being readily available but not be otherwise representative. To what extent should one talk to informants about each other, ascertain their reputation in the community? There is no end to the questions of selection and relationship.

A former professor of mine, experienced for decades in linguistic field research among American Indians, put it this way: "Your relationship to your informants is a uniquely satisfying one. He is one of the few people whom you don't contradict, with whom you never disagree." One must be able to trust one's informants; otherwise there is no security. Purposely or from ignorance, they may give misinformation, but even the selection of this misinformation on their part may tell us something about the culture. Of course fieldworkers often do argue with their informants, about facts, money, roles. And yet the relationship is surely unique. They are our teachers, but unlike those from whom we learn our own culture, they have no real stake in the student's success and need not regard him as a potential competitor.

Ideal ethnomusicological fieldworkers are formidable individuals indeed. According to various writers on the subject (e.g. Jacobs in Freilich 1970, Hood 1971), they should control several disciplines—anthropology, history, art, religious studies, biology, psychology—besides their musical training. They must be talented musicians so that they can quickly learn a strange system. They must know the languages of peoples they are studying. They should excel as recording engineers and cinematographers. They must be able to stay in the field for long periods but not lose themselves in it, have prodigious energy in order to comprehend without much help materials of great complexity under difficult physical conditions. They must have outgoing personalities. On and on. To do the job right, all say emphatically, one cannot just go somewhere and turn on a tape recorder. It has been suggested that teamwork by a group of specialists is the solution. There is just too much to do to prepare really well, to make really complete use of the field opportunities. Yet almost all that has been accomplished has been the work of individuals. How can one be confident in the face of the insuperable demands of one's own scholarly community and of the culture and its material that is waiting to be interpreted? Well, things may not be all that bad. As previously suggested, the way in which one samples repertories, informants, musicians, audiences, villages, periods in a short span of history depends on the approach to fieldwork. Since this is very much a personal matter, ethnomusicology has rarely shown itself to be a replicable science. In fieldwork there is less standardization than in other activities of the research process; it is more art than science.

But the ethnomusicologist is himself also a sample. Just as one cannot study the whole musical culture but must experience it in samplings, one cannot satisfy all desired approaches but must depend on one's own capacities. Rarely in a position to be part of a team that provides expertise in language, performance ability, technology, anthropological theory, and so on, one must be willing to live with these limitations. If expert in one or two of these respects and at least aware of the basic problems of the others, one will have a chance of succeeding in providing some reliable information and a credible interpretation. One must view one's self as a sample of ethnomusicological method and technique. The purpose of this point is to discourage those who say that if someone has visited a society and made recordings, its musical culture has been "researched." There is no single way to go about a task, and each contribution is at best partial. It is a great mistake to feel that a particular culture or music has "been done" because someone has worked with it in the field. The idiosyncratic nature of fieldwork assures the value of each serious attempt, and the more any one society is studied, the more of interest emerges to be done.

Direct inspection at the source: the closest thing to science, but it turns out to be an art. Yet in one important sense we expect a standard from fieldworkers. We expect of them respect for their material and for the people with whom they work. The informants, the teachers, are keenly aware of its presence or absence; they test the fieldworker to determine if he or she is serious and takes them seriously. It is mainly for that reason that they so often start out by saying, "Come back and see me next Tuesday."

Chapter 19

You Will Never Understand This Music

THE UGLY ETHNOMUSICOLOGIST

I was about to leave my lesson of Persian music in the spacious old house in south Teheran when my teacher suddenly fixed me with his forefinger: "You will never understand this music. There are things that every Persian on the street understands instinctively which you will never understand, no matter how hard you try." Startled, but still knowing what he meant, I blurted out, "I don't really expect to understand it that way, I am just trying to figure out how it is put together." "Oh, well, that is something you can probably learn, but it's not really very important." It was clear to my teacher that a member of a society may understand a culture quite differently from even an informed outsider. End of lesson.

Years later, in an American classroom, I was confronted by a young man from Nigeria. "With what rationale do you study the music of other cultures?" The tone implied that this was a most unnatural thing to do, he seemed hostile, and a lot of discussion could not satisfy him that I was doing something legitimate.

My teacher didn't think there was anything wrong with my *trying* to understand Persian music in the way Iranians understood it but only thought it was futile. The West African questioned the morality of even trying. The distinction has come to play an important role in ethnomusicological thinking and discussion, though somewhat less in publication (but see Gourlay 1978 for a critical appraisal). The difference between my Iranian teacher's understanding and mine is recognized by Mantle Hood in what has the significance of a concluding and conclusive statement in his book *The Ethnomusicologist* (1971:374): ". . . the American or French or British ethnomusicologist because of *who* he is—that is to say, what he has succeeded in becoming through years of training—is capable of insights and evaluations, as a transmitter of a non-Western music, which no Javanese, even with training abroad in Western methods, could ever duplicate." The converse is true of the Javanese scholar. Recognizing the difference between the insider's and the outsider's perspectives, Hood asserts that each makes a contribution.

But others—and not exclusively members of "Third World" societies—question the validity of cross-cultural approaches on intellectual and moral grounds. Daniélou (1973:34–35) indicts the profession of ethnomusicology for dealing with non-European music in a condescending way, treating it as something quaint or exotic, failing to make the kinds of distinction between fine art and folk genres conventionally made among strata and degrees of learning in Western culture. In this chapter we are primarily concerned with the intellectual problems that face the outsider *because* of who he is and only secondarily with the morality of dealing with the music of another culture or the ethical questions confronting the fieldworker, which we save for Chapter 22. But of course it is difficult to separate these issues.

The young Nigerian's question had emotional overtones. Perhaps he could not have put his finger on the reasons for his anger, but there is cause for questioning the activities of ethnomusicologists who come in many guises, have many roles. In all cases there is an anomaly, an imbalance. They come as students but quickly pretend to become masters. The theory is that intercultural studies are a reciprocal affair, but they proceed to study non-Western music on their own terms, and also expect non-Western scholars to study Western music in Western terms.

Some ethnomusicologists define themselves as those who, as outsiders, study the musical cultures of the world's societies. But, in fact, the overwhelming majority are simply members of Western society who study non-Western music, members of affluent nations who study the music of the poor. The imbalance might not have arisen if there had been, from the beginning, a network of intercultural scholarship consisting of individuals from many societies who studied each other's musics from many perspectives, more or less evenly distributed. This is in the realm of the "it might have been," but we can get glimpses of the kinds of insights of which we have been deprived by the one-sided history of our field.

A new graduate student from West Africa appeared in my class. He had studied Western music in Europe, but as a villager in his youth had also mastered the percussion ensemble music of his native tradition. My course dealt with North American Indian music, a field that Americans are inclined to study primarily in terms of its melodic aspects. As students of Western music we had learned how to deal with and to perceive melodic material reasonably well, felt confident that we could also do this for Indian songs, but were rather at a loss to treat rhythm in a very sophisticated way. Yet from the beginning the African student turned to the complex relationships between the rhythmic structures of drum and voice, able to comprehend them readily. Throughout the semester he enriched the class with insights that came from the African drummer's thorough grounding in the perception of rhythmic phenomena. If Western ethnomusicology, because of Western preoccupation with melody in its classical system, has always been better at dealing with the pitch-derived aspects of music, it is conceivable that an "African" ethnomusicology, more qualified to deal with rhythm, would have given us a different "outsider's" picture of American Indian music, had there been scholars encouraged to carry out such work (see Cachia 1973 for a parallel case). Such unrealized possibilities boggle the imagination. So why, in the real world, should one indeed ask, "With what rationale do you study the music of other cultures?"

Here are some of the frequently heard objections to ethnomusicological outsiders. They represent a kind of musical colonialism, manipulating the societies they visit, keeping them from controlling their own musical destiny. They may encourage the retention of old materials or segments of a repertory, and they take away music—at the same time leaving it behind, to be sure, but perhaps polluted by having been removed, recorded, its secrecy violated—for their own benefit and that of their society. They take advantage of their membership in a wealthier society, with economic and military power, to cause musical turmoil and dissent, giving allegiance to a few sycophants who may then artificially become an elite because of the association. Walking with heavy tread, they leave footprints after their departure.

We aren't all like that, they may say; sometimes the natives even love us. One needn't swallow such an apocalyptic version of the ethnomusicologist's effect. Yet Alan Merriam, surely a sensitive and careful observer who participated in his host culture only to a small extent, found upon his return to a village in Zaire where he had worked fourteen years before that his earlier visit was the most significant event in musical life in remembered history (Merriam 1977b). Ethnomusicologist outsiders affect the "field," and their very presence can get in the way of their own research.

But if no actual harm comes from the visit of an ethnomusicologist, one is often asked just what good such a study does the people whose music is investigated. Consideration of this issue is properly taken up in Chapter 22, as it is essentially political. The major *intellectual* objection (with its own political overtones) to fieldwork by an outsider is based on the belief that musical systems are essentially untranslatable. There are field situations in which the ethnomusicologist is viewed as a threat because of the comparative approach, sometimes explicitly presented in speaking of "Eastern," "Oriental," "African," "Western" styles, all concepts that assume comparison of musics. The adverse reaction results from three beliefs typically held in the host cultures. (a) The ethnomusicologist comes to compare a non-Western music to his or her own, not to study the non-Western system because it is interesting or significant, and does not respect it for its own sake. The purpose is, so it is thought, to make comparisons in order to show that the outsider's own music is superior, and that the host music is merely a stage in the development of the perfect music. Needless to say, this kind of primitivism is distasteful to thoughtful members of non-Western societies. (b) Ethnomusicologists want to use their own approaches to non-Western music, but these will not work and without doubt result in misunderstandings. Non-Western scholars tend to regard European and American publications as full of errors. What is really significant cannot be learned, as my teacher said, at least not with an essentially comparative approach. As we have seen (in Chapter 5), this belief is shared by some Western scholars. (c) They come with the assumption that there is such a thing as African or Asian or American Indian music, disregarding boundaries obvious to the host. Thoughtful members of all societies regard their own music as something special, and the ethnomusicologist is accused of underrating its musical diversity.

Political and intellectual issues overlap and coincide. Ethnomusicologists take advantage of the members of the host society for personal and in some cases national benefit. In order to do this efficiently, they proceed with bias, approaching a non-Western music with the methods of Western music, making invidious comparisons with evolutionist overtones, imposing research methods so that their findings will accommodate the basic assumptions. Many Asian and African intellectuals think that this is the way it has been done.

One may argue that things have not always been so bad, that ethnomusicologists do better by a musical system than do the other Western musicians who come into contact with the Third World, that they help tradition-minded musicians maintain the independence of their art and aid in the revival of native musics about to disappear. They maintain that they are aware of the limitations of their approaches, are doing the best they can, and accomplish at least something to help international understanding. They often take political stances in opposition to their own countries' foreign policy or at least remain neutral. In the face of this, they often seem to hear, "Never mind, we'd rather take care of things ourselves." It is a personal and disciplinary dilemma.

But we come to yet another objection, given already by implication in Mantle Hood's statement (above). The culture's "insider" and "outsider" provide different interpretations, both valid. Reasoned thought accords primacy to the former view; it is the more important. It is the insider who provides the perspective that the culture has of itself. The outsider, with an essentially comparative and universalist approach, merely adds something less significant. If we as Western scholars believed that Indian and Chinese scholars had something to tell us about Western music, which they could study as outsiders free of our biases and special emotional attachment to this art, we would nevertheless reject the relegation of our own findings and interpretations to background status but would expect the Indian and Chinese insights to remain supplementary. Conversely, non-Western scholars resent being put in the role of minor contributors to the understanding of their own music.

As my teacher said, it may be that I will never understand his music the way his countrymen do, and that the best I can expect is to be able to point out some interesting things they hadn't noticed.

WHO IS AN INSIDER?

One of the major events in ethnomusicology since 1950 is the development of scholars in non-Western nations who study, if not the music of their personal tradition, then that of their nation or region (see e.g. Mapoma 1969 and Euba 1971). The relative roles of Western and non-Western scholars in ethnomusicology have been debated at international gatherings, where it was sometimes shown how many modern nation-states in the Third World exist in violation of culture boundaries otherwise determined, such as tribal and language groups, urban and rural cultures. It is taken for granted that an Englishman doing research in Nigeria is an outsider, but that a Nigerian of Yoruba background is an insider in relationship to his Hausa compatriot. Yet it is only the coincidence of British colonization that threw these peoples, as it were, into the same nation. The same is true of the Javanese studying in Sumatra, though he may have politically and intellectually greater claims to insidership; so does the Bostonian in the Louisiana bayous, but you wouldn't know it from talking to the Cajuns. It is interesting, however, to see that scholars in the more industrialized Third World nations are beginning to admit that they, like European and American fieldworkers, are also outsiders to the rural societies with which they deal. They admit this as a liability to their scholarship but may also insist that their political right to be "insiders" remains unimpaired. On that front, there is even a tendency for insidership to be accorded to residence on a continent. Asian music should be studied by Asians (Koizumi 1977), African music by Africans, one sometimes hears, contrary to the also widely heard insistence that major cultural and musical boundaries crisscross these continents. The concepts of continent, nation, and ethnic group or enclave play parallel, different, alternating roles. Development of the world as "global village" may make everyone potentially an insider to all societies as musical homogenization grows. Conversely, alienation will make it impossible for someone to be anything but an outsider to all but his immediate environment.

The question of the outsider's intellectually meaningful and valid contribution has been muddied by political issues, by the guilt the industrialized nations have to bear for colonizing the others, and whites for enslaving other populations. But it must be possible to lay aside the feelings of professional inadequacy born of this guilt and address the intellectual issues alone. Going back to Mantle Hood's differentiation of insider and outsider, how can outsiders be sure that they are making contributions that are distinctive and yet valid to both insider and international scholar?

Some possibilities:

Calling upon the relativism that is their hallmark, they can stimulate the musical public in their own society to become respectful of other musical systems. This requires a delicate balance between the music lover's enthusiasm, which may result in the impression that non-Western musics are easy to learn and understand, and the scholar's assertion of the insurmountable difficulties of understanding a non-Western music as an outsider. In this context I should once more comment on the widespread tendency for American and some European institutions to teach the performance of non-Western music. (See Hood 1957 for a seminal discussion.) An extremely useful educational device if regarded as a component of ethnomusicology, this practice can nevertheless be abused. One gets the impression from some students and teachers that playing in a Javanese gamelan or a West African percussion ensemble can be learned easily and quickly. Indeed, a group of such students can readily learn to produce sounds that approximate what one might hear in Java or Ghana, but they rarely and only with difficulty attain the expertise to produce them acceptably to the informed native listener. In the fashion of ensembles in American music departments, such groups may quickly forsake their laboratory function and move to the public stage, performing for an uninformed audience which assumes that all gamelans sound like this, that the music is simple and primitive and can be absorbed in one semester. Nothing may be further from the mind of the ethnomusicologist-instructor, but with this process the inner complexities of the music may fall by the wayside, and some of its major components such as improvisation may be replaced by the time-honored Western technique of memorizing.

I would not deny the excellence of certain of these student ensembles, nor would I impugn the values and intentions of the teachers. But one should try to be sure that in the long run one is not doing in the West what the introduction of Western music via a junior high school orchestra would do in Asia or Africa. If non-Western musicians could be sure that their art is treated with proper respect abroad by ethnomusicologists, they might be more trusting. If they could also be sure that where possible they would benefit from the exchange, perhaps by being appointed to teach their music abroad instead of having it taken from them and taught at second hand by their Western students, they might regard the situation as equitable.

It can come as a surprise to fieldworkers that the people with whom they work and from whom they learn want to know what good this work will do them, what they will get out of it. The days of glass beads as the colonialist's universal answer are long gone, but beyond being paid in some way for their time, informants want to know what of real value they will receive in return for having provided a unique service, for having taught what no one in the fieldworker's own culture can teach, what cannot be found in books, what even few in their own society can command. In somewhat the same way the officials in the ministry of culture want to know how the cultural life of the nation will benefit. What is given has value and can in a sense be marketed. Will the nation benefit if its music is recorded, if works are published about it, if its records are disseminated by European scholars, institutions, companies? Or is it better to wait until the nation's own facilities and personnel are up to the task? Many other questions flow from this.

Exposure involves risk. Informants risk the disapproval of their fellows, ridicule if the visiting foreigner later misinterprets what has been learned or takes unfair advantage. They expose the vital organs of their culture, bound to include a component of secrecy. I am not referring only to those societies in which the recording of ritual music would automatically invalidate the ritual. Every society wants to keep aspects of its culture to itself. The way it lives provides social integration; all peoples wish to exclude others from certain of their ways. To teach an outsider your culture is a kind of sharing, sharing of yourself with one who will not remain but will discard you once he has what he wants. You ask yourself to what extent you should share your culture for pay or prestige or just out of the goodness of your heart, and at what point it is no longer worth the money—and at what point your fellow villagers will think you have gone too far and thus make *you* something of an outsider.

SO THAT PEOPLE WILL UNDERSTAND

Looking at a few experiences in the field, I ask myself what it was that my teachers and informants wanted out of their exchange with me. Indeed, they wished the world to have respect for their music, and in time they could be convinced that sharing with me might work to that end. Some wanted adequate pay for their time. They wanted to be treated like human beings, like friends, teachers, associates, not like robot-informants or clerks in a department store. Beyond this, they wanted their material to be used in accordance with their ideas. Plains Indian singers wanted to be sure that records would not be issued, since they were on the verge of issuing their own. They wanted to be sure that, in teaching, I would treat their music as something integral to their culture. They wished to avoid misinterpretation, and they wanted to know that I applied to their music those standards which I applied to my own. If as a music teacher I were careful to teach what I considered the best music of my culture, they wanted this attitude taken also with theirs, given, of course, different criteria. They did not want much of what they said to be widely publicized, did not wish individuals to be mentioned or singled out for attention. And they expected help with their problems, felt it would be improper for me not to be concerned with these, even if I had no legal or official obligation to do so.

In Iran it was somewhat similar, except that my teacher insisted that if he spent his time with me, what I learned must be imparted to the world. "When you return to America, you will write a book about what I have taught you?" "Well, I didn't really have that in mind; maybe I'll never know enough." "But you must, you must write such a book, so that people in America will understand. . . ."

As a matter of fact, it is not clear that the host society always prefers the "participant" approach. If the fieldworker wishes to change from outsider to something approaching insidership, participation seems the most logical route. It is often the most comfortable to the local musicians, who prefer teaching foreigners as they teach their own students and who are uncomfortable in the face of unexpected questions or when asked to play into a microphone. But there are also cases in which members of a society do not wish participation but are willing to be observed.

In the classical music world of Iran participation to a degree was, in my experience, essential. My teacher was willing to have me play the role of observer, but he was not impressed; only when I indicated a desire to learn like his local students did I achieve some credibility. Even then, my observer-like insistence on recording particular things that I requested from a large group of musicians remained an enigma to him. But had I, visiting the villages and small towns of Iran, tried to learn the trade of a motreb, a minstrel, this would have been seen as an intolerable violation of many rules. I was from the wrong place, in the wrong social class, from the wrong family, wrong religion. Even if I learned the material correctly, an unlikely prospect, I simply wasn't the kind of person who could become a motreb. Similarly, Indians of the northern Plains may be ambivalent (though not forbidding) about a white person who tries to sing Indian social dance songs but negative about one who tries to intrude in ceremonies. Some Indian peoples of the Southwest would take a harsher view. If ethnomusicologists want to be welcome in a Third World society, they must behave as much as they can in accordance with its standards.

One day I tried out one of my hare-brained theories about the interrelationships of *gushehs* in the Persian *radif* on my teacher. "My goodness, I never thought of that; of course you're right, and what you said underscores what I've been telling you about the magnificence of our *radif.*" Perhaps an outsider could be of some use after all. My teacher could accept the idea that an outsider, because of who he is, as Hood says, can make a significant contribution even to the insider's understanding. But the matter must be approached carefully, under the right conditions. A foreign student submitting to the same discipline (well, close to the same) as the Iranian students gained the privilege of making her own discoveries, making use of her special outsider role. This is quite different from the Western scholar who draws conclusions from distant observation.

And so, noting or discovering things that are meaningful to a society but not part of its ordinary musical thought can have the effect of mitigating political and intellectual objections to the ethnomusicologist's presence. He or she may determine such odd bits of information as the number of songs or pieces comprising the total repertory of a musician, or play records of strange musics, Western and other, in order to elicit commentary to approach the principles of an aesthetic. These are things of which Third World musicians might not think or, for that matter, Western musicians either—they are a bit strange—but in most cases they do not really violate the rules of music-making and social relationships.

The idea of joint research by an "insider" and an "outsider" has often been mentioned as a way of bridging chasms. In the strictest sense it has not often occurred; there are few articles and books with the names of Western and Indian, Japanese, or African scholars as co-authors. Fieldwork is in all respects a cooperative enterprise, and the major informants and teachers should properly be the co-authors of most studies. The inclusion of a scholar native to the nation whose musical culture is being investigated may be of great scholarly value, and as better communication develops between Western and Third World ethnomusicologists, one may expect to see more such publications. But to enlist the cooperation of an Indian, Nigerian, or Ecuadorian ethnomusicologist only for essentially political reasons seems of doubtful value. The villager may regard the scholar from the capital as much of an outsider as he does the American, and with the suspicion in which he holds bureaucrats of all sorts. There may be resentment at intrusions by an urban government-connected person whose intranational colonialism is every bit as distasteful to the villager as the international colonialism foisted upon him from the outside. Tension between urban and rural, government official and peasant, rich and poor, majority and minorities within Third World nations is a fact of everyday life. The inclusion of native scholars may provide needed musical and cultural expertise, and it may also please the academic community and the ministries in the capital, but such scholars are not necessarily "insiders."

If Third World scholars begin in large numbers to engage in ethnomusicological research, one may ask whether this will greatly change the intellectual stance of the field. Perhaps so. For example, there is a long-standing tradition of musical scholarship in India, and Indian scholars publish widely. While it is difficult to characterize, their work has a unique flavor and character. A book resulting from a conference on Asian music attended only by Asian scholars and musicians (Koizumi and others 1977:11) emphasizes the need of developing the concept of "ethnomethodology," derived from but not precisely parallel to the concept thus named by Garfinkel (1967), approaching research by going deeply into a society's own way of organizing its thinking and actions. The authors of this book, largely Japanese, are critical of ethnocentrism and perceive much research by Europeans and Americans to be thus flawed. But they are also keenly aware of ethnocentrism in an Asian context. "A close observation . . . will soon reveal a conspicuous attitude, i.e., comparing Japanese music with other Asian musics. One may call it 'Japan-centrism.' However, it is not meant so. Rather, it is meant that such a perspective is only one among many that deserve attempting. Other perspectives must be fully explored in the future by ethnomusicologists of various nationalities" (Koizumi 1977:viii).

A wise statement, for it does not simply replace Western objectivism or universalism (which is sometimes a mask for Western ethnocentrism) by the generalization that Asians are one and automatically "have it right," an attitude sometimes heard among other non-Westerners, or yet by a mindless anticomparativism. Rather, Koizumi espouses the concept that one can only study from one's own viewpoint, but that a comparison of viewpoints may give the broadest possible insight; in any case, comparative study is "the principal means by which the quest for knowledge is pursued" (Koizumi 1977:5). Armed with such wisdom, scholars of the future, among them many from what is now the Third World, can proceed with confidence. Anthropologists have also for long suggested the same thing but observed it, it seems, mainly in the breach (Hsu 1973). Firth speaks of the need for "expert anthropologists coming from a great range of countries . . . not only to study the problems of their communities but also to give that useful comparative analysis of each other's problems" (1944:22).

Ethnomusicologists are often compared to the historian of European music; the former are said to work outside their culture, but the latter, within it. But there is reason to ask whether there is ever a true "insider" in this kind of work. The American student of German music of 1830 is greatly removed from the culture that produced this music. By chance, music from 1830 is still performed, and thus its sound constitutes a part of the musical culture of 1980. But no doubt the modern student understands the music of Schumann and Mendelssohn quite differently from the way in which it was perceived in their day, and in a way contemporary students of Indian and Japanese music are at an advantage because they can at least observe at first hand and study with living teachers. If Schumann could speak to Americans of 1980, he might also say, "You will never understand this music," and yet our ability to understand it is taken almost for granted. It is hardly necessary to go further, to the Middle Ages and Renaissance, to make the point. Some historians believe that an "insider" cannot write history, that one needs the perspective of distance, of elapsed time. At one time ethnomusicologists took the analogue for granted as well, realizing that they provided a particular perspective. More recently, the division of roles has been muddied. But I believe that the best approach is to reconcile one's self to being an outsider, providing a limited if unique view. In the end, this is our proper role, whether it is as a European or American working in Turkey, a university-educated African or Indian working in a village, a woman from the countryside who has been trained to look at her culture in special ways not shared by her fellows, or an American trying to find rhyme and reason in the musical life of his own urban community.

Chapter 20

Hanging on for Dear Life

ARCHIVES OF THE WORLD, UNITE!

Of the many definitions of ethnomusicology, none explicitly or implicitly includes the concept of preservation as a major purpose or component of the field. Yet the preservation of music in various forms has all along been one of the major activities. The early history of our field is particularly characterized by this urge, but it continues with us in the present. For example, in 1963, at the sixteenth annual conference of the International Folk Music Council in Jerusalem, a major session was held on "preservation and renewal of folk and traditional music," and in 1978, at the World Congress on Jewish Music in the same city, the concept of preservation again surfaced prominently. As a matter of fact, many musicologists at all times have been motivated by the belief that the interesting music of the world is disappearing, and that one must hang on for dear life, recording and notating and storing against some kind of musical famine. It's a warning that has been promulgated for almost 150 years, and yet music is as interesting as ever!

Of course it is clear that one must collect and preserve materials in order to study them, and the role of the tape recorder as part of the ethnomusicologist's equipment should need no further justification. But collecting and preserving have sometimes become ends in themselves. In the nineteenth century particularly, but also later, many devoted themselves more or less exclusively to preservation. They made recordings, sometimes in enormous quantity, and proceeded to store them in archives, perhaps transcribing them into notation, eventually preserving them in print as well; but often they went no further. Scholars of Western folk music in particular built vast collections, and were followed by a few students of North American Indian music and to a smaller extent by those of African and Asian musics. In the period before 1950 a few major archives, storehouses of recorded collections, were founded, beginning with the Phonogrammarchiv in Berlin, started by Stumpf and Hornbostel in 1901 (see Reinhard 1961) preceded slightly by the less prominent Vienna effort (1899). Also among the most eminent were the German Folk Song Archives in Freiburg (founded in 1914, at first consisting only of manuscripts), the Archive of Folk Song in the Library of Congress (1928), and the Archives of Traditional Music at Indiana University (1948). Since 1950 many universities as well as libraries, state historical institutions, formally constituted tribal organizations, and other kinds of units have built their own archives of (or including) traditional music. Ethnomusicologists at universities wished in the first instance to house materials collected by themselves and their students, eventually in order to provide large collections for teaching, study, and research. National archives, including some in Third World nations established since the 1950s, attempt to make comprehensive collections of national heritage. Some archives are incredibly large; the number of songs and pieces at Indiana University amounts to hundreds of thousands. Even an extremely modest institution such as the Archive of Ethnomusicology at the University of Illinois includes some 300 collections comprising some 10,000 songs and pieces. A few archives, such as that at Indiana, attempt to be comprehensive, providing research materials for all. Some are simply working collections for local products and needs. Others again try to be comprehensive for a special area; the Phonotèque in the Jewish Music Research Center in Jerusalem collects what may by some criterion be considered Jewish music and materials of all types found in Israel.

One of the major problems of an archive is cataloguing, given the many different ways in which the world's cultures classify and identify their musical works, and the problem is exacerbated by the tendency of many recordists to provide insufficient information to place a recording in its proper cultural context. Library cataloguing systems provide imperfect models. Beyond this, the archives of the world have not found a way to cooperate fully in exchanging and combining information. It is extremely difficult to locate all field recordings made in one culture, however small and localized, or all archival versions of one song. An early attempt to list all collections in American archives was published by Herzog (1936b), but this surprisingly large account was made at a time when the making of recordings was difficult and rare, and after the introduction of magnetic tape, archives grew exponentially in size and number. In 1958 Indiana University began the publication of a small periodical whose job it was to exchange information, *The Folklore and Folk Music Archivist,* which continued until 1968. But the task is almost hopeless, as private collections continue also to grow and to play a considerable role. Brieg-leb (ca. 1970) lists and briefly describes 124 archives in the United States and Canada. One would wish to encourage them, if not to combine, at least to unite.

Most of these archives are of great use to individuals more or less permanently at their institutions. As a group, however, they may possibly not justify all the energy that has gone into putting them together. Many of the recordings they contain are restricted by the collectors and may thus be heard but not fully utilized for research. It may amaze the reader that few recordings (some in Eastern Europe are clearly exceptions) are fully used by anyone other than the collectors. While the archives continue to grow, most scholars in their research rely upon their own recordings.

THE OLDIES ARE THE GOODIES

Producing transcriptions and publishing them in large numbers in grand collections is another side of the preservation game, which actually preceded and eventually paralleled recording activity. There are hundreds of relevant publications, but as examples let me mention only the monuments of German folk music (Erk 1893–94, Deutsches Volksliedarchiv 1935–74); the many volumes of Hungarian and other Eastern European folk song produced as a result of the collecting activities of Béla Bartók and Zoltan Kodály (e.g. Corpus 1953–, Bartók 1959–); the collections of English folk songs found in the various states of the United States and in part stimulated in the 1930s by the Works Progress Administration (see e.g. Cox 1939; for discussion, Library of Congress 1942:2–3, Wilgus 1959:186–87, Canon 1963). The two forms of preservation differ fundamentally, for while the record archives might include materials recorded by amateurs who hardly knew what they were doing and by anthropologists whose interests were not specifically musical, the printed collections required musicianship for transcribing and making decisions on classification and order. The students of folk music were certainly interested in preserving a heritage they felt was slipping away, and this feeling of imminent loss was a powerful stimulus for more specifically ethnomusicological inquiry. The point is that these collectors often sought what was specifically old, partly because it was disappearing but partly, one feels, also because what was old was in a sense good. If today's disc jockeys defensively announce "oldies but goodies," many folk music collectors insisted that the oldies were *ipso facto* the goodies. Certain scholars who made truly enormous contributions with their insight into musical and cultural processes, like Bartók and Sharp, were intent upon extracting from modernizing and urbanizing villages and small towns that which was ancient. Some collectors even went out of their way to prove that what they collected was indeed old.

This attitude of preservation was to outlive the early history of our field. The publication of comprehensive collections of national folk music became characteristic of musical scholarship in Eastern Europe after 1950. In the study of non-Western music the idea of comprehensive collecting never became so important, with notable exceptions such as the hundreds of North American Indian songs published by Frances Densmore.

The earliest collectors of non-Western music in the nineteenth century, contrary to those of folk song, probably did not have long-term preservation in mind. They did not, I think, worry much about the fact that music changes rapidly and that much of what they were studying would soon be swallowed up by "pollution" from other cultures. They were aware of the effects of colonization, but I think they also believed that the music of non-Western cultures changes slowly if at all; they perceived, rather, a dichotomy between complete stability and absolute abandonment. The idea of holding fast to early materials was not so much a consideration as was the very discovery of what was then a new phenomenon.

The students of Western folk music, on the other hand, were no doubt affected by the movement in historical musicology to publish series of "monuments" of national music history. Beginning with the German *Denkmäler deutscher Tonkunst* (1892) and the more prestigious Austrian *Denkmäler der Tonkunst in Österreich* (1894), various national series were begun, and much of the energy of music historians in the first half of the twentieth century was directed to the publication, in authentic form, of hundreds of often obscure but "historically" important works. In the end, one would in a sense "have" the materials of art music of a given country. Surely the tendency to publish large folk music collections with attention to their authenticity and to the inclusion of good and perhaps especially old versions and variants was similarly motivated. Folk music scholars and folklorists were interested in the preservation of the most important stories, songs, melodies of the rural societies of Europe and eventually the Americas. I am not sure whether much thought was given to the eventual use of such collections. As in the case of the classical *Denkmäler,* performance was at least sometimes considered. It was assumed, one suspects, that large-scale, artifact-oriented, multipurpose collections would satisfy a number of future needs, historical, ethnographic, practical. It doesn't always seem to have worked out so.

While the collections grew, the scholars who after about 1960 were concerned with increasingly specialized problems in ethnomusicology tended to be less concerned with comprehensive collecting, and there seemed to develop something of a split between them and those we might label professional collectors. Having recognized that music in oral tradition is subject to constant change, that songs, styles, repertories are in a state of flux, we may wonder why so many individuals devoted themselves to collecting largely for the purpose of preserving what was in a sense a piece of ephemera.

Early in the twentieth century there developed an approach to preserving that one might label "applied" ethnomusicology. Practical publications to be used for teaching, the development of records for promulgating what could be of interest to the amateur, the idea of urging people in various communities to continue older practices of music and dance, finding government support for encouraging them and indeed in some ways improving their practice, all these seem to involve preservation in a different sense, holding materials for practical use by peoples thought to be in danger of losing their heritage. This kind of preservation is not a practice always resulting in unmitigated benefit. Much of it, especially in the 1930s, was to take on political and in some cases stridently nationalistic overtones. It also meant that the collector would intrude, trying to persuade people not to change their ways, insisting that it was incumbent on them to retain preindustrial practices. One senses resentment on the part of societies wanting social change and believing that it must be accompanied by musical change. As we have seen in our discussion of the roles of insider and outsider, the ethnomusicologist's lesson about the place of music in culture is one that simpler societies have learned very well. One thus finds interesting examples of conflict. Australian aborigines living in the countryside who did not wish their material to be preserved because the tape recorder would invalidate rituals were opposed by the aboriginals living in cities who felt that they had been deprived of their tribal heritage by their removal to a different setting, and wanted the recordings.

In the 1950s there developed a movement within the field of anthropology conveniently labeled "urgent anthropology," involving the recognition of the imminent destruction of societies, cultures, and artifacts by modernization. It emphasized the need for concentrating anthropological resources upon their preservation. In the case of archeology this might involve the exploration of areas shortly to become inaccessible by the building of dams or roads; in social anthropology it might be addressed to the forced movement of peoples and the dispersal of once homogeneous populations. For the historian such preservation was obviously of paramount importance. For the social anthropologist, who studies change as it occurs, it did not outweigh the study of kinds of change that was constantly occurring; extinction of cultures was, so to speak, an everyday event. So it turned out that the thrust of "urgent anthropology" was mainly the study of the out-of-the-way, with the purpose of gaining insight into human exceptions. Ethnomusicologists, coming out of a long tradition of looking for the exceptional while often virtually ignoring the readily available, would sympathize with this approach. Some, such as Wolfgang Laade (1969, 1971a), participated in the "urgent anthropology" movement in publications and letters noting cultures and musics in danger of extinction. But while we may be bemused by those who wish to exclude all but the exceptional, it is of course true that during the past few centuries many musical cultures have in effect gone out of existence. This fact is particularly relevant to scholars working in the Americas, areas of gradual social change, but even more in nations where culture change has been dramatic, such as Israel, for here obviously a once highly heterogeneous population appears to be on the way to thorough homogeneity. No doubt, then, much ethnomusicology has been motivated by a sense of urgency.

A SAMPLING OF THE INFINITE

We have already viewed the history of ethnomusicological field research as in a sense the history of sampling, and the implications of various attitudes as to what comprises a music. We should now remind ourselves that music is more than sound or artifact, and that sampling involves more than selective sound recording. The methodology of fieldwork of the last two or three decades has been trying to find ways of sampling both music and its cultural context. We have come to believe that more intensive work than results from the mere collecting of musical artifacts on tape can and must be achieved by sophisticated techniques of sampling. For purposes of preservation, we might approach from many directions. The event, the personal repertory, the individual, the variants of one song, the community in one week of its history, all are complementary samplings. The history of preserving, specifically, moves us from very small samples to the making of vast collections for the record alone, then on to practical collections for broadly educational use, then to the urgent, and finally to a realistic if resigned way of looking at a music as something so enormous in quantity that selective forays must be made.

The issue of preservation brings us again to that of transcription and notation. If we need an adequate notation for musical sound, we surely also lack a precise and comparative method for "notating," as it were, or preserving, the cultural context, concepts, and behavior. Despite the development of film and video-tape technique, we do not have techniques that parallel recording machinery. To ask an informant what she thinks of a song, where she learned it, what role it plays in the life of her society (which is what we do as a minimum) is conventional but hardly enough, and yet, beyond ordinary verbal description or film, there simply are no established techniques for specifically preserving these other important sides of the musical universe.

The amount of music in the world is infinite. Its preservation seems to continue to be taken as a fundamental responsibility by the ethnomusicologist. But we need to know what is it that we wish to preserve, and how we should go about it in the future, to build something meaningful rather than, thanks to advanced technology, merely accumulating mass. Let me ask a few more specific questions and suggest possibilities.

What is worthy of preservation? We may wish to preserve what is of high quality, or what is typical, or what a culture considers ideal. The point is that we must make clear our values, decide what we are seeking. The fieldworker needs to grapple with some fundamental issues of ethnomusicological method before simply turning on the tape recorder. There is the question of authenticity, the problem of what is in some way representative of a culture. The point is that before going to work one must face the theoretical issues of sampling, plan one's collecting activities, understand what one is doing. This would be greatly preferable to recording everything within earshot and ending up with a collection with which one can do very little. We should design research carefully and then go after the material we need to carry it out, rather than preserving first and studying later.

Preservation and research may conflict. We may impose special field methods on the society we are studying, methods that will provide us with insights. But we must understand that this imposition may somehow distort what is really going on. Let me refer to a personal experience, my project in Iran in which I tried to study principles of improvisation. I tried to use a single mode, a *dastgāh,* as a sample, and to record as many improvisations in that mode as I could, and I believe I was reasonably successful. However, I am sure I did not arrive at something that is truly representative. All of the performances I recorded, I feel, would be acceptable to the Iranian listener and to the informed Iranian musician. Individually, they are part and parcel of the musical culture. However, since I was there with my tape recorder, requesting and commissioning performances and available for formal events, I no doubt failed to record certain kinds of musical phenomena that would appear only in other, less structured and less formal situations. What I recorded was a group of performances individually part of the culture, but perhaps not a sample representative of the culture in the sense of distribution over its entire universe. I may have found out important things about the way certain things are done in Iranian performance practice, but probably I did not adequately preserve a slice of Iranian musical culture. This kind of conclusion might have to be made in many studies, but particularly in those dealing with improvisation of folk music, where variation from a norm is a major point of observation. In our zeal to preserve, we should be careful to preserve what actually happens in society, or if we can't, at least be aware of the ways in which our work distorts it. If we view ethnomusicology as a science of music history, emphasizing processes and change but insisting on a generalizing and nomothetic approach, preservation pure and simple plays a minor role. But the gathering of data in systematic and controlled forms is important to scholars who need to deal with it in an essentially scientific way. The result of such gathering is in the end also a form of preservation for the future.

At the other end of the spectrum, shall we continue encouraging people to keep up their old practices, asking them to do what they perhaps would not wish to do, just for the sake of the rest of the world? I have no answer. But there is no doubt that ethnomusicologists, simply by their interest in certain kinds of musical phenomena, have stimulated the societies they study to keep up, develop, sometimes isolate and preserve these phenomena in culturally proper or artificial fashion. The role of collectors, with their technology and prestige, has been enormous. Ethnomusicologists must be clear about the part they wish to play. One alternative is for them to study what actually happens, swallowing hard when they find that societies change all the time and allowing precious gems of creation to fall by the wayside. This is necessary in order to provide people freedom to do as they wish (something of an article of faith with me) or are forced by circumstances to do, and then observing what actually happens, because this makes better scholarship than mixing observation with the imposition of one's ideas. Or they may instead take as a basic assumption the idea that preservation on our part and on the part of the cultures of the world is itself a supreme good and must be encouraged at the expense of other factors. An unresolved question for the individual as well as the profession.

Ethnomusicologists in recent years have concentrated on the study of change and need to record and preserve it. How one goes about preserving the record of change, a basic phenomenon of culture but not compatible with our concept of it as a group of "things," is something beyond present-day practicality. But I would suggest that one theoretical direction in which we could move is to add to the musical artifact, the piece, song, individual situation as the focus of study, ways in which the fact and process of change itself can somehow be used as the main focus of attention. There is reason to believe that of the various components of musical culture, using Merriam's model, the musical sound itself changes least rapidly; behavior changes more, and the conception of music most, quickly. The sound of Blackfoot music is much closer to what it was in the nineteenth century than are Blackfoot ideas about music today. If we are indeed to preserve something about music, we must find ways of preserving and recording the concept part of the model; this seems to me to be in fact more urgent ethnomusicology than the continuing preservation of the musical artifact alone. If I am justified in being generally critical of the role of preservation in the ethnomusicology of the past, it is because it has often failed to recognize that there is much more to music than the piece. As the archives of the world continue to grow, those practicing preservation will increasingly need to expand their approaches to the systematic sampling of the infinite musical universe.

Chapter 21

I Am the Greatest

THE LIVES OF THE HEROES

There is a curious disparity. While ethnomusicologists experience a great deal of face-to-face contact with individual informants or teachers in the field and specialize in concentration on a particular person, the literature of the field provides surprisingly little information about the individual in music. Historians of Western music seem (at least on the surface) to be occupied principally with the work of individual composers, their roles and contributions as persons, while ethnomusicologists tend, with a few notable exceptions, to be drawn to the anonymous. Given the kinds of data available, one expects to find such tendencies, but not such an outright split. For a possible explanation, we note that the intrinsic value of non-Western music and folk music has, despite recent thrusts to the contrary, always been questioned, and the attention given to them defended with arguments to the effect that they are, if not great music, at least the music with which large groups of people identify themselves and for that reason worthy of study. The role of the individual in the group is thus easily overlooked. Moreover, the widespread belief that rural communities and tribal groups, and even large nonliterate populations such as the kingdoms of traditional Africa, are homogeneous in their musical and other experience has contributed to this oversight, as has the long-held assumption that music in non-Western and folk cultures is stable and unchanging until polluted by the West.

To reconcile this interest of ethnomusicology in the music of large population groups with the recognition of the fact that proper insight into such groups must include an understanding of the individual, one would expect ethnomusicologists to focus in some of their research on representative musicians, some perhaps outstanding, others more likely average or acceptable, and, further, on the ordinary member of society who participates in musical life but cannot by whatever the criteria the culture uses be called truly a musician. In a humanistic field this may be an odd purpose. We don't wish to explore the mediocre for the mere purpose of giving mediocrity its just representation, though indeed enshrinement in an article in *Ethnomusicology* is hardly an exorbitant reward even for mediocrity. But besides the excellent, the outstanding, who represents the musical ideal in composition or performance, we need understanding of the ordinary but musically acceptable person: the composer who barely makes it in a minor United States campus music department and gets performed occasionally, the kamancheh player who scrounges out a modest living playing at weddings in northern Iran, the person who buys a few records and can't do housework or study without the radio, the lowly player of a kidi drum in a Ghanian drum ensemble led by a master drummer, the seventh-desk orchestra violist, and the member of a third-string singing group at an Indian powwow. It is such people who comprise the real mainstream of musical life in the world, make music a cultural and human universal, constitute the acceptable everyday experience of a culture. But of course we also want to know whether a society distinguishes sharply, gradually, or perhaps not at all between the great and the typical. In order to explore the study of the individual in ethnomusicological fieldwork, we want to look at three selected approaches: biography, personal repertory, and personal performance practice.

The tradition of scholarly biography exists in the literature of non-Western music, but it is not deep. The classical traditions of Asia have produced accounts of the lives of their "great" men who play heroic roles, usually of the past. Indian musical scholarship has accumulated much information about the lives of some of the great composers of the eighteenth and nineteenth centuries, as illustrated best, perhaps, by the large amount of literature about and veneration for Tyagaraja, a holy man who composed hundreds of songs still known and who is honored annually near Tanjore. Much of this kind of information comes from oral tradition, but the typical treatment of Tyagaraja by Indian scholars does not differ greatly from the normal European treatment of a great composer of the sixteenth century. Ethnomusicologists have not often ventured into this kind of scholarly biography, nor have they made much use of what exists for their broader purposes.

By contrast, the use of biography—essentially autobiography, gathered through interviews that must be corroborated and edited—is a major thrust in anthropological field method. The practice goes back to the linguistically oriented text gathering of the late nineteenth century, as verbal material could be conveniently accumulated by asking an informant to tell the story of his life. A thorough biography of an individual who constitutes a sample of a society should provide some information about the role of music in the subject's life. Here and there this actually happens, as in Radin's *Autobiography of a Winnebago Indian* (1963:52–57), first published in 1920, which tells a good deal about the subject's learning of Peyote songs and the interaction of singing with other aspects of the Peyote experience. Studies of individual composers and singers in the realm of folk music are more common, and written with the kinds of perspective also used by historians of classical music (see e.g. Ives 1964, Glassie and others 1970).

Presumably a thorough biography collected and edited by an anthropologist could give one the necessary musical information, within the context of all other aspects of life, to produce a picture of music in the life of an individual. The ethnomusicologist needs to get into the act only because he would wish to deal with those who are particularly active in musical life, or to stress the musical facts in an ordinary person's life, making them the focus. There are, of course, many ways in which individuals can be sketched so as to shed light on their culture; biography is only one.

CAREERS

The range of a composer's stylistic framework in any culture is in part idiosyncratic, but it is also determined by culture patterns, the system of patronage, performance practice, the general attitude toward such concepts as art, innovation, the musician as creator or craftsman, and the state of musical and distributional technology. To ethnomusicology, the range of musical phenomena produced and experienced by one person is of great interest. In certain respects this avenue would parallel one of the main approaches of historical musicology, whose literature is full of studies of the total opus of a composer, stressing what within it is typical, giving its distribution over a lifetime and the boundaries of creativity. The interest to ethnomusicology derives from the fact that the concentration on the study of specific composers provides the opportunity of identifying types and their range in any one culture. For Western music there have been few attempts to classify composers by personality type as expressed in music. Becking's (1928) rhythmic typology, whose exemplars are Mozart, Beethoven, and Bach, a typology supposedly valid for all European music and based largely on very general aspects of rhythmic character, is suggestive. It is tempting to look at typical careers of European composers with the kind of perspective one would wish to use in a comprehensive description of a foreign musical culture. Considering the vast amount of literature in the annals of musicology dealing with individual composers, it seems ridiculous to try to generalize about them. But even an unserious attempt may be instructive. The overarching, sweeping generalizations that we often make about non-Western musics seem incredibly naive when translated into the European context. Although (or perhaps because) there are data, historians avoid the broad view but remain almost inevitably particularistic when concerned with the classical music of Europe. Let me take an ethnomusicologist's bird's-eye view of aspects of Western art music.

Back in the realm of the issue of measuring degrees of similarity, we must take a deep breath. Using diversity of style as a parameter, we might find that Joseph Haydn, Ludwig von Beethoven, and Richard Wagner changed considerably in the course of their careers. Their approximate contemporaries, Mozart, Schubert, and Brahms did so to a lesser degree; perhaps in the case of Schubert and Mozart, this is related to their shorter lifespan. The diversity of work in the opus of these composers seems to exceed substantially that of some others who are thus regarded as lesser artists. Looking back to the early eighteenth century, we would probably regard G. P. Telemann and Antonio Vivaldi as composers with less stylistic spread. But the difference between a Vivaldi and a Beethoven is in part due to differences in such things as patronage and audience expectation. Novelty became more of an issue in the nineteenth century, and indeed has continued to increase in importance until we find composers like Igor Stravinsky and George Rochberg in the course of their careers trying out a number of styles and approaches. This kind of information could lead us to several hypotheses: that European composers, seen as individuals, differ in the stylistic density of their output; that following social change, density decreased from Vivaldi to Rochberg; and that in one period, that of ca. 1775–1890, individuals varied in part in accordance with length of career.

A quick glance at two related kinds of examination: some composers had careers that lend themselves to division into stylistic periods. Beethoven's early, middle, and late works are readily distinguished, but the same is not true of Mozart, who did not effect such relatively sudden breaks. But in both cases changes in musical style are present, and indeed they are expected in the work of European composers, so-called early works being judged in different terms from the mature ones. Obviously, you will say; but it must be noted, for such behavior might not be tolerated in another society. Furthermore, there is a tendency on the part of many Western composers to go back, near the endings of their careers, to musical principles of the past, related perhaps to their early years of study or to predecessors with whom they wish somehow to identify themselves. Thus Brahms's Fourth Symphony contains a passacaglia, a form widespread in the seventeenth and eighteenth centuries, not in imitation of this early period but as a way of reconciling his own approach to music with the past; both Beethoven and Mozart in their later years moved to a more contrapuntal style in certain ways reminiscent of the Baroque period.

One could similarly study performers of the twentieth century, examining a range of recordings of one work or charting the range of works recorded, decade by decade. I don't know whether the reader versed in music history can forgive such a quick glance at Western composers in the style of ethnomusicology, but it may be rewarding in various ways. If one were to look at the literature of music history from the perspective of an anthropologist, trying to see how Western musicians and their audience view the Western composer of the past as individual, one could draw some conclusions about the way composers are seen by their society. Europeans and Americans expect their composers to change musical style; they regard certain works of one composer as clearly superior; they express satisfaction at innovation (the more, the better) but also at the tendency to exhibit earlier influences near the end of life. They perceive that the output is divided into periods, tend to find that abrupt changes in style coincide with changes in residence or position, underscoring the view that the musician composes in part under the influence of particular social and political surroundings. They expect musicians to exhibit the lessons they learn from their teachers but also to depart from these. The expectation of change, of development, and a tension between unidirectional progression and circularity are evident. And so is the expectation that a composer may move from emotional to intellectual focus. Whether this is truly descriptive of the culture or not, it is the way many Western musicians and music lovers seem to see the role of the composer in their own classical system.

There is not the same profusion of biographical data and interpretation for non-Western cultures, but ethnomusicological literature provides some material on the basis of which one can tentatively generalize. In any one culture and in at least certain groups of non-Western cultures that share values, ecology, technology, there are certain typical patterns of biography and perception. The individual is the agent and recipient of change. As already pointed out, Richard Waterman (1956) found music to be used by the people of Yirkalla as a way in which to learn their own culture. The repertory of sacred music was learned gradually, and certain pieces were learned only by elderly men, and thus, assuming a cumulative effect, they were also those who knew the most. Here we are dealing, presumably, not with a population of composers as Western culture would understand the term but of performers and consumers. For a similar example we can look at change in the life of the individual man of Blackfoot culture. He moved through a series of age-grade societies whose activities included ceremonies and music (Ewers 1958:104–5, Lowie 1916). As an individual grew older, he was successively initiated into new societies, learning their songs and dances. Again the oldest men would know the largest amount of music, learned gradually, more or less at four-year intervals. The vision quest of the Plains Indians and of tribes surrounding the Plains exhibited a similarly gradual learning of songs. A so-called "medicine man" would have a succession of visions of his guardian spirit, each time learning more in the way of dealing with the supernatural, which included songs.

This is the traditional picture. For recent times, the tendency to gradual learning of new material is a pattern whose existence is both supported and altered in the career of one Blackfoot singer with whom I worked. Born about 1915, this man was first exposed to Western music through his reservation school, learning French horn, but also—sometimes secretly—he learned a few traditional songs as well. As a young adult he took up the modern, intertribal, "pan-Indian" repertory, which consisted largely of social dance songs without words. In later life he gradually became interested as well in the ancient traditional music, learning it from older men who knew but rarely performed the songs. This sequence has idiosyncratic causes; the third stage coincided with the death of the singer's stepfather, an esteemed tribal leader. But the pattern may also be typical, at least insofar as the most sacred music had long been the province of older men. In this respect my informant, although he was exposed to musics not known in earlier times such as the Pan-Indian songs and the music of the whites, seems to have followed a traditional pattern. But in the sense that he withdrew from interest in one musical repertory as he learned a new one, he probably did not reflect the gradual and cumulative learning of a cohesive musical system. In any event, the concept of pattern in musical life can be found among the ordinary singers of a small tribe as well as the master composers of Western music.

INSIGHTS IN MESHHAD

The biographical approach gives us a special kind of understanding of change in the life of a person. As a field technique for oral history, it is probably superior to asking informants in general how things "used to be," which can provide interesting but in most respects unstructured observation. Musicians may be much better at providing views of their own lives, and while they may indeed wish to cast themselves in a special kind of light, they at least have more factual data available about themselves in memory than they have about the culture of their people as it may have changed over a series of decades. But beyond this, the study of individuals also tells us how they see themselves in their own culture, which may give additional insights into the structure of musical life.

I was visiting Stephen Blum, who was doing fieldwork in Meshhad, Iran, a large religious center that was musically not regarded highly. Through a musicians' agent we chanced to meet and make recordings with a player of the tar, a type of lute widely used in Persian classical, folk, and popular music. Before playing he said, "I am the best tar player." We must have looked incredulous, because we had lived in Iran long enough to know names, to attend formal concerts, take lessons with musicians supported by the government because of their excellence, hear records and radio. "I am the greatest," he reiterated, reminding us of a great American. Then, softening his line a bit, he said, "I and Shahnazi," citing the name of a truly renowned tar player in Teheran. I remembered one of my American teacher's warnings—"Don't argue with your informants"—and thus we proceeded to elicited performance. Disappointing: the man was clearly not an expert; indeed, one would have to assume that he would hardly make a living in Teheran, was perhaps not even in great demand in Meshhad. Even so, other Iranians present at our session did not laugh or contradict him. Clearly he was a long way, to put it mildly, from being a great tar player; he had little technique and seemed to know little repertory.

This experience was the most extreme among a number in Iran in which there seemed to be a need for musicians to describe themselves as experts, as "the best," in contrast to their deferential manner and ceremonial politeness. Without going into further detail, let me move to a possible interpretation. In Islamic Shi'ite societies musicians have not been highly respected, and instrumental music in particular is undesirable, associated with sloth, indebtedness, adultery, prostitution, debauchery. It seems that the only way in which a musician could hold his head up in society was to be a star. In Iranian society it is usually rather easy to persuade individuals who love music to rank musicians, especially on a particular instrument; they readily single out the star, immediately associating an instrument with its best performer: "You want to hear setār? The setār of Ebādi, of course. Or the nai? You mean, certainly, the nai of Kasāi." Thus it seems important for a musician to label himself as a star in order to maintain self-respect. Our moderately competent tar player in Meshhad was not, I believe, trying to fool us. By describing himself as the greatest tar player, he was merely telling us that he was worthy of our attention. The individual Persian musician and his view of himself indicates that in this culture, to maintain this individuality, the musician must think of himself as the best in his field. He does not associate himself readily with a group such as tar players in general. In all of this his behavior reflects important aspects of both the social and the musical systems.

Now, this information did not come from detailed biographical study. But if we had not paid attention to the individual, taken an analytical view of his statements, but had simply assumed that he was lying, or a fool, or making outrageous claims, this interpretation would hardly have come to us. In some respects our tar player acted like a typical Iranian; in some others he exhibited the special character of his role as a musician (see also Sakata 1976). The idea of the musician as a deviant in society, as one who is scorned for abnormal behavior and yet considered indispensable, is analyzed by Merriam (1964:135–37, 1979), with particular attention to the Basongye of Zaire: ". . . being a musician is the only way a male [Basongye] can escape the dominant male role with its heavy load of 'normalcy' and still be tolerated as a useful member of society" (1979:22; see also my Chapter 26).

THE LIFE OF NOUR-ALI KHĀN

The life of my principal teacher in Iran, whom I have frequently mentioned in these pages and whom I greatly revere, illustrates further the interface between musical personality and culture. He was Dr. Nour-Ali

Boroumand, called Nour-Ali Khān by his friends, and he was highly regarded by many Iranians and foreigners engaged in the study of Persian music. There were also others who maintained a more critical view. To what extent was he unusual, in what ways did he reflect ideals of Persian musicianship, and what did he have that was ordinary? His musical biography falls rather conveniently into a number of stages: (1) in childhood, first exposure to classical Persian music and some study of the *radif;* (2) secondary school and medical studies in Germany, and the learning of Western classical music; (3) the onset of blindness, return to Iran, and continuation of study of the *radifs* of several teachers; (4) consolidation of the learned *radifs* into his own version; (5) teaching of his *radif* to a few selected private students; (6) the making available of his *radif* to a wide audience of students at two institutions, and to the general public. In some respects the history is idiosyncratic. Study in Europe and acquaintance with Western music, the teaching of the *radif* only late in life, are not part of the tradition. The fact that he rarely performed in public reflects the Iranian distrust of music and the resulting idealization of the authoritative great amateur, seldom realized in recent decades at any rate. His social and musical conservatism may account for the fact that his contact with Western music does not appear to have influenced his view of Persian music, at least in the direction of Western music, but on the contrary reinforced the view that each culture has and must retain its own music. Studying several *radifs,* by several teachers, in stages from simple to complex, and developing from this his personal *radif,* all this appears to be at least to some degree part of an established tradition. It was the ideal of music study, not possible for many but held to be the best way of establishing oneself squarely in the tradition and at the same time as an individual. Boroumand always maintained that he was the most authoritative Persian musician, not as a performer but as the one who knew the authentic material best.

From Boroumand's musical biography one can receive insights into various aspects of Persian musical culture. Some of these emerge only from such biographical study, others simply underscore what one can observe to be in practice. His emphatic and defensive view of himself as an authority underscores tensions between two extremes in Iranian views of classical Persian music, between respect for authority and desire for change. Those musicians interested in authoritative preservation of the tradition tended to agree that he knew it better than anyone else; those wishing for change and modernization scorned his insistence that the old material must be kept pure and memorized by ear rather than learned from notation, and described him as a man who had done nothing more than memorize a lot of old music and in whom there was no creativeness. No one considered him run-of-the-mill; to some he was the greatest, to others scarcely worthy of attention, reflecting the way in which musicians in general are seen by traditional Iranian society. Boroumand's secretiveness about his knowledge, and his gradual willingness to share, parallel patterns in Iranian culture. The fact that he himself viewed his musical life as consisting of well-defined periods underscores the knowledge that we have of the Iranian intellectual's desire to organize life in relatively discrete units. Modernization and Westernization, processes well known in study in Iran, can be seen as they affect the individual in the course of his life.

Biographical information has also been of interest to students of the music of India who wish to see the role of the musician within the context of his gharana, or school of musicianship. Brian Silver, for example, examines the lives of six musicians of one North Indian gharana, concentrating on their achieving the role of an ustad, or master musician, "through the perfection of required musical skills, the assimilation of certain cultural attributes, and the assumption of various postures characteristic of the ustad as a social type" (1976:29). From this study it is clear that political changes in India during the twentieth century have affected the way in which one becomes an ustad. Of three brothers, the older two fulfilled some of the traditional requirements, while the youngest, who grew up during the transitional stage of Indian independence, had to develop his role in other ways, influenced by the growing modernization of the musical system. Here, as in the case of Boroumand and my Blackfoot informant, Westernization and modernization have played parts in the lives of twentieth-century non-Western musicians, and the role of these processes in musical change becomes clearer through examination of the life story of the individual.

SING ME ALL THE SONGS YOU KNOW

Beyond biography and autobiography, there is also great interest in the study of the total musical activity of one person. It's surprising that this has not frequently been the focus of research, for, after all, many studies in ethnomusicology are essentially based upon the performances and statement of individuals speaking alone for their culture. But while enormous effort has been expended to discover all the musical activities of a Bach or a Mahler, we hardly know what may be the total musical experience, creative and passive, of the person in the street. Do you, dear reader, know very much about your own musical knowledge, how many songs you can sing or have learned, how much music you have heard to the degree of knowing it, recognizing it? Ethnomusicologists should undertake to find out, especially in what we may call the "passive" repertory of music known and recognized. Attempts at ascertaining the total active repertory of individuals have been made, such as Schiørring's (1956) collection of the total repertory of a singer, Selma Nielsen. No doubt many collecting projects in fact though not explicitly produced such data. Let me mention one personal experience.

"Sing me all the songs you know," I asked one Blackfoot singer. The question was an unexpected one for him, but he agreed to try. His reaction was to sing, first, some twenty songs, one after the other, in no special order. He labeled each by function or use, and often indicated whether he liked the song, where he had learned it, and whether it was a song particularly loved by "the Blackfoot people," as he put it. I don't know what it was that led him from one song to another, but the order was not systematic, not determined by uses, associated ceremonies, or dances. After these twenty he had to pause, and to think of new ones gradually; after groping for some time, he asked to be excused in order to think, and to continue the next day. Indeed, the next occasion yielded a shorter string of songs quickly produced, followed again by a period of groping for new material. Some repetitions occurred and were acknowledged. After some five days of this I had recorded about sixty songs, and he decided that he had sung just about all he knew at that time. But he admitted having forgotten songs known earlier in life, and expected to learn new ones from time to time.

Now, I wished to ask whether other members of the Blackfoot tribe have repertories of this size, similarly recalled. I have no direct information, but much earlier, and without the same purpose, had made a similar though less direct attempt to collect all known songs from an Arapaho singer, a man regarded as highly knowledgeable in his tribe but not an acknowledged musical specialist. While this singer had musical knowledge of a completely different scope, concentrating substantially on Peyote songs, the total number was in the same vicinity of sixty. Curiously, this number also coincides with the repertory of Ishi, the last Yahi, who also presumably sang all the songs he remembered for A. L. Kroeber and T. T. Waterman (Nettl 1965), and with the repertories of Shoshoni women as described by Judith Vander (personal communication). It is barely conceivable that this magic number of sixty is somewhere near a norm for the total musical knowledge, at one time, of Plains and perhaps other Indian cultures. If so, this is not readily reconciled with the theory, presented earlier, that musical knowledge is cumulative. Considering that all informants seemed to be in their fifties, we might possibly by happenstance have stumbled upon a typical repertory size for a person of a given age, an intertribal Indian norm.

This is, of course, too speculative even for the most daring of hypothetically oriented ethnomusicologists. The point is that we may get valuable insights into a musical culture by studying the size, scope, and range of an individual's knowledge of music. While from our first, biographical, approach we know a vast amount about certain kinds of Western musicians and have little that is comparable for their non-Western counterparts, the study of musical knowledge, with quantitative orientation, is possibly further along for North American Indian societies than for the average person in Europe and North America.

The kinds of things we might wish to know about the individual's participation in his musical culture are unlimited; asking one to "sing all the songs you know" is a bare beginning. Let me move to yet a third approach in the ethnomusicology of the person, the study of the performance practice of one individual, as compared explicitly and by implication to others in a society or in an intercultural context. Two kinds of studies that have been carried out come to mind. In the one, we would seek to establish the personal practice over the lifetime of one musician. For the second, the purpose is to investigate the range of the characteristics of a personal performance style at one point in a performer's life, or perhaps in a short period such as a few months. For neither approach are there many examples, but musicology of all types would be well served by both.

THE SCOTTISH LADY

Materials for the diachronic kind of study can emerge from biographical repertory studies. Thus the songs of Selma Nielson as edited by Schiørring would indicate something of the person and performance practice of this nineteenth-century singer. The attempts to provide total personal repertories of performers on the Norwegian Hardanger fiddle made by a group of Norwegian scholars (Gurvin 1958–67) gives the basic subject matter, along with some comments, of several personal styles. The musical personality can also conveniently be studied within a microcosm, the ways in which one person performs one song or piece over a long period. James Porter (1976) put together a number of versions of the "Edward" ballad (Child 13) as sung by one Scottish singer, Jeannie Robertson. His conclusions (and they are actually incidental to other aims pursued by this study) show that the singer, over a period of time, changed unidirectionally as influenced by growing fame and personal musical modernization.

Porter identifies three stages in the recorded history of Miss Robertson's singing of "Edward," one representative of her singing before she became widely known and consisting of recordings made when she was forty-four to forty-seven years old; a second, "transitional" stage; and a third, representing a period of singing for large audiences, records, and television. Porter characterizes the stages as "memorial and presentational," "interactional and projective," and "projective and stylized." Whether or not these terms indicate substantive changes in the singer's attitude, Porter notes gradual lengthening of the song, the development of a stable form, and increasing ornamentation. We may speculate about the relationship between increasingly "folk-like" or "exotic" singing style and increasing exposure to urban audiences in the light of theories about the emergence of mannerism as a result of modernization (Katz 1970) and the effect of audience expectation upon a performer from a foreign cultural context. An obviously fertile area for studies of this kind is jazz, and a number of studies (e.g. Owens 1974, Stewart 1973) have made this approach one of the important thrusts in jazz research. Like musical society, the individual is typically influenced by changes in culture, but as we have noted, musical change should not be seen only as change in a piece from one person to another, from teacher to student, in oral transmission, but also in the way an individual transmits, as it were, one piece to him- or herself from performance to performance. While musicians change their ways of performing a piece, they also remain true to themselves. Studies of improvisation in Indian, Middle Eastern, and jazz musics exhibit a wide spread of performances in the repertory of an individual, but distinctly personal styles are developed, and members of a society, like informed analysts from other cultures, can readily learn to recognize a particular musician in a few seconds, just as an aficionado of Western classical music can spot the Mozart or the Schubert fingerprint in a moment of hearing an unknown piece.

Finding the range of performance practice in the work of a single musician at one time in his or her life requires special field techniques. One needs many performances from one person, and this almost inevitably requires elicitation, recording under special or unusual conditions, which may or may not give a true picture. The microcosmic approach—using one piece, or one model for improvisation, as a sample—requires repeated performances of one piece by a musician who may not be at all accustomed to such repetition, as illustrated by the study of Jihad Racy's performances of Nahawand (Nettl and Riddle 1974). The degree to which improvising musicians adhere to patterns may exceed their own knowledge; seeing the result of our analysis, Racy expressed surprise at his predictability. Similar conclusions are found in Albert Lord's (1965) study of improvising procedures among the singers of Yugoslav epics.

Obviously the degree to which an improvisor may depart from a model or a typical formal procedure will vary by culture. In Persian music, to be an acceptable musician, one must toe a line between utter predictability and departure so great that one will be accused of not knowing the model; such a statement is merely a definition of the concept of performance. A musician recognized as great may depart more than another. The difference among allowable variation, substantive change, and unacceptable deviation exists in all cultures, but in some, such as Iran, these are in part defined by the person and the past record of the musician. For our friend in Meshhad to refer to himself as the greatest tar player meant in part that he was claiming a high degree of freedom in improvisation. His performances may not have been stupendous, but we learned more from him than he may have suspected.

Chapter 22

What Do You Think You're Doing?

WHO OWNS THIS MUSIC?

I had given a talk about some field experience at a neighboring university, and afterward we gathered in the back of the room for some coffee and discussion. The American students were deferential, but a young man with the characteristic accent of a West Indian scowled silently for a while, then chimed in: "What do you think you're doing? How do you get away with studying other people's music?" A strange question in a place where everyone was into somebody else's culture. I tried to explain, but he wasn't buying. Since about 1960 such questions have been arising more and more frequently, and in the most recent years ethnomusicologists have had to address their many implications. They have even compartmentalized the aspect of their work that concerns such matters, the ownership of and the right to music and information about it, conveniently if not always with precision labeling it "ethics." The intellectual differences between the insider's and the outsider's understanding, discussed in Chapter 19, are closely related to broader human issues with which the ethnomusicologist must also be concerned.

If scholars have recently decided that music is not a universal language, that there are musics and at least vague boundaries among them, this has all along been obvious to the people who constitute the "field." People everywhere readily speak of "our" music and "theirs," associating themselves with particular musics and caring what outsiders do with them. An ethnomusicologist is not always readily tolerated in the field. "Hey, boy, what you doing around here anyway," was the rhetorical question scornfully asked by the Blackfoot man passing me in the alley. He knew perfectly well and made it clear that he didn't like it, or me, and didn't want to hear explanations. Elsewhere fieldworkers are viewed with more specific suspicion—spies, exploiters, purveyors of invidious comparisons. Or they may be tolerated as necessary evils, aiding in the maintenance of cultural integrity.

The relationship between fieldworker and informant, touched on in Chapters 18 and 19, has larger ramifications, extending to the relationship of one profession, ethnomusicology, to another, musicianship; and of the industrialized first (and second) world to the developing third; of rich to poor; of nation to tribe. It encompasses questions of attitude and of practicality, the respect of scholar for teacher, the etiquette of payment. It includes the degree to which judgments about the greater if unperceived good of a society in which he is a stranger are the privilege of a scholar, and involves the juxtaposition of generally valid and culturally restricted values.

The fundamental question is who owns the music, and what may someone who does not own it do with it. The oral tradition of ethnomusicology has its repertory of horror stories: musicians furious because they were recorded without their knowledge or consent, upset because performances given for study suddenly appear on commercial records, angry at a compatriot who divulged secrets. Asian scholars worried about their inability to get their hands on recordings made in their own tribes but now secluded in European archives; Australian aboriginals disturbed because no one bothered to record their music while it was still widely known; African professors annoyed because they must work with poor equipment while their American colleagues come in with the best and the latest. And so on and on, all the direct or indirect result of the economic and political exploitation of most of the world's peoples by Europeans and North Americans, and of the divergent views that the world's peoples have about the nature and ownership of music, its function and its power.

The annals of ethnomusicology include curiously little about this broadly important and relevant topic. Formal and informal discussion is frequently held at meetings, particularly since 1970 in the United States, when the international relationships implied here were transferred to intranational venues. The Society for Ethnomusicology (1974, 1975, 1977) has a standing committee on "ethics," and the International Folk Music Council has dealt formally with the question in its policy-making organs. But besides the horror stories, there is little conceptualization of the problem or agreement on specific guidelines for the emerging scholar. I should like to look at the problem from three perspectives: the relationship of fieldworker with individual teacher or informant, the attitude of the scholars vis-à-vis the communities in which they work, and the relationship among modern nation-states.

DON'T TELL HIM, IT'S OUR SECRET

In the earlier history of ethnomusicology most publications seemed to strive to give the impression of a homogeneous culture. We are often not told who sang a transcribed song, with the implication that any member of a tribe or village would have sung or said the same. There are notable exceptions: Stumpf, in his landmark study of the Bellacoola (1886), prominently mentions and describes the sessions with his singer, Nuksilusta. Densmore, in her many publications, consistently gives the names of singers below her transcriptions, quoting individual informants at length. But most frequently it was not so. Anthropological literature is parallel, and despite a few notable exceptions of a biographical nature, the identity of informants and their particular standing in their communities are usually left unstated. Setting forth the informant was something underscored as exceptional: "Let it be admitted, too, that the successful outcome of field research depends not only on the anthropologist's own skills, but also on the capabilities and interest of those who teach him their ways," says Casagrande (1960:x) in a book published to counter this cult of impersonality. Incidentally, however, perhaps as a result of their concentration on work essentially within their own culture, folklorists have much longer had a tradition of dealing with informants as people in their publications, and many books and articles from their pens focus on the individual.

It may seem monstrous that members of other societies should be treated impersonally, almost as if they were specimens of flora and fauna. Yet, if ethnomusicologists at one time approached their task thus, it was not with evil intention. Inevitably they made friends with singers and players, became attached, helped them as they could, paid them, but rather than feeling guilty about the inadequacy of these small gestures in the direction of equal treatment for all humans, they tended instead to worry because they were getting involved with trees and ignoring the forest. In the years since 1960 informants and some of their political representatives have fought back, and guilt has been shifted to the callous attitude of the industrial nations and the wealthy classes. Even so, I believe that most ethnomusicologists did not simply ignore the human factor. In the interest of properly scientific inquiry in a field dealing specifically with the music of *groups* of people, they felt that an individual must be regarded primarily as representative of a society. His or her individual talent or accomplishment should be held apart. And thus it came about, I think, that such clearly humane persons as George Herzog (1936) and John Blacking (1967), surely close to their informants and teachers, avoided mentioning names except in broad and general acknowledgments, while Frances Densmore, less interested in being scientific than in showing what Indians could do, gives personal ascriptions.

There are other causes of the widespread avoidance of naming and acknowledging informants. In 1971 the American Anthropological Society (SEM Newsletter Jan.-Feb. 1974) adopted a "Statement of Principles" that speaks to the need and right of informants to remain anonymous in order to safeguard their welfare in their communities and nations. It does not, interestingly, say that they also have the right, if they wish, to be fully acknowledged and quoted by name. Indeed, in my experience, informants and teachers have been more frequently concerned lest their names and attitudes be divulged than that they be given proper credit.

Major changes in the attitude toward informants took place in the period after about 1965, in which ethnomusicologists began to concentrate on the study of Asian classical music. The role of famed teachers and internationally recognized artists in their research motivated scholars to approach these people more in the way historians approach major figures, as representatives of their culture, yes, but also as great artists in their own right. By the 1970s this attitude had spilled over into the study of other societies as well. Berliner (1978) describes many individual Shona mbira players and devotes an introductory chapter to a famed player who had to be convinced, over a period of six years, of Berliner's genuine interest before a central piece of information was given to him. The artist finally concluded, in an announcement to his village, "Well, it seems to me that this young man is serious after all. I suppose I can tell him the truth [about the nomenclature of the keys of the mbira] now." Even then villagers called to the old man, "No, don't tell him; it's our secret" (1978:7). They felt that it was privileged information, that it belonged to them and they had the right to share it or not.

Here a village shared in a musical secret. Elsewhere music may be owned by individuals, clans, tribes, the world. The way in which ethnomusicologists must approach their study depends in large measure on a society's ideas of who owns the music. Again the Blackfoot provide an interesting example. At least at the beginning of the twentieth century they appear to have classed songs in three groups in accordance with ownership (Wissler 1912:27) by tribe or individual, restricted or transferable. By the 1960s strict observance of this system had been abandoned or had little significance. Perhaps it had always been more theoretical than practical, but the fundamental idea that certain songs belonged to particular individuals was still there in 1970. Thus informants singing for my collection would say, "This is my song, because I made it," or "This song was given to me by my mother." Conversation yielded the impression that while no official strictures or sanctions were available, and the matter was not taken all too seriously, a singer/owner would feel a bit uncomfortable if another sang his song. For the Venda, Blacking (1965:36–45) indicates that various levels of chieftainship controlled the performance of many kinds of music, and that certain pieces should not be performed without sponsorship of the proper political echelon. In Iran the teacher of classical music speaks not of teaching but of "giving" material to the student, implying that his *radif* is something that he "has" and is thus free to impart or not. Copyright law in the United States provides a considerable measure of control over a piece of music by its creator, and the special problems of folk music ownership within such a copyright system has been a worry for publishers and authors and the subject of a set of special guidelines proposed by the International Folk Music Council.

Turning to questions of ethics, we assume that ethnomusicologists in the Western world should in the first instance be governed by the ordinary standards of ethical behavior in their own culture. It ought not to be necessary to tell one's students that they should not lie to informants about their intentions of using recordings and information, that one does not record singing without the knowledge and permission of the singer, that one pays what is by some kind of standard a reasonable sum or reciprocates for services rendered. This is all obvious. After all, in Western culture we know that we should not lie. We are up in arms about having offices or bedrooms "bugged" by police, telephone conversations recorded. We may bargain with people about what we pay for services, but not if they are, for example, children unable to bargain effectively. The government provides minimum wage laws to protect those who cannot easily stand up for themselves. We should know enough not to issue records with performances by people who have asked us to refrain from doing so; and so on. It is part of our culture's conception of being a decent human being, and in the field we should adhere to our own standards. Certainly this is also what counts most in fieldwork done in some sense within our own culture area.

But beyond this, the particular question of music ownership in another culture becomes relevant. For example, fieldworkers may be befriended by individuals who live in one way or another on the fringes of their own society—partially Westernized persons in a village that is otherwise traditional perhaps, or outcasts and malcontents. Among them are those who would gladly, for appropriate return or out of sheer dissatisfaction, sing the songs of another or record material not intended for general use. A man in need may succumb to the opportunity of acquiring what seems to him a fortune—little enough for a grant-supported European or American—and divulge the secrets of his society. A fieldworker following through on such opportunities might well do considerable damage to a social (and musical) system and also hurt future opportunities for fieldwork by others. It thus behooves the ethnomusicologist to become sensitive to a society's ideas of who owns music or controls it, and to work within the constraints of the culture.

It is also obvious but sometimes forgotten that teachers and informants have a primary allegiance to their own societies. Paul Berliner's teacher, who waited for six years, had the right to present his system of mbira nomenclature when he was satisfied that Berliner was a serious student. He was an authority, but he allowed the village to assemble and give its assent before proceeding. It was *his* music, but he evidently wanted to be sure that he was following the will of his society. On the other hand, a distinguished Iranian performer, finding that he had been recorded without his knowledge and that a performance he did not regard as worthy of his culture's musicianship standards had been issued on a record, remained suspicious of European and American collectors for years and avoided them. He felt that he had been made ridiculous in the eyes of his colleagues; it was his relationship to his own society that was at issue.

GREAT OFFENSE CAN BE CAUSED

The chairman of the tribal council gave me a piercing look. "What good will it do us if you go around collecting old songs from old-timers?" I explained honestly that it probably would do little good, but that I would pay singers for their efforts, and might write something that would help white Americans understand Indian culture. "Well, you'll probably get it wrong anyway; but go ahead, I guess it won't do much harm." He shrugged his shoulders and continued to take a dim view of me as I worked along, but didn't interfere. I wondered for a while about his hostility.

I had been concerned that I deal fairly and honestly with the individual informants and singers. Probably in the early years of exposure to ethnomusicologists, members of Third World communities regarded this kind of relationship as the paramount issue. As they grew in their experience with fieldworkers—and this was particularly true of North American Indians, who were often swamped (see the well-known joke about the typical Indian family including a father, a mother, three children, and an anthropologist)—they also began to display concern for issues that involved the community and its future. Thus, if one role of the fieldworker was to preserve the culture on film, tape, print, they wished to be sure that the data was "correct," that the truth would be recorded as they perceived it. No doubt, communities both tiny and large have their debates about the nature of their own culture, and these are exacerbated in times of rapid change. Community leaders might well be inclined to direct fieldworkers, to tell them how to operate, and gradually to be frustrated by their inability to keep them in line. Even more disturbing must be certain interpretations: an offhand statement blown up into a major insight; total neglect of a major component of a musical repertory; and of course a group of songs and statements, down to earth, changed into incomprehensible structuralist explanations. All of this can make people suspicious of what may be done with the information they give, with what they teach. Since there is also suspicion that a fieldworker's findings will be used, inevitably, to support some preconceived and probably pejorative notion of the value of a society, a suspicion sometimes justified even where nothing pejorative is intended, the attitude of my council chairman was surely understandable.

Leaders of a community trying delicately to direct their people's survival in a modern cultural ecology may fear that some of the activities of even an ethnomusicologist can cause things to be thrown into an uproar. Some ethnomusicologists, sensitive to this problem and torn between the needs of protecting the integrity of the community and communicating findings to their colleagues, may resort to secrecy, trying to guard against upsetting the people when they see themselves photographed in ceremonies and their statements quoted in books. "Attention fieldworkers: Great offence can be caused if this material is shown to . . . people," says one publication laying out in detail some secret ceremonial material (C. Ellis 1970:207). I wonder whether this is in the end an effective approach. Members of non-Western and folk societies are no longer so isolated from research libraries; they often find out what has been written about them, requesting (and deserving) copies of what is produced. Urban American society has become callous to what is written about it in surveys, since there are so many and so few turn out to be conclusive. But some other societies believe they cannot afford this luxury, knowing that what one scholar writes may for long determine white people's attitude. Thus they are much concerned that they be properly and accurately represented, and that their values be respected.

But more important, beyond his skepticism about my ability to get things right, the council chairman was concerned that what I did should be of some benefit to his people. What difference did that make? His people (and most whose music is studied by ethnomusicologists) were poor and needed help, and he wanted to be sure that time and energy spent in my service would help to improve their lot. There was just too much to be done to permit time to be spent on frivolities. Aware that I would not become wealthy from publishing books or records, he knew that I would nevertheless benefit, was building a career with what his people taught me, and felt that they should also derive benefit.

Just how to act properly in such a context has posed dilemmas of various sorts. If the fieldworker strives to preserve what is old and traditional, this may satisfy, but it may also arouse fear lest the community be viewed as incredibly backward and isolated. Community leaders are not always happy about the encouragement of old musical practices because they readily perceive that these may be symbolic of traditional and no longer competitive ways of dealing with problems of modern economics and technology. Should the collectors do anything beyond simply recording what they find? As far back as 1916 Cecil Sharp, entranced by the old English songs he found in the Appalachians, wrote about what he regarded as the detrimental role of missionaries and their schools. "I don't think any of them [missionaries] realize that the people they are here to improve are in many respects far more cultivated than their would-be instructors. . . . Take music, for example. Their own is pure and lovely. The hymns that these missionaries teach them are musical and literary garbage" (Karpeles 1967:153). Indeed. The statement might have been made about any of hundreds of other societies. But these mountain folk could hardly have survived without some elements of standard education, and Sharp's applauding of a girl who dropped out of school seems at best romantic. Had my council chairman suspected me of urging Plains Indians to avoid learning country-and-western music, he might have demurred, for this is the kind of music that goes with the development of a rural Western lifestyle, the adoption of which may be necessary to the survival of the Indians as a people. Indian leaders know perhaps better than ethnomusicologists the close association of music and the rest of culture. The ethnomusicologist's role in bringing Western music to non-Western societies poses another dilemma. The people and their governments may want it, while the scholar wishes to preserve the world's musical variety. There is no simple solution, but the problem was already understood by the early masters of our field. Hornbostel: "In Africa, the introduction of harmony would check the natural development of polyphonic forms from antiphony. This is . . . regrettable" (1928:42).

In the course of the 1950s there developed a concept and a subdiscipline, "applied anthropology," whose task it was to use anthropological insight to help solve social problems, particularly those occasioned by rapid culture change in the wake of modernization and Westernization. Anthropologists wanted to help but frequently ended up offending the local population and doing what was perceived as harmful. As a result, in the late 1960s and early 1970s they were widely attacked for doing work of no relevance to social problems, of mixing in local politics, of spying (Pelto 1973:282). Ethnomusicologists shared in this criticism.

But the picture is not entirely negative. Some societies are happy to have outsiders come, appreciate their efforts (Pelto 1973:283), their respect for the traditions, and their help in restoring vigor to rapidly disappearing musics (Jairazbhoy 1978:61). Persian and Indian music masters are proud to have Western scholars as students, for it raises their prestige locally and legitimizes their traditional art in the face of modernizing doubters. Even so, there is often the feeling that members of the society itself, given the right training, equipment, and time, could do it better. They sometimes assert that they would benefit if the fieldworker shared with them not only *what* is collected and recorded (in the United States and elsewhere tribal archives have been emerging) but also the research methods. This attitude, along with the belief that the emic viewpoint must be given greater weight than before, has led some ethnomusicologists to espouse fieldwork in which informants become collaborators, the members of a community being studied in effect becoming co-investigators.

But in summary, the general principles in dealing with communities must be that local consensus of what is fair, proper, and true must be respected, and that the sense of the community—not just of the individual informant—must be taken into account.

POLITICS IN THE MODERN WORLD

It will be no surprise that political events of the world since 1945 have had an enormous impact on ethnomusicology, and particularly on fieldwork, as Charles Seeger (1961) was one of the first to recognize. The Third World emerged as a group of nation-states whose boundaries were in many cases, especially parts of Asia and most of Africa, those that had arbitrarily been established by colonizing powers in the centuries before, and which often had little to do with the boundaries of traditional cultural or political units. India, Nigeria, and Indonesia are obvious examples. It goes without saying that eventually these nations, as well as the longer-established ones of Latin America, wished to have the same rights and privileges as those of Western Europe. This began eventually to include the right of determining what kinds of research may be carried out within their borders, and finally of giving their own citizens priority in such research. In the course of the 1960s and 1970s it has become less and less possible for an American or European simply and without question to set up shop and to study music or engage in anthropological fieldwork in Asia, Africa, or, for that matter, Indian lands at home.

A certain amount of distress was registered; it was pointed out that scholars from, say, India and Nigeria were welcome, after all, to study American and European culture in situ. Hardly a fair comparison, for Asian and African scholars beyond the age of graduate study had always come, and would continue to come, in tiny numbers, and carry out their studies in the humanities and social sciences largely under the tutelage and direction of Americans and Europeans. In the Third World fieldworkers from abroad would outnumber native scholars, have superior equipment, decide what and how to study. Just as members of musically small societies had often felt that their heritage was effectively being removed by becoming known and published in the West, so the new nations now began to be jealous of their national heritages, paralleling the attitudes once held by these smaller and organically longer-established culture units such as tribes. They wanted to be sure that the heritage was preserved and studied correctly and that the nation derived benefit from the study. And they wanted a chance to do it themselves.

It was a new ball game. The basic assumption of my chief of the tribal council had been that the members of the tribe would themselves best understand how their culture should be studied and presented. While such a view may not be easily accepted by the comparativist, it is easily justified if one accepts the long-standing integrity of the tribe as a social unit. However, to extend this view to the new nation-state seems less reasonable. It must be admitted that Japanese scholars have greater legal justification than non-Japanese for studying the music of the Ainu, who live in Japan, but the Ainu may feel themselves not much more closely related to the Japanese than to Americans. The Blackfoot people probably couldn't care less whether a fieldworker is a United States citizen or a Canadian or, for that matter, a Frenchman, even though they themselves are United States citizens. And so, at a recent conference at which the familiar question was aired, it fell to Indonesian scholars from Java to point out that they were surely outsiders of a sort when working in Sumatra or the Celebes, and could themselves be blamed for the old problems of colonialism. The university-trained Hausa resident of Lagos may well, for all intents and purposes, be an outsider when working in a Hausa village. The same is true of the Arapaho Indian with a Ph.D. from Harvard. The question, as we have raised it before, is, of course, what makes an "insider," and whether a true "insider" can do fieldwork at all. But beyond this, the identity of culture units is greatly complicated by the vagaries of politics.

I don't need to detail how the peoples of the new nation-states have been exploited—though sometimes less than they think—by the industrial powers of the northern hemisphere. Generally, ethnomusicologists have been among those who have objected. In contrast to the typical missionary, military administrator, or businessman, they have tried to show that the peoples with whom they work have a worthwhile culture, should be treated as equals, should be encouraged to maintain their traditions and become known in the world for their accomplishments. Contrary to the views of some (e.g. Daniélou 1973:34–39), ethnomusicologists have not simply pointed their fingers at the quaintness of the exotic, chuckled at the backwardness, or tried to prove that they were dealing with archaic phenomena. It is curious, therefore, that so many of them feel guilty about what they have done when confronted with the desire of Asians, Africans, and Latin Americans to share in their work.

But share they must and should, for the new nation-states are here to stay, and just as England was once forged into a unified culture from several Germanic tribes, Celtic understructures, and Norman-French invaders, India has become a nation, however internally diverse, and there have come to be national Nigerian and Indonesian cultures. Ethnomusicologists must deal with nations on their terms, not only because their governments control their borders and issue visas but also because the older nations of the West have all along expected this kind of behavior of the Third World governments.

The basic assumption in capitalist as well as socialist nations is that music is a commodity. Governments believe that they own the music within their borders, have the right to control it. The Iranian state radio (before 1978) had no qualms about recording and broadcasting the singing of diverse ethnic minorities in Iran, but the government had definite ideas about who, citizen or foreigner, should be allowed to collect it, and how. It was the *national* government that assumed responsibility (not always well, to be sure) for the welfare of minorities. And so, while some Third World nations have readily admitted fieldworkers while others have not, all maintain the right of control. What, then, do they want, what moral obligations does the fieldworker assume toward them, their musicians and scholars, and what should be done to assure their long-term hospitality and cooperation? What can the ethnomusicologist offer them? Let me mention just two possibilities.

A nation has the right of access to data collected within its borders. For us, this means recordings and supporting data. Depositing copies in national archives or in leading institutions is a convenient and automatic way to satisfy this desire. While this may almost seem like carrying coals to Newcastle, in many nations it is believed that the national heritage is in the process of disappearing. While modern ethnomusicologists may have little interest in it, it is through simple preservation that they seem best able to serve the people with whom they work. A related service is helping local libraries to build the holdings of literature and published records of their national music traditions. Much may have been published in North America and Europe without even the knowledge of local officials and scholars, and they are eager to find out what has been said about them, even if they frequently don't like what they eventually read.

Furthering the training of local individuals as ethnomusicologists, in the field or abroad, is another way in which non-Western research capacity can be aided; related to this is joint research by outsider and local scholars, on an equal and shared basis (Hood 1971:371–75). Actively fostering respect in a Third World government for local musicians follows along the same lines. There is more, but these illustrations serve to make the point. The new governments share the aspirations of informant and tribe. There is a debt that should be repaid, and the new nation-states are the logical recipients.

There are in process various attempts to produce guidebooks on ethical behavior in ethnomusicology (Society for Ethnomusicology 1977). How useful these may be remains to be seen, for each situation requires its own set of considerations. It seems that common sense, the belief that at bottom all humans are equal and their values equally worthy of respect, and some understanding of the subtle concept of music ownership on the part of informant, tribe, village, or nation provide the best guidelines.

The Study of All of the World's Music

Chapter 23

I've Never Heard a Horse Sing

WHY NOT A FOLK SONG?

It is part of the ethnomusicologist's credo that all musics, and all of the music in each society, must be investigated, are worthy of study. All music that is accepted by some community as its own has the minimal qualification by virtue of that fact. Yet ethnomusicologists have from the beginning been concerned with the stratification of music within a society, imposing models such as the folk music–art music dichotomy or the folk-popular-classical continuum and, more recently, trying to determine the hierarchical taxonomies of other cultures. They have also been aware of the fact that subdivisions of a society may identify themselves with particular repertories and styles of music, each regarded as in some way superior by its people. Sometimes they have been drawn into the conflict and come close to establishing groups of scholars extolling the virtues, respectively, of folk, popular, and classical traditions. Among the pervasive issues of ethnomusicology: the identity of "folk music" and the existence of stratification as a musical universal.

Many years ago a few stragglers stayed behind to ask questions after my lecture entitled "Folk Music." "Isn't 'On Top of Old Smoky' a folk song?" asked one. "And how about some of our great hymns, 'Onward, Christian Soldiers,' and such?" Well, I wasn't sure. The questioner hung his head in disappointment. And another: "Don't you think that jazz is *the* true folk music of America?" Well, I wasn't sure about that either. The first retorted more aggressively: "But these are great songs; how can you say they are not folk songs?" I tried to talk about formal criteria, but no luck, and realized that I had offended a lady simply by implying that her favorite songs weren't folk songs. "Why does a song have to be a folk song in order to be respectable to you?" Knowing something about the many uses of the term "folk music," I was tempted to quote the statement attributed to many folk singers who performed for urban audiences, but most frequently tied to Big Bill Broonzy, "All songs are folk songs; I've never heard a horse sing."

The next day in my classroom I saw that one of my colleagues had left some definitions on the board: "A folk song is a song whose composer isn't known. An art song is a fine song composed by a great composer." Why does a song have to have a known composer in order to be a fine song? Tempted to write Big Bill's *bon mot* on the board.

The term "folk song" has strong emotional connotations in Western society, as illustrated already by Julian von Pulikowski (1933), who showed, in a large study of the term, how the concept was batted about by politicians of the left and right, by social reformers, nationalists, educators, antiquarians, musicians theoretical and practical, even in nineteenth-century Germany. In the urban culture of the United States in the period 1930 to 1970, it also came to mean many things to many people: heritage, cultural integrity, a symbol of better things to come, a way to keep a small group intact, a way for people from many groups to communicate. Its prevailingly oral tradition and its supposed association with entire ethnic groups have put it under the particular aegis of ethnomusicology.

It is clear that in modern American urban society music is classified in several categories. There is no single generally accepted system but, except for the small minority who have never heard a horse sing, people consider music as comprising several types or repertories, often in a hierarchical arrangement. The criteria for taxonomy vary with class, education, or ethnicity of the classifier. Two of the most widespread criteria for musical stratification are social classes (with each of which one identified mainly a particular kind of music) and origin (of repertory or individual piece). The criteria lead to similar groupings, and these are the ones most widely used in society at large: primitive, popular, folk, and art or classical music. The educational establishment, as exemplified by the terminology of library catalogues, considers "art" music as the true and central music of the entire society, labeling it simply as "music" while other types have distinguishing adjectives. Some decades ago all non-Western music (or more precisely for the Western classifier, all music from outside his own culture) would have been classed as "primitive." Folk music would have been the music of remote rural populations orally transmitted by nonprofessionals who create variants that must satisfy in order to remain extant. "Popular" music, difficult to distinguish from "folk" or "art" music, would have been that of the lower social and educational classes. Thus four classes of people—urban elite, urban mass, rural, and those totally outside the culture—were socially and musically distinguished by this taxonomy.

The other criterion, origin, tells us that "primitive" music comes from elsewhere and, in the minds of many, a very remote era; folk music is associated with the anonymous mass, art music with specific composers, and popular music mainly with performers (more than with acknowledged composer). Beyond this, people distinguish music by the time of its creation (old and new, or Renaissance, Baroque, Classical, etc.). As it happens, this "folk taxonomy" of Western urban culture was adopted by ethnomusicologists for their work and used widely as a basic guide in research and teaching.

The history of ethnomusicology, however, appears to have gone through several indistinct and overlapping stages. At one time there was a tendency to recognize only two classes, Western art music in the one and everything else in the other (Adler 1885:14). Soon, recognition of the fact that Asian cultures had a stratification of music not unlike that of Europe led to a tripartite model, primitive, art, and folk music. Those cultures with an art music, that is, a kind of music performed by professionals who were highly trained and had the technical and speculative conceptualization of music that we call music theory, were also said to have, in other strata of society or in a different tradition, a folk music. The cultures with no such art music were thought to be "primitive" and thus to have "primitive" music. A third stage is implied in Hood's statement (1963a:316) to the effect that art, folk, popular, and primitive music are the norm. The ethnomusicological study of popular music was, however, slow to be formally accepted (see e.g. Vega 1966). Eventually, further, there also came the realization that each culture has its own way of classifying music, a taxonomy which may have several groupings or perhaps none, and which may exhibit a hierarchical arrangement, or may not. But I suggest that while most cultures do indeed have their own way of classifying music, so that the terms "folk," "art," and "popular" are at best culture-specific to the West, each culture tends to have some kind of hierarchy in its musical system, a continuum from some kind of elite to popular. Where the lines should be drawn is a subject of discussion (see Wiora 1957, Elbourne 1976, Bose 1967, Karpeles 1968).

THE WORLD TURNED UPSIDE DOWN

If we assume that folk music is known to all and performed by the entire community while classical music is only of the elite, or if we believe that in the Asian high cultures we can find the closest approximation of the Western model, we may sometimes find the world turned upside down. Let's look at two familiar cultures. Blackfoot society is usually considered one of the types that have no socio-musical stratification, yet two approaches taken from what is admittedly fragmentary information provide alternate interpretations. Wissler's (1912:263–70) three types of song ownership seem not to have been observed to the letter, but are still evident in vestige today. We can supplement Wissler's statement. Songs of general ownership, for example, were songs of social dances; songs owned individually but transferable included the songs of "medicine men," associated with the medicine bundle ceremonies. Nontransferable songs were to be sung in moments of danger and impending death. There seem also to have been intermediate categories such as the songs of the various men's societies, which were sung only by members but passed on to new generations entering the societies every four years or so.

In certain ways the songs individually owned correspond to the Western conception of art music. They belonged to an elite—religious if not musical, the men with great supernatural power—and were associated with individuals. As a group, they seem to have had a larger variety of style, at least of formal structure. They had greater prestige because of their supernatural power. The social dance songs, known to all, corresponded to folk music. Less emphasis was placed on their specific origin and they had more standardized forms. Although specific statements of value in these earlier times are lacking, they do appear in more recent times. They must be extrapolated from more general information but conform, interestingly, to ways in which modern white or black Americans tend to differentiate and evaluate portions of their own musical culture.

In the 1960s one could distinguish older Blackfoot ceremonial music (i.e. medicine bundle songs) from modern social dance songs by their association with two different groups of people who knew and performed them. Older material was typically known by full-blooded Blackfoot (a cultural category, on the whole comprising individuals who had little or no white ancestry, spoke little English, and were poor). Newer, social dance, and pan-Indian songs were known to the so-called mixed-blood people, typically younger and more Westernized. The older group was smaller and respected for knowledge of the old tribal traditions, and the younger, prized because of its ability to sing. It is a bit like modern Western culture: composers of art music are regarded as intellectually, artistically, and perhaps even morally superior, even when their music is not well understood and liked. Musicians in the popular music field are respected for their entertainment value but are less venerated. The parallel has its limits, of course. But the two strata of Blackfoot music do, perhaps, have something in common with the art-popular or possibly the art-folk dichotomies. Elements of musical hierarchy do exist. A few songs, labeled by the earlier literature and by some singers as "favorite" songs of the people, could be regarded as the classics or, on the other hand, as the true folk songs, beloved by all.

In some Asian societies, especially in India, the distinction between art and folk music seems to be relatively similar to that made in Western music. To a degree, it is so in Iran, although the criteria for distinction are different, and the specialist-generalist dichotomy, widely used to distinguish art and folk music in the West, does not apply. Classical music, thus named by Iranians but also called "original," "noble," or "traditional," the music of the courts of the past, centers on improvised performances and includes an articulated body of music theory. The concept closest to folk music is something most widely called *musiqi-ye mahālli,* literally regional or local music. According to Blum (1975:86), it is distinguished by performance by nonprofessionals, antiquity, cultivation in rural areas, and identification with particular regions. A body of popular music is also recognized and, typically, denigrated; it is of urban provenance and is regarded as a polluted form of classical music by learned musicians, and as sinful by the devout. But in contemporary Iran before the revolution, various kinds of Western music also existed and must be taken into account in an attempt to establish a folk taxonomy and an associated hierarchy.

Here is the stratification of Teheranian musical life, ca. 1970. Venues of performance, evaluations by individuals, cost of tickets, associations with social, economic, and educational classes, all indicate that in modern Teheran the art music of the West (some of it composed, and most of it performed, by Iranians) was at the top of the musical hierarchy. There follow, side by side, Western popular music and Persian classical music. Next is folk music, and finally the Iranian popular music, its styles mixing indigenous, Western, and Asian elements. It is possible to separate the Western and Iranian strands, to see that each has its own classical, popular, and (at least to some extent) folk components, and to find two systems each of which corresponds reasonably well to those of the United States and Europe. However, a perspective of the entire culture exhibits more strata, including, with those already mentioned, religious and other ceremonial music not regarded as truly music by devout Muslims and thus difficult to place in the hierarchy. The complexity of this stratification of music is related to the way in which attitudes toward indigenous culture provide a way for the people to classify themselves.

Now, of course, while a hierarchy is present, it is most clearly articulated by the highest class. Adherents of lower musical classes are understandably unwilling to relegate themselves explicitly to lower categories. In any society there may be classes of music normally associated with subcultures or subdivisions of the society, but their status is usually determined and most typically stated by the highest class. There is a conflict but also a relationship between the librarian and the folk singer. The former, through his catalogue, asserts that "music," "normal" music, is the art music of the highest social class, once aristocracy and court and now educated elite, and that other music is especially labeled "folk," "popular," etc. The folk singer may insist that all music is folk music.

In comparing traditional Iran and the contemporary West, societies with similar kind of strata, we find an interesting difference. In each the member of the elite recognizes classes—art music, folk music, popular music—but in a culture undergoing rapid change the classes become dislocated, reflecting dislocation of standards and social classes. Thus the Western system rises a step, Persian classical music now level with Western popular. In prerevolutionary Iran the Westernized individual had higher status than the member of the traditional elite who had not adopted elements of Western ideology, and it was thus with their music. In comparing folk musicians in

Iran and the urban West (on the basis, one must admit, of very scanty evidence), we find a different situation. The American folk singer is unwilling to admit that there are strata and is inclined to include within his purview all music with which he comes into contact. The musician of Iranian folk culture looks at music as a group of separate, specialized domains, placing them (even within the folk repertoire) in separate categories, with special terms for the repertories of practitioners of music for weddings, narrative songs of a secular nature, songs of religious import performed at teahouses, chants performed at traditional gymnasiums. The tendency is for the two kinds of folk singers to avoid hierarchical thinking, the American tending to lump all music into one category, the Iranian establishing several separate but equal categories.

It may indeed be true that some kind of hierarchical classification of music is present in most cultures. The terms "folk," "art," and "popular" may do, but their specific values differ from one society to the next.

THE RANKING OF MUSICIANS

Blacking (1973) argues for the essential and more or less equal musicality of all humans, laying differences in musical talent and achievement at the door of the tendency for societies to create social classes. Be this correct or not, most societies group musicians by ability and role, and find ways of showing differences of status. Thus, not only do most musical cultures have hierarchies of repertories, they also rank musicians, sometimes by their personal accomplishments but more frequently by their roles in musical and social life.

Merriam (1964:129–30) describes five classes of musicians among the Basongye. The highest, a versatile individual, is truly a full-time professional. The others also have the status of musicians—it is a low status, since musicians are undesirable but indispensable—but are paid very little. Society ranks them, and their pay corresponds roughly to their rank. The basis of the ranking seems to be the importance of percussion instruments in Basongye culture, their status and musical role. The higher-ranking musicians play percussion instruments, the lowest are vocalists. Whether this could be regarded as ranking according to the intrinsic difficulty of the music I cannot say; it does not seem so.

Hood (1972:244–45) describes the relative pay, and thus the status, of musicians in Javanese gamelans. Two kinds of musical roles appear to confer high status: responsibility for keeping the integrity of the gamelan intact, and responsibility for innovation, for departure from the basic melody in carrying out the paraphrasing function. If technical virtuosity itself is rewarded, it is incidental, a function of the other values. In South Indian ensembles the roles of musicians are not as diverse as in a gamelan, and a soloist clearly has higher status than an accompanist. But musicians are evaluated in accordance with criteria similar to those governing the pay scale of gamelan musicians. A musician must respect the musical authority, keep the integrity of the musical system intact, adhere to the principles of the raga and tala if a soloist, follow precisely if an accompanist, or, in other respects, must innovate imaginatively and personally, excel at improvisation.

In the Western symphony orchestra pay and evaluation by the audience tend to go hand in hand. Conductors are highest in both respects, sectional first chairs (i.e. the first viola, or 'cello, or bass player) high, others lower. Conductors have responsibility for both integration and innovation, keeping time, keeping the orchestra together, giving a faithful interpretation of the score, but also imposing their own ideas on it by providing a personal reading. First chairs have only the integrative function; their job is to keep their sections playing together. The concertmaster's task is to hold the integrity of the orchestra, but imaginative playing of solo passages is occasionally part of the job as well, so that he or she shares to an extent the dual responsibility of the conductor and is rewarded for it.

In the South Indian classical music culture of Madras, musicians are judged essentially as technicians. But certain prejudices color the evaluations. There is an underlying assumption, for example, that Brahmins make better vocal soloists, that lower castes are more suited to accompanying, that men are better improvisors than women. Musicians today recognize that this is in fact not so, but the ways in which musical roles were assigned even early in this century, in part by caste and sex, still plays a role in at least the initial expectations of the informed audience.

If one were to look for a ranking of musicians among modern Plains Indians, one could do it most conveniently by comparing ensembles of singers who habitually perform together, and by examining the social and musical structure of the individual ensemble. At an event called "North American Indian Days" on the Blackfoot Reservation in Montana, the most prominent of the secular ceremonies known as "pow-wows," several singing groups alternate, each performing for an hour or two. The groups are associated with towns on and off the reservation—Browning, Heart Butte, Starr School, Cardston (Alberta), etc. Members need not be residents, and membership is informal and floating; a singer from one group may occasionally sing in another. Each group has a leader who begins many but by no means all of the songs and who assembles the singers. Each singer in a group may lead songs, e.g. determine and begin, and there is no set order for the leading of songs. On the surface, at least, the situation is one of informality and equality. Most of the time little is made of distinctions among groups and singers. In the pow-wow sector of the culture there is only one class of individuals who make up something of a musical hierarchy, the class of men known as "singers." But the Blackfoot do distinguish quality and status of musicianship. The singing groups compete for prizes, and during my stay with the Blackfoot there was one that had the reputation of being the best, its superior quality attributed to the members' musicianship, with details unspecified. Individual singers were also singled out as being particularly excellent. The criteria included knowledge of a large repertory as well as the ability to drum well (quality of actual singing was evidently a less important criterion), with emphasis on the ability to drum slightly "off the beat" in relationship to the vocal rhythm, and in perfect unison. Men who made songs were also (automatically) regarded as superior singers but not put into a separate class as composers.

While the Blackfoot singled out excellent musicians, we know that they held a separate category for those who did not sing particularly well but who knew a great deal of older musical material. Musically, these men tended to have lower status than the "singers," perhaps in part because "singers" were usually members of a more modernized and slightly better-off class in the community. The modern social dance repertory has the general character of what Westerners associate with folk music, is widely known and shared by all, and has less diversity of forms and fewer meaningful texts. Yet practitioners have higher status than those who knew something more closely associated with our concept of art music, the more specialized, personal, and sacred repertory. The interface between hierarchies of musicians and of repertories in the world's cultures is fascinating to contemplate.

THE FOLKNESS OF FOLK AND NONFOLK MUSIC

If each culture has its musical strata, from elite to mass, complex to simple, specialized to broadly accepted, cultivated to folk, each also has elements that hold the strata together. They may be stylistic—tonal, rhythmic, formal, harmonic characteristics present at all levels. For example, the singing style of Iranian folk and classical music is more or less the same, and the importance of the triad is readily evident in German classical, popular, and folk music. On the other hand, the common elements may comprise musical content. Alan Lomax puts it in aesthetic terms, maintaining that each culture has a "favored" song style which is a particular reflection of the social and economic core of a culture, and his cantometrics project depends heavily on identifying it (1968:133). What Lomax has in mind, as a matter of fact, is folk music, at least when he deals with European and American cultures. When his considerations move to Africa and the Far East, he is prepared to include classical music, perhaps assuming that it is more favored by the people than is Western classical music by its counterpart—probably an error—or recognizing the different roles of strata in various musical cultures. In any event, we may accept the premise that if a music has several repertory components, each associated with one stratum or segment of society, there is nevertheless one which holds the society musically together, and which symbolizes for it the unity of the entire culture.

But actually identifying the "favored" song style is not easy. To the folk music scholars of the nineteenth and early twentieth centuries, folk music would occupy this role, for it was regarded, after all, as the unchanging, ancient heritage that preceded creation of courts, cathedrals, cities, and the middle class. For those concerned with the cultures of the twentieth century, it is likely to be what we call the "popular" music disseminated through the mass media. In either case it seems to be the music that has a common denominator with other, minority musics. For example, we may consider Anglo-American folk music as the favored style of the Anglo-American culture area for these reasons, among others: (1) It is relatively old and has probably changed more slowly than other genres. (2) It has pentatonic and heptatonic scales commensurate with the popular and classical musics of this area. (3) It prefers a four-line structure also found in hymns, popular songs, and many art songs. On the other hand, if we consider the contemporary popular music—rock and its various predecessors and relatives—we find a simple harmonic structure also basic to (but much more extended in) the classical system, as well as scales and forms also found in church music, folk music, and at least some classical music.

Another approach is to look for a musical system that has a common denominator in another sense. It is a stratum of music that ties together a large number of otherwise musically and culturally diverse segments of society, ethnic groups, geographical areas, because in some way it reflects some of the central values of society. Sometimes this applies to a classical tradition, and, to be sure, in large populations such as those of Europe, India, or China classical systems are readily identified by real or potential listeners as well as those outside this select circle. But even in smaller societies a special, exceptional, and yet favored style can often be identified.

The classical music of today's Iran did not make a distinctive appearance on the stage of history until the late nineteenth century, when it emerged from a period of neglect accompanying the decline of Persian culture and political power under the Qajar dynasty (1797–1925). In recent years, however, there is no doubt that it became a truly classical system in the sense that it was (incorrectly) considered to be very old as well as truly and distinctly Persian. It related to various currents of Iranian life, became regarded as the music of the whole nation, symbolizing its unity and its distinctiveness, in contrast to various folk and popular musics (which spoke to its diversity, regional, cultural, linguistic, religious) and Western music (which bespoke the submersion of distinctiveness in favor of amalgamation with the West). Its structure exhibited certain characteristics of folk musics but developed them further. As we have repeatedly seen, one could trace in it some of the major social values of traditional Iranian society. It drew on material from far-flung parts of Iran. It was associated with the elite population of Iran, court, aristocracy, and eventually the educated but traditional-minded middle class.

In a survey of attitudes a cross-section of Teheranians gave a variety of opinions and evaluations of Persian classical music. Many (including those who hardly knew it) said they liked it, others didn't. Some regarded it as a symbol of an undesirable past, others of what is good, beautiful, truly Persian. To most, however, it was something special.

In India a similar picture emerges in intensified form, the two classical systems transcending the many linguistic and cultural diversities. In another way Western classical music fulfills the same function, for it is a kind of music that, despite regional and national diversity, musically unified Europe and European-derived culture, while national and regional folk musics symbolize this diversity. The popular music of the mass media fulfills this unifying function as well, but with less stability of style and—the popular music repertories of Italy, Germany, and the United States differing more than the repertories of their symphony orchestras and opera houses—uneven geographic distribution. In Western culture, too, only a small part of the population really knows the classical music. It can be accorded "favored" status mainly because of its role as a symbol of what is musically great, the respect it has even among those who do not particularly like it. In most ways it is musically exceptional, differing rather sharply from folk music, popular music, hymns, marches, all of which have elements of form, brevity, and harmonic simplicity in common; it does not provide the stylistic unity of folk or popular music.

In the music of the Blackfoot, something that we could call a "classical" repertory can possibly also be distinguished. Informants give certain songs the status of being "favorite songs of the tribe" (Nettl 1967b:148; see also McClintock 1968). Evidently there are social as well as musical criteria. The songs associated with the most traditional venerated activities may have this status; those that must be sung at certain points in public ceremonies—e.g., while raising the pole of the Sun Dance lodge in preparation for this major tribal ceremony—seem to have been so designated. But the criteria may be musical as well. When a group of songs that have in various ways been labeled as "favorite" by the Blackfoot were compared, as a group, to the rest of the repertory, they showed a slight tendency to be exceptional. Some use more tones in their scales, others have unusual and sometimes more complex forms, or include less repetition. The difference is not great or obvious, but within the Blackfoot repertory these exceptional and favorite songs play a role just a bit like that of classical musics in Europe and Asia.

We may have to find a "favored" song style in a culture by looking for what is common or what is exceptional. Authenticity is a concept most frequently associated with the idea of folk music, but if it is to be used to identify *the* music most central to a society, it may just as frequently have to be applied to other kinds and strata of music. The question of a "favored song style" intersects with the definition of folk music, its relationship to other musics in its society, and its symbolic role. Two contrastive views emerge in the literature.

The first view, widely accepted in modern times, separates classes and suggests that each population group within a society has a primary musical allegiance. Thus in rural Iran the Kurdish, Turkish, and Persian villages, and in an Iranian town the Armenians and Jews as well as the Persian majority, all have their own musics. These may exhibit different musical status, but in any event they correspond to differences of social status. In India various castes and communities have their own musics—the Bauls, the Kota, the Pillai; in the classical music system castes tend to have different roles in an ensemble, lower ones being more frequently the accompanists (Neuman 1980:124–29).

The other view holds that all members of a society are united musically by a fundamental stratum, which is folk music. Wiora (1957:22) states it clearly, in its complexity. "Not all folkish music, [music which is] nonprofessional [and] easily understood, is to be called folk music in the true sense. Rather, this term is used only for that which is properly the culture of the folk. And by 'folk,' we mean not only the totality of the basic strata of society such as peasants, herdsmen, miners, folk musicians, etc., but also that which is truly and generally valid for an entire society" (my translation).

The point Wiora is making is that what may be called the folk music of a society must be held in common by all its components. In the revision of a paper entitled "The Folkness of the Nonfolk and the Nonfolkness of the Folk" (1977b:335–43), Charles Seeger argues that the people of the United States "are divided into two classes: a majority that does not know it is a folk; a minority, that thinks it isn't" (p. 343). Clearly Seeger thought that the whole population had enough in common to constitute, in some sense, a "folk" which shared a folk music, if not as repertory then as conception, and he mourned the lack of awareness. Wiora's and Seeger's emphasis in on what the members of a society musically have in common. Certain individuals may go beyond this basic "folk" stratum to create such things as "art" music, but what ties them together continues to be the common folklore. One result is the revival of folklore and folk music in various kinds of urban contexts, combined in recent German scholarship under the rubric of "Folklorismus" (Baumann 1976).

Another version of this same theme holds that it is rather the classical tradition, the "great tradition," as it is put by Singer and Redfield (Singer 1972:7–10), which holds together people whose folk traditions are actually quite diverse. Various ethnic groups, castes, communities, and religions in India, which have, for their everyday musical experience, a different repertory, nevertheless are united by their respect for, their allegiance to, a common classical repertory. To a smaller extent, this may also be said of Iran.

There are few if any studies of the role of rural folk music in the world's urban cultures, and of the symbolic value of various repertories in an urban society. Emphasis has been on the role of folk music as symbol of the separateness of ethnic groups. But it is not always so restricted. In Central European cities of the first half of this century, a selected body of folk music was known, taught in schools, brought to the attention of middle-class children by nannies from the countryside, and members of this middle class usually knew something they considered to be folk music. To them the folk repertory is a unifying factor because it is a fact of musical life. A "great tradition," functioning more as a symbol, may be a unifying factor in another respect. Many Indians and Iranians do not hear or know their classical traditions but respect them and regard them as symbols of cultural and national identity. It is also as symbol of national identity that the European folk song of the nineteenth and early twentieth centuries served. Following Seeger, we note that either a simple or a complex repertory may fulfill this unifying function. The common stratum may be high or low. Bill Broonzy may be wrong, and all music is not folk music. But all people may have a kind of music that fulfills Wiora's function of folk music, the integration of the larger society.

Chapter 24

We Never Heard a Bad Tune

THE ETHNOMUSICOLOGIST'S VALUES

Ethnomusicologists sometimes appear to be hypocritical. They claim to wish to study all of the world's music, on its own terms, and to introduce only those values that are held by the culture investigated. But their writings readily show their inability (or unwillingness) to avoid injecting certain of their own values. Thus Western ethnomusicologists deal with European folk music, African and Chinese music in ways that reflect their relationships to the values of Western culture, including those that attracted them to these musics in the first place. European folk music research has typically produced large printed collections, while the music of India has stimulated studies revering the wisdom of theorists and the complexity of musical design. African music has often been the vehicle for assessments of intercultural relationships, and South American Indian music, of the complex functions of music in shamanism. Many folk music studies give off a feeling of intimacy; those of Tibetan music, an aura of archeological curiosity; of American Indians, a kind of defensiveness about the importance of *presumably* uninteresting music in the complex organism that is culture.

It has become accepted that we find out how a society evaluates its various musical products, and that we try to see how the fundamental values of a culture may be reflected in its music. We have discussed ethical and social values that determine the kind of person an ethnomusicologist is likely to be or become. But we wish now also to examine some of the values that have moved the profession in particular scholarly directions.

What, by an ethnomusicological standard, is good music? One may say that all music is worthy of equally thorough study, or reply by concentrating on that part of a music which a society itself regards as its most valued. Or one may, as an outsider, identify by one's own criteria the most valuable style for preservation and research. For determining cultural or musical quality or value, a number of criteria appear to have been used, but in all cases they determine music that conforms to an ideal, an ideal which may be the scholar's own.

The concept of the "authentic" for a long time dominated collecting activities, became mixed with "old" and "exotic" and synonymous with "good." Subsuming age and stability under the rubric of authenticity, Charles Seeger (1977:51–53) accuses ethnomusicologists of practicing ethnocentrism in reverse and chides us for the application of preconceived ideas as to what is worthy of study, and thus missing out on much that should have been investigated. Indeed, until very recently, the music most often chosen as the object of ethnomusicological study was that which contrasted most, in any of a number of ways, with the scholar's own musical experience and background. Most typical of these objects was the supposedly pure, unpolluted style of the folk or tribal community. Nineteenth-century ideas of musical and cultural purity held on for decades in the understructure of a field that was striving to separate itself from practical society and politics. Curiously, the concept of a pure music as the mark of a pure and unpolluted society has continued into the late twentieth century. Even a look at our transcriptions and analytical procedures shows that they are conceived for homogeneous, unmixed repertories, and comments accompanying them suggest that what we are looking for is the music unmistakably belonging to a particular society.

Describing his work in the southern Appalachians in 1916, Cecil Sharp reveled in the purity of the folk song style of that isolated area: "When, by chance, the text of a modern street-song succeeds in penetrating into the mountains, it is at once mated to a traditional tune and sometimes still further purified by being moulded into the form of a traditional ballad" (1930: xxvi). His collaborator of many years, Maud Karpeles, describing the same field trip, exulted in the fact that "throughout our stay in the mountains we never heard a bad tune, except occasionally when we were staying at a missionary settlement" (Karpeles 1973:97). The scholarship of Sharp and Karpeles was dominated by the belief that certain kinds of music were good, others bad, and the criteria are evident in these short statements (see also Karpeles 1951). But pollution is inevitable everywhere. "The country has been opened up, roads have been built, and the serpent in the guise of radio and records has penetrated into this Garden of Eden" (1973:98). Never mind that the serpent in this case was the vanguard of Christian Evangelistic missionaries. Sharp evidently did not wish to collect all of the music extant in the Appalachian communities but had specific ideas of what music properly belonged, and it was music believed to be old, to have uniformity of style, and to be unique in comparison to other musics that might be around. These criteria determined purity and authenticity.

Scholars from non-Western musical cultures often share this approach, supplementing it with insights into the practical problems and issues confronting their societies. One of their most articulate, Habib Hassan

Touma, has indicated in various published and oral statements the importance of identifying and studying as authentic that which is regarded as excellent in the culture. Critical of the mixing of Arabic and Western elements in modern Arabic music, he maintains that the typical Arabic musician now "practices a kind of music which is neither genuinely Arabic nor genuinely foreign, but which is greatly influenced by public taste and demand . . . thus the new developments are nothing but incredible deformation of the traditional music through the use of foreign elements from non-Arabic cultures . . ." (Touma 1975:129, my translation). While not explicitly denying the usefulness of understanding modern, mixed styles, he would like to see ethnomusicology support modernization by helping to produce a new music that—in contrast to what has been done—is a genuine continuation of the traditional art music (1975:132). Having stated his cultural and musical values, he builds an approach to fieldwork upon them, using them as criteria to identify the best performers. If one is to understand properly the essence of a musical culture, Touma asserts, one must concentrate on the best musicians (Touma 1968:22).

One can hardly fault a fieldworker for seeking what is in some respect the best. One would surely get a different picture of Western classical music if one studied it through the performances of Isaac Stern and Rostropovich than if one learned from the playing of high school orchestras. Lest we use the latter as norm on account of their frequency, let's remember that high school orchestras would not exist, were not the great virtuosos known and available as ideals. Guidance from informants often pushes one in the direction of looking for the best. Sometimes it is inconceivable to them that a scholar might have anything else in mind. My principal Iranian teacher did not understand why I should have an interest in making comparative studies of several performers. Finally it dawned on him: "You are doing this to show why I am a better musician than the others!" That I might wish to understand what was done by the average musician made no sense to him; after all, these people were trying but failing quite to accomplish what the great musicians succeeded in doing, and they knew it. Why study a culture through what it itself regards as imperfect? Historians of Western music sometimes take the same approach, but since they are not Renaissance or eighteenth-century musicians, they cannot speak with the authority of my teacher, who was, after all, an authentic informant for his culture. But my teacher would have fitted excellently into the framework of modern Western humanism.

In a presentation critical of values used in ethnomusicology, Eugene Helm states the humanist position strongly: ". . . we seem to have forgotten about *quality*. I do not advise my graduate students in historical musicology to resurrect inferior composers of the past, and by the same token I am not ready to treat all non-Western musics as equally worthy of study" (1977:201). Implying a basic difference between science and humanism, he goes on to articulate what seems to him the difference between musicology and ethnology (i.e. sociocultural anthropology), the former selecting music to be studied on the basis of its quality and the latter studying it all because of its role in culture.

One can easily find points of disagreement with Helm's statement. He evidently believes that one can use a kind of universal measuring device for quality, since it is not just the consensus or judgment of a culture upon its musical values with which he is concerned. The claims that some Western composers are better than others is not analogous to the suggestion that some musics are better than others. They are horses of different colors, and combining them sends shivers up the spines of many ethnomusicologists, each of whom would fear that *his* or *her* music could be withdrawn from accreditation. The music historian who studies seemingly insignificant though perhaps in their day popular composers might wish to join them, and the ethnomusicologists would ask whether it is not enough to say that each music, by its own standards, has its good and bad works. The broader question is whether a narrowly humanistic perspective is tenable in a cross-cultural situation.

Music historians have long had to deal with problems occasioned by the relative worthiness of their subject matter. They often find it necessary to justify work with the opus of a particular composer by claiming that it is better on strictly musical grounds than had heretofore been supposed, or that it was historically significant because it exhibits influences and connections. Ethnomusicologists, asked why they work with this or that tribe, may give the equivalent of the mountain climber's answer, "because it is there." But they too are often substantially affected by the belief that one should study what is in some universal (or perhaps Western) sense good or outstandingly important.

UNIFORM AND STABLE

Authenticity, the cultural ideal, is one major criterion of the good. Each culture has music that is in any of several special senses its very own, and ethnomusicologists have concentrated on it. Related to this criterion is the desirability of studying what is not obviously mixed but homogeneous. Perhaps scholars regard unmixed, uniform repertories as better because they seem to exhibit age, stability, authenticity. The conjecture that a musical style is old, "a remnant of the stone age," as it is sometimes put, often rests on its internal uniformity, its rough edges thought to have been smoothed out over the centuries like a pebble on the beach. The conception that the central music of a folk community must be homogeneous, the musical common denominator of an equally homogeneous society, is also widespread.

Aside from ideology, a reason for the value placed on the uniform and unmixed involves ethnomusicological technique. The basic early literature of the field described styles from small samples of musics. Stating what is *the* style of the music of *a* people looms large in our early works; one is tempted to make a case for the belief that ten songs, all rather alike, give such a picture more accurately than a description of ten divergent songs. Of course this is unrealistic. Ten similar songs in a repertory are likely to be an inadequate sample or a small corner of a larger and less unified body. And yet, there is an unspoken assumption in much literature to the effect that the homogeneous sample is the reliable one, that musics are uniform except when disturbed, all of this deriving from the old belief that culture is normally stable. A different set of fundamental values in our operation might have given us the opposite basic assumption, that uniformity is deceptive, that musics are internally (emically and etically) heterogeneous except when unusually isolated. But the analytical and descriptive techniques favored the convenience of seeking out from any music what was homogeneous within it. It is a convenient approach, but we should be careful to understand its limitations.

Throughout most of the history of ethnomusicology the study of polluted styles, hybrid genres partaking of several clearly evident sources, has been avoided. As illustrated by the statements of Cecil Sharp (above), mixed styles were actually decried as resulting from events that should not have taken place. Their practice should be ignored and thus discouraged by ethnomusicologists. Like Sharp and Touma, Daniélou (1973:91) criticizes the changes that were forced on Asian musics by Western musical values. While many other scholars recognize the fact that stability in music is something that members of the world's societies simply do not always want, in their hearts and in their rhetoric they often exhibit a sadness about this state of affairs. Ella Zonis (1973:185) says pointedly that "rapid transformations in modern Iranian life are severely threatening traditional Persian music," though she then goes on to describe what may strike the reader as interesting new developments. Alan Lomax (1968:4) goes further: "To a folklorist the uprooting and destruction of traditional cultures and the consequent grey-out or disappearance of the human variety presents as serious a threat to the future happiness of mankind as poverty. . . ."

And so, beyond criticizing what has happened in the world of music, ethnomusicology until recently tended in the main to ignore the music that seemed to represent instability, in favor of often tiny remnants of traditions that they could assume to have gone unchanged. In his description of Flathead musical culture, as influential a figure as Merriam barely mentions the existence of Western music as a major component of life. Bartók (1931) gives little attention to the "mixed genera" of Hungarian folk song, a style influenced by non-Hungarian and urban sources, despite the fact that in his collection it accounts for the majority of songs. Investigating recent change is a new development.

It is tempting to speculate that the mourning of an ideal, with its social and political implications, has a lot to do with the convenience of a particular view of culture, a view that results from the Western taxonomy of life as a group of objects and concepts which, once made or identified, remain intact. Although anthropology has departed from this view of culture, humanists and other nonanthropologists dealing with the culture concept seem until very recently to have been influenced more by earlier views. Radcliffe-Brown presents an essentially organic view of culture. Schmidt and Graebner see cultures as layers that succeed each other in a population but can still, millennia later, be distinguished. Kroeber and Kluckhohn see culture as a series of interrelated patterns. All use the concept of culture as something essentially static. Social and cultural systems maintain equilibrium until they come into contact with forces from outside, or unless there develops some unsatisfactory inner relationship among the components. After 1950 the study of culture change became more of a norm than an exception in anthropology. But even now, the fact that the term "culture change" is used so widely indicates the degree to which the concept of culture as a stable commodity remains established.

It is obviously more convenient to view a complex system such as a music as something stable; perhaps, as I said, one could not deal with it otherwise. Changing this fundamental position would require enormous readjustments in the musicologist in order for him to focus, instead of on the finished art work, on the relationship between sketch and masterwork, raga and performance, the renditions of 1820 and 1960. But it ought to be clear to us just why ethnomusicologists have in many ways used musical uniformity and stability not just as things to be observed where they occur but as positive values in determining courses of action.

EXOTIC VIRTUOSO AT WORK

A man buttonholed me after the Indian concert. "Fine, fine, I enjoyed it. But how can you call it great music? These people didn't have to study counterpoint to produce those melodies." I could have told him that the musicians had had to study more than he could imagine. But there it was again, the athletic view of music so common among lovers of the Western classical tradition, the expectation of virtuosity. Virtuosity has been a value for ethnomusicologists as well, for to their minds, too, the best music is often that which requires great effort to produce, and perhaps requires effort also on the part of the listener. In composition and performance we want to see the virtuoso at work.

There is no doubt that effort, difficulty, complexity are major values in many non-Western societies as well. The direction of difficulty may vary. Manual dexterity, doing what is physically difficult, is widely esteemed in the West; a great violinist must be able to play passages correctly with lightning speed. Mental dexterity—a simple way of putting it—is also valued, and the composer who can draw musical relationships of the most complex sort, from Bach to Schoenberg, is praised whether the listener can perceive them or not. Precision and length of memory is also important to us, as witness the need to memorize concerts and repertories, notwithstanding the pride that our musical establishment takes in our complex notation system. The conductor who presides without score is praised for this ability. Other values, equally related to the athletic view, are more difficult to describe and isolate. In some tribal and folk societies knowledge of a large repertory is valued. In cultures stressing improvisation it may be the ability to manipulate a vocabulary of components or the courage to take risks in public. Sometimes difficulty shows up in other ways. Subjecting one's self to physical trials, as did Plains Indians in order to learn songs in visions and dreams, is a matter of effort and courage, and it is related to musical creation, but it is not difficulty of a specifically musical sort. Or the issue may not come up at all. Persian classical music, with the exception of the *chahār mezrāb* genre, is not actually thought by Iranians to be especially difficult, and the values associated with it are mood and contemplative quality. Of course the Iranian knows that one must study and practice, but the musician does not, most of the time, try to show that he can do things more difficult than another. The fact that his Hindu counterpart does, however, may be one of the reasons for the major differences in the otherwise related musics.

But as we have said, ethnomusicologists do not just study these values in other cultures, assessing the degree of virtuosity and its direction, but impose their own values as well. The results are sometimes curious. Some of us may exult in the discovery of the fact that a music once thought to be simple and studied only because it satisfies the criteria of age and stability turns out to have the internal complexity taken for granted in Western music and so satisfies the athletic criterion. We are sometimes staggered by the realization that our values are not shared. Eskimos who sing polyphonic and monophonic songs do not appear to regard the two kinds of texture as having different degrees of complexity or difficulty (Pelinski 1981:65–70). Like my friend in the lobby, ethnomusicologists took long to come to the evaluation of even Indian classical music as something equal in complexity, if monophonic, to the polyphony of the West. The ethnomusicologists of the West, finding in non-Western music complexities that are so much part of their own musical culture, may accord them greater importance than does the culture that produced it.

But back to definitions for a moment. Ethnomusicologists don't really like to be defined simply as students of non-Western and folk music, or students of the exotic, but in fact, when they select something to be investigated, it is most frequently what seems to them marvelous and strange. Some early definitions implying this have been discarded, but we sometimes continue to abide by their principles.

And so, despite the large amount of attention given to the need for studying Western musical cultures with the use of ethnomusicological techniques, little has actually been done. Where are the investigations of urban American concert life, of the country-and-western scene, of modern music in the cities of Asia and Africa? There are a few, but the majority of researchers have shied away, for related to the desire to study what is stable, old, uniform, complex, is a taste for a kind of exoticism. We have sought frontiers: North American Indians in the first decades of the twentieth century, unexpected finds of musical archaisms in Italy and the Balkans in the 1950s, South American lowland tribes and New Guinea in the 1960s. While one rarely hears that the music most different from the Western is actually better, it is such explicitly different music and behavior that have received the most attention. We could make a bibliography of works dealing with (to us) odd and even within their cultures rather insignificant phenomena, and project it against blank pages for the paucity of publications on the not-so-strange works that occupy the mainstream of the musical world. Interestingly, even when they turn their attention to Western culture, ethnomusicologists accept the values of the academic music world and turn them over, imposing on them this value of exoticism, in a reversal, as Seeger says (1977:51), of ordinary ethnocentrism. One is tempted to see snobbery on both sides, historians sticking to great works, ethnomusicologists to the weird. In ethnomusicological studies of India, China, Japan the classical music has come first. In all cases the urban, mixed, popular genres, Westernized and sounding familiar, definitely come last.

A small amount of literature of late has come to grips with the need for ethnomusicologists to look at themselves in order to understand their own behavior, their selection of subject matter and their methods (Blum 1975b, Gourlay 1978). Further examination will give interesting insights into the ways in which cultural values affect a discipline that sometimes claims to be above cultural constraints. Ethnomusicology attracts people who are committed to the principles of human, cultural, musical equality. But their selection of subject matter and approach have not always reflected this commitment.

Chapter 25

How Do You Get to Carnegie Hall?

FIRST, THE SCALES

In many societies, including in particular some of those of the South Seas, children and young people learn the important elements and values of their own culture through musical experience, and adults continue to undergo this process into old age (Ramseyer 1970:28–31). Among the people of Yirkalla, South Australia, only old men knew the entire ceremonial musical repertory (R. Waterman 1956:49), and the men in some North American Plains Indian tribes moved every few years into a new warrior society, learning each time new ritual and cosmological materials, education continuing well past middle age. Perhaps music has somewhat of this enculturative function everywhere, but if we have recognized the importance of music in the learning of culture, we have not paid much attention to the way in which people learn music, and surely not to the ways in which the elements and values of a culture affect the learning of music. If we are to take cognizance of all the music of a culture, we must be concerned with the way it is learned and even with the materials that are used to teach it.

In the general Western academic conception of music, learning plays a major role. Study and teaching at all levels come up in many American conversations about music. A large proportion of musicians make their living by teaching, and much of the population spends time and energy in formal learning of music, though in most cases not with the aim of professional musicianship. A large percentage of published music is didactic in nature. We care greatly with whom one studies music and how one goes about learning. If one could monitor all musical sound produced in this society, perhaps the majority would turn out to be for the purpose of learning, in some sense of that word. One reads general statements to the effect that in non-Western cultures, and certainly in nonliterate cultures, learning is "by rote," and there are of course writings about the nature of oral tradition. Often we know little more, even where other components of musical culture are admirably documented. Merriam (1964:145–64) was one of the first to look at the problem as a whole.

There are a number of issues for us to be concerned with; let us look at a few. Most important among them, perhaps: When music is transmitted, what is actually learned? While we assume that a musical system in written or oral tradition is transmitted more or less as a unified whole, there are probably certain things which people learn about a musical system that are most important, and which must be handed down, while others are left more or less to being picked up by chance without special attention or instruction. Another area of interest in this sphere of learning is how people practice, in what activities they actually engage when they are teaching themselves music, when they are carrying out the instructions of a teacher, mediating between the points of instruction and performance. Also related is the use and nature of special materials whose purpose is to help people learn—exercises, etudes, texts on the principles of musicianship. Then there is the identity of teachers and their role in society and in music. And we should know, in an intercultural context, how people in infancy acquire music, and the way in which a musical system, first heard by small children before they are in a position to reproduce it, is perceived by them. There are many other matters that might be of interest, but these issues are sufficient to illustrate a general point that I am trying to make, that a musical system, its style, its main characteristics, its structure, are all very closely associated with the particular way in which it is taught, as a whole and in its individual components.

"How do you get to Carnegie Hall?" asks the newcomer to New York, trying to find his way to a concert. "Practice, practice, practice," replies the Broadway wag. But there are actually many ways in which one arrives at the Carnegie Halls of world music and, like practicing as a concept, "learning music" means many things. One may learn pieces, or a way of performing, or the abstract fundamental principles of a musical system. Perhaps one learns how to listen and appreciate music, perhaps exercises such as scales, or short and easy pieces composed for learning. But each of these, or any combination, amounts to learning a musical system, and this in any case consists of many (and sometimes various types of) discrete units that a musician—composer, performer, improvisor, even informed listener—learns to manipulate. In one way or another the method of teaching breaks a system down into these basic units. In Western academic or classical music they may be pieces or compositions, or smaller ones such as chords, characteristic sequences of chords, or tones in a melody. In order to establish the grammar of a music, one must identify these units and plot their interrelationships. A study of how a music is taught by its practitioners can give insight into the nature of the grammar.

Western academic musical culture is surely one of the most specialized, in the sense that a musician is primarily involved in one aspect of the "music delivery" process—composing, performing, teaching, etc. It is further specialized in rather rigorously separating various kinds of musicians from each other. Singers in the United States are not even members of the musicians' union. Solo violinists rarely play in orchestras. A pianist is regarded mainly as soloist, or accompanist, or jazz ensemble musician. Yet the course of musical education is very much the same for all. One normally begins with an instrument (even if one ends up as a singer), and almost everyone at some point learns to play piano. Piano lessons normally begin with exercises, and the terror of serious beginning students is the requirement that, before all else, they must master the scales in all of the keys and always begin practice with them, with the knowledge that even if they become virtuosos, the need for practicing these scales will not abate. After becoming somewhat proficient on an instrument, one is likely to take up the study of music theory, a subject that is theoretical not in the general sense of the word but rather in that one learns material which does not apply directly to the making of musical sounds but is generalizable to all aspects of musical activity. Until recently, music theory concentrated almost exclusively on harmony and began with types of chords, its basic units.

In both cases, instrumental and theoretical, one first learns things that do not normally constitute music but that must be manipulated and extended in order to be recognized as components of music. Few serious pieces merely use scales or use chord sequences precisely in the way they are learned at the beginning of music theory classes. In Western academic music, then, much of the musical system is learned in the abstract. What the teacher first teaches is largely theoretical concepts and gymnastic exercises rather than units of a higher order, actual compositions.

In most of the world's cultures these compositions are imparted directly by the teacher to the student. Not so in Western academic music—or at least one does not learn the teacher's special approach. Piano students usually do not learn Beethoven sonatas *from* their teacher, with the latter first playing the piece for them, asking them to interpret as they have heard. Rather, the teacher usually confines herself more to general observations, to the instruction of technique and of the materials that make possible the learning of technique, and beyond that asks the students to imbibe Beethoven from the written page, learning, as it were, from the composer. I see our system of teaching as a combination of theoretical and practical materials, with the teacher playing a much larger role in the former.

BUILDING BLOCKS

In the classical music of South India the situation is somewhat similar. While the Western musician learns the basic system through piano and theory classes, the Indian is likely to learn it by exposure to vocal music, even if he turns out an instrumentalist. At the knee of the teacher he studies a long series of exercises that exhibit the characteristics of raga and tala, melody and rhythm, and juxtapose the two in various combinations. These exercises and some simple introductory pieces constitute or include fundamental units such as rhythmic and melodic motifs that are later used in learned compositions and, more important, in the improvisation which forms much of the core of musical performance. The emphasis is upon memorizing materials that will make it possible for one to improvise. Indian composers who, in contrast to improvising, create songs such as the extended South Indian kriti, whose structure has common features with improvisations, evidently undergo training similar to that of the performer. In the Western classical system, by contrast, performer and composer in part at least have rather different kinds of learning experience.

Western and Indian musicianship have in common the concept of discipline, the need to practice the building blocks of music for many hours at a time, directing one's effort only indirectly to what will happen in a performance. A pianist spends much time on scales and exercises, even with a Chopin recital coming up. South Indian singers do not spend their time only trying out various combinations of material and improvising, as they will have to do in public, but also devote hours every day to exercises, from the simple to the very difficult. Indeed, Indian musicians are evaluated by each other only in part in accordance with their musicianship as exhibited in performance or with their knowledge of repertory and in large measure by their reputation for disciplined practice and study, called *riaz* by North Indians (Neuman 1980:32–43). "If a musician wants to celebrate the genius of another musician, he will do so . . . in terms of practice habits" (1980:31).

To these two cultures, Persian classical music provides a contrast. The musician of Iran studies the *radif,* memorizing it precisely from his teacher's version, which may be similar but not identical to that of other teachers. The teacher is concerned only with the student's ability to reproduce what he sings or plays for him with utmost exactness. He does not explain the minutiae of the structure of the *radif,* although the student needs to learn these in order to engage in improvisation, the central activity in true performance. The student must deduce from the *radif,* with its many examples of variation, melodic sequence, extension and contraction of motifs, that its very structure is the guide to improvisatory procedure. Once the *radif* is memorized, the student is considered ready to perform without further instruction. He has learned a theoretical construct and must now suddenly move to improvisation. The Indian musician studies building blocks of varying degrees of complexity, units that gradually become increasingly like real music. The Iranian musician leaps directly from study at only one level of conceptualization into true performance.

By contrast with these three high cultures, we have much less detailed information about teaching and learning from those without musical literacy or articulated theory. The Blackfoot believed that humans learned music in two interconnected ways, from supernatural powers such as guardian spirits in visions and from other humans. The ideal is learning songs from the supernatural, and the concepts of learning and creating music are therefore close. The way in which songs are thought to be learned in visions, normally in a single hearing, influences the concepts that people have about learning music in an entirely human context. In the culture of the Blackfoot, once presumably means four times through, so some repetition is there, but the concept that the guardian spirit teaches you a song by simply *singing* it to you is important, and human teachers worked similarly. Thus a medicine bundle, with its attendant songs, was transferred from one person to another by a single performance of the ceremony, during which the new owner was expected to learn the songs. Today, when people learn songs from each other and recognize the process as such, they indicate that quick learning is desirable and certainly possible, though often violated by the ever-present cassette recorder. The standardization of form and the possibility of roughly predicting the course of a song from its initial phrase as teaching devices are also cases in point.

The varying emphases on various kinds of units and different aspects of the musical system given by a teacher help to identify the building blocks of the music. It is obvious that in northern Plains music the head motifs are the most important things, actually identifying the songs, which frequently do not have names. On the other hand, when I studied the *radif* with an Iranian musician, I was told that parts of it were important, and while these are stressed to some extent in the performances, the fact that they are singled out as important particularly in the teaching of the *radif* may well reflect ideas extremely important in the culture. Those parts of a *dastgāh* that tended to depart from the norm were often stressed by my teacher as being important, and in other respects, in Iranian culture, events or actions that departed from a norm were sometimes particularly valued. By a similar token, the fact that the Western music student learns a theoretical system based largely on a particular part of his repertory, that of the period between 1720 and 1900, indicates rather forcefully what we consider most important in our musical experience and contrasts interestingly with our tendency to prize innovation. While we are surely cognizant of the fact that melody and rhythm are of major importance to our own music-making, the fact that music theory has always stressed harmony indicates that perhaps of all the things that make our music properly an art, the system of harmony is one of the most important.

PRACTICE, PRACTICE, PRACTICE

Not only what is taught, but also the activities involved in learning, can tell us what is valued in a music. A few almost random examples: Western practitioners of art music have many techniques of practicing. For one thing, the repetition of a great deal of didactic material—scales, exercises, and etudes—is standard. Many musicians are unwilling to practice "real" music without first going through theoretical material of the above-mentioned sort. Just what the function of this theoretical material is may not be quite clear, but surely the concept of warming up mentally or physically is rather important. In India musicians have a similar approach to practicing, the daily repetition of exercises being an almost religious necessity, and the function of theoretical materials as building blocks for improvisation is clearer. Elsewhere again, among the Shona people of Zimbabwe, where virtuosity certainly also exists, the idea of warming up is combined with the introductory section of a formal performance.

In a second aspect of practicing, Western academic musicians try to memorize things that might not really have to be memorized, mainly in order to show ability to absorb musical materials. One might have thought that the development of notation could lead specifically to the opposite. Third, the habit of singling out short bits of music in order to repeat them indicates the great stress on technical proficiency we have developed in Western music. Indeed, a Western concert is to a large extent an exercise in mental and dexterous ability. The idea of doing something very difficult, of music as a craft, is highly developed. Such a view is also found in India, but to a much smaller extent than in Iran, for the tradition of learning the Persian *radif* was that one had to learn slowly because of the music's essential philosophical and mystical significance. The introduction of Western notation into Iranian music has always been controversial, partly because it made possible the learning of the *radif* very efficiently and very quickly, violating the belief that the music was in itself something to be contemplated. Nour-Ali Khān, for example, wished to teach only a very small amount of it to me every week, saying that it was important for me to play it frequently, to look at it from all sides, listen to it, examine it, contemplate it. Perhaps contemplation acts as a stimulus for students to learn to understand the way the structure of the *radif* teaches the techniques and concepts of improvisation.

What do we know about the way in which North American Indians practiced? There is evidence that those cultures in which the precise rendering of music for validation of religious ritual was very important also had systematic musical competition, practicing, and rehearsing. We are told this about the Navajo and the north Pacific Coast peoples (Herzog 1938:4, 1949:106–7; McAllester 1954:76–77; see also Frisbie 1980 for discussion of various cultures of the Southwest). Rehearsing was essential, mistakes were punished, rituals in which mistakes were found would have to be repeated entirely or in part in order to be valid. The northern Plains Indians took a somewhat less formal attitude. Having been learned largely from visions for the use of one person, music was more closely associated with the individual and private rituals, and therefore the control of the community over musical performance was less highly developed. Evidently a man who learned a song in a vision would use his walk or ride back to camp as an opportunity to rehearse or work it out. No doubt, actual composition took place along this walk; the inspiration from the white heat of the vision would be rationally worked out. Practicing took place at this point, and the song would be readied for presentation to the other members of the tribe. But since music was primarily a personal and individualistic activity and experience, practicing was not done systematically to any large extent and not much heed was paid to the accuracy of performance. Just as composing and learning are related concepts, composing and practicing overlap.

The introduction of Western notation to many non-Western cultures accompanied and perhaps caused changes in practicing. The various types of notation long used in Asian societies (Kaufmann 1967) have hardly been used for reading while performing, but have functioned as references and perhaps even more as aids to scholarly discussion of music (Hickmann 1970:45–47). Along with Western music, mainly in the nineteenth and twentieth centuries, came the idea of learning music visually rather than aurally. In Iran and India musicians critical of notation realized that it was more than a mechanical convenience, and that fundamental changes in the music system would result from its use.

GURUS, SPIRITS, MOUTHS OF BABES

One might expect notation to become so thoroughly developed that from it a student could learn an entire musical system without hearing it, and without human intervention. We haven't yet arrived at that point, and, indeed, the learning of music is almost everywhere an experience of intense relationship between student and teacher. The identity, social role, and approach of the music teacher is an important component of a socio-musical system, and ethnomusicologists have in recent times come to describe some instances very thoroughly. (See the following publications for examples: Neuman 1980, Berliner 1978, Tracey 1948, Daniélou 1973, Nettl 1974a, and in a very unusual way Mitchell 1978, in which an Indian singer describes his own learning in detail.)

It is interesting that in many cultures, including those used to illustrate this chapter, there is some difference between practicing musician and master teacher. To be sure, ordinary musicians do teach, but great teachers are often people who know material well but are not necessarily best at rendering it. The concept of the specialist music teacher actually exists in a large number of societies. In Western music we have, of course, a large group of professionals who do little beyond teaching. They are often people who are not highly respected and may be denigrated by performers and composers as people who have not made it in the practical field and are therefore relegated to teaching. Actually, society does not treat them all that badly. It is interesting to see that most performers are paid worse than teachers, that teachers develop certain kinds of job security not shared by performers and composers, all of which may be related to the low evaluation of music and the somewhat higher value of the concept of education. Interpreting much more broadly, it may be that in our culture the handing on of the tradition is regarded as more important than its expansion.

In India as well, great teachers are not necessarily great performers, but they are renowned for their *riaz*. For a performer it is important, even more than elsewhere, to be associated with a highly qualified teacher. The genealogy of student-teacher relationships is typically recited in introducing Indian concerts, and a performer is praised for carrying on the tradition of his teacher's gharana. It is therefore interesting to see that in the most recent period of Western culture the Indian concept of guru has come to symbolize the idea of devoted study and teaching. In fact, two terms are widely used in India, "guru" (originally associated with Hinduism) and "ustad" (of Muslim origin). The two concepts are no longer limited to religious or ethnic groups and are more or less interchangeable in actual use. But they represent two approaches to the concept of teaching (Neuman 1980:44–45), with both terms applied to the same person. The ustad, best translated as "master" or even "professor," symbolizes the technical expertise of the teacher, his musical ability and knowledge. The term "guru" symbolizes the teacher's role in molding not only the student's musical learning but also his adoption of an appropriate lifestyle, his absorption of music as a part of culture.

In the classical tradition of India one was expected to become a particular kind of person in order to be recognized as a musician. As modern and Western approaches to music teaching came to be used in the twentieth century, there developed a bifurcation between those who studied in the traditional way, with guru-ustad, and those who went to music schools, spending three years in a conservatory atmosphere taking courses with various professors and emerging with a B.A. The latter might be given credit for excellent knowledge and technique, but they were accorded little respect by those more traditionally schooled. It would seem that they lacked the close personal association, comprising much more than simply music, with the figure of authority.

Normally, music teachers are human, but some, like certain figures in Indian music history, have become mythological figures, the subjects of stories of incredible accomplishment. Ustad Alluddin Khan, father of the modern development of North Indian classical music, is said to have mastered eighty instruments. Another musician was said to have practiced daily for sixteen hours without interruption. Of course there are also many legends about the ability of master musicians to affect the course of nature and history through their control over ragas. Stories about the power of music are almost universal, and familiar from the figures of Orpheus and

Tamino, but in India the powers of the great teacher seem to be particularly stressed. In yet other cultures we find the music teacher to be a directly supernatural figure. The Plains Indians learn their songs from beings who appear in dreams, and the concept, though not the process, of teaching songs appears very prominently in folklore and mythology. But in modern Blackfoot culture there is also a sharp distinction between individuals who, in guru-like fashion, know the older traditions but do not perform in public, and others who sing for social dances. A mixed system of supernatural and human teachers is described by Berliner (1978:136–45) for mbira players of the Shona of Zimbabwe. The spirits are thought to encourage students and players in dreams, and also to teach the instrument and its repertory. The human teachers of the Shona use a number of ways of approaching their task. Some (Berliner 1978:140–41) break down the music into component phrases, teaching them one at a time. Others teach the part of each plucking thumb separately, then combine the two. Berliner stresses the lack of a common method, which goes no further than an insistence that there be a proper approach (whatever that may be in the individual case), and on developing a good memory. This diversity of method must be related to the highly individualistic approach that Shona musicians have to their instruments and their repertory. Again, the musical system results from, but also determines, the way of teaching.

In connection with the techniques and technicalities of studying to be a musician, we must also consider the fact that individuals learn the fundamentals of their own music very early in life, somewhat as they learn language. They learn to recognize music as a category separate from other types of sounds and, it seems likely, to distinguish new sounds that belong to a particular music from those that do not. Actually, what little is known about the process of music acquisition comes almost exclusively from Western culture. It is an area surely important to a comparative study of all musics, particularly in view of what has been said about the effect of learning systems on final products.

Ethnomusicologists have been variously concerned with children's music, and while this is a subject for Chapter 26, I mention it here because it provides clues to the understanding of music acquisition. Most societies recognize it as a separate category that differs in style from the rest of the repertory. Further, various kinds of children's music around the world have certain things in common, particularly short forms, restricted scales using intervals from semitone to minor third, repetitive rhythms. In Western culture there is some evidence that children learn to recognize the components of music in a determined order (Nettl 1956a, c; Werner 1917; Serafine 1980). Certain intervals and rhythmic patterns come before others, some of these appearing in the sounds of babies under a year old and preceding the distinction that eventually appears between singing and speaking. But there is also an order to the learning of music proper. To an extent this is determined by the styles of music to which children are first exposed, but there are certain things young children seem to learn to do correctly earlier than others; for example, major seconds seem to be sung in tune before minor seconds. Given the small amount of data, the idea of a correlation between what is learned earliest among Western children and what is most widespread among musical characteristics of the world seems suggestive. It may be that children learn first the universals of music, in the particular form in which they appear in their own musical systems, and then go on to those traits of their music that are less widespread in the world (Nettl 1956a). The implications of the relationship are certainly not clear, but a similar phenomenon was, long ago, noted by Roman Jakobson (1941) in regard to language learning: those phonetic distinctions most widespread in the world were also those that could first be made by children in their learning of their own language. Some fundamental problems of our field could perhaps be solved by what comes from the mouths of babes.

Many of the sounds humans produce while teaching and learning are not properly music, but they must be studied as part and parcel of a musical culture.

Chapter 26

Vive la Différence

THERE IS REALLY VERY LITTLE DIFFERENCE . . .

This is the beginning of an ancient joke. More seriously, the bulk of ethnomusicological literature looks at the musical culture of a society as something essentially homogeneous. Here we wish to explore a music as something consisting of contributions from a number of diverse elements of society—men, women, children, members of minorities. It goes without saying that these groups of people differ greatly, but in some ways we may derive insights from a brief consideration of women, children, and minorities as similar groups, In many societies they exist outside the most powerful and influential segments of society, but their impact on the musical culture of the entire society may be significant and often overpowering.

People seem to believe that the differences between men and women are few but good. Actually, in ethnomusicology the roles of male and female scholars have been closer to equal than in most other academic fields. Throughout its history the contributions of female scholars have been great. Among the early or older ones we find prominently the names of Frances Densmore, Alice Fletcher, Helen Roberts, Gertrude Kurath, Maud Karpeles, Eta Harich-Schneider. Later, many many others joined this group, and it would be futile and undignified to make a list. The field of North American Indian music research in particular seems at times to have been dominated by women. Also, the membership of the Society for Ethnomusicology is about 50 percent female, women accounting for a high proportion of authors, editors, readers of papers, and contributors to the profile of the field.

Of course, on the whole, women in ethnomusicology have shared the problems of women in all academic fields. One may then ask why, in comparison to other humanistic disciplines, they have made disproportionately large contributions to ethnomusicology. Perhaps the model of a few early figures who arrived by chance and through personal interest and determination, such as Densmore and Fletcher, stimulated the others. Franz Boas encouraged women to enter anthropology in its early American years. Considerable female participation may be characteristic of new and yet unestablished fields; ethnomusicology was not taken as seriously as ancient history and Latin philology for example, thus permitting women easier access. The fact that American and English women are particularly well represented in this group may also be related to the substantial relegation of music in these cultures to women, and to the fact that music departments in North America were first introduced at women's colleges.

A question arising from these facts is, however, whether the large proportion of women in ethnomusicology has had an effect on the nature of research; whether theory, method, approaches are different from what they would have been, had women accounted for a much smaller proportion of the scholars. Among the kinds of effects one might expect are certainly the use of women as informants, the explication of a women's musical culture or subculture where such exists, and the analysis of a total musical culture from the viewpoint of the female segment of the society.

On the whole, but with significant exceptions, this hasn't happened. Good or bad, it seems fair to say that in quality and style of ethnomusicological research, there is relatively little difference between the work of male and female. This may result from the dominant role of men in determining approaches and methods, and perhaps be related to the disinclination of humanistic scholars to deal with population groups on the basis of biological differences. Male and female ethnomusicologists have described musical cultures largely as they were presented by male informants, and usually assumed that the picture was complete. But of course a vast number of songs and pieces performed by women is found in ethnomusicological archives. A considerable portion of the literature does deal with the musical culture of subdivisions of society that are biologically determined—I have in mind children, who are biologically different from adults in a different sense, or racial and ethnic minorities. So if we are to consider briefly the question of women's music in any society, it makes sense to do so in the context of various other divisions of society that are biologically determined. After all, if men and women behave differently, the substantial biological differences must be taken into account as possible causes.

In most cultures the life of women is quite different from that of men. Practically everywhere there is a basic division of labor and social responsibility. One would therefore expect women in most societies to occupy distinctive musical roles and to have distinct repertories. Some cultures make it clear that the differences are there, even on the surface of musical taxonomy. The song repertory of Serbo-Croatians is divided into "men's" and "women's" songs, the first comprising epics, and the second, all kinds of lyrical songs that may be sung by women or men (Bartók and Lord 1951: 247). But, generally speaking, ethnomusicologists have not frequently tried to contrast what women do musically with the activities of men. They've usually focused on the total repertory of a society or community, happy to get what they could, seeking informants as was possible, regardless of sex. On the surface, at least, it appears that in many societies men engage in more musical activity than women. This at any rate is the impression one gets from the bulk of field collections and publications, and while such a state of affairs may be a result of the somewhat larger number of male fieldworkers, the collections by female scholars reflect more or less the same tendency. Whether men really are more active musically than women is difficult to determine; it may simply appear so because in many cultures men are the people who live a more or less public life and are thus responsible for dealing with the outside world—which includes ethnomusicologists. The fieldworker may encounter difficulty in attracting female informants.

A sampling of field experience: Catherine Ellis describes the beginning of her work with a specifically women's ceremony among Australian aboriginal people (1970:101):

> Initial contact with Andagarinja women's ceremonies was made in 1963, at the reserve in Port Augusta. The women were very shy, and hesitated to perform at all. It was not my suggestion that they sing, but rather their own husbands', who were themselves familiar with the idea of the collection of their songs, and who recognized the value of the preservation of the women's songs in this manner, by a woman collector. At first the women sang (their efforts interspersed with a great deal of giggling) and the men stood by and encouraged them, and offered explanations of the songs. After only one session, the women came to me independently and asked if I would go away from the camp with them, where they could sing their secret songs to me without fear of the men overhearing.

Here it was obviously necessary to single out women's music; they had, at least in part, a separate repertory. The men of the society valued it and recognized its importance, but recording it was certainly facilitated by a female collector. Male collectors may be much less fortunate, as illustrated by a somewhat similar event that occurred among Amish people in Indiana, where a female colleague and I had attempted to persuade women to sing. They were too shy, felt it necessary to ask their husbands for permission, which was denied, though what they were to sing were hymns that could be sung by mixed congregations, normally led by men. Again, among the Blackfoot I found it difficult to persuade women to sing alone, although they sometimes sang along with men, helping them, as they put it, in a repertory that consisted of songs normally sung by men. In Middle Eastern Muslim societies, where women are frequently shielded from any kind of public exposure and associate mainly with relatives, the field recordings seem to reflect mainly men's performances. But the existence of a rich separate women's repertory in the Middle East is illustrated by Racy

(1971), who in a study of Druze funeral music from Lebanon, his home country, presents a repertory of thirty-nine women's songs and only thirteen men's songs, and stresses difference in performance practice and style. On the other hand, Densmore (1918), working with the Sioux, seems to have persuaded several women to sing songs that do not, in function or style, differ from those of men. Among Indians of the Southwest women have been shown to participate in ritual dramas in a large variety of ways, including performance, composition, sponsorship, criticism, and response to modernization (Frisbie 1980:319–21).

From this smattering of examples it is clear that women's performances have been recorded frequently enough. But for the vast majority of cultures it is an as yet incomplete task to separate out what is regarded as specifically women's music in order to see to what extent and how it differs from the music of men, in content or style. What little is known seems to indicate that while content may differ, major distinctions in musical style should not normally be expected. Thus in the group singing of the northern Plains Indians minor significant differences in singing style between men and women can be identified but not in scale, form, rhythm.

There are societies in which the social distinctions between men and women are symbolized by the development of different forms of language for the two groups. Among them are the Nootka, Eskimo, and the Yahi, the people of Ishi, where two easily separable dialects of the language were used, one by men, the other by women and by men when speaking to women. Women, however, knew and understood the men's dialect (T. Kroeber 1961:21–31). When songs of this extinct people were sung by Ishi for the anthropologists T. T. Waterman and A. L. Kroeber to record, women's songs were included and labeled, but their musical style appears to be like that of the men's songs; indeed, variants of a tune would appear in both men's and women's songs. Of course, the women's singing style, if distinct, is unknown to us. But we could guess that the sharp societal division by language was not reflected in musical style or even, as far as we can tell, content.

There are societies in which the social roles of men and women are not so different, with many activities readily shared. Folk singing in recent Western society is a case in point. In rural England and North America the same songs were sung by men and women at private and semipublic occasions such as informal social gatherings. There is evidence that in many societies the bulk of the work of transmitting the cultural tradition is the province of women, who, after all, are mainly concerned with the early rearing of children. Thus it is interesting to see that in the thousands of publications and recordings of Child ballads examined by Bronson (1959–72), the majority were sung by women. Female representation in many of the larger collections of European folk music is about half, and it often seems to be particularly the women who know older material. Scandinavian and Scottish collections devoted to the songs of one informant have been made from the singing of women. Farther from modernized Western Europe, the songs recorded by Vikár and Bereczki (1971) indicate the superior position of women in the preservation of the oldest part of the Cheremis folk heritage.

In maintaining a musical tradition it is clear that cultures vary greatly in the relative prominence of women compared to men. Among the modern Blackfoot, women probably sang little (my informant regarded it as evidence of immodesty) but "helped" the men, had some songs of their own, seemed to know—though not to sing—many of the men's songs. In Asian Indian classical music females rival men in fame as singers but have a clearly subordinate role as instrumentalists. In the Middle East women specialized in genres such as funeral songs, provided musical entertainment at courts, became world-famous singers in classical and popular music after the coming of mass media, but never became a major force as instrumentalists. In Northern European folk music they seem at times to have been the major carriers of the general tradition. In Australia they had their separate secret ceremonies. Among the Havasupai they had a separate repertory of songs (but also sang men's songs; Hinton, personal communication), stylistically not readily distinguishable from the rest. Ames and King (1971) indicate a small but specifically delineated role for various types of female musicians among the Hausa. Given the large number of female ethnomusicologists, if an unbalanced picture of world music has been presented, scholars of both sexes bear the responsibility.

INTIMATE RELATIONSHIPS

If there is in some cultures such a thing as a separate women's music, as well as a variety of ways in which women participate in a generally known repertory, there is also the relationship of the sexes to be explored as a factor in the determination of the general musical style of a society. These intimate relations have played a role in the history of ethnomusicological theory. Two suggestive examples:

Curt Sachs (1943:40) proposed a basic difference between men's and women's singing in tribal societies: "If singing is indeed an activity of all our being, sex, the strongest difference between human beings, must have a decisive influence on musical style." In dancing, he noted, men strive for strong motions forward and upward while women's motions are diminutive; they move "inwardly" and keep to the ground. "In the same way, the sexes also form opposite singing styles." He goes on to give examples: "Boat songs of the Eskimo rest on the third; when women row, they sing the same songs with infixes to avoid masculine stride." It remains to be seen whether these examples represent a chance distinction; they certainly are not part of a universal norm.

But the distinction of musical styles suggested by Sachs, between widely ranging melodies with large intervals and songs with narrow ambit and small intervals, may have another sort of sexual significance. There was once a long-held belief that certain societies are dominated by principles of male psychology and physiology and, indeed, dominated by men; in others, the same is true of the female. Associating agriculture with domination by women, Sachs wrote, "the more a people is marked by planter culture, the more closed is its dance; the more completely it is totemistic and patriarchal, the more it will make use of the leap" (1937:33). Sachs found it possible to equate small steps in dance with small musical intervals and symmetrical forms, and leaps with large intervals and wildly irrational forms. Thus "the same contemplative, patient, imperturbable, introvert disposition which through ascendancy of female characteristics creates a predominately feminine culture . . . makes itself felt in dance and music through close movement and through an urge toward the static and the symmetrical. The alert, impatient, vivid, and impulsive extrovert disposition which leads to the dominance of the masculine qualities in a culture and to hunting and cattle-breeding, is reflected in dance and music through expanded movement and through the urge toward the dynamic and the asymmetrical" (1937:203). Later Sachs suppressed the forcefulness of this view, though he did not entirely abandon it, still in his last book maintaining that "women seemed to prefer smaller steps, just as they do in dancing" (1961:62).

The belief that some societies are dominated by men and others by women has for many decades ceased to have much credence in anthropology. "Matriarchy has never existed," says Harris without reservation (1971:582), and in more detail: "Despite the persistent popular notion that the presence of matrilineal descent groups reflects the political or economic domination of men by women, it is the men in these societies no less than in patrilineal societies who control the corporate kin group's productive and reproductive resources" (Harris 1971:328). Sachs's attempt to classify musics by sexual dominance may not be tenable, but nevertheless suggests that one may instead relate musical style to the quality of relationships between the sexes. Sachs begins, after all, with a hypothesis that men and women are prone to sing differently; observes that in some societies all people sing in a way that appears to him like that of men, and in others, women; and concludes that this is a function of type of relationship, that is, which sex dominates.

The thread was later picked up by Alan Lomax, who after examination of a broad sample of world music finds correlation between musical style and six aspects of culture, two of which are severity of sexual mores and balance of dominance between male and female (1968:6). In several publications and many statements he stresses his belief that relative equality of women and men produces well-blended ensemble singing and a relaxed, unembellished vocal technique, while suppression of women produces, in both men and women, a nasal, narrow, ornamented vocal technique. Lomax places the burden of musical style differences among cultures very heavily on the quality and type of relationship between the sexes. His findings are best taken as tentative; the sampling is somewhat uneven, and other factors may not be given enough recognition. But the general conclusions should be taken seriously. Nowhere has there been found a rigid separation of repertories, and everywhere do people hear and seem to understand the music of the opposite sex. Yet it seems reasonable to believe that the great differences in musical style among the peoples of the world can in good measure be attributed to the way in which people relate to each other, and a major aspect of this relationship is sexual.

IN LEAGUE WITH THE DEVIL

The nature of music being what it is, quality of relationship as a determinant of style makes more sense than trying to identify the dominant sex. There are too many examples of music as a central domain of "antistructure" in which the forces governing other aspects of life are contradicted. The special role and reputation of musicians as eccentrics or even social deviants (Merriam 1979) attests to the powerful musical roles of nondominant segments of society. It may seem odd to associate women with strangely behaving men as objects of ethnomusicological inquiry. But if the world's public music-makers are most frequently men, the carriers of musical tradition, the teachers of children are more typically women. But the men emerge as a curious lot, strange people with odd habits, and surprisingly often they are members of ethnic or racial minorities. Like women, they are often objects of discrimination. So if we contemplate women's music and musical behavior as a separate category in ethnomusicology, one approach may be to take a perspective similar to the study of the music of minorities.

A vast proportion of ethnomusicological literature deals with minorities, but there is little in the way of generalization or theory about the musical behavior of these groups and about the special role of music in minority cultures (see Qureshi 1972 and Porter 1978 for attempts). I shall skip over the technical problems of defining minorities, and avoid devoting much space to such obvious things as the fact that every person is in some way a member of one or several minorities. What I am concerned with is population groups, numerically small, who share a language and a culture that contrasts substantially with those of the dominant population among whom, in some sense, they happen to live. Additionally, I am concerned with population groups that are distinguished from the majority by descent, and sometimes only slightly if at all by culture or language. It seems further logical to divide all of these groups into (1) minorities that have been established as such within a dominant culture for a very long time, perhaps beyond the reach of ascertainable records, such as the Jewish populations of Iran; (2)

those that became established through immigration but have retained minority status, such as the German-descended Amish of the Midwest; (3) those that have immigrated from one area to another, occupying the role of minority temporarily while completing a process of acculturation to the dominant culture, including many European ethnic groups in North America, such as Irish and Scandinavians; and (4) those who have become minorities by virtue of becoming surrounded by a newly arrived majority, such as the North American Indians. In all of these cases the minority lives with or in a dominant majority. But there are also other kinds of situations: the caste or community in the culture of India, each a minority where there is no true majority, or the black people of South Africa, numerically not a minority but dominated by another group.

While it might be difficult to show that musical style is directly affected by minority status, we should first ask just what is *the* music of a minority. It's related to an earlier question, what indeed is *the* music of any culture group? To answer it, one might include all of the music the group knows and in some way uses, or only that part of the total musical experience the groups regards as uniquely its own and with which it identifies itself. In the case of certain majorities these two ways of defining a culture's music may substantially overlap. In the case of minorities there is normally a difference. They may participate in the music of the majority, which is in a way also their music, but they identify themselves with a particular repertory that is not shared.

American Indian peoples of the northern Plains readily distinguish between Indian music and white music, both of which they perform and hear. The two are symbolic of the cultures in which the Indians move. "White" social contexts, such as drinking in a bar or going to a Christian church, are accompanied by white music performed by Indians. The traditional contexts of Indian music may be largely gone, but when the people are engaged in activities in which they want to stress their Indian identity, such as pow-wows, social dances, or gambling games, they use Indian music.

Similarly, Iranian Jews residing in Israel participate in the general, largely Western-derived musical culture of Israel. But in social contexts in which the Iranian heritage is stressed—and this extends from weddings to social gatherings to which only Iranians are invited, carried out in an unmistakably Iranian middle-class style—the music is Persian. We find this trend also among Greek-Americans, Irish-Americans, etc. What is interesting in all of these cases is the great importance of music in the minority-specific social contexts. When the minority engages in activities whose role is to symbolize group identity, to strengthen the integration of the group, music is essential and almost ubiquitous.

But what of the specifically musical relationship between the minority and the dominant majority? It depends on many factors such as the degree of stylistic similarity between minority and majority musics. A people who have been thrown into a minority situation may react musically in various ways, but in many cases they are affected by the musical style of the majority. The folk music of Greek-Americans has adopted Western European urban instruments, functional harmony, ideas of ensemble playing. The people of the Andean Highlands, a cultural though not a numerical minority, have adapted their orchestras of panpipes and their melodic style to a Western harmonic base. But it is also well known that minorities sometimes react by maintaining their unique style and, indeed, exaggerating the difference between it and that of the majority.

A typical minority seems to wish to maintain, even in the face of massive contrary evidence, the belief that it has a unique music with a separate style. In a meeting with a group of urban aboriginal people in Australia, I heard complaints about the loss of their traditional culture, aboriginal language, ceremonies, songs, customs. Nevertheless, they keenly felt that they were a separate group from whites, who were of course treating them as a minority. I asked whether there was not some kind of music they thought was really their own, with which they identified themselves *as* aboriginals. The surprising answer, from a man with whom others were quick to agree: "The Old Rugged Cross." But this is a song also sung by white people, I insisted, and the reply was, "Yes, but we sing it differently," so they proceeded to gather around the piano to show me. I could find no difference between this performance and what I expected of white Australians and, unless more thorough analysis shows otherwise, suspect that the *idea* of having a unique *style,* if not a unique repertory, was important to them as a symbol of group identity.

In many societies minorities play a special musical role vis-à-vis the majority. One may ask whether there is a relationship between this fact and the tendency of many minorities to turn particularly to music as an integrative device. In the Middle East the general suspicion especially of instrumental music among devout Muslims evidently led to the partial turning over of musical activity to religious minorities who do not share the proscription. Chief among these are Jews, who, in Iran and Arabic countries, appear for a long time to have held a disproportionate number of musical positions. In early twentieth-century Iran they played roles as professional entertainers at weddings and other Muslim events, participating in and developing the Iranian musical systems, in towns and small cities such as Kerman and Yazd. More recently in Teheran they have played a role somewhat disproportionate to their numbers in the classical music but a still much larger one in the popular music, which was regarded as even less desirable by observant Muslims. As far as I can tell, other minorities did not stand out as much, but some of them also had special roles to play in music. Thus in the village culture in northeast Iran the Kurds, who typically lived in separate villages close to and associating with Persian-speaking ones, were thought in the folklore of the culture to be particularly great singers and also, for that matter, particularly great lovers. The Armenians, largely an urban minority in Iran, maintained a somewhat separate musical culture, but in Teheran they were also specialists in the making of instruments. Interestingly, they did not specialize in retail sale of instruments, which was more of a Jewish trade, nor were they in disproportionate numbers performers. To be sure, the lines of these specialties in Teheran were not drawn tightly, and there were also Persian-speaking Muslims among musicians, instrument makers, and salesmen.

A special musical role for minorities is, of course, found in the West as well. There is much speculation about the reasons for the large number of Jewish musicians; their minority status may itself be a contributing factor. Similarly, black Americans have interacted with whites more in the field of music than in many other aspects of life, in ways too numerous to mention, and other minorities, Irish, Italians, Germans, have at times played special musical roles within the Anglo-American context. Actually, the idea of the foreign musician, of music as something especially reserved for strangers, is a widespread phenomenon in European history. One could even suggest a distant relationship between the popularity of the gypsy musician in European villages and the tendency of American symphony orchestras to have foreign conductors (or at any rate hardly ever selecting one of their own members for the job). In a broad band of cultures from South Asia westward, music is viewed with some suspicion by ordinary folk: entertainment, associated with acrobatics and sports in medieval Europe and modern America; something not for serious people; a difficult activity, properly learned only by strange individuals who may even be in league with the devil (Halpert 1943) in order to learn their uncanny skills. It is something reserved in many societies for people with low status who are nevertheless indispensable. As Merriam (1979) suggests, it is frequently the province of deviants—people who engage in unacceptable behavior, debtors, promiscuous persons, homosexuals, drunkards, drug addicts, keepers of odd hours, lazybones, temperamental figures, but then also of members of strange cultures and minorities, people who somehow behave differently from and in ways unacceptable to the majority. This concept of the musician as an unconventional character is so widespread that if we look at the issue in the broadest possible terms, the questions arise whether this may not be related to the universal and ancient role of music as a mediator between humans and the supernatural. Certainly the special role of minorities in the musical life of dominant cultures seems to be part of a larger picture involving various components of the role of music and musicians in society.

THE YOUNGEST MINORITY

The children of the world participate in music-making in various ways, but societies differ in the degree to which they create a separate repertory for children or designate certain songs or pieces as children's music. Merriam's survey of children's music learning (1964:147–50) indicates that their activities are largely directed to learning the music of adults. But children are also musically separate, the youngest minority. In Western cultures their songs are a separate category with a distinctive musical style that, according to Herzog (1935b:10), is the same all over Europe "no matter what the specific traits of the individual folk music styles in which they are carried along." As for other cultures, a brief look at ethnomusicological literature indicates that there are special children's songs in Chinese (Reinhard 1956:170), Japanese (May 1963), Arabic (Simon 1972:24), Nootka Indian (Densmore 1939:229–41), Sioux (Densmore 1918:492–94), Ashanti (Nketia 1974:36), Australian (Kartomi 1980), and Venda (Blacking 1967) repertories, to name just a few. A glance at examples of this children's music indicates that much of it is quite different from that of adults. Some of it is just simpler, comprised of limited range and scale and of short, repetitive forms. But simplicity may not be the only diagnostic trait of distinction. Blacking's findings in an African tribe are suggestive: "I was also puzzled by the apparent lack of relationship between the styles of children's songs and other Venda music. This seemed illogical in a society in which there was no nursery culture, and in which children were frequently involved in adult activities, though as junior spectators. . . . Children's songs are not always easier than adult songs, and children do not necessarily learn the simple songs first" (1967:28–29). Similarly, in writing about Australian aboriginal children, Kartomi (1980:211) says: ". . . this difference in style between adult and childlike music exists . . . because the children perform, reproduce, and create according to their own sense of priorities as children. . . ."

If children are capable of learning music equal to that of adults in complexity, why does children's music frequently have a separate style? It may have to do with the quality of adult-child relationships. Throughout the world children's music has several uses. There are lullabies or other kinds of songs sung by adults to quiet and amuse children; songs associated with children's games and with play; and music, perhaps instrumental, that is itself play. There are songs intended to help children learn their own culture, with the words of proverbs or stories from which one may draw conclusions to guide behavior. And there is music intended to teach rudiments of musicianship. In only a few cases might one find a truly separate children's tradition as suggested for the Australians, and for the Venda by Blacking (1967: 29), who believes that it is "conceivable that many of the songs were composed by children, and not handed down to them."

In most cases it seems to be adults who decide how children should sing. They teach a separate style, but one they share for particular purposes. The simple style of European children's songs is found in some children's repertories elsewhere, in American Indian, Middle Eastern, and Oriental cultures. It is also present in certain groups of adult songs, typically those of games (e.g. gambling songs of North American Indians) and of outmoded rituals (e.g. vestiges of pre-Christian seasonal rites in Europe). In Europe, too, simple children's instruments such as rattles, the bullroarer, flutes without finger holes are found in entertainments descended from serious ceremonies no longer in use and eventually attached to Christian feast days such as St. John of Austria's, Christmas, and Easter.

One can only speculate why adults should have chosen a particular kind of music to give to children. There may be everywhere the assumption that simple music is appropriate because of children's abilities and preferences. Beyond this, and perhaps more significant, is the need to symbolize for children their separate status in society, a status necessarily devoid of many adult responsibilities and privileges. Children's songs thus logically related to earlier rituals, no longer functional or taken seriously, but a heartwarming reminder of the cultural past, as a child is a reminder to the adult of his own past.

In many cases, then, children's songs are not simply a kind of *gradus ad parnassum* through which one learns, in stages, the music-making capacity of adults. The separateness of children's repertories is actually of considerable significance. Blacking concludes that it marks children as a separate social group, that children do not perform adult music because "each social group has its associated style of music, its audible badge of identity" (1967: 29). Society treats children, even musically, like a minority, and they look upon themselves as such, continuing even to teen-age to symbolize the social separateness by adhering to their own music, often to the despair of parents desperately fighting the superior power of the loudspeaker. If ethnomusicology claims to study all of the world's music, it must, in addition to explicating the central repertory and style of a society, make special efforts to understand as well the music of those subdivisions of society that live outside the mainstream, and this includes the musical cultures of minorities, of children, and of the female half of the population.

Chapter 27

Cultural Grey-Out

WE ARE LIVING IN A NEW ERA

At cocktail parties of ethnomusicologists one often hears about the demise of musics. If there is one commonly held fear, it is that in the twentieth century we will see the complete homogenization of world music, resulting in incredible boredom and the de-employment of all ethnomusicologists. Although never on as large a scale, musical homogenization has surely occurred before, as presumably in the expansion of Chinese culture in the fourteenth century, the Islamic wars of conquest, or perhaps the course of Aztec or Inca expansion. The twentieth century is different. We are living in a new era, having entered a period of history in which the world is, in a special sense, a single unit of culture. In ethnomusicology we have come to view the twentieth century as a unique period. Since about 1880 the relationships among many of the world's cultures have become so close that cultural interaction, viewed through music, has become a major focus of ethnomusicological research. We have come full circle: beginning with attempts to see the whole musical world in its diversity and its unity, we moved to a high degree of specialization, but now that the world has, as we often hear, shrunk to a "global village," we are again becoming interested in the course of human music, particularly the most recent segment of its history.

The literature that bears on this subject is almost unlimited; for bibliography and discography, works by Laade (1969, 1971a) and Günther (1973) should be mentioned. Although little interest was evident before 1950, Frances Densmore (1934) was one of the first to attend to the issue. By then the practical effect on non-Western musicians and musical life had become a factor, resulting in a landmark conference of Middle Eastern and European musicians and scholars in Cairo (1932), and later of others including one in Teheran (1961) (see Archer 1964b). The parts of the world first subject to thorough study of the interaction of traditional and Western music were those in which Europe and sub-Saharan Africa were musically juxtaposed.

By the 1970s Western influence had been shown to be powerful even in such genres as Javanese gamelan music, once thought to be relatively immune (Becker 1972). The study of the interaction of musics has more recently given rise to a subfield called urban ethnomusicology, whose studies are based on the characteristic of modern cities to be composed of a variety of ethnic groups, in varying degrees affected by modern Western musical culture (see Nettl 1978a). A paradigm that may serve as a point of departure for systematization of the ethnomusicological study of the twentieth-century world is Wiora's (1965b:147–97) description of the last of his four ages of music as "global industrial culture." Wiora sees the twentieth century, perhaps rather pessimistically, as a period of musical homogenization.

Recently often affecting an uncaring attitude, ethnomusicologists have actually spent much time sorrowing inwardly at the disappearance of musics, of styles, genres, instruments. It is difficult not to share this sorrow. But I would so far hardly agree that the greying-out of musical diversity, foreseen by Alan Lomax (1968:4), is actually taking place. True, the typical Third World music now available for study is the result of a mix of stylistic and conceptual elements from traditional and Western cultures. Far from turning our back on these results of the misfortunes of pollution, we should pay attention to them because they constitute the bulk of non-Western musical experience, and because they provide us with an opportunity for observing the musical outcome of cultural interaction at first hand. Whether the twentieth century is such a bad period for world music is arguable. After all, one of its characteristics is the enormously increased availability of many kinds of music to most people. The musical experience of the average individual is much broader than in the past. The hybrids and mixes could be interpreted as enrichment, and old traditions as a class have not simply disappeared. What is perhaps most significant is the diversity of reactions of other cultures to the introduction and importation of Western music and musical thought. In this chapter it is this large group of reactions with which we are concerned.

I should like to view the musical world not so much as a group of musics but as a large network of musical interrelationships. In discussing ways in which musics affect each other, the extant ethnomusicological literature revolves about two major concepts, relative complexity and degree of compatibility. These concepts overlap, and both involve us in difficulties of definition and interpretation. One implied reason generally accepted for the great influence of Western music upon all others is its presumably great complexity, and that of its accompanying technology and economic power. This assumption derives in part from Western views of world music but also from the nature of the particular Western music that has generally been presented to non-Western cultures—classical music to a small degree, classical-derived or related military, church, and popular music to a much greater extent, rural folk music hardly at all. Using the idea essentially as a quantitative concept, the presumably great complexity of Japanese and Indian music and the greater simplicity of North American Indian music have been considered as predictors of musical response. As the reader knows, we have no precise measurements of musical complexity, but the literature is full of intuitive statements not to be rejected out of hand. If we equate complexity in some way with quantity of components and of their interrelationships, we may be justified in making some working hypotheses. For example, a purely oral tradition will normally be simpler than a partially written one (see Nettl 1956d); a tradition with music theory of an articulated sort, more complex than one lacking it; and traditions with professional training of musicians, more complex than those that lack it. We may, indeed, be able to rate overall complexity of a musical system on a continuum and get reasonable agreement even among observers from a variety of cultures.

But according to the standard ethnomusicological literature, a more important predictor of musical history than complexity is the compatibility of musics; in somewhat simpler words, this may just mean degree of significant similarity (see Wachsmann 1961; R. Waterman 1952; Katz 1968, 1970). Some classical studies (e.g. R. Waterman 1952, Merriam 1955b, J. Roberts 1972) have tried to show that African and Western musics are more compatible than are Western and American Indian, bringing about certain musical effects. To be sure, the assessment of compatibility comes from examination of the results, perhaps in the end a circular argument.

QUESTIONS OF MOTIVE AND ENERGY

In all of these considerations the desires or motivations of non-Western societies as expressed in their musical behavior are of great importance. The motivations are not exclusive; one people may have many, and social groups, strata, and individuals will differ. In any one instance one or two motivations may dominate. As a beginning, let me suggest three major *types* or groups of motivation. At one end of a continuum would be the desire to leave traditional culture intact, survival without change. We have noted the fact that practically all cultures have changed quite perceptibly in the twentieth century. Yet the desire for unchanging survival may have been present here and there; it is thus possible that the people of Ishi wished such survival and preferred disappearing from the face of the earth to relinquishing their tradition.

Complete Westernization, that is, simple incorporation of a society into the Western cultural system, is the opposite end of the continuum. While it has perhaps not happened anywhere in its extreme form, some Australian aboriginals claim that this has indeed been their fate. There are cultures that have in essence become part of the West, even though the population was once culturally non-Western and is biologically descended only in small measure from Europeans. Mexico might possibly serve as an example. I am not maintaining that Mexican culture is indistinguishable from European, but the difference between Mexican and Spanish is possibly no greater than that, say, between Spanish and Norwegian. Of course, the concept of *a* Western cultural system may be a vast oversimplification.

Between these extremes, a third kind of motivation is modernization, a term used in many ways in the literature of anthropology and history. Here I define it as the adoption and adaptation of Western technology and other products of Western culture, as needed, simultaneously with an insistence that the core of cultural values will not change greatly and does not match those of the West. Perhaps most non-European societies wish to move in this direction (see Steward 1967 and Singer 1972 for discussion and illustration). These three approaches to motivation are purely typological constructs; reality no doubt exhibits a vast variety of degrees and combinations.

Music may, of course, simply change in accordance with these broad cultural trends. A modernizing culture may also simply modernize its musical system; another, trying to survive without change, may seek to prevent Western music from making a dent in its structure and sound. We assume a norm of parallel motion between music and the rest of culture. But we have already noted that music in certain cases may play a contrastive role. A number of examples bring out the fact that while a people is being driven to move in one major direction, to channel all of its various activities to accomplish one main goal—for example, economic survival, military victory, adoption of a new cultural system—this same people may use music to provide relief, to say to itself, as it were, that there is also a desire for the opposite, to protest against a fate forced on it. While certain contemporary North American Indian peoples may wish to live like white Americans, traditional music and dance, in particular, underscore for them their Indian identity. Cultural minorities may be particularly susceptible to this kind of bifurcation between music and other forms of behavior. So, while we may wish to identify the major goals of peoples in their confrontation with Western culture during this century, and while we may find in these an explanation of the development of musical styles and musical behavior, we should also consider that sometimes music, because it *is* music, does quite the opposite, provides the counterpoint necessary for equilibrium.

Non-Western musics have been changed under the impact of the West in a number of ways. Many of the changes can be interpreted as strategies for survival, attempts to change aspects of the old system in order to save its essence. They differ by culture, but in common they address the need to balance advantages of old and new. A way of explaining the variety of strategies, which result in specific musical responses along a single continuum, is to introduce a concept I shall, for lack of a more elegant term, call "musical energy." In each culture, I would hypothesize, a certain maximum amount of energy is available for musical creativity and activity. The term "energy" may be fashionable, but others such as "capacity" or "limit" might also be applicable. In any event, it must be stressed that what is involved is a theoretical construct which makes comparison convenient, and which accompanies the hypothesis that additions to the musical culture of a society require adjustments in the tradition already present.

There may be an absolute human maximum of musical energy, but each culture no doubt has its own. Some peoples are presumably willing to expend large amounts of energy on musical activity at the expense, perhaps, of visual or verbal art, or of technology. Others keep music to a minimum, forging ahead or at least holding their own in other aspects of life. Again, one culture may be prepared to expend much energy on the musical activity of a few of its members, providing them training, pay, equipment, status, and a docile audience; others expect less but closer to equal involvement on the part of the majority of their populations. Now, if this concept has any validity at all, we certainly know very little about it, but it may have some use in the comparative study of musics, for my basic assumption is that the amount of energy that a culture is willing to expend on music remains more or less constant over long periods, changing only slowly. We must thus assume that additions to the musical life of a people must be balanced by loss, by ways of achieving conservation of musical energy.

We may therefore think of the responses that non-Western peoples have made to Western music essentially as choices. A society might thus choose between on the one hand allowing a large part of a musical repertory to be forgotten, and on the other hand permitting it to remain intact but in simplified form, requiring less energy to learn and maintain. Another may divide the population into those who maintain the tradition but learn little of newly introduced materials, and others who do the opposite, reducing the number of individuals who retain the tradition. Finer points of musical change can also be explained in this framework. When new material is introduced, it must replace, in *some* way (but there are many options), part of what was there before. This notion of a maximum and more or less fixed amount of musical energy accounts, along with the other determinants discussed above, for the variety of responses; this idea also makes it possible to put the many kinds of changes—changes in individual pieces of music, attitudes, styles of entire repertories, and the substitution of parameters and of compositions—so to speak under one umbrella. It is the base line for comparison.

EIGHT LIMITED RESPONSES

Here now is an initial group of eight non-Western responses to Western music, put together on the basis of analysis of actual music—pieces, recordings—produced in non-Western societies, but not necessarily on the basis of field observations of behavior. Some apply to entire repertories, some to individual pieces or performances, and others only to specific aspects of one piece. They overlap and are present in varying degrees and proportions in any one culture. They are examples of the kinds of things that happen when musics confront each other and vie for the allegiance of one population, and in a sense they represent the rejection mechanisms of musics being invaded by transplants. Other groupings and classes have also been suggested (see, e.g., Kartomi 1981).

The type of response about which we have heard the most in the way of laments is total loss, *abandonment* of the musical tradition. As already stated, this seems rarely if ever to have happened quite so completely. It seems doubtful that there is a population which has remained biologically alive but whose musical experience has been completely replaced, without trace, by the Western counterpart. Certainly sectors of repertories have disappeared, and something fairly close to abandonment has probably occurred here and there. But unless we define as "Western" all of the music *affected* by the West and now practiced in non-Western nations (conceivable in certain folk evaluations), we must admit at least the coexistence of traits, traditional and Western, in the same piece of music, or the coexistence of pieces in two contrasting styles, in the experience of the people. Indeed, in some instances one may feel that specifically music was singled out for survival in comparison with the abandonment of other forms of traditional behavior, but this tendency in certain societies has already been touched upon. The coming of Western music has not stamped out the existence of non-Western styles; it may have reduced them, changed them, recast them for different uses, but in some they have continued to exist in changed form.

This statement is close to what may be taken as a value judgment, something from which I wish to refrain. Whether what has happened is good or not must be judged by the people to whom it has happened. I am making an "etic" statement. There may be peoples who believe that their traditional music has disappeared, outsiders who still detect its presence in substance or vestige notwithstanding. Changes in instruments, disappearance of traditional religious uses of music, changes from three-quarter tones to semitones in a scale may make all the difference in the world to their owners. So, admittedly, the statement that non-Western musics continue to exist everywhere, like the majority of descriptions of the other responses below, stem from general, comparative, and, of course, Western-oriented views which try to take into consideration, but which perforce cannot adopt outright, the views of all or indeed any non-Western cultures.

If complete abandonment of traditional music has not taken place, there certainly has been the abandonment of components, or substantial *impoverishment,* resulting from shifts in musical energy. Some North American Plains Indian cultures once had a vast quantity of religious music; today there is little but, instead, much music for a small number of social dances. The total traditional repertory of a typical Indian tribe seems now to be very much smaller, in number of songs or of song types, than in the past. The repertories in Japanese classical music have shrunk. Mervyn McLean (1965) similarly describes the process and function of "song loss" among the Maori. Elsewhere instruments are lost and replaced by Western counterparts; traditional technology is lost and replaced. Standardization (as in the forms of the Plains Indian songs) and simplification (as in rhythmic patterns of African drumming in the Caribbean) may release energy to be expended on the absorption of Western music. A point to be contemplated is that if we divide music into sound, behavior, and concept, in many cultures there is maintained a distinct musical sound, based at least in part on its older musical tradition, but the musical behavior has often been abandoned in favor of Western counterparts—concerts, paid musical professionalism, records and radio, sitting on chairs to perform, clapping after a performance. The traditional concepts of music, how it comes about, what it is, how it is defined, its major role in life, what power it has, all of this may, curiously, be closest to being abandoned by the cultures of the world in favor of Western concepts of music.

Another response to Western music is the artificial or perhaps *isolated preservation* of the tradition in a restricted environment, relegation, as it were, to a museum (see Archer 1964b for a sample of approaches). The mainstream of functional musical life of a people changes to Western patterns, and in some cases to Western musical forms merely influenced by the native tradition. But the music that a people regard specifically as their own traditional heritage is preserved in isolated pockets of existence, often under the protection and patronage of government agencies. The population recognizes this music but regards it as something belonging to the past or as a musical ideal rarely experienced and reserved for special purposes, events, social classes. Musical organizations are created and tour the nation in order to exhibit its own musical past. In some countries, such as South Korea, distinguished older musicians are formally given special status as "national treasures." The desire is to preserve this older music without change, to give it a kind of stability that it in fact probably did not experience in the past, and to do this at the expense of permitting it to function as a major musical outlet for the population. Sometimes this sort of artificial separation and preservation was used as a temporary expedient. In Iran, for example, classical music was for a time preserved under the aegis of the Ministry of Fine Arts; then, in the period after 1968, it again began to play more of a role in everyday life and thus began to undergo more change. This temporary preservation of music by artificial means, followed by reintroduction in new forms into the mainstream of musical life, seems also to be a characteristic of twentieth-century Western musical culture. We have preserved older European classical music, medieval, Renaissance, Baroque, and certain kinds of folk music in educational institutions and with government support, in a decidedly static and museum-like environment. Some of it is now again in the mainstream.

We come to a group of phenomena more readily found in small segments of repertories and unlikely to be representative of the musical behavior of an entire society. *Diversification* of styles in unified contexts is the combination of diverse elements into a single musical or social context. Thus Iranian and Indian films may include, in one musical number or in a single sequence of pieces, a number of different styles originating in various regions and exhibiting among themselves several different kinds of response to Western music. *Consolidation,* related to but also in a sense opposite to diversification, has occurred often as a function of the creation of nation-states from what once were groups of politically separate entities, tribes, chiefdoms, kingdoms, or of the change of a people from independence to colonized minority. The establishment of a reasonably compact and, in terms of musical energy, not very demanding North American Indian style to replace what was once a large variety of tribal repertories is an example. So also is, in another sense, the establishment of African repertories presented by especially trained troupes of musicians and dancers whose purpose is to consolidate a nationally recognized music from a number of once more distinct traditions.

An interesting although probably not widespread development of the nineteenth and twentieth centuries is the *reintroduction* of musical styles to their place of origin after a sojourn elsewhere. For example, African music was taken to various parts of the New World by slaves, changed and developed through contact with Hispanic and British music, and returned to Africa, influencing modern African music. The music of overseas Indians may in time have a similar effect. *Exaggeration* is a phenomenon resulting from the Western listener's expectation of great exoticism in the sound of non-Western music. In some non-Western cultures music appears to have changed in order to conform to the European and the Westernized native's conception of what the tradition should be, stressing the difference and emphasizing what is, from the European viewpoint, an exotic musical sound. Ruth Katz (1970) shows certain modern Arabic music to have exaggerated traits that Westerners would regard as particularly Arabic; modern Plains Indian songs seem also to have exaggerated their peculiarly Indian characteristics, possibly in deference to ideas originating with white Americans. Finally, a response evident in only a few pieces of music, but worthy of note nevertheless, is the *humorous juxtaposition* of Western and non-Western elements, humorous in the thinking of Western, Westernized, and traditional listener. Music stimulating this reaction seems to have arisen in certain American Indian and African cultures, in some of the film music of India, and in the performance of Western classical pieces in popular style by Mexican mariachi bands.

SYNCRETISM, WESTERNIZATION, MODERNIZATION

We turn now to three broader concepts relating non-Western to Western music, processes of which the responses in the preceding list may be a part: syncretism, Westernization, and modernization. In their original uses these concepts do not readily form a group, but as processes they can be distinguished in part by their use of centrality of traits in a musical style, that is, the proposition that a style is comprised of certain traits essential to its identity and others that are more expendable (see also Chapter 4).

Syncretism is defined as "fusion of elements from diverse cultural sources" by the *Encyclopedia Britannica,* but is used more specifically in anthropology to explain the growth of culturally mixed phenomena when the elements are similar or compatible (see Merriam 1964:313–15). It has been widely used in ethnomusicology, most notably to explicate the broad spectrum of styles in African-derived cultures from the New World to Africa. It has also been touched upon as a contributing factor in the evolution of modern Middle Eastern, Indian, and African musics. The development of mixed or hybrid styles is, of course, a characteristic of twentieth-century world music, and these seem to have developed most readily when the sources are similar, compatible, and, most important, share central traits.

Many societies are torn, musically, between attempts to maintain their tradition in a modern environment compatible with Western-derived political, social, and economic institutions, and the desire to enter the Western cultural system without completely changing the traditional music. Evidence for this tension, which no doubt can be traced to the nineteenth century (see Günther 1973) or even earlier, is readily found in government documents, newspapers, statements by informants of all types. Circumstantially it can be discerned in the musical product as well. The distinction between modernization and Westernization is made by anthropologists at least in theory, although the difference is not always clear (see Rudolph 1967; Singer 1972:265–66, 386–89; Steward 1955:334–35). It can be of value for musicological work.

Some societies appear to have changed their traditional musical culture in the direction of the Western by taking from the latter those elements they consider to be central to it; this is Westernization. The centrality of these characteristics in such a situation must, I think, be somehow agreed upon by both cultures involved in the exchange. Foremost among them are functional harmony, prominence of the large ensemble, emphasis on the composed piece performed more or less unchanged, simple but stable metric rhythms. These features are incorporated whether they are compatible with the traditional music or not. In the case of modernization, compatible but noncentral elements have been adopted. Scales have been slightly adjusted, concert situations altered, notation introduced, patronage systems changed. In both instances the musical actions may be interpreted as adaptations of the musical system for survival. I present this distinction between Westernization and modernization only as a working hypothesis against which a plethora of known facts and as yet uncollected data would have to be tested. But clearly, it seems to me, some non-Western music has been changed to make it in the minds of everyone concerned a particular kind of Western music. In other cases the desire has been to create a new, adapted, modernized version of the original. (See Deva 1974:145–48 for an example of this juxtaposition.)

Thus, to summarize rather rigidly and as simply as possible: syncretism results when the two musical systems in a state of confrontation have compatible central traits; Westernization, when a non-Western music incorporates central, non-compatible Western traits; modernization, when it incorporates noncentral but compatible Western traits.

However great the effects of the Western musical world on all cultures have been, there are related events, such as the diffusion of Middle Eastern styles into the rest of the Muslim world in Asia and Africa, and the effects of non-Western musics on Western culture, that should also be investigated by ethnomusicologists. The twentieth century may in fact not be all that unusual. It is the laboratory in which we find ourselves, providing tantalizing opportunities for observing the different reactions of a variety of cultures faced with essentially the same musical event. For the time being, the conclusion of such study can only be that as long as music remains a major symbol of cultural identity, a high degree of musical diversity will continue in existence.

Postlude

The Grand March

SHOULD ETHNOMUSICOLOGY BE ABOLISHED?

A friend accompanied me to a meeting of the Society for Ethnomusicology. "Good heavens, it certainly is colorful," was his comment upon seeing professional-looking types delivering papers in one room, a group of dashiki-clad Americans giving their all to a set of drums, bells, and rattles before an obviously empathic audience in the next, and some students in jeans looking at kits for making sitars at a table in the hall. Then, upon attending a panel discussion, he gave a different sort of comment: "They're beautiful people, but each of them knows something different, and there doesn't seem to be much that they all know." Perhaps a bit of exaggeration.

At another meeting: "The development of ethnomusicology is the most significant thing that has happened in musicology since 1950." A statement made by a music historian. And at a third: "Should ethnomusicology be abolished?" Title of a panel. No one wanted to remove the ethnomusicologists from their teaching positions, libraries, laboratories, or relegate their publications (all of them, at any rate) to the memory hole. But wasn't it perhaps time to call them, again, just plain musicologists, or anthropologists, or whatever it was that they came from?

The implication of these vignettes is that there sometimes appears to be little to hold ethnomusicology together and much to tie it to older, more established fields. It is a tempting suggestion. One might be able to separate those interested in serious scholarship from those seriously interested in hearing interesting music or learning to play and sing. There seem to be many people doing many things, some intellectually more removed from each other than any one of them is from Western music history, music theory, anthropology, folklore. As for the scholars, their approaches and their substance can be of great service to these disciplines, and they would in turn benefit from exchange. It is gratifying to realize that now, more than in the past few decades, the ideas which are the stock in trade of ethnomusicology have begun to have an impact on related fields.

If there seems to be little that ethnomusicologists have in common, the disciplinary identity of ethnomusicology, its own unity and its relationship to other fields, is certainly one of the major issues of the past but even more of the present. There are those who would like to unite (or reunite) all branches of musicology, and this may well be the proper direction to be followed in the future. My purpose here is not to make recommendations. But I would argue that the great diversity of ethnomusicology is in some measure illusory. If one is to understand certain important aspects of the state of music research of the present, one must recognize that ethnomusicology has a unified past and a tradition which is to a considerable degree its own. It has its separate history of ideas, its culture heroes and heroines, its landmarks, its moments of glory and of pathos, its own grand march of history.

To be sure, this history is at many points closely tied to that of other disciplines. Vincent Duckles (in Brook and others 1972:39) suggests that seven main motivations set the stage for musicological inquiry in the nineteenth century and earlier, including among them the music of the ancients, the discovery of world music, and the discovery of national song, all clearly leading to what later became ethnomusicology, along with more specifically historical drives such as chant reform and the arts of custodianship. On the other hand, anthropology has also been involved. The role of musical scholarship in the work of the German diffusionist school of anthropology has been pointed out (Chapter 16), as has the degree to which American anthropologists such as Boas and Herskovits affected the work of scholars such as Herzog, Waterman, and Merriam.

But the history of ethnomusicology is not simply as a subdivision of musicology and/or anthropology. Nor is it simply the sequence of events in the research of individual world areas. If it makes sense to view the history of our field as a unit, it is so because there have been events of general significance to all who identify themselves with it.

In what has come to be one of the most popular interpretations of his field, Thomas Kuhn (1970) describes the history of science in terms of a series of paradigms, defining these as "accepted examples of scientific practice—examples which include law, theory, application, and instrumentation together—that provide models from which spring particularly coherent traditions of scientific research" (1970:10). Scientists come to agree on the fundamental nature of a phenomenon or a process. Once established, however, such a paradigm leads to dissatisfaction, then further research, diversity of opinion, confusion, even chaos, and eventually the formulation of a new paradigm, often the result of a forceful statement by one scholar, a single major finding resulting in a revolution. The nature of scientific progress is the solved problem, and there is agreement that a solution works while science moves on to new problems, continuing its own grand march.

This interpretation of the history of knowledge may be labeled as the "sudden breakthrough" theory, and its opposite number can be conveniently called "gradual insight." The latter is perhaps more readily applied to the humanities, in which the appearance of specific findings of broad, general significance to an entire profession such as art history, literary scholarship, or historical musicology may be difficult to identify. One might best interpret the history of ethnomusicology with the use of the "gradual insight" approach, but I suggest that there have also been breakthroughs, that paradigms have periodically been established, some of them eventually found wanting and replaced, others becoming part of the permanent intellectual arsenal.

The question is not whether ethnomusicology is a science but, rather, whether there are serious generalizations of substance, procedure, method, and theory upon which ethnomusicologists have agreed at the beginning of their work, and whether there are others upon which they later came to find themselves in agreement. One could hardly find a group of scholars more contrastive to the community of chemists, physicists, and biologists. For a century or more there have been a great many scientists, many even in subspecialties like high-energy physics or microbiology. But there have always been very few ethnomusicologists. Scientists have rigorous and fairly unified kinds of training; ethnomusicologists come from several disciplines—or from none. International and intercultural communication among scientists has been relatively easy; they speak more or less one language. Communication about music is mired in the emic-etic dichotomy. The facts that members of different societies think and speak differently about music, and that scholars coming from these societies may disagree about their relationship to the musical substance which they study, are not to be ignored or obviated but are things of which one takes positive advantage. Kuhn suggests that scientific paradigms appear in some of the world's great classics, such as Newton's *Principles* or Lavoisier's *Chemistry*. Ethnomusicology must be more modest: it has a shorter history and is, let's face it, of less immediate importance to most of the world's people. And in ethnomusicology it is often hard to identify consensus.

Given these caveats, let me briefly examine some aspects of the history of ethnomusicology along lines suggested by Kuhn's *Structure of Scientific Revolutions*.

THE STRUCTURE OF REVOLUTIONS

If there have been revolutions, they are not sudden or convulsive, but the way in which the field has changed indicates that they have nevertheless come about. My point of orientation is the four fundamental beliefs of ethnomusicology, stated in my "Prelude" and used as the principle of organization for this volume: ethnomusicology as the comparative study of musical systems, as the study of music in culture, as the result of field research, and as the comprehensive study of all sorts of music and musical phenomena.

Contributions to ethnomusicological insight go back to the Renaissance (see Harrison 1973). But it was in the period in which ethnomusicology developed as a distinct field, between 1880 and 1900, that a group of first paradigms was established. Most important among them was a consensus to the effect that in certain ways, at least, it was reasonable to consider all musical systems as equal. The implications of cultural evolutionism, leading through various stages to the rational tonal system of modern Europe, had been dominant in the nineteenth century and has, for that matter, continued its effect. But at some point there emerged the belief that all musical systems—as represented particularly by the parameter of scales and tone material—were equally natural or, if you will, equally unnatural. The influential publication that resulted in this acceptance was A. J. Ellis's study *On the Musical Scales of Various Nations* (1885), and from that time stems a general belief in relativism as at least the intellectual point of departure.

There followed a new paradigm, represented by the work of Hornbostel and his colleagues and students, in the period shortly after 1900: the establishment of a method of description and analysis more or less applicable to all cultures. This was developed further by Herzog, who refined the method by taking the relationship of music and culture into account; by Kolinski, who formulated ways of making rigorous comparisons of scales, forms, rhythms; by Wiora, who added comparative study of musical content to that of style; and later again by Lomax, who added emphasis on singing style and performance practice. It is interesting that these approaches to analysis and comparison were, for these scholars, by-products of work directed elsewhere.

But if the broad, comparative approach of Hornbostel was followed by these scholars, it was also in large measure gradually replaced, in the work of others such as Jaap Kunst, Mantle Hood, and J. H. Nketia, by a more culture-specific approach. Thoroughly established in the 1950s, it regarded the study of individual musics on their own terms as paradigmatic. A new wave of comparative study appeared in the 1970s, and elements of the older approaches are still with us. But the bulk of the ethnomusicological population in its view of music itself has shifted directions several times in the twentieth century.

The study of music as an aspect of culture is harder to pinpoint historically. As a diagnostic criterion it belongs among the first paradigms, as indicated in Guido Adler's designation of ethnomusicology as having "ethnographic purposes" (1885:17). Two paradigmatic directions appear early in the twentieth century: the designation of cultural context for each recorded artifact by many collectors, and the use of music-culture relations for historical insights by the German diffusionist school. After several decades the proposition of a view of ethnomusicology primarily as the study of music in culture, by Waterman, Merriam, and a large group of American scholars following in their footsteps in the 1950s and early 1960s, and culminating in Merriam's *Anthropology of Music* (1964), represents a major shift resulting from dissatisfaction with the emphasis on comparatively oriented descriptions of style. This change was mainly responsible for an increased interest in processes and in the discovery of patterns. The thesis that musics, like species, change to accommodate changed musical and cultural environments, a return of sorts to evolutionist views discarded in the 1930s, is illustrative. A new paradigm in the making may be the gradually expanding view of music as something to be studied mainly as a symbol or set of symbols.

There is no doubt about the first paradigm of ethnomusicology as based upon fieldwork. It is the invention of sound recording in the 1880s leading to the first recordings of American Indian music by Walter Fewkes in 1889, and the recognition of its importance by the leaders of the mainstream (Hornbostel and Abraham 1904). Soon there was added a second fundamental paradigm: ethnomusicology as the study of music by an outsider of the culture. This continued in effect until the 1950s, when new principles appeared: first, that in addition to making recordings and observations, fieldworkers could and should learn, by studying performance, participation in the cultures they study; and second, that non-Western scholars, insiders to the culture, should be accepted to the field. Both of these changes—and they, too, truly had the impact of revolutions—owe much to the work of Mantle Hood.

It seems likely in the period before and shortly after 1900 that the ultimate purpose of scholars was to study all of the world's music. If direct statements to that effect are lacking, publications by such people as Ellis and Hornbostel certainly display a catholic taste. But the concept of authenticity was also present, with its insistence that each culture had a music that was properly its own, with avoidance of the exceptional and the mixed. The paradigms along this line of inquiry move us to more sophisticated views of the musical world, and to a greater inclusiveness.

When, perhaps around 1900, comparative musicologists first began to have a sense of the musical map of the world, they tended to divide musical cultures into two groups, the "traditional" ones, which were assumed to have a high degree of stability, and Western music, which changed constantly. This belief is rarely articulated but is clear in the essentially synchronic approach of early ethnomusicological literature. At some point this view changed to one that substitutes a continuum for the dichotomy, the rapidly changing Western music at one end, some highly stable tribal musics at the other, most musics of the world at various intermediate points. The change in views was again gradual, but perhaps the pendulum had swung by the early 1960s.

If the history of ethnomusicologists' views of musical change is the establishment of a dichotomy later replaced by a continuum, this same kind of history characterizes other aspects of research. When we began to know something about world musics, we established a dichotomy between classical and folk traditions. Again, more recently, we have come to realize that to split the world of music into these two types is unrealistic, that musical cultures adhere in varying degrees to the diagnostic features of folk (or tribal) and classical musics. In step with this realization, ethnomusicologists have lately but with considerable force come to include what we usually call popular music. Similarly, the once powerful difference between notated and oral traditions has shrunk to a continuum extending from the absolutely written of some of the newest Western art music, to more traditional Western notations, to Oriental notations that are used much less in performance, on to traditions with oral notations, and so on to the completely oral. And the acceptance of universals as possible concepts for research in the 1970s draws the field further yet into the insistence that all of the world's music is involved.

THE SHAPE OF THE STORY

The comprehensive history of ethnomusicology remains to be written, and when this is done, my group of examples of paradigms will be corrected and surely greatly expanded. But even those I present demonstrate that the history is not simply a sequence of events, one discovery or one monograph leading to the next, but that it has a structure, times of stress and of consolidation, diverse activity alternating with concerted effort. Two more aspects of this history are worthy of brief mention here.

In viewing research in individual areas of the world, one may see a shape of peaks and valleys, the peaks representing not paradigms proper, since they need not have broad methodological or theoretical significance, but rapid advances of knowledge. The study of North American Indian music begins with a cluster of significant works in the decade 1880–90: the first scholarly book on the subject by Baker (1882), the first solid monograph on one tribe by Stumpf (1886), the first recordings in 1889. Some dozen years later, on another peak, we find the application of Hornbostel's descriptive paradigm to Indians (Abraham and Hornbostel 1906), major monographs of great scope by Alice Fletcher (e.g. 1904), serious books for the general reader by Natalie Curtis (1907) and Frederick R. Burton (1909), and the first major monograph by Frances Densmore (1910). In the middle 1930s there appeared several major studies by George Herzog (1934, 1935a, b, 1936a, 1938) and Helen Roberts's (1936) significant designation of musical areas. In the late 1940s and early 1950s we find a clustering of publications including important studies by McAllester (1949, 1954), and much field research by Gertrude Kurath, Alan Merriam, and Willard Rhodes. The

1970s saw a renewed interest in the subject, including many studies of music in culture, modernization and Westernization, historical and archeological work. Thus, the shape of the history of scholarship in one world area.

The general history of ethnomusicology, however, taking together the paradigms of theory and method and the ups and downs of individual continents and cultures, can be seen as comprising three general periods, vague and overlapping but nevertheless much in evidence. They are in some ways related to periods in the course of historical musicology, anthropology, folklore, and perhaps the humanities and social sciences at large. But primarily, they reflect the broad progression of one field with a high degree of cohesion.

The first period is one of initial examination and discovery, and of generalization. It is characterized by the attitudes that non-Western and folk musics are worthy of study, that comparisons among them can be made and historical insights gained from them, and that a relativistic approach is best. It includes separation of field and laboratory work, and the insistence on the collection and preservation of authentic artifacts. We still have much from this early period with us. But soon (perhaps beginning by the 1930s) a period of specialization replaced it. The leadership of a Hornbostel, trying his hand at many cultures, was replaced by individual and idiosyncratic research by many scholars, each devoted perhaps throughout a career to one or two of the world's societies. This approach seems to have culminated in the 1950s and 1960s, but it too is very much with us still.

More recently, perhaps beginning in the middle 1960s, a third period emerged. It is one of consolidation of gains from the many specialized studies, and of resumed and increased interest in generalized theory and methodology. Old problems are brought back and viewed with greater sophistication: the matter of origins of music, universals, comparative study. There are attempts to be nomothetic about the way in which music is related to culture. Analytical approaches from linguistics and semiotics begin to play a major role. Scholars are still interested in how a particular culture and its musical system work, but this interest is tempered by a conviction that their own approaches and procedures must be carefully honed to produce credible findings and interpretations.

This is a history with great diversity of ideas and methods, but with a mainstream of paradigms articulated by a dominant group of scholars whose work is of abiding value but which was periodically the object of intellectual revolutions. Ethnomusicology is closely related to other fields of inquiry, perhaps even part of them, but it also brings to these other fields a unique perspective. With its group of distinctive problems and approaches, it has made and continues to make distinctive contributions.

Publications Cited

ABBREVIATIONS

AA — American Anthropologist
AM — Asian Music
EM — Ethnomusicology
IFMC — International Folk Music Council
JAF — Journal of American Folklore
JAMS — Journal of the American Musicological Society
MQ — Musical Quarterly

Aarne, Antti A.
1961 *The Types of the Folktale. . . .* trans. and enlgd. Stith Thompson, 2d rev. ed. Helsinki: Suomalainen Tiedeakatemia.

Abraham, Otto, and E. M. von Hornbostel
1903 "Tonsystem und Musik der Japaner." *Sammelbände der internationalen Musikgesellschaft* 4:302–60.
1906 "Phonographierte Indianermelodien aus Britisch-Columbia." In *Boas Anniversary Volume.* New York: G. E. Stechert, pp. 447–74.
1909–10 "Vorschläge für die Transkription exotischer Melodien." *Sammelbände der internationalen Musikgesellschaft* 11:1–25.

Adams, Charles R.
1976 "Melodic Contour Typology." *EM* 20:179–215.

Adams, Richard N.
1975 *Energy and Structure: A Theory of Social Power.* Austin: University of Texas Press.

Adler, Guido
1885 "Umfang, Methode und Ziel der Musikwissenschaft." *Vierteljahrschrift für Musikwissenschaft* 1:5–20.

1930 Ed., *Handbuch der Musikgeschichte.* 2d ed. Berlin: H. Keller.

Allen, Warren Dwight

1939 *Philosophies of Music History.* New York: American Book Co.

Ambros, August Wilhelm

1862 *Geschichte der Musik.* Breslau: F. E. C. Leuckart.

Ames, David W.

1973a "Igbo and Hausa Musicians: A Comparative Examination." *EM* 17:250–78.

1973b "A Socio-Cultural View of Hausa Musical Activity." In Warren L. d'Azevedo, ed., *The Traditional Artist in African Societies.* Bloomington: Indiana University Press, pp. 128–61.

Ames, David W., and Anthony V. King

1971 *Glossary of Hausa Music and Its Social Contexts.* Evanston, Ill.: Northwestern University Press.

Amiot, Père

1779 *Memoire sur la musique des chinois.* Paris: Chez Nyon l'ainé.

Ankermann, B.

1902 "Die afrikanischen Musikinstrumente." Dissertation, University of Leipzig.

Anttila, Raimo

1972 *An Introduction to Historical and Comparative Linguistics.* London: Macmillan.

Apel, Willi

1969 *Harvard Dictionary of Music.* 2d ed. Cambridge, Mass.: Harvard University Press.

Archer, William Kay

1964a "On the Ecology of Music." *EM* 8:28–33.

1964b Ed., *The Preservation of Traditional Forms of the Learned and Popular Music of the Orient and the Occident.* Urbana: University of Illinois Institute of Communications Research.

Baily, John

1976 "Recent Changes in the Dutar of Herat." *AM* 8/1:29–64.

Baker, Theodore

1882 (1976) *On the Music of the North American Indians.* Trans. Ann Buckley. Buren, Netherlands: F. Knuf.

Barbeau, Marius

1934 "Asiatic Survivals in Indian Songs." *MQ* 20:107–16.

1962 "Buddhist Dirges of the North Pacific Coast." *Journal of the IFMC* 14:16–21.

Barkechli, Mehdi

1963 *La musique traditionelle de l'Iran.* Teheran: Secretariat d'état aux beaux-arts.

Barnett, H. G.

1953 *Innovation: The Basis of Cultural Change.* New York: McGraw-Hill.

Barry, Phillips
1910 "The Origin of Folk Melodies." *JAF* 23:440–45.
1914 "The Transmission of Folk-Song." *JAF* 27:67–76.
1933 "Communal Re-Creation." *Bulletin of the Folk-Song Society of the Northeast* 5:4–6.
1939 *Folk Music in America.* New York: Works Progress Administration, Federal Theatre Project, National Service Bureau Publication no. 80-S.

Barth, Frederick
1969 Ed., *Ethnic Groups and Boundaries.* Boston: Little, Brown.

Bartók, Béla
1931 *Hungarian Folk Music.* London: Oxford University Press.
1935 *Melodien der rumänischen Colinde (Weihnachtslieder).* Wien: Universal-Edition.
1959 *Slovenske l'udove piesne.* Bratislava: Akademia Vied.
1967 *Rumanian Folk Music.* Vol. 1. The Hague: M. Nijhoff.

Bartók, Béla, and Albert B. Lord
1951 *Serbo-Croatian Folk Songs.* New York: Columbia University Press.

Baumann, Max Peter
1976 *Musikfolklore und Musikfolklorismus.* Winterthur: Amadeus.

Bayard, Samuel P.
1942 "Ballad Tunes and the Hustvedt Indexing Method." *JAF* 65:248–54.
1950 "Prolegomena to a Study of the Principal Melodic Families of British-American Folk Song." *JAF* 63:1–44.
1953 "American Folksongs and Their Music." *Southern Folklore Quarterly* 17:130–38.
1954 "Two Representative Tune Families of British Tradition." *Midwest Folklore* 4:13–34.

Becker, Judith
1972 "Western Influence in Gamelan Music." *AM* 3/1:3–9.

Becking, Gustav
1928 *Der musikalische Rhythmus als Erkenntnisquelle.* Augsburg: B. Filser.

Belzner, William
1981 "Music, Modernization, and Westernization among the Macuma Shuar." In Norman E. Whitten, ed., *Cultural Transformations and Ethnicity in Modern Ecuador.* Urbana: University of Illinois Press, pp. 731–48.

Benedict, Ruth
1934 *Patterns of Culture.* Boston: Houghton Mifflin.

Berliner, Paul
1978 *The Soul of Mbira.* Berkeley: University of California Press.

Bingham, W. V.
1914 "Five Years of Progress in Comparative Musical Science." *Psychological Bulletin* 11:421–33.

Blacking, John

1965 "The Role of Music in the Culture of the Venda of the Northern Transvaal." *Studies in Ethnomusicology* (New York) 2:20–53.

1966 Review of *The Anthropology of Music,* by Alan P. Merriam. *Current Anthropology* 7:218.

1967 *Venda Children's Songs: A Study in Ethnomusicological Analysis.* Johannesburg: Witwatersrand University Press.

1970 "Tonal Organization in the Music of Two Venda Initiation Schools." *EM* 14:1–56.

1971 "The Value of Music in Human Experience." *Yearbook of the IFMC* 1:33–71.

1972 "Deep and Surface Structure in Venda Music." *Yearbook of the IFMC* 3:91–108.

1973 *How Musical Is Man?* Seattle: University of Washington Press.

1977 "Can Musical Universals Be Heard?" *World of Music* 19/1-2:14–22.

1978 "Some Problems of Theory and Method in the Study of Musical Change." *Yearbook of the IFMC* 9:1–26.

Blaukopf, Kurt

1951 *Musiksoziologie: Eine Einführung in die Grundbegriffe mit besonderer Berücksichtigung der Soziologie der Tonsysteme.* Vienna: Verkauf.

1970 "Tonsysteme und ihre gesellschaftliche Geltung in Max Webers Musiksoziologie." *International Review of Music Aesthetics and Sociology* 1:159–68.

1979 "The Sociography of Musical Life in Industrialised Countries—A Research Task." *World of Music* 21/3:78–81.

Bloomfield, Leonard

1951 *Language.* Rev. ed. New York: Holt.

Blum, Stephen

1972 "Musics in Contact: The Cultivation of Oral Repertories in Meshhed, Iran." Dissertation, University of Illinois.

1975a "Persian Folksong in Meshhed (Iran), 1969." *Yearbook of the IFMC* 6:68–114.

1975b "Towards a Social History of Musicological Technique." *EM* 19:207–31.

Blume, Friedrich

1949–79 Ed., *Die Musik in Geschichte und Gegenwart.* Kassel: Bärenreiter.

Boilès, Charles

1967 "Tepehua Thought-Song." *EM* 11:267–92.

1973a "Reconstruction of Proto-Melody." *Yearbook for Inter-American Musical Research* 9:45–63.

1973b "Sémiotique de l'Ethnomusicologie." *Musique en jeu* 10:34–41.

1978 *Man, Magic, and Musical Occasions.* Columbus, Ohio: Collegiate Publishing.

Bose, Fritz
1952 "Messbare Rassenunterschiede in der Musik." *Homo* 2/4: 1–5.
1953 *Musikalische Völkerkunde.* Zurich: Atlantis.
1959 "Western Influences in Modern Asian Music." *Journal of the IFMC* 11:47–50.
1966 "Musikgeschichtliche Aspekte der Musikethnologie." *Archiv für Musikwissenschaft* 24:239–51.
1967 "Volkslied—Schlager—Folklore." *Zeitschrift für Volkskunde* 63:40–49.

Brailoiu, Constantin
1960 *Vie musicale d'un village: Recherches sur le repertoire de Dragus (Roumaine) 1929–1932.* Paris: Institut universitaire roumain Charles Ier.
1973 *Problèmes d'ethnomusicologie: Textes reunis et prefaces par Gilbert Rouget.* Geneva: Minkoff Reprint.

Briegleb, Ann
ca. 1970 *Directory of Ethnomusicological Sound Recording Collections in the U.S. and Canada.* Ann Arbor, Mich.: Society for Ethnomusicology.

Bright, William
1963 "Language and Music: Areas for Cooperation." *EM* 7:26–32.

Bronson, Bertrand H.
1949 "Mechanical Help in the Study of Folk Song." *JAF* 62:81–90.
1950 "Some Observations About Melodic Variation in British-American Folk Tunes." *JAMS* 3:120–34.
1951 "Melodic Stability in Oral Tradition." *Journal of the IFMC* 3:50–55.
1959 "Toward the Comparative Analysis of British-American Folk Tunes." *JAF* 72:165–91.
1959–72 *The Traditional Tunes of the Child Ballads.* Princeton, N.J.: Princeton University Press.

Brook, Barry, and others
1972 Ed., *Perspectives in Musicology.* New York: Norton.

Brown, Howard M.
1976 *Music in the Renaissance.* Englewood Cliffs, N.J.: Prentice-Hall.

Buecher, Carl
1902 *Arbeit und Rhythmus.* 3d ed. Leipzig: Teubner.

Bukofzer, Manfred
1937 "Kann die Blasquintentheorie zur Erklärung exotischer Tonsysteme beitragen?" *Anthropos* 32:402–18.
1947 *Music in the Baroque Era.* New York: Norton.

Burling, Robbins
1964 "Cognition and Componential Analysis: God's Truth or Hocus-Pocus?" *AA* 66:20–28.
Burman-Hall, Linda C.
1975 "Southern American Folk Fiddle Styles." *EM* 19:47–65.
Burney, Charles
1776–89 (1935) *A General History of Music.* New York: Harcourt, Brace.
Burton, Frederick R.
1909 *American Primitive Music.* New York: Moffat, Yard.
Cachia, Pierre
1973 "A 19th Century Arab's Observations on European Music." *EM* 17:41–51.
Canon, Cornelius Baird
1963 "The Federal Music Project of the Works Progress Administration: Music in a Democracy." Dissertation, University of Minnesota.
Caron, Nelly, and Dariouche Safvate
1966 *Iran (Les traditions musicales).* Paris: Buchet/Castel.
Casagrande, Joseph B.
1960 Ed., *In the Company of Man.* New York: Harper and Row.
Cassirer, Ernst
1944 *An Essay on Man.* New Haven, Conn.: Yale University Press.
Caton, Margaret
1974 "The Vocal Ornament *Takiyah* in Persian Music." *UCLA Selected Reports in Ethnomusicology* 2/1:42–53.
1979 "Classical and Political Symbolism in the Tasnifs of 'Arefe Qazvini.'" Unpublished paper read at the 1979 meeting of the Society for Ethnomusicology.
Chandola, Anoop C.
1970 "Some Systems of Musical Scales and Linguistic Principles." *Semiotica* 2/2:135–50.
Chase, Gilbert
1958 "A Dialectical Approach to Music History." *EM* 2:1–9.
Chenoweth, Vida, and Darlene Bee
1971 "Comparative-Generative Models of a New Guinea Melodic Structure." *AA* 73:773–82.
Christensen, Dieter
1960 "Inner Tempo and Melodic Tempo." *EM* 4:9–13.
Chrysander, Friedrich
1885 "Über die altindische Opfermusik." *Vierteljahrschrift für Musikwissenschaft* 1:21–34.
Clark, Henry Leland
1956 "Towards a Musical Periodization of Music." *JAMS* 9:25–30.

Cohen, Dalia
1971 "The Meaning of the Modal Framework in the Singing of Religious Hymns by Christian Arabs in Israel." *Yuval* 2:23–57.
Cohen, Dalia, and Ruth Katz
1968 "Remarks Concerning the Use of the Melograph in Ethnomusicological Studies." *Yuval* 1:155–68.
Cole, Hugo
1974 *Sounds and Signs: Aspects of Musical Notation.* New York: Oxford University Press.
Collaer, Paul
1958 "Cartography and Ethnomusicology." *EM* 2:66–68.
1960 *Atlas historique de la musique.* Paris: Elsevier.
Cooke, Deryck
1959 *The Language of Music.* London: Oxford University Press.
Cooper, Robin
1977 "Abstract Structure and the Indian Raga System." *EM* 21:1–32.
Corpus
1953 *Corpus musicae popularis hungaricae.* Budapest: Akademiai Kiado.
Cox, John Harrington
1939 *Folk-Songs Mainly from West Virginia.* New York: National Service Bureau, Works Progress Administration (American Folk-Song Publications, no. 5).
Curtis-Burlin, Natalie
1907 *The Indians' Book.* New York: Harper.
Cutter, Paul F.
1976 "Oral Transmission of the Old-Roman Responsories?" *MQ* 62:182–94.
Dahlback, Karl
1958 *New Methods in Vocal Folk Music Research.* Oslo: Oslo University Press.
Dahlhaus, Carl
1971 Ed., *Einführung in die systematische Musikwissenschaft.* Cologne: Hans Gerig.
1977 *Grundlagen der Musikgeschichte.* Cologne: Hans Gerig.
Danckert, Werner
1939 *Das europäische Volkslied.* Berlin: J. Bard.
1956 "Tonmalerei und Tonsymbolik in der Musik der Lappen." *Musikforschung* 9:286–96.
Daniélou, Alain
1966 "The Use of the Indian Traditional Method in the Classification of Melodies." *Journal of the IFMC* 18:51–56.
1973 *Die Musik Asiens zwischen Misachtung und Wertschätzung.* Wilhelmshaven: Heinrichshofen.

Densmore, Frances
1910 *Chippewa Music.* Washington: Smithsonian Institution (Bull. 45 of the Bureau of American Ethnology).
1913 *Chippewa Music II.* Washington: Smithsonian Institution (Bull. 53 of the Bureau of American Ethnology).
1918 *Teton Sioux Music.* Washington: Smithsonian Institution (Bull. 61 of the Bureau of American Ethnology).
1927a "The Study of Indian Music in the Nineteenth Century." *AA* 29:77–86.
1927b "The Use of Music in the Treatment of the Sick by the American Indians." *MQ* 13:555–65.
1929a *Papago Music.* Washington: Smithsonian Institution (Bull. 90 of the Bureau of American Ethnology).
1929b *Pawnee Music.* Washington: Smithsonian Institution (Bull. 93 of the Bureau of American Ethnology).
1934 "The Songs of Indian Soldiers during the World War." *MQ* 20:419–25.
1939 *Nootka and Quileute Music.* Washington: Smithsonian Institution (Bull. 124 of the Bureau of American Ethnology).

Deutsches Volksliedarchiv
1935–74 *Deutsche Volkslieder mit ihren Melodien.* Berlin: De Gruyter.

Deva, B. C.
1974 *Indian Music.* Delhi: Indian Council for Cultural Relations.

Douglas, Mary
1966 *Purity and Danger.* New York: Praeger.
1970 *Natural Symbols.* New York: Pantheon.

Draeger, Hans-Heinz
1948 *Prinzip einer Systematik der Musikinstrumente.* Kassel: Baerenreiter.

Driver, Harold E.
1961 *Indians of North America.* Chicago: University of Chicago Press.

Dumont, Jean-Paul
1978 *The Headman and I.* Austin: University of Texas Press.

Durbin, Mridula A.
1971 "Transformational Models Applied to Musical Analysis: Theoretical Possibilities." *EM* 15:353–62.

Einstein, Alfred
1947a *Music in the Romantic Era.* New York: Norton.
1947b *A Short History of Music.* New York: Knopf.

Elbourne, Roger P.
1976 "The Question of Definition." *Yearbook of the IFMC* 7:9–29.

Ellis, Alexander J.
1885 "On the Musical Scales of Various Nations." *Journal of the Royal Society of Arts* 33:485–527.

Ellis, Catherine J.
1970 "The Role of the Ethnomusicologist in the Study of Andagarinja Women's Ceremonies." *Miscellanea Musicologica* (Adelaide) 5:76–208.

Elschek, Oskar
1977 "Zum gegenwärtigen Stand der Volksliedanalyse und Volksliedklassifikazion." *Yearbook of the IFMC* 8:21–34.

Elschek, Oskar, and Doris Stockmann
1969 Ed., *Methoden der Klassifikazion von Volksliedweisen.* Bratislava: Verlag der slowakischen Akademie der Wissenschaften.

Elschekova, Alica
1966 "Methods of Classifying Folk Tunes." *Journal of the IFMC* 18:56–76.

Elsner, Jürgen
1975 "Zum Problem des Maqam." *Acta Musicologica* 47:208–39.

Erdely, Stephen
1964 "Folksinging of the American Hungarians in Cleveland." *EM* 8:14–27.
1965 *Methods and Principles of Hungarian Ethnomusicology.* Bloomington: Indiana University Publications.
1979 "Ethnic Music in America: An Overview." *Yearbook of the IFMC* 11:114–37.

Erickson, Edwin Erich
1969 "The Song Trace: Song Styles and the Ethnohistory of Aboriginal America." Dissertation, Columbia University.

Erk, Ludwig
1893–94 *Deutscher Liederhort . . . neubearbeitet und fortgesetzt von Franz M. Böhme.* Leipzig: Breitkopf und Härtel.

Euba, Akin
1971 "New Idioms of Music-Drama among the Yoruba: An Introductory Study." *Yearbook of the IFMC* 2:92–107.

Ewers, John C.
1958 *The Blackfeet: Raiders on the Northwestern Plains.* Norman: University of Oklahoma Press.

Feld, Steven
1974 "Linguistic Models in Ethnomusicology." *EM* 18:197–217.

Ferand, Ernst
1938 *Die Improvisation in der Musik.* Zurich: Rhein-Verlag.

Firth, Raymond
1944 "The Future of Social Anthropology." *Man* 44/8:19–22.
1973 *Symbols, Public and Private.* Ithaca, N.Y.: Cornell University Press.

Fletcher, Alice C.
1904 *The Hako: A Pawnee Ceremony.* Washington: Smithsonian Institution (22nd Annual Report of the Bureau of American Ethnology, pt. 2).

Födermayr, Franz
1971 *Zur gesanglichen Stimmgebung in der aussereuropäischen Musik.* Vienna: Stiglmayr.
Fox-Strangways, A. H.
1914 (1965) *The Music of Hindostan.* Oxford: Clarendon Press.
Foster, George M., and Robert V. Kemper
1974 Ed., *Anthropologists in Cities.* Boston: Little, Brown.
Freeman, Linton C., and Alan P. Merriam
1956 "Statistical Classification in Anthropology: An Application to Ethnomusicology." *AA* 58:464–72.
Freilich, Morris
1970 Ed., *Marginal Natives: Anthropologists at Work.* New York: Harper and Row.
1977 *Marginal Natives at Work: Anthropologists in the Field.* New York: Schenkman.
Frisbie, Charlotte Johnson
1967 *Kinaaldá, a Study of the Navaho Girls' Puberty Ceremony.* Middletown, Conn.: Wesleyan University Press.
1980 Ed., *Southwestern Indian Ritual Drama.* Albuquerque: University of New Mexico Press.
Garfinkel, Harold
1967 *Studies in Ethnomethodology.* Englewood Cliffs, N.J.: Prentice-Hall.
Geertz, Clifford
1971 Ed., *Myth, Symbol, and Culture.* New York: Norton.
1973 *The Interpretation of Cultures.* New York: Basic Books.
Georges, Robert A., and Michael O. Jones
1980 *People Studying People: The Human Element in Fieldwork.* Berkeley: University of California Press.
Gillis, Frank, and Alan P. Merriam
1966 *Ethnomusicology and Folk Music: An International Bibliography of Dissertations and Theses.* Middletown, Conn.: Wesleyan University Press.
Glassie, Henry, Edward D. Ives, and John F. Szwed
1970 *Folksongs and Their Makers.* Bowling Green, Ohio: Bowling Green University Popular Press.
Goertzen, Christopher
1979 "'Billy in the Low Ground,' a Tune Family Study." Unpublished paper, University of Illinois.
Golde, Peggy
1970 Comp., *Women in the Field.* Chicago: Aldine.
Goldstein, Kenneth S.
1964 *A Guide for Field Workers in Folklore.* Hatboro, N.J.: Folklore Associates.
Gourlay, K. A.
1978 "Towards a Reassessment of the Ethnomusicologist's Role." *EM* 22:1–36.

Graf, Walter

1966 "Zur Verwendung von Geräuschen in der aussereuropäischen Musik." *Jahrbuch für musikalische Volks- und Völkerkunde* 2:59–90.

1968 "Das biologische Moment im Konzept der Vergleichenden Musikwissenschaft." *Studia Musicologica* 10:91–113.

1972 "Musikalische Klangforschung." *Acta Musicologica* 44:31–78.

Grame, Theodore

1962 "Bamboo and Music: A New Approach to Organology." *EM* 6:8–14.

Greenway, John

1953 *American Folksongs of Protest.* Philadelphia: University of Pennsylvania Press.

Grinnell, George Bird

1920 *Blackfoot Lodge Tales.* New York: Scribner.

Gronow, Pekka

1963 "Phonograph Records as a Source for Musicological Research." *EM* 7:225–28.

1978 "The Significance of Ethnic Recordings." In Howard W. Marshall, ed., *Ethnic Recordings: A Neglected Heritage.* Washington: Library of Congress.

Günther, Robert

1973 Ed., *Musikkulturen Asiens, Afrikas und Ozeaniens im 19. Jahrhundert.* Regensburg: G. Bosse.

Gurvin, Olav

1958–67 Ed., *Norsk folkemusikk—Norwegian Folk Music.* Oslo: Universitetsforlaget.

Haas, Robert

1931 *Aufführungspraxis der Musik.* Potsdam: Athenaion.

Haas, Wilhelm

1932 *Systematische Ordnung Beethovenscher Melodien.* Leipzig: Quelle & Meyer.

Halpert, Herbert

1943 "The Devil and the Fiddle." *Hoosier Folklore Bulletin* 2:39–43.

Harich-Schneider, Eta

1973 *A History of Japanese Music.* London: Oxford University Press.

Harris, Marvin

1968 *The Rise of Anthropological Theory.* New York: Crowell.

1971 *Culture, Man, and Nature.* New York: Crowell.

Harrison, Frank

1973 *Time, Place, and Music.* Amsterdam: Knuf.

1977 "Universals in Music: Towards a Methodology of Comparative Research." *World of Music* 19/1–2:30–36.

Harrison, Frank, Mantle Hood, and Claude Palisca

1963 *Musicology.* Englewood Cliffs, N.J.: Prentice-Hall.

Harwood, Dane L.
1976 "Universals in Music: A Perspective from Cognitive Psychology." *EM* 20:521–33.

Helm, E. Eugene
1977 Response to F. Lieberman, "Should Ethnomusicology Be Abolished?" *College Music Symposium* 17/2:201–2.

Henry, Edward O.
1976 "The Variety of Music in a North Indian Village: Reassessing Cantometrics." *EM* 20:49–66.

Henry, Jules
1963 *Culture against Man.* New York: Random House.

Herndon, Marcia
1974 "Analysis: The Herding of Sacred Cows?" *EM* 18:219–62.

Herndon, Marcia, and Norma McLeod
1980 *Music as Culture.* Darby, Pa.: Norwood.

Herskovits, Melville J.
1945 "Problem, Method, and Theory in Afroamerican Studies." *Afroamerica* 1:5–24.

Herzog, George
1928 "The Yuman Musical Style." *JAF* 41:183–231.
1930 "Musical Styles in North America." *Proceedings of the 23rd International Congress of Americanists* (New York), pp. 455–58.
1934 "Speech-Melody and Primitive Music." *MQ* 20:452–66.
1935a "Plains Ghost Dance and Great Basin Music." *AA* 37:403–19.
1935b "Special Song Types in North American Indian Music." *Zeitschrift für vergleichende Musikwissenschaft* 3/1–2:1–11.
1936a "A Comparison of Pueblo and Pima Musical Styles." *JAF* 49:283–417.
1936b *Research in Primitive and Folk Music in the United States.* Washington: ACLS (Bulletin 24).
1936c "Die Musik der Karolinen-Inseln aus dem Phonogrammarchiv Berlin." In Anneliese Eilers, *Westkarolinen.* Hamburg: De Gruyter, pp. 263–351.
1938 "Music in the Thinking of the American Indian." *Peabody Bulletin* (May), pp. 1–5.
1939 "Music's Dialects—A non-Universal Language." *Independent Journal of Columbia University* 6:1–2.
1945 "Drum Signalling in a West African Tribe." *Word* 1:217–38.
1949 "Salish Music." In Marian W. Smith, ed., *Indians of the Urban Northwest.* New York: Columbia University Press, pp. 93–109.
1950 "Song." In M. Leach, ed., *Funk and Wagnall's Standard Dictionary of Folklore, Mythology and Legend.* New York, 2: 1032–50.

1957 "Music at the Fifth International Congress of Anthropological and Ethnological Sciences." *Journal of the IFMC* 9:71–73.

Hickmann, Hans

1970 "Die Musik des arabisch-islamischen Bereichs." In *Handbuch der Orientalistik,* 1. Abt., Ergänzungsband IV. Leiden: Brill, pp. 1–134.

Hinton, Leanne

1967–68 Personal communication and unpublished papers on Havasupai music, University of Illinois.

Hoebel, E. Adamson

1949 *Man in the Primitive World: An Introduction to Anthropology.* New York: McGraw-Hill.

Hohmann, Rupert Karl

1959 "The Church Music of the Old Order Amish in the United States." Dissertation, Northwestern University.

Honigmann, John J.

1976 *The Development of Anthropological Ideas.* Homewood, Ill.: Dorsey Press.

Hood, Mantle

1957 "Training and Research Methods in Ethnomusicology." *Ethnomusicology Newsletter* 11:2–8.

1959 "The Reliability of Oral Tradition." *JAMS* 12:201–9.

1960 "The Challenge of Bi-Musicality." *EM* 4:55–59.

1963 "Music, the Unknown." In Harrison, Hood, and Palisca (1963).

1966 Review of *Africa and Indonesia,* by A. M. Jones, *EM* 10:214–16.

1971 *The Ethnomusicologist.* New York: McGraw-Hill.

1977 "Universal Attributes of Music." *World of Music* 19/1–2:63–69.

Hopkins, Pandora

1966 "The Purposes of Transcription." *EM* 10:310–17.

1977 "The Homology of Music and Myth: Views of Lévi-Strauss on Musical Structure." *EM* 21:247–61.

Hornbostel, Erich M. von

1905 "Die Probleme der vergleichenden Musikwissenschaft." *Zeitschrift der internationalen Musikgesellschaft* 7:85–97.

1906 "Phonographierte tunesische Melodien." *Sammelbände der internationalen Musikgesellschaft* 8:1–43.

1907 "Notiz über die Musik der Bewohner von Süd-Neu-Mecklenburg." In E. Stephan and F. Graebner, *Neu-Mecklenburg.* Berlin: D. Reimer, pp. 131–37.

1910 "Über einige Panpfeifen aus Nordwest-Brasilien." In Theodor Koch-Gruenberg, *Zwei Jahre unter den Indianern.* Berlin: E. Wasmuth, 2:378–91.

1911 "Über ein akustisches Kriterium für Kulturzusammenhänge." *Zeitschrift für Ethnologie* 3:601–15.

1912 "Melodie und Skala." *Jahrbuch der Musikbibliothek Peters* 20:11-23.

1917 "Musikalische Tonsysteme." In Friedrich Trendelenburg, ed., *Handbuch der Physik.* Berlin: J. Springer, 8:425-49.

1928 "African Negro Music." *Africa* 1:30-62.

1933 "The Ethnology of African Sound Instruments." *Africa* 6:129-57, 277-311.

1936 "Fuegian Songs." *AA* 38:357-67.

1975- *Hornbostel Opera Omnia.* Ed. Klaus Wachsmann and others. The Hague: Nijhoff.

Hornbostel, Erich M. von, and Otto Abraham

1904 "Über die Bedeutung des Phonographen für die vergleichende Musikwissenschaft." *Zeitschrift für Ethnologie* 36: 222-33.

1909 "Vorschläge zur Transkription exotischer Melodien." *Sammelbände der internationalen Musikgesellschaft* 11:1-25.

Hornbostel, Erich M. von, and Curt Sachs

1914 "Systematik der Musikinstrumente." *Zeitschrift für Ethnologie* 46:553-90. English translation by Anthony Baines and K. P. Wachsmann, "Classification of Musical Instruments," *Galpin Society Journal* 14:3-29, 1961.

Hsu, Francis L. K.

1973 "Prejudice and Its Intellectual Effect in American Anthropology." *AA* 75:1-19.

Hustvedt, Sigurd Bernhard

1936 "A Melodic Index of Child's Ballad Tunes." *Publications of UCLA in Languages and Literature* 1/2:51-78.

International Folk Music Council

1952 *Notation of Folk Music: Recommendations of the Committee of Experts.* Geneva.

Ives, Edward D.

1964 *Larry Gorman: The Man Who Made the Songs.* Bloomington: Indiana University Press.

Izikowitz, Karl Gustav

1935 *Musical and Other Sound Instruments of the South American Indians.* Göteborg: Kungl. Vetenskaps-och Vitterhets-Samhälles Handlingar.

Jackson, George Pullen

1943 *White and Negro Spirituals.* Locust Valley, N.Y.: J. J. Augustin.

Jacobs, Norman

1966 *The Sociology of Development: Iran as an Asian Case Study.* New York: Praeger.

Jairazbhoy, Nazir A.

1971 *The Rags of North Indian Music.* London: Faber and Faber.

1977 "The 'Objective' and Subjective View in Music Transcription." *EM* 21:263-74.

1978 "Music in Western Rajasthan: Continuity and Change." *Yearbook of the IFMC* 9:50–66.

Jairazbhoy, Nazir A., and Hal Balyoz

1977 "Electronic Aids to Aural Transcription." *EM* 21:275–82.

Jakobson, Roman

1941 *Kindersprache, Aphasie, und allgemeine Lautgesetze.* Uppsala: Almquist & Wiksell.

Járdányi, Pál

1962 "Die Ordnung der ungarischen Volkslieder." *Studia Musicologica* 2:3–32.

Jones, A. M.

1954 "African Rhythm." *Africa* 24:26–47.

1959 *Studies in African Music.* London: Oxford University Press.

1964 *Africa and Indonesia: The Evidence of the Xylophone.* Leiden: Brill.

Kaemmer, John E.

1980 "Between the Event and the Tradition: A New Look at Music in Socio-Cultural Systems." *EM* 24:61–74.

Kaplan, David, and Robert A. Manners

1972 *Culture Theory.* Englewood Cliffs, N.J.: Prentice-Hall.

Karpeles, Maud

1951 "Concerning Authenticity." *Journal of the IFMC* 3:10–14.

1958 Ed., *The Collecting of Folk Music and Other Ethnomusicological Material: A Manual for Field Workers.* London: IFMC.

1967 *Cecil Sharp, His Life and Work.* Chicago: University of Chicago Press.

1968 "The Distinction between Folk Music and Popular Music." *Journal of the IFMC* 20:9–12.

1973 *An Introduction to English Folk Song.* London: Oxford University Press.

Kartomi, Margaret J.

1973 *Matjapat Songs in Central and West Java.* Canberra: Australian National University Press.

1980 "Childlikeness in Play Songs—A Case Study among the Pitjantjara at Yalata, South Australia." *Miscellanea Musicologica* (Adelaide) 2:172–214.

1981 "The Processes and Results of Musical Culture Contact: A Discussion of Terminology and Concepts." *EM* 25:227–50.

Katz, Ruth

1968 "The Singing of Baqqashot by Aleppo Jews." *Acta Musicologica* 40:65–85.

1970 "Mannerism and Cultural Change: An Ethnomusicological Example." *Current Anthropology* 2/4–5:465–75.

1974 "The Reliability of Oral Transmission: The Case of Samaritan Music." *Yuval* 3:109–35.

Kauffman, Robert
1973 "Shona Urban Music and the Problem of Acculturation." *Yearbook of the IFMC* 4:47–56.
1980 "African Rhythm: A Reassessment." *EM* 24:393–416.

Kaufmann, Walter
1967 *Musical Notations of the Orient.* Bloomington: Indiana University Press.

Keesing, Roger M.
1976 *Cultural Anthropology, A Contemporary Perspective.* New York: Holt, Rinehart & Winston.

Keil, Charles
1979 *Tiv Song.* Chicago: University of Chicago Press.

Keil, Charles and Angeliki
1966 "Musical Meaning: A Preliminary Report." *EM* 10:153–73.

Kemppinen, Ivar
1954 *The Ballad of Lady Isabel and the False Knight.* Helsinki: Kirja-Mono Oy.

Key, Mary
1963 "Music of the Sirionò (Guaranian)." *EM* 7:17–21.

Kiesewetter, Raphael
1842 *Die Musik der Araber.* Leipzig: Breitkopf und Härtel.

Kneif, Tibor
1974 "Was ist Semiotik der Musik?" *Neue Zeitschrift für Musik* 135/6:348–53.

Knepler, Georg
1961 *Musikgeschichte des 19. Jahrhunderts.* Berlin: Henschelverlag.

Kodály, Zoltan
1956 *Die ungarische Volksmusik.* Budapest: Corvina.

Koetting, James
1970 "Analysis and Notation of West African Drum Ensemble Music." *UCLA Selected Reports* (Institute of Ethnomusicology) 1/3:116–46.

Kohs, Ellis B.
1976 *Musical Form: Studies in Analysis and Synthesis.* Boston: Houghton Mifflin.

Koizumi, Fumio, and others
1977 Ed., *Asian Music in an Asian Perspective.* Tokyo: Japan Foundation.

Kolinski, Mieczyslaw
1936 "Suriname Music." In M. Herskovits, ed., *Suriname Folklore.* New York: American Folklore Society.
1956 "The Structure of Melodic Movement, a New Method of Analysis." In *Miscelanea de Estudios Dedicados al Dr. Fernando Ortiz.* Havana: Sociedad Economica de Amigos del Pais), 2:879–918.

1959 "The Evaluation of Tempo." *EM* 3:45–57.
1961 "Classification of Tonal Structures." *Studies in Ethnomusicology* (New York) 1:38–76.
1962 "Consonance and Dissonance." *EM* 6:66–74.
1965a "The General Direction of Melodic Movement." *EM* 9:240–64.
1965b "The Structure of Melodic Movement—A New Method of Analysis." *Studies in Ethnomusicology* (New York) 2:95–120.
1971 Review of *The Ethnomusicologist,* by Mantle Hood. *Yearbook of the IFMC* 3:146–60.
1973 "A Cross-Cultural Approach to Metro-Rhythmic Patterns." *EM* 17:494–506.
1978 "The Structure of Music: Diversification versus Constraint." *EM* 22:229–44.

Koller, Oswald
1902–3 "Die beste Methode, volks- und volksmässige Lieder nach ihrer melodischen Beschaffenheit lexikalisch zu ordnen." *Sammelbände der internationalen Musikgesellschaft* 4:1–15.

Koning, Jos.
1980 "The Fieldworker as Performer." *EM* 24:417–30.

Kroeber, Alfred Louis
1947 *Cultural and Natural Areas of Native North America.* Berkeley: University of California Press.
1948 *Anthropology.* New ed. New York: Harcourt, Brace.

Kroeber, Theodora
1961 *Ishi in Two Worlds.* Berkeley: University of California Press.

Krohn, Ilmari
1902–3 "Welche ist die beste Methode, um volks- und volksmässige Lieder nach ihrer melodischen (nicht textlichen) Beschaffenheit lexikalisch zu ordnen?" *Sammelbände der internationalen Musikgesellschaft* 4:643–60.

Krohn, Kaarle
1926 *Die folkloristische Arbeitsmethode.* Oslo: Oslo University Press.

Kubler, George
1962 *The Shape of Time.* New Haven, Conn.: Yale University Press.

Kuhn, Thomas S.
1970 *The Structure of Scientific Revolutions.* 2d ed., enlgd. Chicago: University of Chicago Press.

Kunst, Jaap
1950 *Musicologica.* Amsterdam: Royal Tropical Institute.
1954 *Cultural Relations between the Balkans and Indonesia.* Amsterdam: Royal Tropical Institute.
1959 *Ethnomusicology.* 3d ed. The Hague: M. Nijhoff.

Kurath, Gertrude P.
1960 "Panorama of Dance Ethnology." *Current Anthropology* 1: 233–54.

Laade, Wolfgang
1969 *Die Situation von Musikleben und Musikforschung in den Ländern Afrikas und Asiens und die neuen Aufgaben der Musikethnologie.* Tutzing: Hans Schneider.
1971a *Gegenwartsfragen der Musik in Afrika und Asien: Eine grundlegende Bibliographie.* Heidelberg: W. Laade.
1971b *Neue Musik in Afrika, Asien und Ozeanien.* Heidelberg: W. Laade.
1975 *Musik der Götter, Geister und Menschen.* Baden-Baden: Valentin Koerner.
1976 *Musikwissenschaft zwischen gestern und morgen.* Berlin: Merseburger.

Labov, William
1972 *Sociolinguistic Patterns.* Philadelphia: University of Pennsylvania Press.

Lach, Robert
1924 *Die vergleichende Musikwissenschaft, ihre Methoden und Probleme.* Vienna: Akademie der Wissenschaften.

Lachmann, Robert
1929 *Musik des Orients.* Breslau: Jedermanns Bücherei.

Langer, Susanne K.
1942 *Philosophy in a New Key.* New York: Mentor.
1953 *Feeling and Form.* New York: Scribner.

LaRue, Jan
1970 *Guidelines for Style Analysis.* New York: Norton.

Leach, Edmund
1970 *Claude Lévi-Strauss.* New York: Viking Press.

Levant, Oscar
1940 *A Smattering of Ignorance.* New York: Doubleday, Doran.

Lévi-Strauss, Claude
1963 *Structural Anthropology.* New York: Basic Books.
1969 *The Raw and the Cooked: Introduction to the Science of Mythology.* Trans. from the French. New York: Harper and Row.
1971 *Mythologiques IV: l'homme nu.* Paris: Plon.

Lewis, Oscar
1951 *Life in a Mexican Village: Tepotzlán Restudied.* Urbana: University of Illinois Press.
1956 "Comparison in Cultural Anthropology." In W. L. Thomas, ed., *Current Anthropology, a Supplement to Anthropology Today.* Chicago: University of Chicago Press, pp. 259–92.

Library of Congress
1942 *Check-List of Recorded Songs in the English Language in the Archive of American Folk Song to July, 1940.* Washington.

Lidov, David
1975 *On Musical Phrase.* Montreal: Les Presses de l'Université de Montréal.

Lieberman, Fredric
1969 *The Music of China,* vol. 1 (Notes to the record, Anthology AST-4000). New York: Anthology Record and Tape Corp.

Lieberman, Philip
1975 *The Origins of Language.* New York: Macmillan.

Lindley, Mark
1980 "Composition." In S. Sadie, ed., *The New Grove.* London: Macmillan, 4:599-602.

List, George
1963a "An Approach to the Indexing of Ballad Tunes." *Folklore and Folk Music Archivist* 6/1:7-15.
1963b "The Boundaries of Speech and Song." *EM* 7:1-16.
1963c "The Musical Significance of Transcription." *EM* 7:193-97.
1968 "The Hopi as Composer and Poet." *Proceedings of the Centennial Workshop in Ethnomusicology,* pp. 42-53.
1974 "The Reliability of Transcription." *EM* 18:353-77.
1979a "The Distribution of a Melodic Formula: Diffusion or Polygenesis?" *Yearbook of the IFMC* 10:33-52.
1979b "Ethnomusicology: A Discipline Defined." *EM* 23:1-6.

Loeb, Laurence D.
1972 "The Jewish Musician and the Music of Fars." *AM* 4/1:3-14.

Lomax, Alan
1959 "Folksong Style." *AA* 61:927-54.
1960 *The Folk Songs of North America.* New York: Doubleday.
1962 "Song Structure and Social Structure." *Ethnology* 1:425-51.
1968 *Folk Song Style and Culture.* Washington: American Association for the Advancement of Science.
1976 *Cantometrics.* Berkeley: University of California.

Lord, Albert B.
1965 *The Singer of Tales.* New York: Atheneum.

Lorenz, Alfred Ottokar
1928 *Abendländische Musikgeschichte im Rhythmus der Generationen.* Berlin: M. Hesse.

Lowie, Robert H.
1916 "Plains Indian Age-Grade Societies: Historical and Comparative Summary." *Anthropological Papers of the American Museum of Natural History,* 11, pt. 13:877-1031.
1937 *The History of Ethnological Theory.* New York: Rinehart.

Lowinsky, Edward
1946 *Secret Chromatic Art in the Netherlands Motet.* New York: Columbia University Press.

Lyons, John
1977 *Noam Chomsky.* Rev. ed. New York: Penguin Books.

Malinowski, Bronislaw
1935 *Coral Gardens and Their Magic.* New York: American Book Co.
1954 *Magic, Science, and Religion; and Other Essays.* New York: Doubleday.
1967 *A Diary in the Strict Sense of the Term.* New York: Harcourt, Brace and World.

Malm, William P.
1959 *Japanese Music and Musical Instruments.* Tokyo: C. E. Tuttle.
1969 "On the Nature and Function of Symbolism in Western and Oriental Music." *Philosophy East and West* (Honolulu) 19/3:235–46.
1972 "On the Meaning and Invention of the Term Disphony." *EM* 16:247–49.
1977 *Music Cultures of the Pacific, the Near East, and Asia.* 2d ed. Englewood Cliffs, N.J.: Prentice-Hall.

Manners, Robert Alan, and David Kaplan
1968 Ed., *Theory in Anthropology, a Sourcebook.* Chicago: Aldine.

Mapoma, Isaiah Mwesa
1969 "The Use of Folk Music among Some Bemba Church Congregations in Zambia." *Yearbook of the IFMC* 1:72–88.

Maraire, Abraham Dumisani
1971 "Mbiras and Performance in Rhodesia." Notes to the record *Mbira Music from Rhodesia,* UWP-1001. Seattle: University of Washington Press.

Marcel-Dubois, Claudie
1972 *Pour une analyse de contenu musical.* Paris: Musée national des arts et traditions populaires.

Massoudieh, Mohammad T.
1968 *Awas-e-Šur.* Regensburg: G. Bosse.
1978 *Radif vocal de la musique traditionelle de l'Iran.* Teheran: Ministry of Culture and Fine Arts.

May, Elizabeth
1963 *The Influence of the Meiji Period on Japanese Children's Music.* Berkeley: University of California Press.

McAllester, David P.
1949 *Peyote Music.* New York: Viking Fund Publications in Anthropology, no. 13.
1954 *Enemy Way Music.* Cambridge: Peabody Museum Papers, vol. 41, no. 3.
1971 "Some Thoughts on 'Universals' in World Music." *EM* 15: 379–80.

McClintock, Walter
1910 (1968) *The Old North Trail.* Lincoln: University of Nebraska Press.

McCollester, Roxane
1960 "A Transcription Technique Used by Zygmunt Estreicher." *EM* 4:129–32.

McFee, Malcolm
1972 *Modern Blackfeet: Montanans on a Reservation.* New York: Holt, Rinehart and Winston.

McLean, Mervyn
1965 "Song Loss and Social Context among the New Zealand Maori." *EM* 9:296–304.
1971 "An Analysis of 651 Maori Scales." *Yearbook of the IFMC* 1: 123–64.
1979 "Towards the Differentiation of Music Areas in Oceania." *Anthropos* 74:717–36.

McLeod, Norma
1964 "The Status of Musical Specialists in Madagascar." *EM* 8:278–89.
1966 "Some Techniques of Analysis for Non-Western Music." Dissertation, Northwestern University.

Mead, Margaret
1973 "Changing Styles of Anthropological Work." *Annual Review of Anthropology* 2:1–26.

Merriam, Alan P.
1954 "Song Texts of the Bashi." *Zaire* 8:27–43.
1955a "Music in American Culture." *AA* 57:1173–81.
1955b "The Use of Music in the Study of a Problem of Acculturation." *AA* 57:28–34.
1959 "African Music." In William R. Bascom and Melville J. Herskovits, eds., *Continuity and Change in African Cultures.* Chicago: University of Chicago Press, pp. 49–86.
1960 "Ethnomusicology: Discussion and Definition of the Field." *EM* 4:107–14.
1964 *The Anthropology of Music.* Evanston, Ill.: Northwestern University Press.
1967a *Ethnomusicology of the Flathead Indians.* Chicago: Aldine Press.
1967b "Music and the Origin of the Flathead Indians." In *Music in the Americas.* The Hague: Mouton, pp. 129–38.
1969a "The Ethnographic Experience: Drum-Making among the Bala (Basongye)." *EM* 13:74–100.
1969b "Ethnomusicology Revisited." *EM* 13:213–29.
1973 "The Bala Musician." In Warren L. d'Azevedo, ed., *The Traditional Artist in African Societies.* Bloomington: Indiana University Press, pp. 250–81.
1975 "Ethnomusicology Today." *Current Musicology* 20:50–66.
1977a "Definitions of 'Comparative Musicology' and 'Ethnomusicology': An Historical-Theoretical Perspective." *EM* 21:189–204.

1977b "Music Change in a Basongye Village (Zaire)." *Anthropos* 72:806–46.

1979 "Basongye Musicians and Institutionalized Social Deviance." *Yearbook of the IFMC* 11:1–26.

1981 "African Musical Rhythm and Concepts of Time-Reckoning." In Thomas Noblitt, ed., *Music East and West: Essays in Honor of Walter Kaufmann.* New York: Pendragon Press, pp. 123–42.

Metfessel, Milton E.

1928 *Phonophotography in Folk Music.* Chapel Hill: University of North Carolina Press.

Meyer, Leonard B.

1956 *Emotion and Meaning in Music.* Chicago: University of Chicago Press.

1960 "Universalism and Relativism in the Study of Ethnic Music." *EM* 4:49–54.

1967 *Music, the Arts, and Ideas: Patterns and Predictions in Twentieth-Century Culture.* Chicago: University of Chicago Press.

Mitchell, Frank

1978 *Navajo Blessingway Singer. . . .* Ed. Charlotte Frisbie and David P. McAllester. Tucson: University of Arizona Press.

Moser, Hans Joachim

1954 *Die Musik der deutschen Stämme.* Vienna: E. Wancura.

Mueller, John H.

1951 *The American Symphony Orchestra: A Social History of Musical Taste.* Bloomington: Indiana University Press.

Murdock, George Peter

1956 "How Culture Changes." In H. L. Shapiro, ed., *Man, Culture and Society.* New York: Oxford University Press, pp. 247–60.

Nadel, Siegfried

1930 "The Origins of Music." *MQ* 16:531–46.

Naroll, Raoul, and Ronald Cohen

1973 Eds., *A Handbook of Method in Cultural Anthropology.* New York: Columbia University Press.

Nattiez, Jean-Jacques

1971 Ed., *Sémiologie de la musique. Musique en jeu,* vol. 5.

1972 "Is a Descriptive Semiotics of Music Possible?" *Language Sciences* 23:1–7.

1973 "Linguistics: A New Approach for Musical Analysis." *International Review of the Aesthetics and Sociology of Music* 4/1:51–68.

1975 *Fondements d'une sémiologie de la musique.* Paris: Union génerale d'éditions.

Naumann, Hans

1921 *Primitive Gemeinschaftskultur.* Jena: E. Diederichs.

Nettl, Bruno

1954a *North American Indian Musical Styles.* Philadelphia: American Folklore Society.

1954b "Text-Music Relations in Arapaho Songs." *Southwestern Journal of Anthropology* 10:192–99.

1956a "Infant Musical Development and Primitive Music." *Southwestern Journal of Anthropology* 12:87–91.

1956b *Music in Primitive Culture.* Cambridge, Mass.: Harvard University Press.

1956c "Notes on Infant Musical Development." *MQ* 42:28–34.

1956d "Unifying Factors in Folk and Primitive Music." *JAMS* 9: 196–201.

1957 "The Hymns of the Amish: An Example of Marginal Survival." *JAF* 70:323–28.

1958a "Historical Aspects of Ethnomusicology." *AA* 60:518–32.

1958b "Some Linguistic Approaches to Musical Analysis." *Journal of the IFMC* 10:37–41.

1960 "Musical Cartography and the Distribution of Music." *Southwestern Journal of Anthropology* 16:338–47.

1961 "Polyphony in North American Indian Music." *MQ* 47: 354–62.

1963 "A Technique of Ethnomusicology Applied to Western Culture." *EM* 7:221–24.

1964 *Theory and Method in Ethnomusicology.* New York: Free Press.

1965 "The Songs of Ishi." *MQ* 51:460–77.

1967a "Aspects of Folk Music in North American Cities." In *Music in the Americas.* The Hague: Mouton, pp. 139–47.

1967b "Blackfoot Music in Browning, 1965: Functions and Analysis." In *Festschrift Walter Wiora.* Kassel: Bärenreiter, pp. 593–98.

1967c "Studies in Blackfoot Indian Musical Culture," pts. I and II. *EM* 11:141–60, 293–309.

1968 "Studies in Blackfoot Indian Musical Culture," pts. III and IV. *EM* 12:11–48, 192–207.

1969 "Musical Areas Reconsidered." In *Essays in Musicology in Honor of Dragan Plamenac.* Pittsburgh: University of Pittsburgh Press, pp. 181–90.

1974a "Nour-Ali Boroumand, a Twentieth-Century Master of Persian Music." *Studia Instrumentorum Musicae Popularis* 3: 167–71.

1974b "Thoughts on Improvisation, a Comparative Approach." *MQ* 60:1–19.

1976 *Folk Music in the United States, an Introduction.* Rev. and expanded ed. by Helen Myers. Detroit: Wayne State University Press.

1978a Ed., *Eight Urban Musical Cultures: Tradition and Change.* Urbana: University of Illinois Press.

1978b "Musical Values and Social Values: Symbols in Iran." *Journal of the Steward Anthropological Society* 10/1:1–23.
1978c "Some Aspects of the History of World Music in the Twentieth Century: Questions, Problems, Concepts." *EM* 22:123–36.

Nettl, Bruno, and Bela Foltin, Jr.
1972 *Daramad of Chahargah, a Study in the Performance Practice of Persian Music.* Detroit: Information Coordinators.

Nettl, Bruno, and Ronald Riddle
1974 "Taqsim Nahawand, a Study of Sixteen Performances by Jihad Racy." *Yearbook of the IFMC* 5:11–50.

Neuman, Daniel M.
1977 "The Social Organization of a Music Tradition: Hereditary Specialists in North India." *EM* 21:233–46.
1980 *The Life of Music in North India.* Detroit: Wayne State University Press.

Nketia, J. H. Kwabena
1962 "The Problem of Meaning in African Music." *EM* 6:1–7.
1974 *The Music of Africa.* New York: Norton.

Nohl, Ludwig
1883 *Life of Haydn.* Trans. Geo. P. Upton. Chicago: Jansen, McClurg.

Obata, Juichi, and Ryuji Kobayashi
1937 "A Direct-Reading Pitch Recorder and Its Application to Music and Speech." *Journal of the Acoustic Society of America* 9:156–61.

Olsvai, I.
1963 "Typical Variations, Typical Correlations, Central Motifs in Hungarian Folk Music." *Studia Musicologica* 4:37–70.

Osgood, Charles E., and others
1975 *Cross-Cultural Universals of Affective Meanings.* Urbana: University of Illinois Press.

Owens, Thomas
1974 "Charlie Parker: Techniques of Improvisation." Dissertation, UCLA.

Pelinski, Ramon
1981 *La musique des Inuit du Caribou.* Montreal: Les Presses de l'Université de Montreal.

Pelto, Pertti J. and Gretel H.
1973 "Ethnography: The Fieldwork Enterprise." In J. Honigmann, ed., *Handbook of Social and Cultural Anthropology.* Chicago: Rand McNally, pp. 241–88.

Petrovic, Radmila
1968 "The Concept of Yugoslav Folk Music in the Twentieth Century." *Journal of the IFMC* 20:22–25.

Poladian, Sirvart
1942 "The Problem of Melodic Variation in Folksong." *JAF* 55: 204–11.

Porter, James

1976 "Jeannie Robertson's *My Son David,* a Conceptual Performance Model." *JAF* 89:7–26.

1977 "Prolegomena to a Comparative Study of European Folk Music." *EM* 21:435–52.

1978 "Introduction: The Traditional Music of Europeans in America." *UCLA Selected Reports in Ethnomusicology* 3/1:1–23.

Powdermaker, Hortense

1967 *Stranger and Friend.* New York: Norton.

Powers, Harold S.

1970 "An Historical and Comparative Approach to the Classification of Ragas." *UCLA Selected Reports of the Institute of Ethnomusicology* 1/3:1–78.

1979 "Classical Music, Cultural Roots, and Colonial Rule: An Indic Musicologist Looks at the Muslim World." *AM* 12/1:5–39.

1980 "Language Models and Musical Analysis." *EM* 24:1–60.

Pulikowski, Julian von

1933 *Geschichte des Begriffes Volkslied im musikalischen Schrifttum.* Heidelberg: C. Winter.

Qureshi, Regula

1972 "Ethnomusicological Research among Canadian Communities of Arab and East Indian Origin." *EM* 16:381–96.

Racy, Ali Jihad

1971 "Funeral Songs of the Druzes of Lebanon." M.M. thesis, University of Illinois.

1976 "Record Industry and Egyptian Traditional Music, 1904–1932." *EM* 20:23–48.

Radcliffe-Brown, A. R.

1952 *Structure and Function in Primitive Society.* London: Cohen and West.

Radin, Paul

1963 *The Autobiography of a Winnebago Indian.* New York: Dover.

Ramseyer, Urs

1970 *Soziale Bezüge des Musizierens in Naturvolkkulturen.* Bern: Francke.

Rawlinson, H. G.

1952 *India, a Short Cultural History.* 2d rev. ed. New York: Praeger.

Redfield, Robert

1930 *Tepotzlán, a Mexican Village.* Chicago: University of Chicago Press.

Reese, Gustave

1954 *Music in the Renaissance.* New York: Norton.

Reinhard, Kurt

1956 *Chinesische Musik.* Kassel: E. Röth.

1961 "Das berliner Phonogrammarchiv." *Baessler-Archiv, neue Folge* 9:83–94.

1968 *Einführung in die Musikethnologie.* Wolfenbüttel: Mösiler.

Rhodes, Willard

1952 "Acculturation in North American Indian Music." In Sol Tax, ed., *Acculturation in the Americas (Proceedings of the 29th International Congress of Americanists),* 2:127–32.

1958 "A Study of Musical Diffusion Based on the Wandering of the Opening Peyote Song." *Journal of the IFMC* 10:42–49.

1962 "Music as an Agent of Political Expression." *African Studies Bulletin* 5/2:14–22.

Riemann, Hugo

1959-67 *Riemann Musik Lexikon.* 12th ed., ed. Willibald Gurlitt. Mainz: Schott.

Roberts, Helen H.

1936 *Musical Areas in Aboriginal North America.* New Haven, Conn.: Yale University Publications in Anthropology, No. 12.

Roberts, John Storm

1972 *Black Music in Two Worlds.* New York: Praeger.

Roberts, Warren E.

1958 *The Tale of the Kind and the Unkind Girls.* Berlin: De Gruyter.

Robertson-DeCarbo, Carol

1974 "Music as Therapy: A Bio-Cultural Problem." *EM* 18: 31–42.

1977 "Tayil as Category and Communication among the Argentine Mapuche." *Yearbook of the IFMC* 8:35–52.

Rouget, Gilbert, and Jean Schwarz

1970 "Transcrire ou décrire? Chant soudanais et chant fuegian." In Jean Pouillon and Pierre Maranda, eds., *Échanges et communications: Mélanges offerts à Claude Lévi-Strauss. . . .* The Hague: Mouton, 1:677–706.

Royce, Anya Peterson

1977 *The Anthropology of Dance.* Bloomington: Indiana University Press.

Rudolph, Lloyd I. and Susanne H.

1967 *The Modernity of Tradition: Political Development in India.* Chicago: University of Chicago Press.

Ruwet, Nicolas

1966 "Méthodes d'analyse en musicologie." *Revue belge de musicologie* 20:65–90.

1967 "Linguistics and Musicology." *International Social Science Journal* 19:79–87.

1975 "Théorie et méthodes dans les études musicales. . . ." *Musique en jeu* 17:11–36.

Sachs, Curt

1929 *Geist und Werden der Musikinstrumente.* Berlin: J. Bard.

1930 (1959) *Vergleichende Musikwissenschaft—Musik der Fremdkulturen.* Heidelberg: Quelle und Meyer.
1937 *World History of the Dance.* New York: Norton.
1940 *The History of Musical Instruments.* New York: Norton.
1943 *The Rise of Music in the Ancient World, East and West.* New York: Norton.
1946 *The Commonwealth of Art.* New York: Norton.
1948 *Our Musical Heritage.* New York: Prentice-Hall.
1953 *Rhythm and Tempo.* New York: Norton.
1962 *The Wellsprings of Music.* The Hague: M. Nijhoff.

Sachs, Nahoma
1975 "Music and Meaning: Musical Symbolism in a Macedonian Village." Dissertation, Indiana University.

Sahlins, Marshall D.
1960 *Evolution and Culture.* Ann Arbor: University of Michigan Press.

Sakata, Lorraine
1976 "The Concept of Musician in Three Persian-Speaking Areas of Afghanistan." *AM* 8/1:1–28.

Salmen, Walter
1960 *Der fahrende Musiker im europäischen Mittelalter.* Kassel: Hinnenthal.

Salzer, Felix
1952 *Structural Hearing.* New York: C. Boni.

Śarana, Gopala
1975 *The Methodology of Anthropological Comparisons: An Analysis of Comparative Methods in Social and Cultural Anthropology.* Tucson: University of Arizona Press (Viking Fund Publications in Anthropology, no. 53).

Schaeffner, André
1936 *Origine des instruments de musique.* Paris: Payot.
1956 "Ethnologie musicale ou musicologie comparée." In Paul Collaer, ed., *Les colloques de Wégimont.* Brussels: Elsevier, pp. 18–32.

Schering, Arnold
1936 *Beethoven und die Dichtung.* Berlin: Junker und Dünnhaut.
1941 *Das Symbol in der Musik. . . .* Leipzig: Koehler und Amelang.

Schinhan, Jan Philip
1937 "Die Musik der Papago und Yurok." Dissertation, University of Vienna.
1957 *The Music of the Ballads.* Durham, N.C.: Duke University Press.

Schiørring, Nils
1956 *Selma Nielsens viser.* Copenhagen: Munksgaard.

Schmidt, Wilhelm
1939 *The Culture Historical Method of Ethnology.* New York: Fortuny's.

Schneider, Albrecht

1976 *Musikwissenschaft und Kulturkreislehre.* Bonn: Verlag für systematische Musikwissenschaft.

1979 "Vergleichende Musikwissenschaft als Morphologie und Stilkritik: Werner Danckerts Stellung. . . ." *Jahrbuch für Volksliedforschung* 24:11–27.

Schneider, Marius

1934 *Geschichte der Mehrstimmigkeit.* Vol. 1. Berlin: J. Bard.

1951 "Die historischen Grundlagen der musikalischen Symbolik." *Musikforschung* 4:113–44.

1957 "Primitive Music." In Egon Wellesz, ed., *Ancient and Oriental Music.* London: Oxford University Press, pp. 1–82.

Schünemann, Georg

1923 *Das Lied der deutschen Kolonisten in Russland.* Munich: Drei Masken Verlag.

Sebeok, Thomas A.

1977 Ed., *How Animals Communicate.* Bloomington: Indiana University Press.

Seeger, Anthony

1979 "What Can We Learn When They Sing? Vocal Genres of the Suya Indians of Central Brazil." *EM* 23:373–94.

Seeger, Charles

1941 "Music and Culture." *Proceedings of the Music Teachers National Association for 1940* 64:112–22.

1950 "Oral Tradition in Music." In Maria Leach, ed., *Funk and Wagnall's Standard Dictionary of Folklore.* . . . New York, 2: 825–29.

1953a "Preface to the Description of a Music." *Proceedings of the 5th Congress of the I.M.S.* The Hague: Trio, pp. 360–70.

1953b "Toward a Universal Music Sound-Writing for Musicology." *Journal of the IFMC* 5:63–66.

1958 "Prescriptive and Descriptive Music Writing." *MQ* 44: 184–95.

1960 Review of *New Methods in Vocal Folk Music Research,* by Carl Dahlback. *EM* 4:41–42.

1961 "Semantic, Logical, and Political Considerations Bearing upon Research into Ethnomusicology." *EM* 5:77–80.

1966 "Versions and Variants of the Tunes of 'Barbara Allen'." *UCLA Selected Reports of the Institute of Ethnomusicology* 1/1: 120–67.

1971 "Reflections upon a Given Topic: Music in Universal Perspective." *EM* 15:385–98.

1977 *Studies in Musicology 1935–1975.* Berkeley: University of California Press.

Serafine, Mary Louise

1980 "The Development of Cognition in Music." Paper presented at a meeting of the Society for Music Theory, Nov. 6–9.

Shapiro, Ann Dhu
1975 "The Tune-Family Concept in British-American Folk-Song Scholarship." Dissertation, Harvard University.

Sharp, Cecil J.
1932 (1952) *English Folk Songs from the Southern Appalachians.* London: Oxford University Press.
1965 *English Folk Song: Some Conclusions.* 4th ed., ed. Maud Karpeles. Belmont, Calif.: Wadsworth.

Shiloah, Amnon
1970 "The Aliyya Songs in the Traditional Folk Literature of Israel" (in Hebrew). *Folklore Research Center Studies* (Jerusalem) 1:349–68.
1974 "The Status of the Oriental Artist." *Ariel* 36:79–83.

Silver, Brian
1976 "On Becoming an Ustad." *AM* 7/2:27–50.

Simon, Artur
1972 *Studien zur ägyptischen Volksmusik.* Hamburg: K. D. Wagner.
1978 "Probleme, Methoden und Ziele der Ethnomusikologie." *Jahrbuch für musikalische Volks- und Völkerkunde* 9:8–52.

Simpson, Claude M.
1966 *The British Broadside Ballad and Its Music.* New Brunswick, N.J.: Rutgers University Press.

Singer, Milton
1972 *When a Great Tradition Modernizes.* New York: Praeger.

Slobin, Mark
1976 *Music in the Culture of Northern Afghanistan.* Tucson: University of Arizona Press.

Slotkin, J. S.
1952 *Menomini Peyotism. Transactions of the American Philosophical Society,* new series, vol. 42, pt. 4.

Smith, Richard Chase
1971 "Deliverance from Chaos for a Song: A Preliminary Discussion of Amuesha Music." Unpublished paper, Cornell University.
1974 *The Amuesha People of Central Peru: Their Struggle to Survive.* Copenhagen: International Work Group for Indigenous Affairs.

Society for Ethnomusicology
1974 "Special Ethics Issue." *SEM Newsletter* 8/1.
1975 "Ethics Committee Report." *SEM Newsletter* 9/6:8.
1977 "Ethics Committee Report." *SEM Newsletter* 11/1:8.

Sperber, Dan
1975 *Rethinking Symbolism.* Cambridge: Cambridge University Press.

Spindler, George D.
1970 Ed., *Being an Anthropologist: Fieldwork in Eleven Cultures.* New York: Holt, Rinehart & Winston.

Springer, George
1956 "Language and Music: Parallels and Divergences." In *For Roman Jakobson.* The Hague: Mouton, pp. 504–13.

Stam, James H.
1976 *Inquiries into the Origin of Language: The Fate of a Question.* New York: Harper and Row.

Stauder, W.
1967 "Ein Musiktraktat aus dem zweiten vorchristlichen Jahrtausend." In *Festschrift Walter Wiora.* Kassel: Bärenreiter, pp. 157–63.

Steward, Julian
1955 *Theory of Culture Change: The Methodology of Multilinear Evolution.* Urbana: University of Illinois Press.
1967 *Contemporary Change in Traditional Societies.* Vol. 2. Urbana: University of Illinois Press.

Stewart, Milton Lee
1973 "Structural Development in the Jazz Improvisational Technique of Clifford Brown." Dissertation, University of Michigan.

Stockmann, Doris
1966 "Das Problem der Transkription in der musikethnologischen Forschung." *Deutsches Jahrbuch für Volkskunde* 12: 207–42.
1979 "Die Transkription in der Musikethnologie: Geschichte, Probleme, Methoden." *Acta Musicologica* 51:204–45.

Stockmann, Doris, and Jan Steszewski
1973 Eds., *Analyse und Klassifikation von Volksmelodien.* Krakow: Polskie wydawnictwo muzyczne.

Stockmann, Erich
1972 "The Diffusion of Musical Instruments as an Inter-Ethnic Process of Communication." *Yearbook of the IFMC* 3:128–37.

Stumpf, Carl
1886 "Lieder der Bellakula-Indianer." *Vierteljahrschrift für Musikwissenschaft* 2:405–26.
1911 *Die Anfänge der Musik.* Leipzig: J. A. Barth.

Sturrock, John
1979 Ed., *Structuralism and Since.* Oxford: Oxford University Press.

Sturtevant, William
1964 "Studies in Ethnoscience." *AA* 66, pt. 2:99–131.

Symposium
1964 "Symposium on Transcription and Analysis: A Hukwe Song with Musical Bow." *EM* 8:223–77.

Szabolcsi, Bence
1959 *Bausteine zu einer Geschichte der Melodie.* Budapest: Corvina.
1965 *A History of Melody.* New York: St. Martin's Press.

Tappert, Wilhelm
1890 *Wandernde Melodien.* 2. vermehrte und verbesserte Ausgabe. Leipzig: List & Francke.
Thompson, Stith
1946 *The Folktale.* New York: Dryden Press.
1953 "The Star Husband Tale." *Studia Septentrionalia* 4:93–163. Reprinted in Alan Dundes, *The Study of Folklore.* Englewood Cliffs, N.J.: Prentice-Hall, 1965, pp. 414–74.
Touma, Habib Hassan
1968 *Der Maqam Bayati im arabischen Taqsim.* Berlin: H. Touma.
1975 *Die Musik der Araber.* Wilhelmshaven: Heinrichshofen.
Tracey, Hugh
1948 *Chopi Musicians: Their Music, Poetry, and Instruments.* London: Oxford University Press.
1954 "The Social Role of African Music." *African Affairs* 53:234–41.
Tran Van Khê
1977 "Is the Pentatonic Universal?" *World of Music* 19/1–2:76–84.
Treitler, Leo
1974 "Homer and Gregory: The Transmission of Epic Poetry and Plainchant." *MQ* 60:333–72.
1975 "Centone Chant: Übles Flickwerk or E pluribus unus?" *JAMS* 28:1–23.
Truitt, Deborah
1974 *Dolphin's Porpoises: A Comprehensive Annotated Bibliography of the Smaller Cetacea.* Detroit: Gale Research Co.
Tsuge, Gen'ichi
1974 "Avaz: A Study of the Rhythmic Aspects of Classical Iranian Music." Dissertation, Wesleyan University.
Turner, Victor
1974 *Dramas, Fields, and Metaphors.* Ithaca, N.Y.: Cornell University Press.
Tyler, Stephen A.
1969 Ed., *Cognitive Anthropology.* New York: Holt, Rinehart & Winston.
Tylor, E. B.
1871 *Primitive Culture.* London: J. Murray.
1889 "On a Method for Investigating the Development of Institutions." *Journal of the Royal Anthropological Institute* 18:245–72.
Vansina, John
1965 *Oral Tradition, a Study in Historical Methodology.* Chicago: University of Chicago Press.
Vega, Carlos
1966 "Mesomusic: An Essay on the Music of the Masses." *EM* 10:1–17.

Vikár, László, and Gábor Bereczki
1971 *Cheremis Folksongs.* Budapest: Akademiai Kiado.
Villoteau, G. A.
1809 "De l'état actuel de l'art musical en Egypte." In *Déscription de l'Egypte.* Paris: Commission des monuments d'Egypte, 1:609-846.
Viswanathan, T.
1977 "The Analysis of Raga Alapana in South Indian Music." *AM* 9/1:13-71.
Voget, Fred W.
1975 *A History of Ethnology.* New York: Holt, Rinehart & Winston.
Wachsmann, Klaus
1961 "Criteria for Acculturation." In *Report of the 8th Congress of the International Musicological Society.* Kassel: Bärenreiter, pp. 139-49.
1971a Ed., *Essays on Music and History in Africa.* Evanston, Ill.: Northwestern University Press.
1971b "Universal Perspectives in Music." *EM* 15:381-84.
Waengler, H. H.
1963 "Über Beziehungen zwischen gesprochenen und gesungenen Tonhöhen in afrikanischen Tonsprachen." *Jahrbuch für musikalische Volks- und Völkerkunde* 1:136-45.
Walin, Stig
1952 *Die schwedische Hummel.* Stockholm: Nordiska museet.
Wallaschek, Richard
1893 *Primitive Music.* London: Longmans, Green. German ed. 1903, with title *Anfänge der Tonkunst.*
Ward, John M.
1980 "The Hunt's Up." *Proceedings of the Royal Musical Association* 106:1-25.
Warwick, Donald P., and Samuel Osherson
1973 Eds., *Comparative Research Methods.* Englewood Cliffs, N.J.: Prentice-Hall.
Waterman, Christopher A.
1979 "The Effect of Western Functional Harmony on Persian and sub-Saharan African Music." Unpublished paper, University of Illinois.
Waterman, Richard A.
1948 "'Hot' Rhythm in Negro Music." *JAMS* 1:24-37.
1952 "African Influence on American Negro Music." In Sol Tax, ed., *Acculturation in the Americas.* Chicago: University of Chicago Press, pp. 207-18.
1956 "Music in Australian Aboriginal Culture—Some Sociological and Psychological Implications." *Music Therapy* 5:40-50.

Wax, Rosalie H.
1971 *Doing Field Work: Warnings and Advice.* Chicago: University of Chicago Press.

Weber, Max
1958 *The Rational and Social Foundations of Music.* Carbondale: Southern Illinois University Press. First published in German, 1921.

Weber-Kellermann, Ingeborg
1957 *Ludolf Parisius und seine altmärkischen Volkslieder.* Berlin: Akademie-Verlag.

Wenker, J.
1970 "A Computer-Oriented Music Notation Including Ethnomusicological Symbols." In B. S. Brook, ed., *Musicology and the Computer.* New York: City University of New York Press, pp. 91–129.

Werner, Heinz
1917 *Die melodische Erfindung im frühen Kindesalter.* Vienna: Akademie der Wissenschaften Wien, Phil.-hist. Klasse, Sitzungsberichte 182, no. 4.

Wertheimer, Max
1909/10 "Musik der Wedda." *Sammelbände der internationalen Musikgesellschaft* 11:300–304.

White, Leslie
1949 *The Science of Culture.* New York: Farrar, Strauss & Giroux.

Wieschoff, Heinz
1933 *Die afrikanischen Trommeln und ihre ausserafrikanischen Beziehungen.* Stuttgart: Strecker und Schröder.

Wilgus, D. K.
1959 *Anglo-American Folksong Scholarship since 1898.* New Brunswick, N.J.: Rutgers University Press.

Wilkens, Eckart
1967 *Künstler und Amateure im persischen Santourspiel.* Regensburg: G. Bosse.

Wiora, Walter
1953 *Europäischer Volksgesang.* (Das Musikwerk, no. 4.) Cologne: Arno Volk. English trans. ca. 1966, Robert Kolben, *European Folk Song: Common Forms in Characteristic Modification.* New York: Leeds.
1956 "Älter als die Pentatonik." In *Studia Memoriae Belae Bartok Sacra.* Budapest: Academia Scientiarum Hungaricae, pp. 185–208.
1957 *Europäische Volksmusik und abendländische Tonkunst.* Kassel: J. P. Hinnenthal.
1965 *The Four Ages of Music.* New York: Norton.
1970 "Das Alter des Begriffes Volkslied." *Musikforschung* 23:420–28.

1972 "Reflections on the Problem: How Old Is the Concept Folksong." *Yearbook of the IFMC* 3:23–33.

1975 *Ergebnisse und Aufgaben vergleichender Musikforschung.* Darmstadt: Wissenschaftliche Buchgesellschaft.

Wissler, Clark

1912 *Social Organization and Ritualistic Ceremonies of the Blackfoot Indians.* American Museum of Natural History, Anthropological Papers, no. 7.

1917 *The American Indian.* New York: McMurtrie.

Witmer, Robert

1973 "Recent Change in the Musical Culture of the Blood Indians." *Yearbook for Inter-American Musical Research* 9:64–94.

Wulstan, D.

1971 "The Earliest Musical Notation." *Music and Letters* 52:365–82.

Wundt, Wilhelm

1911 *Völkerpsychologie, eine Untersuchung der Entwicklungsgesetze von Sprache, Mythus und Sitte.* 3d ed. Leipzig: Engelmann.

Zonis, Ella

1973 *Classical Persian Music, an Introduction.* Cambridge, Mass.: Harvard University Press.

INDEX

A Note on the Author

Bruno Nettl was born in Prague, Czechoslovakia, in 1930 and immigrated to the United States as a young boy. He received A.B., M.A., and Ph.D. degrees from Indiana University, as well as a M.A.L.S. from the University of Michigan. After ten years at Wayne State University, he came to the University of Illinois in 1964, where he is now professor of music and anthropology. He was one of the founders of the Society for Ethnomusicology and has served it as member of the executive board, councillor, and president. Among his numerous publications are *Music in Primitive Culture* (1956), *Introduction to Folk Music in the United States* (now in its third edition), *Theory and Method in Ethnomusicology* (1964), *Contemporary Music and Musical Cultures* (with Charles E. Hamm and Ronald Byrnside, 1975), and another book from the University of Illinois Press, *Eight Urban Musical Cultures* (1978). He has done fieldwork among the Blackfoot people of Montana, in Iran, and in Madras, India.